COMMONΙ
CARIBE___
INSURANCE LAW

This book sets out in a clear and concise manner the central principles of insurance law in the Caribbean, guiding students through the complexities of the subject. This book features, among several other key themes, extensive coverage of:

- insurance regulation;
- life insurance;
- property insurance;
- contract formation;
- intermediaries;
- the claims procedure; and
- analysis of the substantive laws of several jurisdictions.

Commonwealth Caribbean Insurance Law is essential reading for LLB students in Caribbean universities, students in CAPE Law courses, and practitioners.

Lesley A. Walcott is a Senior Lecturer in Law at Cave Hill, University of the West Indies, Barbados.

COMMONWEALTH CARIBBEAN LAW SERIES

The Commonwealth Caribbean Law Series is the only series of law books that covers the jurisdiction of the English speaking Caribbean nations. The first titles in the series were published in 1995 to acclaim from academics, practitioners and the judiciary in the region. Several editions followed, and they have now become essential reading for those learning and practising Caribbean law.

This must-have series is required holdings for any law library specialising in Caribbean legal information.

Titles in this series include

Commonwealth Caribbean Insurance Law
Lesley A. Walcott

Judicial Review in the Commonwealth Caribbean
Rajendra Ramlogan

Commonwealth Caribbean Administrative Law
Eddy Ventose

Commonwealth Caribbean Contract Law
Gilbert Kodilinye and Maria Kodilinye

Commonwealth Caribbean Employment and Labour Law
Natalie Corthésy and Carla-Anne Harris-Roper

Commonwealth Caribbean Tort Law
Gilbert Kodilinye

Commonwealth Caribbean Property Law
Gilbert Kodilinye

Commonwealth Caribbean Business Law
Natalie Persadie and Rajendra Ramlogan

Commonwealth Caribbean Corporate Governance
Edited by Suzanne Ffolkes-Goldson

Commonwealth Caribbean Family Law: Husband, Wife and Cohabitant
Karen Nunez-Tesheira

Forthcoming titles

Commonwealth Caribbean Intellectual Property Law
Eddy Ventose

Commonwealth Caribbean Administrative Law (Second Edition)
Eddy Ventose

Commonwealth Caribbean Tort Law (Sixth Edition)
Gilbert Kodilinye

COMMONWEALTH CARIBBEAN INSURANCE LAW

Lesley A. Walcott

Routledge
Taylor & Francis Group

LONDON AND NEW YORK

First published 2019
by Routledge
2 Park Square, Milton Park, Abingdon, Oxon OX14 4RN

and by Routledge
52 Vanderbilt Avenue, New York, NY 10017

Routledge is an imprint of the Taylor & Francis Group, an informa business

British Library Cataloguing-in-Publication Data
A catalogue record for this book is available from the British Library

Library of Congress Cataloging-in-Publication Data
Names: Walcott, Lesley A., author.
Title: Commonwealth Caribbean insurance law / Lesley A. Walcott.
Description: New York : Routledge, 2019. | Series: Commonwealth Caribbean law | Includes
    bibliographical references and index.
Identifiers: LCCN 2018054359 | ISBN 9781138491878 (hardback) | ISBN 9781138491885 (pbk.)
Subjects: LCSH: Insurance law—West Indies, British.
Classification: LCC KGL5300 .W35 2019 | DDC 346.729/086—dc23
LC record available at https://lccn.loc.gov/2018054359

ISBN: 978-1-138-49187-8 (hbk)
ISBN: 978-1-138-49188-5 (pbk)
ISBN: 978-1-351-03178-3 (ebk)

Typeset in Baskerville
by Apex CoVantage, LLC
Printed by CPI Group (UK) Ltd, Croydon CR0 4YY

For my father, Edward H. Walcott, and for Dr. Leonard Shorey

CONTENTS

FOREWORD

During her career as a member of the academic staff of the Faculty of Law of The University of the West Indies, Lesley Ann Walcott has published legal articles in a wide variety of journals. It was therefore only a matter of time before she undertook the task of writing a textbook on law. She has chosen to discuss the law of insurance as it applies across the disparate jurisdictions of the Commonwealth Caribbean.

That is no mean feat, because the discussion must necessarily embrace examination and analysis of the statutory and common law underpinnings of insurance law in the several islands of the Commonwealth Caribbean. Ms Walcott has succeeded admirably in producing in the chapters of this book, a clear exposition of the relevant principles of law interlarded with robust discussion and critical analysis of judicial decisions.

Our understanding of the law of insurance in its Commonwealth Caribbean context has been greatly enhanced by this volume. Judges and practitioners of law will find in this work a storehouse of information and a research tool that will surely illuminate any dark areas of inquiry and shine a spotlight on possible solutions to problems.

When the Faculty of Law was inaugurated in 1970, insurance law was not included in the curriculum for undergraduates. That is no longer the case as both undergraduate and graduate students are now exposed to courses in that field of law. I anticipate that this book will be a compulsory text for students reading the law of insurance. It deserves to be, as it will make an indelible contribution to a subject that is so relevant to the commerce of our everyday living and whose importance has been highlighted by the collapse of the CLICO group of companies and the consequential financial tragedy that has befallen policyholders.

I know the CLICO disaster was a factor motivating Ms Walcott to produce this text. I heartily commend her for the high scholarship evident in the pages of this work and I commend it to the widest possible readership.

Sir David Simmons Q.C.
Former Chief Justice of Barbados
May 2018

PREFACE

The idea of writing a textbook on insurance law in the Commonwealth Caribbean derives from a fascination with the mixture of separate areas of the law – contract, crime, family law and finance – all entwined in the practice of insurance business. Immediately upon consideration of insurance law this connectivity reveals itself. I began working on the project while on sabbatical at American University Washington College of Law. Progress, in part, was almost guaranteed by the fact that I was teaching insurance law to both graduates and undergraduates in the Faculty of Law at Cave Hill, the Barbados campus of The University of the West Indies. This diverse community of students hailed from Canada to Guyana, often encompassing nationals of all the CARICOM (Caribbean Community) member countries.

An element of uniqueness – the multi-jurisdictional nature of insurance law in the Commonwealth Caribbean – at times presents differences with more than the typical level of complexity to be resolved. This realisation, that true understanding requires creation of a road map of insurance law in the region, led me to the task I deemed necessary: to describe and explain the evolution of insurance law in the Commonwealth Caribbean. As work on the material progressed, placing me at a good place in comfort with what I had achieved, most jurisdictions in the region were hit without warning by the CLICO collapse. CLICO had succeeded the Colonial Life Insurance Co. Ltd, founded in 1936. This event forced revision of the text as the jurisdictions of the Commonwealth of the Bahamas, St Kitts and Nevis and Trinidad and Tobago scrambled to (and did) succeed in reforming their laws. I have tried to incorporate all the legislative reform and their implications for the insurance business. My hope is that this text will be of benefit generally to the Caribbean and of assistance specifically to students of the law, judges, lawyers engaged in its practice and those toiling in the academic vineyard.

In bringing the material from idea to publication I have been assisted by the searching questions of my students as well as comments of those – referenced in the acknowledgements – who have been kind enough to devote their time, despite grueling schedules, to read and comment on different parts of the book. That said, I must insist that they bear no responsibility for any lingering infelicities that have yet found themselves into the text – these I lay claim to, solely.

ACKNOWLEDGEMENTS

Several people assisted in seeing this text to completion. I would like to thank the Honourable Justices Rolston Nelson and Winston Anderson of the Caribbean Court of Justice (CCJ), who provided my first introduction to the nuances of insurance law. My sincere thanks also to Dr David Berry, Dean of the Cave Hill Campus Faculty of Law of The University of the West Indies. He was a continuing source of support and encouragement throughout my work. Thanks also to my students Notori Bobb and Shamar Mondere, and Faculty of Law staff Renaldo Arthur, Beal Mapp, Karen Pyrmus and Larry Craig. The entire law library staff assisted way beyond the normal call of duty. I want to thank also the late Leonard Shorey for editorial work on my first draft. My husband, Ian Carrington, has been a source of support particularly by exercise of his enduring patience, and my mother, Ercil Walcott, has always believed in me. I must thank Dr Sean Marquez for bolstering my spirits and Wilberne Persaud for inspiration at difficult moments and editorial assistance.

INTRODUCTION

This text explores insurance law in the Commonwealth Caribbean as it evolves amidst dynamic reorganisation in global commerce with concomitant responses in the law. Commonwealth Caribbean jurisdictions are 16 in number: Anguilla, Antigua and Barbuda, the Bahamas, Barbados, Belize, British Virgin Islands, Dominica, Grenada, Guyana, Jamaica, Montserrat, St Kitts and Nevis, St Lucia, St Vincent and the Grenadines, Trinidad and Tobago and Turks and Caicos. The reader will immediately note two apparent contradictions: Belize is located in Central America, and Guyana is located on the northern edge of South America. These two jurisdictions are members of the Commonwealth. History therefore binds them in the evolutionary process of the legal system associated with centuries of British colonial rule.

Growth and development of the insurance industry highlights the socio-economic relevance to the region of the legislative framework from its colonial roots to the current position as an amalgamation of Australian, British, United States, Canadian and Caribbean law. The regional integration movement and the Treaty of Chaguaramas,[1] the Caribbean Law Institute and the model Insurance Bill[2] embody the construct for harmonisation of insurance law in the region.

HISTORICAL DEVELOPMENT OF THE INSURANCE INDUSTRY

During the period of colonial rule, the Commonwealth Caribbean insurance industry reflected its umbilical tie to the United Kingdom. Historically British insurance companies operated through agencies – generally called branches – that possessed local underwriting powers.[3] Examples include the Phoenix Assurance Group, a British insurance entity with Barbados operations dating back to 1804. Another, Standard Life, established in Edinburgh in 1825, began business in Barbados in 1846. Sun Life of Canada established operations in Barbados, Jamaica and Trinidad and Tobago in 1879. The Manufacturers Life Insurance Company (Canadian), less than a decade after incorporation by an Act of Parliament, established a Bermuda-based agency in 1893; Jamaica and Trinidad quickly followed in 1894.[4] Indeed, although British firms predate North American companies' regional operations, the latter, principally Canadian, subsequently achieved dominance of the insurance market until as late as the early 1970s.[5]

There were, however, indigenous institutions: the oldest indigenous life insurance concern in the British Caribbean, the Barbados Mutual Assurance Society, opened its doors on Barbados as early as 1840. This eventually became The Mutual as a result of a takeover of Life of

---

1   Civil Code 1879, Civil Code (Amendment) Ordinance 1956, Cap 242. See further D. White, 'Some Problems of a Hybrid Legal System: A Case Study of St Lucia' (1981) 30 *ICLQ* 862.
2   See the preamble to the Revised Treaty of Chaguaramas, 2001 (www.CARICOM.org).
3   C. A. Karch, *The Rise of the Phoenix: The Barbados Mutual Life Assurance Society in Caribbean Economy and Society 1840–1990* (Ian Randle Publishers: 1997), p. 28; C. H. Denbow, *Life Insurance Law in the Commonwealth Caribbean* (Butterworths: 1984).
4   The Canadian Encyclopedia (www.thecanadianencyclopedia.ca/en/article/manulife-financial-corporation); see also L. A. Winter, *The First Sixty Years, 1887–1947: A History of the Manufacturers Life Insurance Company* (Manufacturers Life Insurance Company: 1947). See www.thecanadianencyclopedia.ca/en/article/manulife-financial-corporation.
5   US insurance companies included American Life Insurance Company (ALICO) and British American Insurance Company (BAICO).

Barbados. It subsequently expanded throughout the neighboring British colonies during the 1850s and 1860s.[6]

During the nineteenth century, and continuing until the post-independence period in the latter half of the twentieth century, the insurance industry in the Caribbean developed with certain well-defined structural features.[7] Considering the process of financial intermediation, compared to commercial bank operations there was a much larger number of registered insurance companies conducting business in this relatively small market.[8] A majority of the companies were foreign owned and controlled, engaging primarily in non-life-insurance business.[9] In the post-colonial period a shift in government policy resulted in a reduction of foreign insurance companies' sphere of influence.[10] Significant income repatriation to their head offices constituted an unacceptable drain on foreign exchange reserves.[11] As a result, governments sought to indigenise insurance activities as they enacted legislation to regulate and modernise the conduct of insurance business. National savings and investment became a priority as some governments introduced legislation requiring majority share control to be in the hands of nationals, while in other cases subtle pressure was exerted on foreign companies to incorporate locally.

The result was that the influence of foreign insurance companies gradually diminished as indigenous operations grew. The industry was the subject of significant structural change; heightened merger and acquisition activity influenced by the global financial services sector blurred the distinction between commercial and investment banks, insurance companies and asset management firms.[12]

LEGISLATIVE HISTORY

Statutory regulation of insurance contracts remains rooted in the region's colonial legacy.[13] Thus the United Kingdom's Life Assurance Act of 1774,[14] Marine Insurance Act of

---

6   Antigua and Barbuda in 1863; Dominica in 1868; Grenada in 1858; Montserrat in 1863; Demerara, Guyana, in 1866; St Kitts in 1861. The Barbados Mutual Assurance Society was formed under deed of settlement in 1840 in Barbados. It has subsequently undergone significant corporate reconstruction. In the late 1990s the process of de-mutualisation was initiated, creating Sagicor Insurance Co. Ltd. Subsequently in 2002, Sagicor Insurance Ltd acquired Life of Barbados Insurance Company, a company listed on the Barbados Stock Exchange. Sagicor Insurance Co. Ltd is listed on the stock exchanges of both Barbados and Trinidad and Tobago. Sagicor operates in 20 countries across the Caribbean and in the United States. On 30 September 2005 the company acquired American Founders Life (AFL) for $58 million, providing a US presence as a licensed insurer in 41 states and the District of Columbia and a licensed reinsurer in 45 states and DC. On 14 February 2007 Sagicor Financial Corp. was listed on the London Stock Exchange (LSE). See further www.sagicor-international.com and www.sagicor.com/countries.aspx.
7   M. A. Odle, *The Significance of Non-bank Financial Intermediaries in the Caribbean: An Analysis of Patterns of Financial Structure and Development* (Institute of Social and Economic Research, University of the West Indies: 1972), p. 11.
8   Odle, ibid., reports that in 1962 there were 41 companies operating in Guyana, 66 in Trinidad and Tobago and 140 in Jamaica.
9   Odle, supra n. 7, reports that in 1972 there were 24 life and 42 non-life insurance companies in Trinidad and Tobago, 24 life and 116 non-life companies in Jamaica and 24 life and 17 non-life companies in Guyana. In Guyana, of the 41 companies registered, 34 were foreign.
10 The impetus for these changes may be attributed to various socio-economic and political factors. In the 1970s there occurred a rise of the Black Power movement and national pride, in part reflecting changing international conditions linked to Martin Luther King Jr and the Civil Rights protest movement embracing 'non-violence.'
11 C. H. Denbow, *Status Report on Insurance Law in the Commonwealth Caribbean* [1995] April, *Caribbean Law & Business.*
12 It is estimated that the value of global mergers and acquisitions peaked at about US$2.4 trillion in 1998, compared to an estimated value of US$500 billion in 1990.
13 See further D. Morrison, 'The Reception of Law in Jamaica' [1979] 2 *W.I.L.J.* 43; K. Patchett, 'The Reception of Law in the West Indies' (1973) *J.L.J.* 17; R. M. B. Antoine, *Commonwealth Caribbean Law and Legal Systems* (Cavendish: 1999).
14 14 Geo. 3, c. 48.

1906,[15] Married Women's Property Act of 1882[16] and the Gaming Act of 1845,[17] for the most part, continue to define West Indian insurance law. As Caribbean territories secured independence from Britain and ownership and control of insurance business transitioned from foreign to local hands, national Insurance Acts supplementing the British legislative base were enacted[18] with each territory implementing its own administrative and deposit requirements. Throughout most of the twentieth century, legislation governing insurance operations in the Commonwealth Caribbean was largely inadequate as it related to the requirement of insurable interest and the status of the beneficiary. This deficiency meant that the legislation had to be supplemented by an application of the common law and the still relevant eighteenth- and nineteenth-century legislation from the United Kingdom.[19] More importantly, the fact of Canadian firms' dominance in the market meant adherence to Canadian law practice effectively therefore, that

> life insurance law in the Caribbean while founded on English law, has been by reason of the slow development of English law and the historical control of the market place by Canadian companies significantly influenced by law derived from countries other than England.[20]

It was not until the late twentieth century, with the advent of the Caribbean Law Institute (CLI), that significant insurance law reform took place. In the 1990s, the CLI's Insurance Committee set forth several recommendations for reform of insurance law in the region.[21] The Institute's proposals have been adopted by Barbados, Guyana, Jamaica, the Bahamas and most of the OECS (Organisation of Eastern Caribbean States) member countries. In effect, Caribbean insurance law – a work in progress – is a distinct 'hybridist' model reflecting early colonial domination of the insurance industry during the eighteenth and nineteenth centuries with subsequent later twentieth-century American and Canadian[22] entry into the jurisdiction.

---

15   28 Geo. 3, c. 56.
16   45 & 46 Vict., c. 75.
17   8 & 9 Vict., c. 109; Barbados Gaming Act No. 4 of 1891.
18   Anguilla Insurance Act, Cap 218; Antigua and Barbuda Insurance Contracts Act No. 10 of 1964, Insurance Act No. 10 of 1967, Insurance (Licence) Act No. 11 of 1967, Insurance Levy Act No. 6 of 1977; the Bahamas Insurance Act Chapter 317; Barbados Insurance Act No. 13 of 1972, Cap 310; Belize Insurance Act No. 15 of 1975, Cap 208; Cayman Islands Insurance Act of 1979; Dominica Insurance Act Chapter 78: 40; Grenada Insurance Act No. 2 of 1973; Guyana Insurance Act No. 3 of 1968; Jamaica Insurance Act No. 8 of 1971; St Kitts and Nevis Insurance Act of 1968; Trinidad and Tobago Insurance Act of 1966; Turks and Caicos Insurance Ordinance of 1989.
19   Road traffic legislation was introduced much earlier in the 1930s. Consider Barbados Road Traffic Act No. 40 of 1931; Jamaica Motor Vehicles Insurance (Third Party) Risks Act Chapter 257; Trinidad and Tobago Road Traffic Act 1931, replaced by the Motor Vehicles Insurance (Third Party) Risks Act No. 48:51 of 1981; Guyana Motor Vehicles Insurance (Third Party) Risks Act, Chapter 51:03; St Vincent and the Grenadines Motor Vehicles Insurance (Third Party) Risks Act (replaced by the Motor Vehicles Insurance (Third Party Risks) Act No. 4 of 2003). In the Privy Council decision of *Presidential Insurance Company v Stafford* on appeal from Trinidad and Tobago No. 4 of 1999, commenting on the scheme of motor insurance legislation noted that 'the Act requires drivers to have compulsory third party insurance to cover "in respect of any liability which may be incurred by him or them in respect of the death or bodily injury to or damage to the property of any person caused by or arising out of the use of the motor vehicle on a public road".'
20   Denbow, supra n. 3.
21   Caribbean Law Institute Model Motor Vehicles Insurance Bill of 1993; Insurance Association of the Caribbean [2000 Rev.]; Caribbean Law Institute Model Insurance Bill 1993; Insurance Association of the Caribbean (IAC) [2000 Rev.].
22   St Vincent and the Grenadines Insurance Act No. 45 of 2003 adopts a composite approach regulating the carrying on of insurance business together with the operation of pension funds. The difference between St Vincent and the Grenadines is marginal as, for the most part, it reflects enhanced regulatory scrutiny and mirrors the CLI position with respect to insurable interest and the named beneficiary.

Within the colonial framework two significant points of departure exist. First, in the jurisdictions of St Lucia, with its French civil law,[23] and Guyana, with its Roman-Dutch law,[24] the
principles of insurance, contract and agency reside within a civil code. The legal system of St
Lucia has been described as a 'fascinating blend of Quebec, French, English and indigenous
law.'[25] Article 917A(1) of the St Lucia Civil Code[26] applied the law of England for the time
being relating to contracts and quasi-contracts, in the absence of local statutory provision.[27]
This code operated until the enactment of the Insurance Act of 1968,[28] which was eventually
repealed by the 1995 Insurance Act.[29] In Guyana, the conflict between Holland and Britain
during the period 1781–1803 produced a Roman-Dutch legacy upon which British law is juxtaposed. The curious amalgam of civil law and English common law is reflected for instance in
Section 13 of the Guyana Civil Law Act.[30] This section states:

> In every suit, action and cause having reference to questions of fire and life assurance which are
> hence forth brought in the high court or in any other competent court of this colony, the law
> administered for the time being in the high court of justice in England, so far as that law is not
> repugnant to, or in conflict with any act now in force in Guyana, shall be the law to be adminis-
> tered by the high court or other competent court.

This code expressly incorporated British insurance law as the law of the territory. Accordingly,
in *New India Assurance Company v Bacchus*,[31] the Federal Supreme Court used the Civil Law Act to
apply the Marine Insurance Act of 1906 (UK) to British Guiana. Section 3 thereof provides:

> From and after the commencement of this Act all questions arising within Guyana relating to
> the following matters, namely, ships and the property therein and owners thereof; the behaviour
> of the masters and mariners and their respective rights, duties and liabilities as regards the
> carriage of passengers and goods by ships; stoppage in transit; freight; demurrage; Insurance;
> salvage; average; collision between ships; bills of lading; and all rights, liabilities, claims, con-
> tracts, and matters arising in respect of a ship or any such question as aforesaid, shall adjudged,
> determined, construed and enforced according to the law of England applicable to that or the
> like case.

As observed by the Federal Supreme Court, the purpose of this Civil Law Act was to introduce
into Guyana the law of England with regard to merchant shipping and matters connected
therewith.

---

23 See further K. D. Anthony, 'Historical Aspects of the Evolution of Caribbean Legal Systems' (1996) *Com-
     parative Law Studies*, 1996 Washington OAS, General Secretariat, 29.
24 See further Antoine, supra n. 13. In Chapter 2, Antoine describes the legal tradition which took hold in Guy-
     ana via Roman-Dutch law. The author notes that

      The Order of the Netherlands Government in 1629 affirmatively applied Roman-Dutch law,
      The Political Ordinance of 1580, to the Colonies; Roman-Dutch law prevailed until the cessation
      of Guyana to the British, which signified the 'steady erosion of the Roman civil tradition.'

      The jurisprudence of Guyana is hybridist in nature 'deriving its principles from both the civil and com-
      mon law and produced Anglo-Roman jurisprudence.' See Antoine, p. 50.
25 V. Flossaic, 'The Interpretation of the Civil Code of St Lucia,' unpublished paper, in Antoine, supra n. 13,
     p. 51, n. 29.
26 Supra n. 1.
27 St Lucia Civil Code Article 917A(1), Cap 242 to apply the law of England for the time being relating to
     contract and quasi-contract, in the absence of local statutory provision; Insurance Act No. 3 of 1968.
28 St Lucia Insurance Act No. 3 of 1968.
29 St Lucia Insurance Act No. 6 of 1995.
30 Chapter 6:01.
31 WIR (1986), p. 33.

A second area of departure is the palpable influence of the Australian Life Insurance Act on Caribbean legislatures.[32] Australian life insurance law itself and regulation of insurance companies modified many common law principles. Insurable interest was addressed and modern legal doctrines governing the relationship between the assured and the insurance company were introduced. After the CLI Insurance Law Committee's recommendations, Barbados enacted the Insurance Act of 1996 and Guyana enacted the Insurance Act of 1998. Jamaica replaced the Insurance Act of 1971 with the Insurance Act of 2001.[33]

REGIONAL HARMONISATION

The West Indies Federation

The West Indies Federation was a short-lived federal initiative that existed from 3 January 1958 to 31 May 1962. It encompassed ten colonies of the United Kingdom: Antigua and Barbuda, Barbados, Dominica, Grenada, Jamaica, Montserrat, the then St Kitts-Nevis-Anguilla, St Lucia, St Vincent and Trinidad and Tobago. The expressed intention was creation of a viable political unit that also potentially should exhibit what the Colonial Office termed 'financial viability' prior to achieving independence from Britain as a single state.[34] It collapsed due to internal political conflict,[35] but during its existence the Marine Insurance Act of 1959 was passed by the legislature of the West Indies Federation as federal law. The Marine Insurance Act of 1959[36] was short-lived, much like the West Indies Federation itself. In 1962, Britain instituted The West Indies (Dissolution and Interim Commissioner) Order in Council,[37] a statutory instrument which dissolved the West Indies Federation. Section 16 of this Act vested power in a commissioner to determine which laws passed by the federal legislature would continue to apply after its dissolution. The Marine Insurance Act of The West Indies Federation was eventually repealed.

CARICOM

The regional harmonisation effort must be understood in the context of economic integration, the establishment of a single economic space and the liberalisation of trade in goods and services within the Caribbean Community.[38] This process, punctuated as it is by a series of

---

32 Sections 95–99, Australia Life Insurance Act 1945–1973, Schedule 6.
33 Jamaica Insurance Act No. 26 of 2001; Trinidad and Tobago Insurance Act Chapter 84:01; Section 4, St Lucia Insurance Act No. 6 of 1995.
34 T. A. Carmichael, *Passport to the Heart: Reflections on Canada Caribbean Relations* (Ian Randle Publishers: 2001); A. R. Stewart, 'Canadian–West Indian Union, 1884–1885' (1950) 4 *Canadian Historical Review* 31, 369–389; C. Fraser, *Ambivalent Anti-colonialism: The United States and the Genesis of West Indian Independence, 1940–1964* (Greenwood Press: 1994); H. Ghany, *Kamal: A Lifetime of Politics Religion and Culture* (Multimedia Production Centre, University of the West Indies: 1996); R. Gonsalves, *History and the Future: A Caribbean Perspective* (Quik-Print: 1994); F. A. Hoyes, *The Rise of West Indian Democracy: The Life and Times of Sir Grantley Adams* (Advocate Press: 1963); W. Mahabir, *In and Out of Politics* (Inprint Caribbean: 1978); P. W. Wickham, 'Factors in the Integration and Disintegration of the Caribbean,' in J. G. LaGuerre, ed., *Issues in the Government and Politics of the West Indies* (Multimedia Production Centre, University of the West Indies: 1997).
35 See further J. Mordecai, *The West Indies: the Federal Negotiations*, with an epilogue by W. A. Lewis (George Allen and Unwin: 1968) and E. Wallace, 'The Break-up of the British West Indies Federation,' in H. Beckles and V. Shepherd, eds, *Caribbean Freedom: Economy and Society from Emancipation to the Present* (Ian Randle Publishers: 1996), p. 455.
36 1959, Cap 711.
37 S.I. 1962/1084.
38 See wwmfaft.gov.jm/Intl_Community/CARICOM.htm.

accords and protocols, can be traced to the Treaty of Chaguaramas[39] representing the construct for harmonisation of law in the Commonwealth Caribbean.[40] The aim of the Treaty of Chaguaramas is to coordinate economic and foreign policy[41] to achieve a sustained global economic presence based on international competitiveness. Revised in 2001 and culminating with the creation of the Caribbean Single Market and Economy (CSME),[42] the Treaty with its core principles has operated as the catalyst for regional law reform in the region.

CSME, unlike the European Union (EU) – an integrated supra-national body created by the single European Act and its attendant legislative powers in the form of EU Directives – does not remove the element of discretion from member states. No similar integrated autonomous body exists in the CSME. Indeed it does not appear – certainly not publicly – to be contemplated. With no institution having supranational authority, reliance 'must instead be placed on regional inter-governmental cooperation and the sharing and exchange of information among regulatory agencies.'[43] Caribbean insurance companies are thus subject to what may be termed a potential maze of initial and continuing financial and regulatory obligations that may indeed differ among member states in which they operate. Consequently, this bureaucratic labyrinth of regulatory requirements for stipulated deposits, maintenance of statutory funds and share capital renders region-wide operation difficult.

At the heart of the absence of regulatory certainty as to whether local companies are to be treated equally for all Caribbean jurisdictions is the core distinction made in domestic legislation between foreign and local insurance companies, and 'off-shore'[44] versus domestic insurance regimes. Several papers and studies have attempted to advance this process. They have identified the logistical and administrative hurdles such as the CARICOM Enterprise Regime (CER),[45] the CARICOM Financial Services Agreement[46] and more recently the CARICOM Agreement on Investment.[47] CARICOM, admittedly, has made progress for special recognition to be afforded to a company incorporated in one Caribbean country when it seeks to operate in another. Protocol II to the Treaty of Chaguaramas addresses the status of CARICOM nationals' rights of establishment, the provision of services and the free movement of capital within the Community without impediments and restrictions.[48] Article 38 of the Revised Treaty specifically requires member states to remove discriminatory restrictions on banking, insurance and other financial services. This article confers a right, identical to that afforded a

---

39 CARICOM was established at Chaguaramas in Trinidad and Tobago on 4 July 1973 by countries of the Commonwealth Caribbean.
40 This treaty and its annex is referred to as the Treaty of Chaguaramas. Earlier on 1 April 1973, an agreement was concluded establishing the Caribbean Community in Guyana – the Georgetown accord. The community was seized with three areas of activity: (1) economic integration through the Caribbean Common market, (2) common services and functional cooperation and (3) coordination of foreign policy among independent countries. Members of the community include Antigua and Barbuda, the Bahamas, Barbados, Belize, Dominica, Grenada, Guyana, Jamaica, Montserrat, St Kitts and Nevis, St Lucia, St Vincent and the Grenadines, Suriname and Trinidad and Tobago.
41 Supra n. 2.
42 Barbados, Belize, Jamaica, Trinidad and Tobago, Guyana and Suriname are the only countries to date that have signed on to the CSM. The member states of the Organisation of Eastern Caribbean States (Dominica, St Lucia, Grenada, and St Vincent and the Grenadines) became signatories by the end of 2006.
43 L. A. Walcott, 'In the Interest of the Insured Policy-holder; Law Reform in the Commonwealth Caribbean' (2009) *Common Law World Review.*
44 Barbados Exempt Insurance Act of 1983, Cap 308A.
45 This came into operation in 1988 upon the ratification by four countries of the CARICOM group: St Lucia, St Kitts and Nevis, Antigua and Barbuda and Guyana.
46 CARICOM Financial Services Agreement, prepared by the Economic Intelligence and Policy Unit, CARICOM Secretariat, November 2004.
47 CARICOM Agreement on Investment – Economic Intelligence and Policy Unit, CARICOM Secretariat, revised March 2005.
48 Articles 30–50, Revised Treaty of Chaguaramas 2001.

national of any state within the region, on CARICOM nationals: to establish insurance business, provide insurance services and deploy insurance capital. Given the free movement of labour and the freedom of establishment protocols to the Treaty of Chaguaramas, a formal inter-regional oversight structure would buttress the establishment of the Caribbean Court of Justice to replace the Privy Council as the final appellate court, thereby advancing the integration process.[49] Additionally, the CLI Insurance Bill of 1993[50] and its recommendations on reform of Caribbean insurance business and insurance law have been a useful mechanism in furtherance of this process.[51]

THE CLI INSURANCE COMMITTEE

The Insurance Committee of the Caribbean Law Institute produced a Status Report on Insurance Law in the Commonwealth Caribbean. The report reviewed the statutory framework governing the conduct of insurance business in the region and the substantive law of insurance with special emphasis on identifying areas of disharmony among various countries and areas where the law was considered outdated. Several jurisdictions have enacted significant insurance law reform,[52] either expressly or impliedly incorporating the Caribbean Law Institute's Insurance (CLI) Bill. The CLI model significantly tightens the regulatory regime governing the industry by bestowing, *inter alia*, the power to search and seize on the regulator,[53] imposing stringent regulatory and financial obligations on insurance companies in relation to stipulated deposits,[54] statutory funds,[55] the maintenance of stipulated share capital, while the insurance company's investment strategy is channelled in accordance with state policy.[56] Consequently,

---

49 The Caribbean Court of Justice was established in 2005 in order to, *inter alia*, enhance access to justice in terms of reducing distance and expense for the population of the Caribbean community (www.jis.gov.jm/special_sections/CARICOMNEW/ccj.html). See further R. M. B. Antoine, *Commonwealth Caribbean Law and Legal Systems* (Cavendish: 1999), Chapter 14.
50 In April 1989, the CLI produced a Survey Report on the Status of Insurance Law in the Commonwealth Caribbean. This report identifies a number of areas where existing law in the Commonwealth Caribbean could be harmonised and modernised. As a consequence, in November 1990 the CLI established an Insurance Law Advisory Committee.
51 Caribbean Law Institute Model Motor Vehicles Insurance Bill of 1993; Insurance Association of the Caribbean [CLI/CLIC 2000 Rev.]; Caribbean Law Institute Model Insurance Bill 1993; Insurance Association of the Caribbean [2000 Rev.].
52 Anguilla Insurance Act R.S.A. 2000 c. I1215; Barbados Deposit Insurance Act No. 29 of 2006, Insurance Act No. 32 of 1996; Belize Insurance Act No. 14 of 2005; British Virgin Islands Insurance Act No. 15 of 1994; Cayman Islands Insurance Law No. 24 of 1979, Insurance Law [1995 Rev.] G6/1995; Dominica Insurance Act Chapter 78:49 [1990 Rev.]; Guyana Insurance Act No. 20 of 1998; Grenada Insurance Act No. 26 of 2001, Insurance Act No. 10 of 2002, Cap 150; Montserrat Insurance Act No. 2 of 1977; Jamaica Insurance Act No. 10 of 2001; St Lucia Insurance Act, Cap 12:08 [2001 Rev.]; St Vincent and the Grenadines Insurance Act No. 45 of 2003.
53 Section 53 of the Barbados Insurance Act No. 32 of 1996, Cap 310, empowers a magistrate or justice of the peace:

> [if] he is satisfied on information on oath laid by the Supervisor or any person authorised by the Supervisor for the purpose that there are reasonable grounds for suspecting that there are on any premises any securities, books, accounts, documents or statistics production of which have not been produced . . . the magistrate or justice of the peace may issue a warrant authorising any member of the police force together with any other persons to enter the premises, search, and seize.

See also Section 49 of the Jamaica Insurance Act No. 26 of 2001.
54 Ibid.
55 Section 25, Barbados Insurance Act No. 32 of 1996, Cap 310; Section 46, Guyana Insurance Act of 1998.
56 See for example Section 12 of the St Lucia Insurance Act, which stipulates share capital for long-term insurance as $1 million for a local company and $2 million for a foreign company; Section 13, Trinidad and Tobago Insurance Act Chapter 84:01.

modern regional insurance legislation provides for ongoing monitoring obligations including restrictions on borrowing powers, the obligation to file annual financial returns and submit audited accounts, all of which buttress the initial compliance requirements.[57] The critical underlying objective of these reforms is an economic one – solvency – to ensure the insurance company's ability to honour and discharge its obligations when due.[58] In addition, mirroring the ancillary but fundamental social reform that has taken place regionally with respect to status of children,[59] family law[60] and domestic violence,[61] modern regional Insurance Acts abolish the application of the Married Women's Property legislation and recognise 'unions, other than marriage' for the purposes of insurable interest and for the status of the beneficiary.[62]

INSURANCE BODIES OPERATING IN THE COMMONWEALTH CARIBBEAN

Insurance bodies providing educational and technical assistance exist in all Commonwealth Caribbean territories.[63] In addition, regionally two main insurance bodies monitor the industry's operation. These are the Insurance Association of the Caribbean (IAC)[64] and the Association of Insurance Institutes of the Caribbean (AIIC).[65] Additionally, external bodies such as the International Association of Insurance Supervisors (IAS),[66] the International Monetary Fund (IMF), and the Caribbean Association of Insurance Regulators provide technical assistance by issuing guidelines and assisting in the setting of standards providing a critical external regulatory function.

---

57 See for instance the Second Schedule to the Barbados Insurance Act No. 32 of 1996, Cap 310; Fourth Schedule to the Insurance Act of St Lucia No. 6 of 1995.
58 Section 6, Jamaica Insurance Act 2001; Section 4, St Lucia Insurance Act No. 6 of 1995; Section 11, Trinidad and Tobago Insurance Act Chapter 84:01.
59 Antigua and Barbuda Status of Children Act, Cap 414; Barbados Status of Children Reform Act of 1979, Cap 220; St Vincent and the Grenadines Status of Children Act, Cap 180 [1990 Rev.]; Trinidad and Tobago Status of Children Act of 1976, No. 46:07.
60 Anguilla Matrimonial Proceedings and Property Ordinance 1996; Antigua and Barbuda Divorce Act of 1997; Barbados Family Law Act, Cap 214; Barbados Marriage Act, Cap 106; Guyana Adoption (Amendment) Act of 1997; Trinidad and Tobago Cohabitational Relationships Act of 1998; Section 2(6)(a)(i) of the Guyana Family and Dependent Provisions Act No. 22 of 1990 states that 'a "wife" shall include a single man in a common law union for seven years immediately preceding the date of his death.' Jamaica, Matrimonial and Causes Act 1989; Trinidad and Tobago Cohabitational Relationships Act 1998. See also Robinson, 'New Directions in Family Law Reform in the Caribbean' (2000) 10 *Caribbean Law Review* 101; Roberts, 'Developments in Family Law Since Emancipation' [1985] *W.I.L.J.* 9; S. Owuso, 'Unions Other Than Marriage Under the Barbados Family Law Act, 1981' [1992] 21 *Anglo-Amer. L. Rev.* 53.
61 Barbados, Domestic Violence (Protection Orders) Act of 1992.
62 See for instance Sections 114–126 of the Barbados Insurance Act No. 32 of 1996, Cap 310.
63 See for instance www.attic.org.tt. The Association of Trinidad and Tobago Insurance Companies (ATTIC) was formed in Trinidad and Tobago in 1966 by Colonial Fire and General Insurance Co. Ltd, GTM Fire Insurance Co. Ltd, TATIL and Winsure Life and General Insurance Co. Ltd. In the mid- to late 1970s there was a marked increase in localisation of activities and a rejuvenation of ATTIC, which joined forces with Life Office Association and the local rating committee. Over the past 40 years, ATTIC's membership has grown from five companies to embrace all the life insurance companies and a majority of the general insurance companies in the country.
64 See www.iac-caribbean.com. The Insurance Association of the Caribbean (IAC) was established in 1974 in Kingston, Jamaica, and incorporated in August 1990 in Bridgetown, Barbados. It was formed in response for the need of an umbrella organisation to be an agent for carrying out the mandate of several insurance firms in the Anglophone Caribbean.
65 See www.iac-caribbean.com/institute/AIIC/About/asp. This association was established on 11 September 1989 by the insurance institutes of Barbados, Guyana, Jamaica, St Lucia and Trinidad and Tobago. Its primary focus is the harmonisation of educational efforts.
66 See www.iaisweb.org. The International Association of Insurance Supervisors (IAIS) was established in 1994 and represents insurance regulators and supervisors in some 180 jurisdictions in more than 130 countries. This body formulated essential criteria on 17 principles of insurance regulation.

CHAPTER 1

INSURANCE REGULATION

1.1   INTRODUCTION

The Commonwealth Caribbean insurance industry is regulated by statute, associated regulations and the common law. Statute vests responsibility for insurance administration in the regulator – historically described variously as Supervisor,[1] Registrar or Commissioner[2] of Insurance, depending on jurisdiction. This arrangement for oversight of financial services represents a sectoral approach, which in the modern era has been abandoned in favour of consolidated super-regulators known as Financial Services Commissions. Variance in descriptive title notwithstanding, regional Insurance Acts bestow on the regulator powers relating, *inter alia*, to registration of insurance companies and qualification of insurance personnel[3] for which regulatory approval must be had. The Bahamian decision *Commonwealth General Insurance Co. Ltd v The Minister Responsible for Insurance et al.*[4] illustrates this. The issue was whether the company was transacting life insurance business for which it had no licence. Applying Section 2 of the Insurance Act[5] and *Prudential Insurance Co. v I.R.C.*,[6] the Court found that appellant did indeed carry on life insurance business for which it had no licence. The action failed. More recently, actions of regulators and governments were addressed by the Privy Council in *United Policyholders Group et al. v Attorney General*.[7] The Privy Council decision stands atop an unsettled environment, triggering jurisprudence with assertions of guarantee and legitimate expectation. This places regulators under the microscope while reflecting the significance of the CLICO collapse in the Commonwealth Caribbean.

---

1   Prior to regulatory consolidation in the sectoral approach to oversight of the financial services sector, Barbados Insurance Act No. 32 of 1996, Cap 310 and St Vincent and the Grenadines Insurance Act 45 of 2003, for instance, referred to a 'Supervisor of Insurance.'

2   The Guyana and Jamaica Insurance Acts refer to the 'Commissioner' of insurance: Guyana Insurance Act No. 20 of 1998; Jamaica Insurance Act No. 26 of 2001. Section 5 of St Kitts and Nevis Insurance Act No. 22 of 2009, Cap 21:11 empowers the Registrar of Insurance to have responsibility over the general administration of the Insurance Act. Section 4(1) of The Bahamas Insurance Act No. 23 of 2009, Chapter 347 states that:

> there is hereby established for the purposes of this act, a body corporate to be known as the insurance commission of the Bahamas. (2) the commission shall be a body corporate, having perpetual succession and a common seal, with power to purchase, lease or otherwise acquire and hold and dispose of land and other property of whatsoever kind. (3) the commission may sue or be sued in its corporate name, and service up of any document of on whatsoever kind.

3   See further J. Hellner, 'The Scope of Insurance Regulation: What is Insurance for Purposes of Regulation?' (1963) 12 *Am. J. Comp. L.* 494; C. Bowyer, 'The Concept of Economic Law in England: Revisited to Consider the Regulation of General Insurance' [1995] *Anglo-Amer. L. Rev.* 259; R. Brophy, 'Development of Insurance Regulation in Ireland,' (2012) 2 *Journal of Financial Regulation and Compliance* 3, 249.

4   BS 1998 SC 8.

5   Section 2 of the Insurance Act, Chapter 317 defines 'life assurance business' as

> insurance of human lives and insurance appertaining thereto or connected therewith and includes the granting of annuities, endorsement benefits, sinking fund benefits and benefits in the event of death or disability by accident or sickness, provided that such insurance against disability by accident or sickness is included as additional benefit in a life policy.

6   [1904] 2 K.B. 658.

7   [2016] UKPC 17.

1.2   CARIBBEAN LAW INSTITUTE INSURANCE BILL

The Caribbean Law Institute's Insurance (CLI) Bill, adopted throughout the Caribbean in varying versions, has strengthened the regulatory regime. The preamble to the Barbados Insurance Act captures the object and intent of CLI's reforms:

> An Act to revise the law regulating the carrying on of insurance business in Barbados in order to strengthen the protection given to policyholders under the existing Act; to increase the capital and solvency requirements of insurance companies; to expand the existing regulatory framework to include the regulating of all insurance intermediaries; and to give effect to matters related thereto.

Effectively, response to the CLICO collapse expands the regulator's power in many jurisdictions by incorporating CLI's position. Far more expansive than earlier Insurance Acts, the current Acts exhibit, *inter alia*, increased financial requirements, more robust corporate governance safeguards and recognition of spousal relationships. The latter, if not for purposes of insurable interest, then certainly for recognition of the distinction between revocable and irrevocable beneficiaries. Undoubtedly, in light of disputes surrounding the validity of 'policies' such as Executive Flexible Premium Annuity (EFPA) as true insurance contracts and not fixed interest deposits, some jurisdictions have made provision for variable life products. Mindful of life insurance companies' creativity, Section 152 of the St Kitts and Nevis Insurance Act 2009,[8] for instance, describes a 'variable product' as meaning 'a variable life insurance policy, a variable annuity contract, or a universal life insurance policy.' Such a concept was foreign to Insurance Acts of the 1960s.

1.3   STATUTORY REQUIREMENTS

To mitigate the risk of corporate failure, recent regional insurance legislation imposes more robust regulatory and financial obligations, the underlying objective being maintenance of solvency – solvency of course being the prerequisite for insurance companies' ability to honour obligations when, as probabilities dictate, they shall become due. Regulatory oversight therefore provides added policyholder protection.[9] The regulator's function ensures requirements are met as conditions precedent to registration. The Act in most jurisdictions expressly stipulates that 'no person other than a body corporate may carry on insurance business.'[10] The regulator must be satisfied that the entity is a company before authorising registration of an insurance company. This is not the case, however, in St Vincent and the Grenadines Insurance Act No. 45 of 2003, which recognises an Association of Underwriters and further makes provision for unauthorised insurers to conduct insurance business.[11] Apart from the latter category, in order to be registered the insurer must have a minimum paid-up capital which varies in accordance with the nature of the insurance business being conducted (i.e. whether long-term, general or motor vehicle insurance business). For instance, the Barbados Insurance Act stipulates that the

---

8   St Kitts and Nevis Insurance Act No. 45 of 2009.
9   Antigua and Barbuda Insurance Act, Cap 218; the Bahamas Insurance Act Chapter 317; Belize Insurance Act Chapter 208; Trinidad and Tobago Insurance Act Chapter 84:01; Guyana Insurance Act of 1998; St Lucia Insurance Act No. 6 of 1995.
10   Section 9(1), Barbados Insurance Act, Cap 310; Section 6, Jamaica Insurance Act No. 26 of 2001; Section 11, Trinidad and Tobago Insurance Act Chapter 84:01.
11   Section 9, St Vincent and the Grenadines Insurance Act No. 45 of 2003.

company must have paid-up capital not less than $3 million for long term insurance business and $3 million for general insurance business. In the case of composite insurance business, the requirement is $5 million.[12] Other financial prerequisites to registration apart from minimum paid-up capital exist. These include the payment of a prescribed deposit to the regulator[13] and the maintenance of a statutory fund. A statutory fund requires an insurance company's placement in trust of assets equal to the company's liabilities and reserves.[14] In Guyana, for instance, Section 46 of the Insurance Act provides that insurers registered to carry on business 'shall establish and maintain a statutory fund in respect of each class of insurance business.'[15] The classes of insurance business in Schedule 2 annexed to the act, are accident and liability, auto, marine and aviation and fire. Finally, before the insurer is entitled to receive a registration certificate, the company must disclose the nature of business to be pursued and the qualifications of key personnel. The regulator, upon receipt of an application, may request additional information considered relevant. Once satisfied of the insurance company's solvency, the adequacy of the reinsurance arrangements for that class of insurance business[16] and the fitness and suitability of each of the persons managing or controlling the company, a certificate of registration in the prescribed form will be issued.

The initial statutory requirements for registration may be summed up as follows:

1 The insurer must be a body corporate;
2 The insurer must have a minimum paid up capital;
3 A deposit must be lodged with the regulator;
4 A statutory fund must be created and maintained;
5 Disclosure of the nature of business to be pursued and the qualifications of key personnel.

1.4 IMPOSITION OF PENALTIES

In some jurisdictions, an insurer's failure to observe any of the requirements under the Act triggers subjection to a penalty. Accordingly, Section 6 of the Jamaica Insurance Act imposes a penalty on the insurance company if it conducts insurance business without being an authorised body corporate, fails to satisfy deposit requirements and/or fails to submit the names and addresses of persons resident in Jamaica who are authorised to accept, on behalf of the body corporate, service of process in legal proceedings.[17] The consequences of breach are severe. By virtue of Section 6(3), any person found to be in contravention shall be guilty of an offence and liable on summary conviction in a Resident Magistrates Court to a fine not exceeding $3 million or to imprisonment for a term not exceeding three years or to both such fine and imprisonment. In St Vincent and the Grenadines, by virtue of Section 24 of the Act, a company that fails to comply with the deposit requirement is liable on summary conviction to a fine of $10,000 and in addition to any other punishment is liable to having its certificate cancelled.

12 Section 9(1), Barbados Insurance Act No. 32 of 1996, Cap 310; under the St Lucia Insurance Act No. 6 of 1995, the share capital for long term insurance is $1 million for a local company and $2 million for a foreign company, to be fully paid up in cash and for other types of insurance, not less than $750,000 for locals and $1.5 million for foreign companies.
13 Section 9, Barbados Insurance Act No. 32 of 1996, Cap 310; Section 40, Guyana Insurance Act No. 20 of 1998; Section 21, Trinidad and Tobago Insurance Act Chapter 84:01.
14 Section 25, Barbados Insurance Act No. 32 of 1996, Cap 310; Section 46, Guyana Insurance Act No. 20 of 1998.
15 Guyana Insurance Act No. 20 of 1998.
16 See for instance Section 12, Barbados Insurance Act No. 32 of 1996, Cap 310.
17 Jamaica Insurance Act No. 20 of 2001.

1.5   FINANCIAL MECHANISMS

In addition to the initial requirements, regional statutes also contain financial mechanisms aimed at ensuring the financial viability of insurance operations. These mechanisms can be grouped into two categories: provisions governing the insurer in the conduct of insurance business, and provisions which, although inherently part and parcel of the conduct of insurance business, specifically pertain to the supervisory powers of the regulator.

1.6   PROVISIONS GOVERNING OPERATIONS OF THE INSURER

In addition to the initial requirements for registration, regional Insurance Acts contain provisions governing the operation of insurance business. These include the requirement that insurance companies file annual financial returns and submit audited accounts.[18] Restrictions are also placed on the insurer's borrowing powers,[19] and the insurer's investment strategy is circumscribed by specific rules on the insurer's asset to debt ratio and the percentage of equity investment. The restrictions on the insurer's investment strategy essentially channel investment to meet the state's objectives while additionally serving to mitigate the risk of financial distress. This approach is evident in Section 55 of the Guyana Insurance Act,[20] which lays out with some particularity rules regulating the insurer's investment strategy:

> every insurer carrying on long-term insurance business in Guyana under this Act shall have assets in Guyana and shall maintain such assets in an amount of not fewer than 85 per cent of its statutory fund, provided however that for each percentage point of its assets invested in the common stock or long term debt of a company in Guyana, the 85 percent minimum may be reduced by one percentage point, up to a maximum of a ten-percentage point reduction.

Collectively, these ongoing mechanisms buttress the solvency mandate of the St Kitts and Nevis Insurance Act.[21] Section 33 of the Act provides:

> '(1) a registered insurance company that transacts more than one class of insurance business shall maintain records which accurately identify the assets comprising each insurance fund: (2) a registered insurance company shall, within four months of the end of each financial year, furnish a statement showing particulars of (a) liabilities in respect of each insurance fund and (b) assets comprising each insurance fund. Additionally, in the same act, section 34 prescribes rules governing the investment of insurance fund in assets: (1) an insurance bond shall be invested only in the assets prescribed in the fourth schedule; (2) the Minister may, by order published in the *Gazette* amend the fourth schedule.'

1.7   SUPERVISORY POWERS OF THE REGULATOR

Throughout the Caribbean, mechanisms for financial services regulation are transitioning from a sectoral to a consolidated approach. Historically, the region embraced the sectoral approach

---

18   Part VIII, Guyana Insurance Act No. 20 of 1998.
19   Section 160, St Lucia Insurance Act No. 6 of 1995.
20   Guyana Insurance Act No. 20 of 1998.
21   Cap 21:11.

to regulating both financial and non-financial institutions. Contemporary mechanisms clearly reject the view that the segregated approach is inefficient, wasting resources by duplication without enhancing or improving solvency outcomes of supervised entities. Admittedly, Caribbean commercial practice reflects connectivity among securities, banking and insurance activities, necessitating dialogue and cooperation among otherwise independent commissions. Fortunately, the Basel Committee's prudential financial guidelines apply across sectors including insurance. Underlying insurance regulation is the ultimate fact: prudent, sound financial practice begets solvency, *ergo*, policyholders are protected.[22] As a result, super 'one-stop' regulators have emerged in Barbados, Jamaica, the Organisation of Eastern Caribbean States (OECS) and Trinidad and Tobago. Emergence of regulatory convergence is attributable to many factors including, *inter alia*, the example and influence of the United Kingdom's Financial Services Authority.[23]

Jamaica established its Financial Services Commission (FSC)[24] in the aftermath of the dramatic collapse of its domestic financial services sector in mid-1996. The OECS established a Financial Services Authority in response to CLICO's failure. These new institutional mechanisms provide for continuous oversight and monitoring of financial services in general. With respect to insurance and the law however, the regulator – apart from central banks – occupies the summit of the regulatory regime in its vital supervisory role.

Insurance Acts give the regulator considerable powers. The regulator is empowered to prohibit the insurer from writing new policies[25] and ultimately, to suspend and/or cancel registration[26] (i.e. its ability to carry on business). Additionally, the regulator may initiate investigation of insurance operations[27] and is empowered to search and seize property. This is seen in the Insurance Acts of Barbados, Guyana, Jamaica and St Vincent and the Grenadines.[28] Section 53 of the Barbados Insurance Act[29] empowers a magistrate or justice of the peace,

> [if] he is satisfied on information on oath laid by the Supervisor or any person authorised by the Supervisor for the purpose that there are reasonable grounds for suspecting that there are on any premises any securities, books, accounts, documents or statistics production of which have not been produced in compliance with the requirement, the magistrate or justice of the peace may issue a warrant authorising any member of the police force together with any other persons to enter the premises, search, and seize.

The 'reasonable grounds for suspecting' requirement works as a necessary safeguard against abuse of the considerable powers the law gives to the regulator.

---

22 Hellner, supra n. 3.
23 The Financial Services and Markets Act 2000; see further J. Marsh, 'Disciplinary Proceedings against Authorised Firms and Approved Persons under the FSMA 2000', in John De Lacey, ed., *The Reform of United Kingdom Company Law* (Cavendish Publishing: 2002), p. 439; Bowyer, supra n. 3; E. Ferran and C. A. E. Goodhart, eds, *Regulating Financial Services and Market in the 21st Century* (Hart: 2001).
24 Jamaica Insurance Act No. 10 of 2001.
25 See for instance Section 73, St Vincent and the Grenadines Insurance Act No. 45 of 2003.
26 Section 46, Jamaica Insurance Act No. 26 of 2001.
27 Section 49, Jamaica Insurance Act No. 26 of 2001; Section 47, St Vincent and the Grenadines Insurance Act No. 45 of 2003.
28 Barbados Insurance Act, Cap 310.
29 Section 26, Jamaica Insurance Act No. 10 of 2004.

1.8   ONGOING MONITORING MECHANISMS

The ongoing monitoring mechanisms may therefore be summarised as follows:

1   Preparation and submission of annual accounts;[30]
2   Audited financial statements and accounts;[31]
3   Maintenance and separation of funds;
4   Restriction on borrowing powers;[32]
5   Restrictions on investment strategy;
6   Continuous oversight by the supervisor and accompanying powers.

1.9   JAMAICA INSURANCE ACT OF 2001[33]

Passage of the Jamaica Insurance Act of 2001 came on the heels of the collapse of the indigenous financial services sector in mid-1996. In the period prior to its collapse, the insurance sector managed more than half the country's pension funds. In 1997, when Jamaica Stock Exchange (JSE) requirements mandated filings for the previous year, this eventuality meant open declaration of the sector's insolvency. The government's response was creation of a resolution institution, The Financial Sector Adjustment Co. Ltd (FINSAC), with an initial J$6.3 billion (US$180 million at then then ruling exchange rate) loan assistance programme for distressed financial institutions. Insurance companies would absorb the lion's share.[34] Collapse of the domestic financial services sector and the attendant need to rebuild public confidence acted as a catalyst for implementation of the Deposit Insurance Act[35] and the Insurance Act of 2001.[36]

---

30 Section 28, Jamaica Insurance Act No. 10 of 2004; Section 61, the Bahamas Insurance Act No. 14 of 2009; Dominica Insurance Act, Cap 21:11.
31 St Lucia Insurance Act No. 6 of 2013.
32 Supra n. 19.
33 Jamaica Insurance Act No. 26 of 2001.
34 Assistance was sought by Dyoll Life, Mutual Life Assurance Society, Island Life and Life of Jamaica. A negative offshoot of this rescue package was the diversion of tax dollars and continuing reduced confidence in local companies operating in the financial system. Whereas extant media reports suggest causal factors that highlight anti-inflation policy, high interest rates and a tight liquidity regime maintained by the government (essentially: blame the government), Persaud attributes this more to imprudent risk management, regulatory arbitrage and failures made possible by inadequate legislation and supervisory personnel. He argues that connected interests sought to control the public narrative of causal factors in order to downplay poor investment policies and choices; mismatch of assets with liabilities – short-term funds used to acquire long term assets; disturbing management and control failures; burgeoning hubris and in some cases, deliberate fraudulent intent. Subsequently validated suit no. CL 1996/C330 – *Financial Institutions Services Ltd v CNB Holdings et al.* For description and analysis of this collapse, see W. H. Persaud, *Jamaica Meltdown: Indigenous Financial Sector Crash 1996* (iUniverse Inc.: 2006); Wilbern Persaud, *Jamaica: Post-colonial Struggles for Dignity, Equity and Development* (Harpy Research Centre: 2013).
35 Jamaica Insurance Act No. 3 of 1998.
36 G. Bonnick, 'Storm in a Tea Cup: Crisis in Jamaica's Financial Sector,' Adlith Brown Memorial Lecture, 13th Annual Conference of the Caribbean Centre for Monetary Studies (Nassau, the Bahamas, October 1998). In 1997, the insurance sector, which controlled half the total managed pension funds, stood on the brink of insolvency. The Jamaican government's solution was a massive bailout by the Financial Sector Adjustment Company (FINSAC) with an initial $6.3 billion (US$180 million) loan assistance program for troubled companies including Mutual Life Assurance, Dyoll Life, Island Life and Life of Jamaica. While some economists point to causal factors such as high interest rates and tight liquidity, the collapse represented a good example of the consequences of imprudent investment decision making and inadequate financial regulation. Newspaper reports reveal that many insurance companies launched into real estate projects – commercial office

From a macro perspective, the Jamaica Insurance Act of 2001[37] is an example of a discernible trend to more robust intervention in the affairs of the insurer.[38] Insurance Acts in jurisdictions using this approach stand apart from their regional counterparts both with respect to ongoing financial restrictions placed on insurance companies and extensive corporate governance rules to which companies operating in the jurisdiction are subject.

1.10 CORPORATE GOVERNANCE

The Jamaica Insurance Act predates the Sarbanes-Oxley Act in the United States,[39] but we should indicate that in addition to the broad financial restrictions that obtain in other regional Insurance Acts, it exhibits features similar to Sarbanes-Oxley relating to corporate governance. By importing corporate governance principles to the Insurance Act (corporate governance is identified as one of the 16 core principles of insurance regulation)[40] the financial relevance of the industry to the state is recognised, accompanied by an unwillingness, in the wake of the experience of the 1990s, to leave corporate governance principles to be narrowly defined as purely external to the purview of insurance legislation.

Thus, the Act contains detailed provisions on an array of issues. There are provisions governing the appointment of the auditor[41] and the auditor's report,[42] which extend beyond registered insurers to agents and brokers.[43] The Act furthermore demands that insurance companies appoint an actuary.[44] The duties imposed on the insurer, accompanied by a detailed monitoring mechanism – a system of continuous notification by the insurer to the Commission at every stage of the insurance operation – have been described as burdensome by multi-jurisdictional companies. Registered insurers must, within 90 days of the end of each financial year, submit to the Commission an annual statement and related documents in the prescribed form and containing the prescribed information.[45]

Within 14 days of the date of document submission, an audited financial statement must be published in a daily newspaper,[46] and insurers must exhibit throughout the year a copy of the latest financial statement in a conspicuous position.[47] The annual statement must be certified by the company's independent auditor and, should a document furnished by the insurer be incorrect or incomplete, the Commission may, by notice in writing, require the company to amend the document.[48] The Act mandates that the company's accounts be audited annually by

---

towers, beach resorts and golf courses – without proper due diligence and secure pre-construction lease arrangements. Persaud (2006), supra n. 34, attributes this to non-arm's-length decisions on loan approval versus investment choice: lender and developer were one and the same!

37   Supra n. 33.
38   See for instance St Vincent and the Grenadines Insurance Act No. 45 of 2003.
39   Pub. L. No. 107–204, 116 Stat. 745.
40   See www.iaisweb.org. The International Association of Insurance Supervisors (IAIS) was established in 1994. It formulated essential criteria on the 17 principles of insurance supervision. These were identified as organisation, licensing, changes in control, corporate governance, internal controls, assets, liabilities, capital adequacy and solvency, derivatives and off-balance sheet items, reinsurance, market conduct, financial reporting, on-site inspections, sanctions, co-ordination and co-operation, and confidentiality.
41   Section 41.
42   Section 40.
43   Section 37.
44   Section 44.
45   Section 26(1)(a).
46   Section 26(1)(b).
47   Section 26(1)(c).
48   Section 26(3).

an independent auditor.[49] Further, insurers conducting long-term insurance business must initiate an investigation into the company's financial position by an actuary valuing the company's liabilities.[50] On completion of the investigation, an abstract of the report must be submitted to the Commission within 90 days.[51] The Commission is to be notified periodically of various matters including the auditor's appointment, removal or any other occurrence that causes a vacancy in the office.[52] These requirements ensure the authorities are kept abreast of the insurer's operations.

Powers of the Commission are far-reaching. The Commission itself has the power to appoint an auditor where the insurer, agent or broker fails to do so.[53] The broad mandate of the Commission is buttressed by wide powers of investigation. The Commission may demand from any insurance company information relating to any matter connected to its insurance business.[54] It has the power to enter, search premises, using such force as is reasonably necessary for the purpose, and seize and remove any securities, books, accounts, documents or statistics.[55] The corporate governance reach of the legislation cannot be disputed. By virtue of Section 23 of this Act, a registered insurer shall not, directly or indirectly:

(1) Every director of a registered insurer who knowingly contravenes subsection (1) and (b) shall be guilty of an offence:[56]

(a) acquire or deal in its own shares or lend money or make advances on the security of its own shares;

(b) lend any of its funds to a director or an officer of the insurer or to the spouse or a child of a director or an officer except on security of the insured's own policies;

(c) grant unsecured credit facilities to any person except for

(i)   temporary cover, not exceeding thirty days in the case of general insurance;

(ii) advances to agents, sales representatives or to full-time employees against commissions or salaries to be earned.

(d) enter into any guarantee or provide any security in connection with a loan by any other person to any person referred to in paragraph (b).

Additionally, as a safety measure, the Commission's written approval must first be obtained before an amalgamation, acquisition and/or transfer of business can take place,[57] thereby curbing the insurer's freedom to embark upon corporate reconstruction. By legislating rigid time lines and importing corporate governance safeguards, the Act plainly reflects a desire to strengthen ethical, prudential and financial soundness and decision-making in the financial sector while simultaneously rebuilding and increasing public confidence in the money management apparatus.

The Act embraces most of the CLI initiatives and has influenced Insurance Acts or rather policy-makers throughout the Commonwealth Caribbean. The Act additionally possesses some notable features which set it apart from its Caribbean counterparts.

---

49   Section 28.
50   Section 30(1).
51   Section 30(2).
52   Supra n. 43.
53   Section 37(3).
54   Section 46.
55   Section 49.
56   See also Section 44, St Vincent and the Grenadines Insurance Act No. 45 of 2003.
57   Section 31.

1.11   THE INTERESTS OF POLICYHOLDERS

An interesting aspect of the Jamaica Insurance Act 2001 is evident in Section 36, which provides:

> For the purpose of discharging his duty to act honestly and in good faith with a view to the best interests of an insurance company, a director or senior officer thereof *shall*[58] take into account the *interests of the company's policyholders.*[59]

It is well-settled that an important component of the underlying rationale of insurance regulation is the protection of policyholders. This is implicit in the preamble to most Insurance Acts and in the powers of the Supervisor to intervene where the interests of policyholders are threatened and/or in the situation of a company unable to pay its debts. Further, it is evident in the express authorisation of the Supervisor to act as an arbitrator in matters of dispute.[60] In light, however, of the express recognition of the 'interests of . . . policyholders' in the Jamaica statute, the approach adopted by its regional counterparts seems relatively benign in comparison. Several theoretical implications arise. The stance adopted by the Jamaica Insurance Act seems to suggest a *communitaire*/stakeholder position – an approach also evident in the residual Jamaica Companies Act.[61] Section 174 of the Companies Act similarly provides that in discharging duties, directors may have regard to the 'interests of shareholders, employees and the *community in which the company operates*'![62] The philosophical implication thereof is beyond the scope of this text. Suffice it to say the laudable resonance of the Insurance Act, by repeating the expansive language of the underlying Companies Act,[63] is recognition that the company's successful operation rests on the quality of its relationships with policyholders.[64] Most regional Company Acts contain broad remedial mechanisms for 'complainants.'[65] Section 225 of the Barbados Companies Act,[66] for instance, defines a 'complainant' as:

(a)   a shareholder or debenture holder of a share or debenture of a company or any of its affiliates;

(b)   a director or officer or former director and officer of the company or any of its affiliates;

(c)   the registrar; or

(d)   any other person who in the opinion of the court is a proper person to make an application under this part.

There is considerable Caribbean case law indicating the willingness of the Courts to exercise judicial discretion under the 'any other person who . . . is a [fit and] proper person to make an application' rubric.[67] With respect to insurance, however, while the social tenor of the Act

---

58   Emphasis added.
59   Emphasis added.
60   Section 5, Barbados Insurance Act, Cap 310; Section 8, Trinidad and Tobago Insurance Act Chapter 84:01.
61   Jamaica Companies Act No. 10 of 2004.
62   Emphasis added.
63   See Section 174 of the Jamaica Companies Act No. 10 of 2004.
64   J. Parkinson, 'Inclusive Company Law,' in J. de Lacy, ed., *The Reform of United Kingdom Company Law* (Cavendish Publishing: 2002), p. 43.
65   See the unreported decisions of *Dabreo and Dabreo v Dolland et al.* (High Court of Grenada No. 81 of 1995); *Grenada General Ins. et al. v Grenada Ins. Services Ltd* (High Court of Grenada No. 12 of 1999); *Ward v Mountgay Rums Co. Ltd* (High Court of Barbados).
66   Cap 308.
67   Recognising parties to a pre-incorporation contract in the Barbadian decision of *Canwest International Inc. et al. v Atlantic TV Ltd et al.* (1994) 48 WIR 40; A corporate customer, in the *Five Star Medical & Ambulance Services Ltd v Telecommunications Services of Trinidad & Tobago Ltd & Samuel Martin*, HCA No. 1593 of 2001; and a former employee in *Lalla v Trinidad Cement Ltd & TCL Holdings* (unreported decision, High Court of Trinidad and Tobago HCA No. Cv. S-852/98).

imports notions of managerial ethics and responsibility, because of the marked absence of a coherent negotiation structure within insurance law or insurance companies for policyholders, unless they are shareholders the end result is that there is no tangible advantage to the mandate placed on directors and officers 'to take into account the interests of the company's policy-holders.' In *Demerara Holdings Ltd et al. v Demerara Life Assurance Co. of Trinidad & Tobago Ltd*,[68] the judgment of Moosai J serves as a focal point for understanding bankruptcy, corporate and insurance law governing mergers and acquisitions, the oppression remedy, insurance business and the solvency of the statutory fund.

In this decision, the first plaintiff sought relief pursuant to Sections 242 and 250 of the Companies Act, complaining that the business or affairs of the first and second defendants, as affiliated companies, are being carried in a manner that is oppressive or unfairly prejudicial to or unfairly disregards its interests as a former shareholder of the first defendant and a share-holder of the second defendant and the interests of the holders of life policies issued by the first defendant for whom it acts as trustee.

(a)   The first plaintiff, for relief pursuant to the provisions of sections 242 and 250 of the Companies Act, under which the first plaintiff complains that the business or affairs of the first and second defendants, as affiliated companies, have been and are being carried on or conducted and are destined to be carried on or conducted, and the powers of the third, fourth and fifth defendants as directors of both companies have been exercised, in a manner that is oppressive or unfairly prejudicial to or unfairly disregards its interests as a former shareholder of the first defendant and a shareholder of the second defendant and the interests of the holders of life policies issued by the first defendant for whom it acts as trustee.

(b)   The second and third plaintiffs, in their capacity as directors of the first plaintiff and as former directors of the first defendant, and the fourth plaintiff as director of the first plaintiff and an officer of the first defendant, for relief pursuant to the provisions of Section 242 and 250 of the Companies Act. Specific to the statutory fund to the fact that the statutory fund deficit had ballooned out of all proportion and the Central Bank required immediate steps to be taken to rectify same.

While at the inception of the merger Demerara Life could have been considered weak, Mega Insurance was disproportionately weaker. Having regard to its historical weakness and inability to satisfy the statutory fund deficit, Mega Insurance poses a threat to the financial security of Demerara Life policyholders in the event that it be allowed to assume legal liability for their policies. Accordingly I hold that there are good grounds for setting aside the Merger Agreement on the basis that the merger would be unfairly prejudicial to and in unfair disregard of the interests of the policyholders of Demerara Life within the meaning of section 242 of the Companies Act.

The utility of complainant provisions under the Companies Act is apparent.

1.12   WINDING UP

The fundamental premise of insurance regulation is to ensure, as far as possible, that the insurer is capable of fulfilling its financial obligations when they become due. Essentially the ultimate objective is to reduce the risk of corporate failure. In this regard, the Commission

---

68   TT 2011 HC 86.

may apply to the court for an order that the insurer be placed under judicial management.[69] Where there is evidence that the liabilities of the company exceed the value of its assets, the relevant provisions governing the winding up of insurance operations contained in the Insurance Act will be triggered.[70] This operates in conjunction with residual companies legislation,[71] upon which the Insurance Act is juxtaposed, and any ancillary bankruptcy legislation.[72]

Section 51 of the Jamaica Insurance Act provides, for instance:

(1) The Court may order the winding up of a company in accordance with relevant provisions of the Companies Act;

(2) A company may be wound up on a petition of –

    (a) ten or more policyholders owning policies of an aggregate sum assured that is equivalent to at least twenty percent of the total sum assured by the company or

    (b) the Commission.

(3) A petition referred in subsection (2) shall not be presented except by leave of the court, and such leave shall not be granted until a *prima facie* case has been established to the satisfaction of the court and until security for costs has been given for such amount as the court may think reasonable.[73]

The St Vincent and the Grenadines Insurance Act expressly pierces the corporate veil to impose liability on directors where in the process of winding up it is discovered that a director, personal representative or officer committed a misfeasance.[74] A claim that insurance is a special regime requiring leave before winding up proceedings could be commenced in *CLICO (Bahamas) Ltd v Supervisor of Insurance RF&G Life Insurance Co. Ltd*,[75] concerned the insolvency of the Caribbean insurance company formerly known as British Fidelity Assurance Ltd, better known as CLICO, part of the CL Financial Group. The proceedings concerned a branch office in Belize ('CLICO Belize'), a subsidiary of CLICO (Bahamas) Ltd ('CLICO Bahamas'), an insurance company incorporated in the Bahamas. CLICO Belize, which is registered in Belize as an overseas company, was formerly under judicial management.

---

69   Section 53, St Vincent and the Grenadines Insurance Act No. 45 of 2003.
70   Section 51, Jamaica Insurance Act No. 26 of 2001.
71   Antigua and Barbuda Companies Act No. 18 of 1995; Barbados Companies Act, Cap 308; Dominica Companies Act No. 21 of 1994; Grenada Companies Act No. 35 of 1994; St Lucia Companies Act No. 19 of 2013; St Vincent and the Grenadines Companies Act No. 8 of 1994.
72   Barbados Bankruptcy and Insolvency Act Chapter 303; St Lucia Bankruptcy & Insolvency Laws Act No. 21 of 1991; Jamaica Insolvency Act 2014.
73   Section 61.
74   Section 65.
75   Supreme Court of Belize No. 12 of 2010. The statute laws applicable to insurance companies in Belize comprise a statute enacted No. 15 of 1975, which came into force on 19 July 1976 (hereinafter referred to as 'the 1975 Insurance Act'), and the other is the Insurance Act 2004 (hereinafter referred to as 'the 2004 Insurance Act'). Both are collectively referred to as 'the Insurance Acts.' The Insurance Acts have made provision for registered insurance companies, such as CLICO Belize, to establish and maintain statutory funds for the benefit and security of each of the many different categories or 'classes' of insurance business to which the Insurance Acts apply, and which was being carried on by any insurance company within Belize. The funds being held by the Liquidator are the balance of funds (approximately BZ$726,353) ('the balance of the statutory funds') remaining after certain statutory funds (approximately BZ$5,643,502) ('the statutory funds') had been split and distributed by the liquidator in various ways with the approval of the SOI. The balance of the statutory funds together with a property owned by CLICO Belize within the Orange Walk district of Belize, is essentially all of the assets remaining in the Liquidation for distribution, to satisfy the substantially greater debts outstanding in the Liquidation, prior to completing the winding up of CLICO Belize.

Liquidation proceedings were commenced and concern related to the limited funds being held by the liquidator of CLICO Belize in its winding-up, how such monies should be distributed and who should benefit from its distribution.

> It is worth noting that the class of 'Annuities' for which Certificates were provided commenced from 1 January 2008 to 31 December 2009, but within the category of 'annuity' was a product known as the 'Executive Flexible Premium Annuity' ('EFPA').[76]

The EFPA product has been the subject of litigation elsewhere in the Caribbean, but within Belize, whether it is more in the nature of a financial product (like a certificate of deposit) than a genuine insurance policy has been a controversial question. That is because it is something of a hybrid 'with the payment of high interest rates which exceeded the market rate' Belize was carrying under the Core Portfolio and the EFPA. The statutory fund of each class of insurance under the Insurance Acts must be used exclusively for only that class. The disagreement is rooted in the fact, as previously noted, that there was a deficiency of the statutory fund being maintained and held by the Supervisor of Insurance (SOI). Also, in relation to the statutory fund, disagreement arose about the nature of the two respective groups of contracts (the Core Portfolio and the EFPA) and the consequence to the statutory funds (and the holders of these products) arising from the differing views being expressed. The disagreement was despite the legal and statutory provision that the management of the company 'vest exclusively in the Judicial Manager, who shall have complete control of the management of the company' (subject of course to the 2004 Insurance Act, wherein the SOI was supposed to have a role subsidiary to the Judicial Manager while both were under the general management or supervision and directions of the Court). As noted above, the grounds on which a company may be wound up include the fact that the company is unable to pay its debts, and that it is just and equitable that the company be wound up. The Companies (Winding-Up) Rules 1909 of England apply to the proceedings in the winding-up under the Companies Act and therefore apply to the winding-up of CLICO Belize. It is clear that the Companies Act provisions, as they relate to winding-up of CLICO Belize, following the provisional order of liquidation and the provisional appointment by the liquidator, are in respect of winding-up by the court only (and not voluntary winding-up or winding-up subject to the supervision of the court).

The court may also have regard to the wishes of the creditors in all matters relating to a winding-up. The liquidator is an officer of the court, who, once appointed with the sanction of the court, has the power to carry on the business of the company, so far as may be necessary for the beneficial winding-up thereof; and without the sanction of Section 130(1)(e) and (f) of the Companies Act 39, Sections 138 and 141 of the Companies Act, Section 169 of the Companies Act, and Section 147(1)(b) of the Companies Act.[77]

---

76 The EFPA product was apparently being sold by CLICO Belize, within Belize, for a long time without a license and outside of the radar of the SOI, and it was not until possibly 2002/2003 that this product was licensed. The EFPA product has been described by the representative of the interested party as 'toxic,' no doubt because

> (1) . . . it would place a severe and debilitating financial burden on the insurer; (2) reinsurance is not available; and 3) matching assets would be required for its transfer. In respect of (3), matching assets equates to refunding EFPA holders their deposits.

77 Sections 130(1)(e) and (f), 138, 141, 147(1)(b) and 169, Belize Companies Act; see also *Gulf Insurance Ltd v The Central Bank of Trinidad & Tobago*, TT 2005 PC 8.

1.13 COMMON LAW

In addition to statute, the common law assists in the determination of whether the company is conducting 'insurance business'; whether, as a consequence of an affirmative finding that it is indeed conducting insurance business, the company falls within the parameters of the Insurance Act; and whether the regulator has acted appropriately and in accordance with the rules of natural justice. The common law also assists in determining the consequences of conducting insurance business without being authorised. The role of the common law in assisting in the determination of whether an insurer is indeed conducting insurance business and so falls within the parameters of the Insurance Act will be dealt with in Chapter 2. Next we consider the role of the regulator and the consequences of failure to comply with statutory requirements.

1.14 COMMON LAW ON THE ROLE OF THE REGULATOR

There is regional case law, *United Security Life & General Insurance Co. Ltd v Supervisor of Insurance*[78] and *Narsham Insurance (Bds) Ltd v Supervisor of Insurance & Another*,[79] illustrating the relative success of administrative law and rules of natural justice in constraining abuse of power by the regulator. In the decision of *United Security Life & General Insurance Co. Ltd v Supervisor of Insurance*,[80] the Supervisor of Insurance failed to furnish, in a timely manner, the plaintiff insurance company with a copy of the auditor's report. In fact, the plaintiff received a copy of the document some seven days after the Supervisor had intervened and some three months after the Supervisor received the Report. The Court, in hearing the action for Judicial Review, interpreted Section 65 of the Trinidad and Tobago Insurance Act, which empowered the Supervisor of Insurance to intervene into the affairs of a company where (i) the interests of the policyholders are being threatened, (ii) the Supervisor is satisfied that it is necessary to intervene to protect the interests of policyholders, (iii) the company is unable to pay its debts, (iv) there has been unreasonable delay in the settlement of claims and (v) the company has furnished misleading or false information. Section 66 of the said Act places an obligation on the Supervisor to provide written notice prior to the exercise of power. The High Court of Trinidad and Tobago held that the failure by the Supervisor to furnish the appellant with a copy of the report vitiated the Supervisor's action. Justice Blackman stated, in reference to the dispute as to the amount of the deficit in the statutory fund:

> I do not think the rules of natural justice and the judicial limitations on the exercise of his powers that the courts should get involved in accounting matters. The courts are not equipped to handle such problems which are better left to the experts.

This decision may be construed as reflective of the judiciary's general reluctance to intervene in commercial matters. In this regard, administrative law operates as a convenient and appropriate device to avoid investigating minutiae of insurance operations.

A similar outcome was reached in the Barbadian Court of Appeal decision of *Narsham Insurance (Bds) Ltd v Supervisor of Insurance and Another*.[81] Here the applicant, an insurance company,

---

78 (1990) 1 Trin LR 410, TT 2005 PC 8.
79 (1999) 56 WIR 101.
80 Note at p. 419 of the judgment, citing *Re Western Ontario Credit Corp. Ltd v Ontario Securities Commission* [1975] 59 DLR (3d) 501 at 511, where Justice Hughes stated: 'Moreover where a regulatory tribunal acting with its jurisdiction, makes an order in the public interest with the experience and understanding of what that interest consists of in a specialized field accumulated over many years.'
81 75 (1999) 56 WIR 101.

failed to file financial returns in accordance with the Insurance Act. After the company was in default for two and a half years, the Supervisor ordered the company to cease writing new business, making new investments and liquidating existing investments. On an application for Judicial Review, the Court of Appeal held that the actions of the Supervisor amounted to a breach of the rules of natural justice. It ruled that the Supervisor's failure to make the Report of the actuary available to the company on a timely basis made his actions vulnerable to review.

The decisions of *United Security Insurance* and *Narsham* demonstrate that administrative law and the rules of natural justice effectively limit the exercise of the regulator's powers. Despite the fact that in both cases there was undoubtedly cause for intervention, the failure by regulators to pay particular attention to required procedural details rendered the action vulnerable to attack. A contrary position is witnessed in *Commonwealth General Insurance Co. Ltd v The Minister Responsible for Insurance et al.*, Supreme Court of the Bahamas, No. 8 of 1998. In this case the issue was whether the insurer was conducting life insurance business without a licence. The regulator wrote to the insurer outlining two options: (1) seek and obtain authorisation to engage in life and health business in conjunction with its property and liability business and after meeting all other requirements (to carry on both general and life and health insurance business, required the deposit of $3 million), establish and maintain a separate account for life and health business; or (2) incorporate a new, separate entity to write life and medical insurance. The Supreme Court reviewed the role of the Regulator under Section 10 of the Insurance Act and the powers of the Minister responsible for insurance. In finding for the regulator, the Court ruled that it is accepted that a person or authority to whom Parliament gives power to do certain things, or whom Parliament indicates is to be satisfied about certain things, cannot normally delegate that power or authority to any other person or body. However, the rule cannot be carried to the point of requiring a Minister of the Crown to give his mind personally to all the things he is empowered to decide.

1.15   UNAUTHORISED INSURANCE

Overview

An insurer is precluded from relying on its non-compliance with the statute in order to avoid obligations to the insured. Where the insurer evades its obligations, there is authority indicating the willingness of Caribbean courts to invoke the equitable maxim, 'He who comes to equity must come with clean hands,' or under the common law maxim, *nullus commodum capere potest de injuria sua propria* ('no one can gain an advantage by his own wrong'). This is seen in the Guyanese decision of *Guyana National General Insurance Co. Ltd v Moore et al.*[82] Here the plaintiff company conducted motor insurance business and issued motor insurance policies under the Motor Vehicles (Third Party Risks) Ordinance.[83] In 1986, the Registrar of Joint Stock Companies informed the plaintiff company that they had not deposited the sum of $50,000 or approved securities to the like amount with the Accountant General as prescribed by Section 2(b) of the Insurance Act.[84] The plaintiff company acknowledged that this was the case and undertook to stop writing any new business and to refund premiums already collected. In the interim, Moore sued G, a policyholder of the company, in respect of motor insurance and obtained a judgment

---

82   77 [1969] *Guy. L. Rev.* 91.
83   Cap 281.
84   Ibid.

by default, calling upon the insurance company to pay the judgment.[85] The judgment was not paid and a levy was executed on the property of the plaintiff company, as the insurers of G, to pay the judgment. The plaintiff company sought a declaration that it was not an authorised insurer under the Insurance Act and that the policies issued were illegal, void and *ultra vires*. Further, that it was not liable to indemnify persons against whom judgments had been given and that the levy executed on its property to satisfy the judgment was irregular and bad in law. Vieira J, in the High Court of Guyana, stated in a strongly worded judgment:

> In my opinion, equity will not permit this company, after having received no doubt thousands and thousands of dollars as premiums for policies issued in respect of third party risks in relation to motor vehicles . . . to now come before this court and piously raise their hands to the heavens and boldly disclaim all or any liability and ask this court, sitting as a court of both law and equity, to countenance such disgraceful conduct by granting them this modern equitable relief.

1.16   STATUTE

Most Insurance Acts in the Commonwealth Caribbean contain a provision to the effect that 'Failure on the part of a company to comply with any provision of this Act shall not in any way invalidate any policy issued by the company.'[86] The obvious purpose and intent of this section is the protection of the insured policyholder against the risk of insurance being effected with an unauthorised insurance carrier. This purposive rationale is, however, capable of being undermined if the section is subjected to a literal interpretation. A closer reading of the section reveals that the scope of the section is capable of being narrowed to (1) bodies corporate and (2) policies of insurance. Thus associations and societies would be excluded as falling outside the purview of the Act, as would a relationship where a clearly discernible policy is absent. An alternative approach however is to have regard and to place appropriate emphasis on the term 'any.' This would give effect to the purpose and intent of the provision so that while statute emphatically provides 'that no person may carry on insurance business unless that person is a company,' an innocent insured will be protected in instances where that 'condition' cannot be satisfied.

Instead, rather than deny the insured's claim, the statutory solution is to impose on the insurer an economic sanction. Hence, regionally, the insurer is instead subject to a penalty ranging from $40,000[87] to $1 million.[88] From the standpoint of the insured consumer, the statutory intervention is welcomed. The risks of effecting cover with an unauthorised insurer have been effectively reduced to an economic public policy rationale, recognition that the purpose of the legislation is to ensure the financial soundness of insurers for the protection of insured persons.

1.17   COMMON LAW ON UNAUTHORISED INSURANCE

The tension between a literal interpretation of the statute and a purposive one is evident in common law construing statutes without an express statutory sanction. In jurisdictions without statutory intervention, the common law must be applied. The common law on point is of

---

85   Section 25, Barbados Insurance Act, Cap 310; Section 46, Guyana Insurance Act No. 20 of 1998.
86   See for instance Section 162 of the Barbados Insurance Act 1996.
87   Section 157, St Lucia Insurance Act No. 6 of 1995.
88   Section 19, Guyana Insurance Act No. 20 of 1998; see also Section 166, Barbados Insurance Act 1996, Cap 32, 310.

marginal assistance as it turns on the construction of the specific statute. In Barbados, Jamaica and Trinidad and Tobago, the express statutory sanction of 'illegal' contracts arguably obviates the necessity of applying the common law. However, in jurisdictions without express statutory guidance, the cases indicate that the precise language used in the statute is of critical importance. There is no general consensus as to the circumstances under which the rights of the policyholder will be sustained despite the insurer not being registered under the Act. On the one hand are the decisions of *Stewart v Oriental Fire & Marine Insurance Co. Ltd*[89] and *Guyana National General Insurance Co. Ltd v Reginald Moore & Others*,[90] which found in favour of the policyholder. In contrast, *Bedford Insurance Co. Ltd v Institutio de Resseguros do Brasil*[91] and *Phoenix General Insurance Company of Greece S.A. v Administrattia Asigualiror de Stat*[92] found that non-compliance by the insurer rendered the contract void and incapable of being enforced.

The cases depict the fine distinction made between 'effecting insurance business' and the 'carrying on of insurance business.' These elements first import the negotiation and conclusion of the insurance contract while the second connotes the execution of the contract by for instance, the payment of claims.[93] In order to determine whether the legislation imposes an express prohibition on effecting and carrying on insurance of an unauthorised class, close attention must be paid to the relevant statute.

In *Stewart v Oriental Fire & Marine Insurance Co. Ltd*,[94] a Lloyd's syndicate insured a risk, written by the syndicate, with the defendants a foreign corporation acting through agents and sub-agents. Neither defendant was authorised to carry on insurance business under the Act. The issue was whether the reinsurance contract was illegal and void on the basis of the earlier decision of *Bedford Insurance Co. Ltd v Institutio de Resseguros do Brasil*.[95] The Court held that the Insurance Companies Act of 1974 did not expressly prohibit the making of a contract of insurance of the classes specified, but merely the carrying on of certain classes of unauthorised insurance business. Since the purpose of the Act was to ensure the financial soundness of insurers for the protection of insured persons, the Court found that there was no sufficient justification on the grounds of public policy for depriving innocent insured persons the benefit of their contracts of insurance. The fact that insurance business was defined by reference to 'contracts of insurance' was not sufficient to prohibit any implication of the making of individual contracts of insurance, and that accordingly, since the syndicate did know that the defendants were carrying on unauthorised and illegal business and since the syndicate did not themselves commit any criminal offence, the reinsurance contract was enforceable at the suit of the plaintiff.

The earlier decision of *Phoenix General Insurance Co. of Greece S.A. v Administratia Asigurarilor de Stat*[96] involved aviation contingency insurance. The insurance company was previously authorised under the precursor to the 1974 Act but regulations were subsequently passed pursuant to the EU directive. On the question of illegality, the Court of Appeal's comments were *obiter* but represent a powerful application of the *Bedford* approach:

> The net point is then that it is settled law that any contract which is prohibited by statute, either expressly or by implication, is illegal and void . . . The Insurance Companies Act, 1974 imposes

---

89 84 [1985] QB 988.
90 [1969] Law Reports of Guyana 91.
91 [1984] 3 WLR 726
92 [1986] 2 Lloyd's Rep 552.
93 J. Birds, *Modern Insurance Law*, 6th edn (Sweet & Maxwell: 2014), p. 26.
94 [1984] 3 All ER 777.
95 [1984] 3 All ER 766.
96 [1987] 2 All ER 152.

a unilateral prohibition on unauthorised insurers. If this were merely to prohibit them from carrying on the business of effecting contracts of insurance

> of a class for which they have no authority, then it would clearly be open to the court to hold that consideration of public policy precludes the implication that such contracts are prohibited and void. But unfortunately the unilateral prohibition is not limited to the business of effecting contracts of insurance

but extends to the business of carrying out contracts of insurance. This is a form of statutory prohibition, albeit only unilateral . . . since the statute prohibits the insurer from carrying out the contract – of which the most obvious example is paying claims – how can the insured require the insurer to do an act which is expressly forbidden by statute? And how can a court enforce a contract against an unauthorised insurer when Parliament has expressly prohibited him from carrying it out?

In this decision, the contracts were held to be illegal, void and unenforceable based on the fundamental principle that the law will not countenance an illegality. In light of these conflicting authorities, what therefore is the approach to be adopted in the Caribbean? In *Guyana National General Insurance Co. Ltd v Reginald Moore & Ors*,[97] decided prior to the decisions of *Bedford* and *Phoenix*, the equitable maxims were used to sidestep the considerations. In *Guyana National General Insurance Co. Ltd v Reginald Moore & Ors*,[98] the Supreme Court of Guyana found that no question of *ultra vires* arose since the company was empowered to carry on the business of motor insurance under its memorandum of association. Further, that the plaintiff could not approach the court for a declaration because no question of *ultra vires* or any compromise thereof was raised in the action upon which the levy was raised.

Consequently several questions remain unresolved. The issue is whether effecting insurance with an unauthorised insurer is a fatal flaw rendering the contract unenforceable. Attention must be paid to the language of the statute. Applying the principle in *Phoenix*, if the prohibition is against carrying on of insurance business of a relevant class without authorisation, then the contract will be unenforceable. In the United Kingdom Acts under consideration, there is no direct reference to contracts of insurance. Such references as exist are imported by the definition clause. The argument here is that because in relation to each class, insurance business is defined as meaning the business of effecting and carrying out contracts of insurance. Insurance business cannot be prohibited without *ipso facto* prohibiting the effecting and carrying out of those contracts of insurance which are meant to be effected.

Fortunately, as noted earlier, in some Caribbean territories statute expressly obviates the need for reliance on the common law. In jurisdictions without such express statutory assistance, the maxim 'He who comes to equity must come with clean hands' or *nullus commodum capere potest de injuria sua propria* ('no one can gain an advantage by his own wrong') as applied in *Guyana National General Insurance Co. Ltd v Moore et al.*[99] is of assistance. Moreover, the so-called anti-insured cases of *Bedford Insurance Co. Ltd v Institutio de Resseguros do Brasil*[100] and *Phoenix General Insurance Company of Greece S.A. v Administrattia Asigualiror de Stat*[101] are distinguishable on the facts. The distinction between effecting and carrying on insurance business as exists in the United Kingdom's Insurance Act 1974 is not present in the Caribbean Insurance Acts.

97 Supra n. 90.
98 Ibid.
99 Ibid.
100 Supra n. 95.
101 Supra n. 92.

1.18   OFF-SHORE INSURANCE

In the twentieth century a robust financial services sector otherwise described as the 'off-shore' sector emerged in the Caribbean. Indeed, the jurisdictions of the Bahamas, Barbados, Bermuda and the Cayman Islands have distinguished themselves in this regard. The off-shore financial industry embraces special vehicle companies which are afforded privileged status, under specific legislation, to establish operations off-shore. Included in the category 'off-shore' are international business companies (IBCs),[102] off-shore banks,[103] off-shore trusts and relevant to present discussion, off-shore insurance. The off-shore insurance industry in Barbados is governed by the Exempt Insurance legislation[104] which falls under the auspices of the Supervisor of Insurance, who is charged with the responsibility of administering the Act and ensuring that all captive/exempt insurance companies are compliant. The Exempt Insurance Act, *inter alia*, requires:

1   The company is incorporated under the Companies Act as a company limited by shares or is a Mutual Insurance company;

2   Its object and activities must be a transaction of captive/exempt insurance business;

3   At least one of its directors must be a resident of Barbados;

4   Its beneficial shareholders must not be persons resident within the Caribbean Community;[105]

5   Its articles of incorporation must be acceptable to the Minister;

6   Its paid-up capital, or in the case of a mutual insurance company its contributed reserves, must accord with specified requirements.

Captive insurance is a vehicle which facilitates 'self-insurance,' whereby an entity is established to assume the risks of its parent and/or affiliate(s).[106] By virtue of this special vehicle legislation, companies are granted a special status attracting a tax rate ranging from zero to 2.5%.[107]

The off-shore industry overshadows the domestic insurance industry in terms of economic contribution to the state's Gross Domestic Product (GDP) and in terms of incorporation figures. The 2006 figures for Barbados reveal that the Supervisor of Insurance regulates 426 exempt insurers in contrast to 27 domestic insurance companies, 10 of which are engaged in life insurance[108] and 17 are involved in general insurance.[109] It is therefore not difficult to

---

102 St Vincent and the Grenadines International Business Companies Act No. 18 of 1996; see also *In the Matter of Mariner International Bank Ltd* (unreported decision, St Vincent and the Grenadines High Court No. 148 of 2002).

103 St Vincent and the Grenadines International Banks Act No. 19 of 1996. In St Vincent and the Grenadines, the industry is regulated by the Off-shore Finance Authority.

104 Barbados Exempt Insurance Act of 1983, Cap 308A.

105 Amended 2001.

106 V. Braithwaite, 'Captive/International Insurance Industry with Special Reference to Barbados,' in R. M. B. Antoine, ed., *Legal Issues in Off-shore Financial Services* (Caribbean Law Publishing Company: 2004), p. 21. Braithwaite categorises the captive industry in Barbados into types 1, 2, 3, and 4. Type 1 is the traditional self-insurance captive. Type 2 is a captive which insures closely controlled third-party risks. In type 3 industries, the captive engages in reinsurance business providing cover to customers of parent and/or its affiliate. Type 4 involves captives that are essentially third party reinsurers in the international reinsurance market.

107 L. A. Walcott, 'Issues Relating to Recent Tax Reform In the Commonwealth Caribbean – Netting the Elusive Taxpayer' (2002) *Carib. L. Rev.* 1; R. Bisvos, ed., *International Tax Competition and Fiscal Sovereignty* (Commonwealth Secretariat: 2000).

108 According to information supplied by the Office of the Supervisor of Insurance, Nicholas House, Bridgetown, Barbados, these ten insurance companies have Gross Direct Premiums written in Barbadian dollars as $186,862,571 million.

109 According to 2004 statistics from the Office of the Supervisor of Insurance, Nicholas House, Bridgetown, Barbados, these 17 insurance companies have approximate Gross Direct Premiums written in Barbadian

appreciate that where the regulator responsible for insurance regulates not only the domestic but also the off-shore insurance industry[110] that the economic relevance of one sector arguably overshadows the other. By extension it can further be canvassed that there is potential for the regulatory function over domestic insurance being sidelined relative to concentration on off-shore insurance.

1.19   CONCLUSION

Regional Insurance Acts are the primary vehicle governing regulation of the insurance industry in the Commonwealth Caribbean. The Insurance Act, administered by the regulator, imposes initial and ongoing obligations on the insurer. These requirements, both conditions prior to licensing and ongoing obligations to be monitored, are so designed collectively to ensure solvency of the insurance operations for the ultimate protection of policyholders. In this regard, administrative law restraints serve as a necessary check against the potential for abuse of power by a regulator. Where the insurer fails to adhere to these statutory obligations, statute expressly preserves the sanctity of the 'contract,' thereby protecting the rights of policyholders.

Regulation is predicated on the insurer conducting insurance business. This in turn begets an inquiry into whether there is a valid contract of insurance. Legislators and judges, as will be seen from Chapter 2, are reluctant to lay down a coherent definition of insurance – a position important from the standpoint of regulation of an industry that, resulting from its evolving nature, is in constant change.

Insurance business today is certainly not the same as that of yesteryear. Hybrid insurance products designed to compete for clients' savings dollars challenge traditional understanding of insurance. Equity-linked, interest-sensitive insurance products,[111] integrated products with holistic financial risk management, have emerged. This creativity, evident for instance in EFPAs, Deposit Administration Contracts and products exhibited in the decision of *Fuji Finance Inc. v Aetna Life Insurance Co. Ltd & Ors*,[112] makes a compelling case for legislation to be both flexible and adaptable. It is the lack of definition which enables the statute to respond. Certainly a definition would assist in determining application of insurance statutes, protocols under the Revised Treaty of Chaguaramas and the relevance of ancillary statutes such as income tax. Arguably however, the absence of a coherent definition assists in regulation of an industry that admittedly continues to evolve. Deliberate silence of the legislation notwithstanding, assisting principles may be and have been extrapolated from the common law.

---

dollars of $420,263,892 million. Of the 27 insurance companies registered, five life insurance companies are currently not writing new business, while two of the companies engaged in general insurance are currently not writing new business.

110 See for instance Barbados Companies (Amendment) Act No. 30 of 2001, which introduced Segregated Cell Companies or rent-a-captive; see also Exempt Insurance Act No. 9 of 1983.

111 In Jamaica in 1989, sales of equity-linked insurance products accounted for 50% of industry sales.

112 [1996] 4 All ER 608.

CHAPTER 2

THE NATURE OF INSURANCE

2.1 INTRODUCTION

Insurance is based on risk pertaining to a future event: 'possible, probable, contingent, fortunate or unfortunate.'[1] The element of risk-shifting is critical to the insurance product for calculating premiums, the quantum to be paid and potential liability under reinsurance. There is mutuality as the insured fulfils his end of the bargain via payments described as premiums; the other party – the insurer – promises to perform its obligation once loss is sustained. Insurance imputes, attributes or prescribes value both to risk and intangible 'peace of mind.' These are viewed as costs the insurer assumes or takes care of. Essentially, insurance attaches a cost to risk aversion. Risk is the measure of a mathematically calculated expectation: the product of the probability of the event multiplied by its agreed value.[2] Risk is the subject matter of insurance. Study of insurance reveals a heady mixture of family law, crime, social and public policy as the insured attempts to shift risk in his or her favour. Uncertainty over risk is an important indicator of the need for insurance.[3]

2.2 APPLICATION

In the United States, the formula is called the known-loss rule. In *Metropolitan Life Insurance Company v The Board of Equalization*,[4] it was said of the definition of insurance in the Californian Insurance Code[5] that it required '(1) a risk of loss to which one party is subject and a shifting of that risk among similarly situated persons.' In *Truta v Avis Rent a Car System Inc.*,[6] it was held that a limit to a collision damage waiver provision in a car rental contract did not amount to insurance because the company did not undertake to assume liability or third party risks, but merely agreed not to insist that the person having the car make payments for certain types of damage which otherwise would be due to the company. Channell J's definition has been approved in several English courts and throughout the Commonwealth Caribbean. In one California case, surrounding the question of service as opposed to indemnity, the court was asked to determine whether a subscriber to a medical contract for the poor was insurance as a service rather than indemnity as its principal object and purpose.[7] In *Re Barrett: Ex Parte Young v NM Superannuation Pty Ltd*,[8] reference was made to Justice Channell's view in *Prudential*, Von Doussa J in the Federal Supreme Court of Australia, where this particular situation was being considered, noted that uncertainty may give rise both to profit and loss to the insurer. This is a distinguishing characteristic of a contract of insurance: a contract based upon speculation.

---

1   F. Ewald (J. M. Dautrey and C. F. Stifler trans), 'Risk in Contemporary Society (2000) *Connecticut Ins. L.J.* 365.
2   Ibid.
3   R. Hodgin, 'Problems in Defining Insurance Contract' [1980] *LMCLQ* 14.
4   Supreme Court of California, 1982 625 P2d 426.
5   Section 22 (2000): 'Insurance is a contract whereby one undertakes to indemnify another, against loss, damage, or liability arising from a contingent on an unknown event.'
6   193 Cal App 3d 802 (California Court of Appeal, 1987).
7   *California Positions Service v Garrison*, 172 P2d 4 (1946).
8   106 ALR 549 (Federal Court of Australia).

Regional legislation is silent on the definition of insurance. absent a coherent, comprehensive definition one must resort to the common law, where the element of risk permeates the entire set of arrangements.[9] Insurance is a mechanism by which the risk of loss is transferred from one person to another. Lord Mansfield in *Carter v Boehm*[10] shared the view that insurance is a contract on speculation. Indeed, one judge refrained from aspiring to lay down an exhaustive definition 'good for all purposes and in all contexts,' doubting whether a satisfactory definition of a 'contract of insurance' will ever be evolved.[11] Sometimes, however, it is necessary to ascertain whether a contract of insurance exists precisely because insurance regulation is predicated on the existence of a contract. Birds suggests a contract of insurance is any contract whereby one party assumes the risk of occurrence of an uncertain event not within his control, happening at a future time, in which event the other party has an interest, and under which contract the first party is bound to pay money or provide its equivalent if the uncertain event occurs. In *Lucena v Craufurd*,[12] Lawrence J stated:

> Insurance is a contract by which the one party in consideration of a price paid to him adequate to the risk, becomes security to the other that he shall not suffer loss, damage, or prejudice by the happening of the perils specified to certain things which may be exposed to them.

In *Castellain v Preston*,[13] it was simply stated that 'insurance provides indemnity against loss.' Likewise, insurance legislation defines insurance business as 'the assumption of the obligations of an insurer in any insurance business and includes reinsurance business.' Since the assumption of obligations is evidenced by the contract of insurance for which there is no adequate definition, assisting principles must be sought from the common law.

2.3   THEORETICAL NOTIONS

Based on the *laissez-faire* doctrine,[14] contract law promotes a classical theory, a sense of individualism with an absence of state interference.[15] Deficiencies in the application of traditional

---

9   J. Lowry and P. Rawlings, *Insurance Law: Cases and Materials* (Hart: 2004), p. 3.
10   [1766] 3 Burr. 1905, 97 ER 1162.
11   *Medical Defence Union Ltd v Department of Trade* [1980] Ch 82.
12   (1802) 2 B & P (NR) 269.
13   (1883) 11 QBD 380; LJQB 368.
14   A. Smith, *An Inquiry into the Nature and Causes of the Wealth of Nations* (Penguin Books: 1986), p. 52:

> The exclusive privileges of corporations, statutes of apprenticeship, and all those laws which restrain, in particular employments, the competition to a smaller number than might otherwise go into them, have the same tendency, though in a less degree. They are a sort of enlarged monopolies, and may frequently, for ages together, and in whole classes of employments, keep up the market price of particular commodities above the natural price, and maintain both the wages of the labour and the profits of the stock employed about them somewhat above their natural rate.

15   M. J. Trebilcock, *The Limits of Freedom of Contract* (Harvard University Press: 1993); M. J. Trebilcock, 'Critiques of the Limits of Freedom of Contract: A Rejoinder.' (1995) 33 *Osgoode Hall L.J.* 2; P. Benson, 'Abstract Right and the Possibility of a Non-distributive Conception of Contract: Hegel and Contemporary Contract Theory' (1989) 10 *Cardozo L. Rev.* 1077; P. Benson, 'Contract' in Dennis Patterson, ed., *A Companion to Philosophy of Law and Legal Theory* (Blackwell: 1996); P. Benson, 'The Idea of a Public Basis of Justification for Contract' (1995) 33 *Osgoode Hall L.J.* 273; Randy Barnett, 'A Consent Theory of Contract' (1986) 86 *Colum. L. Rev.* 269; R. Barnett, 'The Sounds of Silence: Default Rules and Contractual Consent,' (1992) 78 *Va. L. Rev.* 891–911.

theories exist.[16] Within theories postulated by Adam Smith,[17] adherents of free market ideology such as Ludwig von Mises,[18] and Murray N. Rothbard's input itself described as a

> unique contribution . . . the rediscovery of property and property rights as the common foundation of both economics and political philosophy, and the systematic reconstruction and conceptual integration of modern marginalist economics and natural-law political philosophy into a unified moral science: libertarianism.[19]

Regulators in the twenty-first century must acknowledge the value of these economists who collectively shaped and influenced economic thought. According to Kessler,[20] classical contract theory is typified by a bargain freely entered into by parties through the process of offer and acceptance, the consequences of wills or minds, resulting in a bargain freely struck by individuals seeking their own interests. This theory is at odds with others such as responsive theory[21] and adhesive theory.[22] The inequality of bargaining power is entrenched by common drafting techniques with contract and declaration clauses reinforcing the insurer's superiority. Proponents Powell[23] and Verplanck[24] argue that contracts of adhesion[25] are based not on consensus but on adhesion. This necessitates a different interpretive technique, a technique which counters asymmetry in the process thereby enhancing good faith while creating less potentially hazardous economic outcomes/relations.[26] Theoretical/academic pronouncement on the need for differentiation given the potential for unfair exploitation of their market position has led to a profusion of exemption clauses, basically part and parcel

---

16   W. F. M. Bondt and R. Thaler, 'Does the Stock Market Work?' (1985) 40 *Journal of Finance* 793–805; R. B. Ekelund Jr and R. F. Hébert, *A History of Economic Theory and Method* (Waveland Press: 2013); Max Weber, *The Theory of Social and Economic Organization* (Simon & Schuster: 1995).

17   A. Smith, *An Inquiry into the Nature and Causes of the Wealth of Nations* (ed. E. Canaan; The Modern Library: 1937), Vol. I: 524; Vol. II: 568.

18   The acknowledged leader of the Austrian School of economic thought, a prodigious originator in economic theory, and a prolific author. Mises' writings and lectures encompassed economic theory, history, epistemology, government and political philosophy.

19   Murray N. Rothbard, *The Ethics of Liberty* (New York University Press: 1982), p. 2.

20   F. Kessler, 'Contracts of Adhesion – Some Thoughts about Freedom of Contract' (1943) 43 *Colum. L. Rev.* 629, 631, 642:

> This will not be the case so long as we fail to realize that freedom of contract must mean different things for different types of contracts. Its meaning must change with the social importance of the type of contract and with the degree of monopoly enjoyed by the author of the standardized contract.

21   M. A. Eisenberg, 'The Responsive Model of Contract Law' [1984] 36 *Stan. L. Rev.* 1107; A. Schwartz and R. E. Scott, 'Contract Theory and the Limits of Contract Law' (2003) John M. Olin Center for Studies in Law, Economics, and Public Policy Working Papers, Paper 275.

22   The theoretical model of adhesion covers all standard form contracts where the element of factual bargaining is absent.

23   L. F. Powell Jr in Schwartz and Scott, supra n. 21.

24   G. C. Verplanck, 'An Essay on the Doctrine of Contracts: Being an Inquiry How Contracts Are Affected in Law and Morals, by Concealment, Error, or Inadequate Price' (G. & C. Carvill: 1825).

25   Applying these theories to adhesion contracts, where the contract is drafted by the seller and the purchaser merely 'adheres' to it and has little choice as to its terms, it is understandable why many commentators refer to the formalistic classic model as one of unfairness, noting deficiencies in the formal process: the absence of factual assent, lack of informed notice of terms, lack of bargaining power, lack of consent to terms and economic duress. Lowering transaction costs standard by forms obviate the need for bargaining over terms and thereby saves time. To the extent that adhesion contracts de-emphasise bargaining they represent a contract model wholly supportive of the mass market institution.

26   Law Commission Consultation Paper No. 121 (1991) *Privity of Contract: Contracts for the Benefit of 3rd Parties*; A. S. Burrows, 'The Will of Contract Revived – Fried's "Contract as Promise"' (1985) *Current Legal Problems* 141.

of allocating contractual rights and liabilities. Exemption clauses enable the stipulator to enjoy all the advantages without necessarily having to bear the burden of corresponding obligations and potential liabilities. Their effect is to deprive the weaker party of rights which, without more, may accrue.[27]

Once one applies these theories to adhesion contracts, the view of many commentators who refer to the formalistic model of unfairness, noting deficiencies in the formal process, becomes perfectly understandable. The absence of factual assent, lack of informed notice of terms, lack of bargaining power, lack of consent to terms and economic duress all lead to this conclusion.[28] Lowering transaction costs obviates the need for bargaining over terms and thereby saves time. To the extent that adhesion contracts de-emphasise bargaining they represent a contract model wholly supportive of the mass market institution.

Burgess departs from Lenhoff's treatise[29] introducing a distinction between adhesion contracts and commercial standard form contract.[30] According to Burgess, this latter type standard form contract is customary between parties possessing relatively equal bargaining power engaging in trade, business or commerce. These clauses, settled over the years by negotiation among established commercial interests, have been widely adopted as experience demonstrated effective facilitation in conduct of trade.[31]

Burgess contends that the contract of adhesion involves downgrading the element of bargaining in the classical contact sense, as Lord Denning stated in *Levison v Patent Steam Carpet Cleaning Co. Ltd*,[32] the weaker party is simply presented with a form to sign and told: 'sign here.' The contracting process therefore consists of cooperative acts by the weaker party done in agreement rather than by way of negotiating an agreement. The contract is essentially a public contract. Traditionally contract is perceived as a private matter between private individuals and that there is an area of contract outside private contract where the public interest is best served by restrictions and regulations on the individual's private right of freedom of contract. Referring to Atiyah,[33] Burgess contends that the major characteristic of the public contract is that

> contracts falling within it have the potential to affect a wide and indiscriminate range of persons in society either directly because these persons become parties to the contract or indirectly, because the operation of the contract could disrupt fundamental social and economic norm.

---

27 Supra n. 15.
28 A. Lenhoff, 'Contracts of Adhesion – The Freedom of Contract' (1962) 36 *Tulane. L. Rev.* 48.
29 A. Burgess, 'Adhesion Contracts & Unfair Terms: A Critique of Current Theory and a Suggestion' [1985] *Anglo-Amer. L. Rev.* 8.
30 M. P. Furmston, *Cheshire, Fifoot & Furmston's Law of Contract*, 15th edn (OUP: 2007), p. 779, n. 130; E. McKendrick, *Contract Law – Cases and Materials* (OUP: 2005); P. S. Atiyah, *The Rise and Fall of Freedom of Contract* (Clarendon Press: 1979); R. E. Barnett, *Contracts* (Aspen Publishers: 2003); S. Fruehwald, 'Reciprocal Altruism as the Basis for Contract' (2009) 47 *Univ. of Louisville L. Rev.* 489.
31 *Schroeder Music Publishing Co. Ltd v Macaulay* [1974] 1 WLR 1308 HL. The House of Lords held the standard form agreement could not be justified as moulded under the pressures of negotiation, competition and public opinion. Macaulay had no bargaining power. The defendants purported to be able to arbitrarily decline to exploit the plaintiff's work, in which event the plaintiff's remuneration under the agreement would be limited to a £50 advance payable thereunder during the five-year period. The defendants' power to assign precluded the argument that the restrictions would not be enforced oppressively. The defendants had failed to justify restrictions which appeared unnecessary and capable of oppressive enforcement.
32 [1977] 3 WLR 90 CA.
33 P. S. Atiyah, 'An Introduction to the Law of Contract' (1943) 43 *Colum. L. Rev.* 629, 631.

It cuts across a number of transactional situations. Acceptance of this theoretical model assists in understanding insurance contracts.[34]

2.4 THE COMMON LAW

The contract must exhibit certain characteristics in order for it to amount to a contract of insurance.[35] These characteristics as stated were laid down in the decision of *Prudential Insurance Co. v Commissioner of Inland Revenue*.[36] Channell J, although eventually concluding that this was not an exhaustive definition, stated that there were three requirements for a valid contract of insurance. First, it must be a contract whereby for some consideration, usually but not necessarily for periodical payments called premiums, some benefit for the policyholder is secured on the occurrence of some event. Second, the occurrence should involve some element of uncertainty. Third, the uncertain event should be *prima facie* adverse to the interests of the insured. Channell J's definition as noted above has been approved in subsequent decisions in Australia, New Zealand and in the Commonwealth Caribbean. In *Department of Trade & Industry v St Christopher Motorists' Association Ltd*,[37] the court was presented with the opportunity to revisit the question, 'What is insurance?' Here, according to the terms of the agreement, disqualified or injured motorists were entitled to a driver and, if necessary, a car and driver for up to 40 hours a week for a maximum of 12 months. The court was concerned with whether the association was carrying on insurance business and was an insurance company to which the Insurance Act 1985[38] applied. Templeman J, in finding that a contract of insurance existed, accepted that Channell J's pronouncement in *Prudential* was not an exhaustive definition of the contract of insurance, finding no logic in distinguishing between the benefit of a sum of money and the provision of services.[39]

Subsequently, in the important decision of *Medical Defence Union Ltd v Department of Trade*,[40] the issue was whether the term 'contract of insurance' applied to a contract under which the benefit was discretionary and not obligatory. Here a member's contractual right under the rules was no more than a right to require the union to properly consider a request for assistance. Construing the term insurance business in accordance with general law, Sir Robert Megarry VC concluded a contract of insurance did not exist since the presence of a discretionary benefit robbed the agreement of contractual force. Applying the principles laid down in *Prudential*

---

34 *Re Digital Satellite Warranty Cover Ltd* [2011] EWCA Civ 1413. The Court of Appeal held that 'extended warranty contracts' covering satellite television equipment were contracts of insurance. The businesses selling them were carrying out regulated activities that required FSA authorisation. The businesses involved sold extended warranty contracts relating to electrical equipment, targeting people whose warranties were about to run out. The warranty by Digital Cover indicated that it would cover breakdown and accidental damage. A customer would receive a warranty certificate which did not exclude accidental damage. The question is whether these contracts were contracts of insurance and therefore needed to be regulated. The Court of Appeal held risk covered by a contract which provides for repair and replacement and a contract which covers for loss is essentially the same. The risk is the breakdown of equipment.

35 *Flood v Irish Provident Assurance Co. Ltd* [1912] 2 Ch 597; *Gould v Curtis* [1913] 3 KB 84; *Fuji Finance Inc. v Aetna Life Insurance Co. Ltd* [1997] Ch 173.

36 Supra n. 6.

37 [1974] 1 All ER 395.

38 C. 6.

39 Lord Justice Templeman could find no all-embracing definition of insurance. Stating one had to peruse the rules and regulation of the society. Ruling the member was contractually bound that the provision of services other than a monetary payment was still within the essence of the insurance contract. There was no logical difference between paying a chauffeur and paying a sum of money to a member which would represent the cost to him of engaging a chauffeur.

40 [1979] Lloyds Rep 499.

Insurance v IRC and *Gould v Curtis*,[41] Megarry VC preferred the wider approach in *St Christopher's* but suggested that one should proceed with caution in permitting benefits other than money, continuing that he was unable to see any justification for replacing money or its equivalent by benefit as a constituent part of the definition of the contract of insurance. Megarry VC laid down the following principles: (1) the contract must be one which entitles the insured to some benefit, (2) there must be some uncertainty and (3) the insured must have an insurable interest in the subject matter. Megarry VC refrained from 'aspiring' to lay down an exhaustive definition, 'good for all purposes and in all contexts,' doubting whether a satisfactory definition of a 'contract of insurance' will ever be evolved, further noting that 'it may be a concept which it is better to describe than to attempt to define.'

Assistance in determining what constitutes insurance business can be seen in *R v Wilson*.[42] Here the appellant was charged with carrying out insurance business without authority from the Secretary of State contrary to Sections 2 and 14 of the Insurance Companies Act 1982.[43] The appellant contended that it was the company which was in breach of legislation. The Court of Appeal affirmed the conviction of the appellant and dismissed the appeal, contending that a person who solicited business and held himself out as having authority to make insurance contracts and receive premiums on behalf of the insurer whether or not any contract was entered into 'was playing an active and significant part in selling insurance and he did this in contravention of section 2.' Evan LJ, in referring to Section 2(1),[44] interpreted 'carrying on business' as encompassing preliminary negotiations. He regarded them as a necessary integral part of the process. 'Effecting and carrying out' includes the processes of negotiation.

In the earlier decision of *Scher and Ackman v Policyholders Protection Board & Ors*,[45] the issue was the insurer's liquidation, which raised the issue whether policyholders were entitled to be indemnified by the Protection Board. The Board was established under the Policyholders Protection Act 1975[46] for the purpose of assisting or protecting policyholders who had been or might be prejudiced as a result of the inability of authorised insurance companies carrying on business in the United Kingdom to meet liabilities under policies issued by them. The Court held that although the claims were to be paid in the United States and Canada, the performance nevertheless constituted 'carrying on' by the insurers of insurance business in the United Kingdom. The policy under consideration in Section 4 was not so much protecting the domestic consumer as the protection of the assured who obtained cover on the London market against the insolvency of insurers, the wider range of protection being matched with a wider range for the imposition of a levy. Central to the construction of Section 4(2) is the concept of carrying on by the insurer of insurance business. Carrying on insurance business is constituted by the erecting and carrying out of contracts of insurance.

In *Fuji v Aetna*,[47] the plaintiff company effected a policy of insurance, described as a policy of life assurance or capital investment bond, with an insurance company whose business was

---

41 [1913] 3 KB 84, CA.
42 [1913] 3 KB 84, CA.
43 Director ordered to perform 100 hours of community service. It was disqualified under the evidence that appellant (individual) gave individual brochures and other documents purportedly issued by a limited company which offered a debt collection and debt indemnity service.
44 'Subject to the following provision in this section, no person shall carry on any insurance business in the United Kingdom unless authorised to do so [by the Secretary of State].'
45 [1993] 3 All ER 384.
46 C. 75.
47 [1997] Ch 173, CA.

shortly thereafter taken over by the defendants, the life assured being that of T., who was concerned in the management of the plaintiff. Under the policy, a sum calculated by reference to the price of units currently allocated to the policy was payable on the death of the life assured or on its earlier surrender. The policy provided that on surrender within the first five years, the amount payable was to be reduced by a discontinuance charge. The plaintiff paid a single premium of £50,000, which was applied to secure units in a variety of internal funds administered by the insurance company. The policyholder had the option to switch units allocated to his policy between the funds. By taking advantage of the defendants' procedure for fixing the price of the units, the plaintiff was able to increase the surrender value of the policy from £50,000 to over £1 million in six years. The defendants then altered the procedure for switching units so that the plaintiff was unable to continue to make profits as before. The plaintiff claimed that by altering the terms of the switching procedures the defendants had committed a repudiatory breach of contract and surrendered the policy. The defendants paid the plaintiff the surrender proceeds, which amounted to £1,110,758.

The plaintiff brought an action for damages for breach of contract. The trial of preliminary issues focused on whether the policy was a policy of life insurance within Section 1 of the Life Assurance Act 1774 so as to be void because the plaintiff had no insurable interest in the life of T., or, if not, whether it was unenforceable under Section 16 of the Insurance Companies Act 1982, the judge held that since the same sum was payable on surrender of the policy as on the death of T., the policy was not a contract of insurance on the life of T. and was therefore not rendered void by Section 1 of the Act of 1774, and that a policy issued in good faith, albeit in breach of Section 16 of the Act of 1982, was not thereby rendered unlawful and unenforceable.

2.5 CAPACITY

In the absence of a statute to the contrary, the prevailing modern rule is that a minor's contracts are voidable. Nevertheless, it also is well established that a minor may be liable for the value of necessaries furnished to him or her. This doctrine, eponymously referred to as insurance, dislodges the general rule regarding minors – in law, a minor is a person under a certain age, usually the age of majority, which legally demarcates childhood from adulthood. The age of majority depends upon jurisdiction and application, but is generally 18 years of age. These age limits are often different from the age of majority. In St Kitts and Nevis Insurance Act Section 117(1), a minor who has obtained an age of ten years not exceeding 16 years may, with written consent of his or her parent or of a person standing in *loco parentis* to the minor,

> (a) effect a policy upon his or her own life or upon another life in which he or she has an insurable interest; or (b) take an assignment of a policy. (2) a minor who has obtained the age of sixteen years (a) may effect a policy upon his or her own life or upon another life in which he or she has an insurable interest; or (b) may take an assignment of a policy; and (c) subject to subsection (3) is competent in all respects and exercise the powers and privileges of a policyholder of full age in relation to a policy of which he or she is holder. (3) a minor who has obtained the age of sixteen years may assign or mortgage a policy with the prior consent in writing of his or her parent or other person standing in *loco parentis* to the minor. (4) this section does not (a) impose on a minor, any liability to which the board this section, he or she would not be subject; (b), confer on a minor any power or capacity that, but for this section, the minor would not have not have; (c) validate a receipt, a discharge for a surrender of, or security over a policy given by a minor, if, but for this section, that receipt, discharge, surrender or security would not be valid; or (d) validate any assignment of the policy that, but for this section, would not be valid.

2.6   WRITTEN POLICY

Early twentieth-century case law suggests criteria beyond that postulated by Channell J is required. *Hampton v Toxteth Co-operative Society Ltd*[48] and *Hall D'Ath v British Provident Association for Hospital & Additional Services*[49] suggest that there can be no insurance business carried on in the absence of a stipulated policy and a stipulated premium. In *Hampton v Toxteth Co-operative Provident Society Ltd*,[50] the plaintiff was a member of an industrial society and had received from them a share book, a membership card, a purchase book and a copy of the rules of the society. It was held that there was no carrying on of life insurance business within the meaning of the Insurance Act of 1909 – Assurance Companies Act 9 Edw. 7, c. 49. Although the rules provided that the society had the power to carry on insurance business, and under Rule 14A, the committee of management were authorised to appropriate money *inter alia* for providing a sum to be paid on the death of a member or the wife or husband of a member, such sum to be proportional to one year's average purchases of the member from the society during the three years immediately preceding death, the society advertised free life assurance as an inducement to persons to become members. The plaintiff claimed that the society had paid large sums of money in respect of life insurance within the meaning of the Assurance Companies Act 1909 without having paid the deposit of £20,000. The majority of the Court of Appeal regarded the absence of a policy as crucial, since under the rules of the society there was no enforceable contractual right to the sum assured. Since policies must be in writing and no policy issued, no premium had been paid. There was no obligation on the society to appropriate any further sum to the insurance fund and the arrangement might at any moment be terminated by a general meeting.

Lord Cozens-Hardy MR's judgment follows in part:

> I think there is no carrying on life assurance business within the meaning of the Act. No policy has been issued, no premium has been paid, there is no obligation upon the society to appropriate any further sum . . . the arrangement seems to me to lack every element necessary to constitute carrying on the business of life assurance. It is nothing more than an appropriation of income, or possibly of capital . . . I cannot part with the case without referring to advertisements and notices issued by the society which are inaccurate, misleading and highly improper . . . they cannot by calling something which is not an assurance and by that name make it a policy of assurance within the meaning of the Act.

Similarly, in *Hall D'Ath v British Provident Association for Hospital & Additional Services*[51] the Court held that the Association was not conducting insurance business within the meaning of Section 1 of the Assurance Act 1909. Although the prospectus made an offer to provide certain benefits, and this offer when accepted by a subscriber constituted a binding contract to pay benefits according to the prospectus, the combined effect of the prospectus and the subscription was insufficient to constitute a policy and hence the business being conducted was not illegal/*ultra vires*.

Considering that these cases were decided in 1915, it is doubtful whether the requirement of written policies would be rigidly adhered to, given advances in technology and e-commerce.[52]

---

48   [1915] 1 Ch 721.
49   [1953] 48 LTR 240.
50   Supra n. 48.
51   [1932] 48 LTR 240.
52   Consumer Guarantees Act, Cap 326E; Consumer Protection Act, Cap 326D; Control of Standards Act; Fair Competition Act, Cap. 326C; Fair Competition Act, Cap 326E; Fair Trading Commission Act, Cap 326B.

The Barbados Electronic Transactions Act[53] defines records as information that is inscribed on a tangible medium and retrievable in perceivable form. At Cap 308B the Act establishes that 'Security procedure means a procedure established by law or agreement or knowingly adopted by each party that is employed for the purpose of verifying that an electronic signature' has validity. It continues: 'Signature includes any symbol executed or adopted, or any methodology or procedure . . . adopted by a person with the intention of authenticating a record, including electronic or digital methods.'

Despite its failure to define the term 'policy,' twenty-first-century legislation adopts facilitation of electronic transactions as its mandate. In some jurisdictions, statute establishes that a life insurance policy means any instrument by which the payment of money is assured on death, or the happening of a contingency dependent on human life, or any instrument evidencing a contract which is subject to the payment of premiums for a term dependent on human life, but does not include an instrument by which the payment of money is assured only on 'accidental death'[54] In St Kitts and Nevis, 'a policy is defined as a valid insurance contract, whatever the form in which the rights and obligations of the parties to the contract are expressed or created, and includes a sinking fund policy,' but does not include an insurance contract which relates to exempt insurance business. While these provisions seemingly import a broad notion of what constitutes a policy, at the same time the Acts unhelpfully define a policy as a 'policy issued.'[55] An argument may therefore be made that informality will thrust the arrangement beyond the ambit of the Act merely by the presence of the word 'policy' as opposed to 'contract.'

2.7   CONTRACTS OF GUARANTEE VERSUS CONTRACTS OF INSURANCE

A Contract of guarantee is a performance bond or other type of *guarantee* in which the guarantor effectively becomes a co-signatory to the underlying *contract*. Unlike a demand *guarantee* (standby letter of credit), the guarantor acquires certain rights under the *contract* and can challenge the obligee's demand for payment of the *guaranteed* sum. Vaughn Williams LJ distinguished a contract of insurance from a contract of guarantee:

> the distinction in substance, in cases in which the loss insured against is simply the event of the non-payment of a debt, seems to be, as I read the judgment of Romer LJ in *Seaton v Heath* [(1899) 1 QB 782], between contract in which the person desiring to be insured has means of knowledge as to and the insurer has not the same means, and those cases in which the insurer has the same means.

Templeman LJ cautions in *Department of Trade v St Christophers' Motorists' Association*:

> There may well be some contracts of guarantee, some contracts of maintenance which at first appear to have some resemblance to the definition laid down by Channell J and which, on analysis, are not found to be true contracts of insurance at all.

There are several cases which raise the issue. In *R v Wilson*,[56] the appellant was charged with carrying on insurance business without authority from the Secretary of State contrary to Sections 2

---

53   Cap 308B.
54   Section 2, Jamaica Insurance Act No. 26 of 2001.
55   Ibid.
56   [1997] 3 WLR 1247.

and 14 of the Insurance Companies Act 1982.[57] The appellant contended that it was the company which was in breach of the legislation. The Court of Appeal affirmed the conviction of the appellant, dismissing the appeal, contending that a person who solicited business and held himself out as having authority had the requisite authority.

Evan LJ, referring to Section 2(1),[58] interpreted 'carrying on business' as encompassing preliminary negotiations, regarding them as a necessary integral part of the process, the jury finding that the appellant was playing an active and significant part in selling insurance and he did this in contravention of Section 2 and failed to discharge the burden of proof. Earlier, in *Scher v Policyholders Protection Board & Ors*,[59] on the insurer's liquidation, the issue arose as to whether the policyholders were entitled to be indemnified by the Protection Board (this board had been established under Policyholders Protection Act 1975 for the express purpose of assisting or protecting policyholders who had been or might be prejudiced as the result of the inability of authorised insurance companies carrying on business in the United Kingdom to meet liabilities under policies issued by them).

Jurisdiction under Section 41(1) of the 1975 Act was confined to UK policies. The Court held that although claims to be paid in the United States or Canada perform and nevertheless constitute carrying on by the insurers of insurance business in the United Kingdom, the policyholder under consideration in Section 4 was not so much protecting the domestic consumer but rather ensuring protection of the assureds who obtained cover on the London market against the insolvency of insurers. Thus the enhanced protection was being matched by a wider range for the imposition of a levy. Central to the construction of Section 4(2) is the concept of 'carrying on by the insurer of insurance business.' Carrying on insurance business is constituted by erecting and carrying out of contracts of insurance.

Legislators and judges, however, are reluctant to lay down a coherent definition. This lack of definition assumes importance from the standpoint of effective regulation of an industry in constant change. Contemporary insurance business is decidedly not the insurance of yesteryear. Hybrid insurance products designed to compete for savings dollars challenge traditional understanding of insurance. Equity-linked, interest-sensitive insurance products[60] and others integrated with holistic financial risk management have emerged. Such creativity, evident for instance in *Fuji Finance Inc. v Aetna Life Insurance Co. Ltd & Ors*,[61] compels flexibility and adaptability in the legislative process.

Absence of definition enables a functional statutory response. Certainly a settled definition would assist in determining the application of insurance statutes, protocols under the Revised Treaty of Chaguaramas and ancillary statutes such as those applicable to income tax. Yet admittedly, these benefits do not deny the fact that regulation of a constantly evolving industry would be rendered particularly hazardous in face of a time-bound, concrete definition. Simply put, a contract of guarantee is a promise to perform the promise, or discharge the liability, of a third person in case of his default. A guarantee may be either oral or written. The person who gives the guarantee is called the surety, the person on whose default the guarantee is given is called the principal debtor, and the person to whom the guarantee is given is called the creditor. Legislative silence notwithstanding, assisting principles are readily gleaned from the case law.

---

57 The director was ordered to perform 100 hours of community service. It was disqualified under the evidence that appellant (individual) gave individual brochures and other documents purportedly issued by a limited company which offered a debt collection and debt indemnity service.
58 Supra n. 44.
59 Supra n. 45.
60 In Jamaica in 1989, new sales of equity-linked insurance products accounted for 50% of industry sales.
61 [1996] 4 All ER 608.

2.8   CLASSIFICATION OF INSURANCE

Assurance versus insurance

One area of potential difficulty rests on practices common during the nineteenth century when the terms 'assurance' and 'insurance' were used synonymously. There is however, a subtle distinction. 'Assurance' is used in those contracts which guarantee the payment of a certain sum on the occurrence of a specified event which is bound to happen – for example attainment of a certain age, or death. Thus life policies come under 'assurance.' Insurance, on the other hand, contemplates granting agreed compensation on occurrence of specific events stipulated in the contract. These may not be expected, they may not even be anticipated but may happen – examples are risk relating to fire, accident or a ship sinking as in marine insurance coverage. There are a number of classifications in insurance law recognising differences based on the nature of the risk covered by the insurance contract. Thus the law recognises life, fire, marine and accident and casualty insurance. Within these broad categories further classifications exist, which we explore below.

2.9   WHOLE LIFE

Whole life relates to a life insurance policy that pays a specified amount only on the death of the person insured. It possesses both an insurance and savings feature. Whole life insurance is considered an entire, permanent life insurance. Coverage and premiums last for the insured's entire life. As long as premium payments are made as agreed, insurance coverage is maintained throughout life, with the death benefit being a guaranteed amount. Premium payments are a set, level amount that cannot be increased. There are several distinct types of whole life insurance.

Ordinary life insurance

Premiums are paid either throughout the lifetime of the person insured or until the person reaches a pre-determined specified age (50, 60, etc.), at which point the policy will continue without the payment of additional premiums. This type of policy has a conservative rate of return.

Limited payment

Limited payment policies are life insurance policies where premiums are paid during a specified number of years or until a specified event occurs. Premiums on *limited payment life insurance* are paid for a *limited* number of years. Premiums are payable for 10, 15 or 20 years depending on the policy selected. Premiums can be paid monthly, quarterly, semi-annually or annually. Guaranteed cash value grows.

2.10   SINGLE PREMIUM PAYMENT

Single premium payment is an immediate annuity, also known as an income or single premium immediate annuity (SPIA). SPIA is a contract between the insured and the insurer designed for income purposes. Unlike a deferred annuity, it skips the accumulation stage and begins paying out income either immediately or within a year of purchase.

Individuals approaching retirement age choose this type of annuity because they will be able to make large contributions without the limitations of Registered Retirement and other retirement plans. Single premium immediate annuities allow seniors to supplement Social Security income and pension plans, which may not provide enough to cover retirement living expenses. The danger of single premium payments is the capacity to be abused for money laundering. Essentially this is where a large policy is purchased for a lump sum premium. To cover a large risk, the risk attaches, the person who bought the risk makes a claim on the company – a payout. 'Dirty' money goes in, and 'clean' money comes out as compensation.

2.11 JOINT LIFE INSURANCE

Husband and wife jointly purchase a single policy, paying a single premium. There is a certain assumption that both parties fulfil their end of the bargain. The obvious danger of such a policy emerges when the relationship becomes strained, acrimoniously ending in divorce, with obligations left in tatters.

2.12 UNIVERSAL LIFE

Universal life distinguishes between the portion of the premium attributed to insurance protection coverage and that portion allocated to an investment, attracting higher rates of return as the increased investment portion increases the cash returns associated with the policy.

2.13 ENDOWMENT

Endowment life insurance policies provide for the payment of specified amount in the event of death before the end of the endowment period – usually 20 years. This can be seen in *Re Englebach's Estate*.[62]

2.14 TERM LIFE INSURANCE

Term life insurance provides for the payment of a specified amount if death occurs within the time period designated in the policy. Term period may, for example, be five to 20 years and is generally used to secure a mortgage. Within term life insurance there are several variables. For instance, a convertible term insurance contains the right to convert the policy into whole life or endowment. A renewable term insurance confers the right to renew for an additional term without regard to health at the time of exercising the option. Generally, this form of insurance attracts the lowest premium.

2.15 SPECIAL CLASSES

Industrial life

This term refers to a type of life insurance that is marked by frequent premiums typically written to cover small coverages for accident and health of industrial workers. Frequency of premium payments (e.g. weekly) distinguishes this type of policy from group insurance.

---

62 [1924] 2 Ch 348.

Annuities

An annuity contract generally provides for the payment of a fixed dollar annual benefit commencing at a specified date and continuing as long as the annuitant lives. The uncertainty is the risk of long life, in which case the annuity contract will pay the annuitant substantially more than the company received. If the annuitant dies before annuity payments begin or within some specified period after annuity payments begin, the company will pay a specified sum as a refund of a part of the premium or premiums paid to purchase the contract. Variable annuities are designed to provide retirement income.

Indemnity

Essentially an indemnity policy indemnifies an insured only in respect of loss suffered, if it is actually suffered and only then to the amount of the loss suffered has certain characteristics. First it should be noted that the risk insured against may never occur.

Principle of Indemnity

This principle is applicable in case of fire and marine insurance only. It is not applicable in case of life, personal accident and sickness insurance. A contract of indemnity means that the insured in case of loss against which the policy has been insured shall be paid the actual cost of loss, not exceeding the amount of the insurance policy.

Subrogation

Flowing from the principle of indemnity is the doctrine of subrogation. As stated, the purpose of contract of insurance is to place the insured in the same financial position as he was before the loss. Bishop J, in *Lascelles De Mercado & Co. Ltd v King Et,*[63] referred to the seminal decision *Burnand v Rodocanachie & Sons & Co.,*[64] stating:

> I am of the opinion within the law or doctrine of subrogation has been clearly stated in the case *Burnand v Rodocanachie & Sons Co.,*[65] . . . and I can do no better than to repeat in part the statement of Lord Blackburn in that case
>
>> The general rule of law (and it is obvious justice) is that where there is a contract of indemnity (it matters not whether it is a marine policy, or a policy against fire on land, or any other contract of indemnity) and a loss happens, anything which reduces or diminishes that loss reduces or diminishes the amount which the indemnifier is bound to pay; and if the indemnifier has already paid it, then, if anything which diminishes the loss comes into the hand of the person to whom he has paid it, it becomes an equity that the person who has already paid the full indemnity is entitled to be recouped by having that amount back.

63   LC 1968 HC 35.
64   (1882) 7 AC 333.
65   Ibid.

2.16   PRINCIPLE OF CONTRIBUTION

The principle of contribution is a corollary to the doctrine of indemnity. It applies to insurance which is a contract of indemnity. So, it does not apply to life insurance. A particular property may be insured with two or more insurers against the same risks. In such cases, the insurers must share the burden of payment in proportion to the amount insured by each. If one of the insurers pays the whole loss, he is entitled to contribution from other insurers.

2.17   PREMIUMS

Premiums can be considered (*Currie v Misa*)[66] a badge of enforceability, operating as the 'consideration' – part and parcel of general contract law[67] as some right, benefit, or interest, profit accruing to one party or some forbearance, detriment or loss to the promisor in exchange for his promise and responsibility, given, suffered or undertaken by the other. To constitute consideration: (1) a performance or return promise must be bargained for; (2) a performance or return promise is bargained for if it is sought by the promisor and given by the promisee; and (3) the performance may consist of (a) an act other than a promise or (b) a forbearance, the creation, modification or destruction of a legal relation in accordance with the common law cemented regionally in *Williams v Persaud*[68] and *BGTM Life Insurance Co. Ltd v Harry*,[69] something which is of value in the eyes of the law, moving from the plaintiff.

The practice of antedating insurance contracts by using the date of an agreement to apply for insurance coverage which usually coincides with the payment of the premium receipts is a step in the right direction, but it hardly goes far enough. The applicant, if he is protected against the risk of delay, is only protected if he has paid the first premium in full. He is not protected, for instance, if he has only made a down payment on the first premium, as illustrated by *Swentusky v Prudential Ins. Co.*[70] Whether and to what extent the applicant is protected depends on the type of the premium receipt used. Premiums are closely related to the *causa* of the civil law – they provide motive for contracting and justification for the arrangement being enforced.

Generally, resulting from Commonwealth Caribbean Insurance Acts' failure to define 'premium,' it is left to the common law to ascertain its legal meaning and effect.[71] The premium can be a single payment or a series of payments. According to *Prudential Insurance Co. v Commissioner of Inland Revenue*,[72] Channell J stated: 'it must be a contract whereby for some consideration, usually but not necessarily for periodical payments called premiums, some benefit for the policyholder is secured on the occurrence of some event.' There is no actual requirement for all premium payments to be made prior to execution of an insurance policy. The correct mode of payment is cash or cheque, and an insured is entitled to periods of lapse known as 'days of grace' when the premium is due but not paid. This is an allowance by the insurer. An insured is entitled to a return of premium where there has been a total failure of consideration, in accordance with the decision of *Tyrie v Flecture*.[73] The rationale for this rule is that there has

---

66   Ibid.
67   *Currie v Misa* (1857) LR 10 Ex 153.
68   (1968) 12 WIR 261.
69   (1962) LRBG 39.
70   116 Conn. 526.
71   *Lewis v Norwich Union Fire Insurance Co.* [1916] AC 509.
72   [1904] 2 KB 658.
73   (1777) 2 Cowp. 666.

been a total failure of consideration so that the insurer was never at risk. The action is in quasi-contract for money had and received. The principle applies because the insurer was not in place or not authorised at the time. While silent, legislation notably intervenes with respect to payment of insurance premiums by the insured to the agent. In this regard, statute expressly abrogates the common law principle that an agent is assumed to be the agent of the insured, and renders the agent as the agent of the insurer, for the purposes of the receipt of premium. Thus, Section 79 of the St Lucia Insurance Act provides:[74]

> an insurance agent, an insurance broker or an insurance salesman is guilty of an offence where he received money from a client for an account of an insurer and fails to pay over the same less any commission and other deduction within thirty days after demand for payment is made in writing.[75]

Failure by the agent to pay the said premium to the insured within the stipulated time period will render the agent personally liable. The utility of these provisions is obvious. The insurer is not free to assert non-receipt of the premium in order to avoid its obligations under the contract of insurance where the premium has already been paid by the insured to the agent. Instead, the statutory solution is to impose personal liability on the agent where he fails to pay over premium within a stipulated time period – 15 days in Barbados and 30 days in St Lucia.[76] Apart from the agent being subject to personal liability for failure to turn over premiums paid in respect of an insurance policy, in some jurisdictions an agent will be rendered personally liable to the insured for unauthorised contracts in the same manner as if he were the insurer. The basis of the liability is knowingly procuring the contract of insurance by fraudulent representation.[77]

Insurance Acts contain provisions regarding premium payments as representing payment to the insurer. It is a question of *quo animo* with what the spirit or intention of the policy is. A legal personal representative of an insured person cannot take advantage of a life insurance company's offer to the insured in his lifetime to accept late payment of premium, as seen by *Zanool Mohammed et al. v Capital Insurance Co. Ltd & All Trinidad Sugar Estates & Factory Workers' Trade Union*[78] and *Byles v Family Guardian Insurance Co. Ltd.*[79] Considering the contract of insurance, its enforcement and the status of insurance policies, confidentiality precludes insurers from disclosing information to the personal representative.

2.18   PRINCIPLES OF INSURANCE

To summarise, the basic principles which govern insurance are:

1   Utmost good faith;[80]
2   Insurable interest;[81]
3   Indemnity;[82]

---

74   St Lucia Insurance Act, Cap 12:08 [2001 Rev.].
75   See Section 90 of the Barbados Insurance Act, Cap 310; Section 82(1), Jamaica Insurance Act No. 26 of 2001.
76   Section 94, Barbados Insurance Act, Cap 310; Section 83, Jamaica Insurance Act No. 26 of 2001; Section 73, St Lucia Insurance Act No. 6 of 1995.
77   See Section 84 of the Jamaica Insurance Act No. 26 of 2001.
78   [1990] 1 TLR 43.
79   BS 2013 SC 84.
80   See Chapter 7.
81   See Chapters 4 and 5.
82   See Chapter 5.

4   Contribution;[83]

5   Subrogation.[84]

2.19   CONCLUSION

It is inscribed in legal doctrine that contracts are created through offer, acceptance and consideration. The rules governing insurance contracts originate from the law pertaining to general commercial contracts. As a special sub-species of contract, insurance contract law fits uneasily into the general notions: offer, acceptance, consideration and intention to form legal relations must be present. Insurance law distinguishes itself in several ways including the concept of insurable interest, contracts secured with Lloyd's and the duty of utmost good faith. In ensuring an insurance contract, special consideration must be given to cover notes, interim insurance and renewals. Note must be taken of the imbalance in bargaining power – weak in the case of the insured who is confronted with standard form contracts. It must be understood that the insurance contract is furthermore distinct because of the multiple players involved in securing the contract (intermediaries): agents, brokers, sub-brokers and loss adjusters. Additionally, there is the procedure of a variety of forms, policies, cover-notes – all juxtaposed in an environment of mass-produced goods and services which collectively constitute the insurance contract. The contract is drafted by the insurer; the insured merely adheres to it, with no choice but acceptance or rejection. The theoretical model of adhesion covers all standard form contracts where the element of actual bargaining is absent.

Differences of opinion prevail regarding how the term 'insurance' should be defined. Regardless, insurance has to contain two central elements: (1) risk pooling and (2) risk transfer. Risk pooling creates a large sample of risk exposure and, as the sample gets larger, the possibility of errant future loss prediction gets lower. This is the law of large numbers. The combination of risk pooling and risk transfer (from the owner of the risk to a third, unrelated party) materially reduces the risk, both in number and in the anxiety it engenders. As such, insurance may be regarded as a beneficial 'social device' enabling groups of individuals to pool and transfer risk to another party who combines or pools all the risk exposure. Pooling the exposures permits more accurate statistical prediction of future losses. Without risk pooling and the technique of avoidance of adverse selection, the negative impacts of unmitigated risk exposure would dominate.

---

83   See Chapter 14.
84   Ibid.

CHAPTER 3

CONTRACT FORMATION

3.1 INTRODUCTION

Because domestic legislation offers little assistance, Commonwealth Caribbean jurisprudence resolves issues and disputes in contract formation – including attendant rules – by application of regional case law[1] augmented by British, Canadian, and Australian jurisprudence.

As established in our previous chapter, the insurance contract is a sub-species of contract.[2] It is therefore from the common law that the general principles of contract formation must be extrapolated. These principles apply equally to contracts of insurance: offer, acceptance, consideration, capacity and an intention to form legal relations. As stated by the Supreme Court in the Jamaican decision of *Bennett v Advantage General Insurance Co. Ltd*:[3]

> it is well established that in order for a binding contract of insurance to arise, there must first be an offer put forward by one party to the contract and the acceptance of it by the other. An offer, it is said, is usually made by the proposer (the proposed assured) who completes a proposal form and sends it to the insurers for their consideration. The insurers would then accept the proposal made leading to an agreement.

In some situations, counter-proposals may be made by the insurer so that negotiations may end with the insurer making a final offer for insurance cover to the proposer, which is up to the proposer to accept by, for instance, tendering the premium due. The general principles of contract law are applicable insurance law. In *Sukhbir v GTM Fire Insurance Co. Ltd*,[4] emanating from the jurisdiction of Trinidad and Tobago, it was stated that there is no rule of common law requiring contracts of insurance to be in any particular form, or in writing at all.[5] Usually these contracts are made by the offer of the proposed insured by the completion of a proposal form which is given to the insurers for their consideration and acceptance. Negotiations may or may not ensue, leading ultimately to the issuing of the policy of insurance. A binding contract of insurance, however, can be made notwithstanding the failure to fill out a proposal form or the issuing of a policy. The only requirement is that there is consensus *ad idem* on the material terms of the policy. This is a fundamental feature of insurance law:

> An acceptance will be of no effect in law unless the parties have agreed upon every material term of the contract they wish to make. The material terms of a contract of insurance cover, the amount and mode of payment of the premium and the amount of the insurance payable in the event of a loss. As to all these there must be a consensus *ad idem*, that is to say, there must either be an express agreement or the circumstances must be agreed.

Once the terms of insurance have been agreed by the parties, there is *prima facie* a binding contract of insurance and the assured is obliged to pay the premium when due and as agreed, and the insurer for their part must deliver a policy containing the agreed terms.[6]

---

1 The Caribbean Court of Justice has marginally considered issues of insurance. *Sea Havens Inc. v Dyrud*, BB 2011 CCJ 7. Insurance was only briefly referenced where the company was in breach of its obligations as to payment of insurance premiums and land taxes. *Canadian Imperial Bank of Commerce v Gypsy International Ltd and Beepat*, BB 2015 CCJ 7.
2 See further G. H. Treitel, *Law of Contract*, 14th edn (ed. E. Peel; Sweet & Maxwell: 2011), Chapters 2–5.
3 JM 2011 SC 98.
4 TT 2006 HC 28.
5 See N. Legh-Jones, J. Birds and D. Owen, *MacGillivray on Insurance Law*, 10th edn (Sweet & Maxwell: 2003), p. 121.
6 *AG of Trinidad and Tobago v Kalackall Bhooplal Smalal* (1987) 36 WIR 382: 'it is essential when weighing the credibility of a witness, to put correctly into the scales the important contemporaneous documents.'

3.2   PRACTICAL PERSPECTIVE

There are, however, several aspects of insurance law unique to the contract of insurance. From a theoretical standpoint, an obvious tension exists between classical contract theory and insurance law. Either as a product of or in an attempt to circumvent this friction, insurance law has some peculiar features in the form of the concept of insurable interest, the doctrine of *umberrimae fides* and the status and rights of the beneficiary.[7] Further, several difficulties are encountered when one attempts to apply general contract principles to the insurance contract. The dominance of a *laissez-faire* philosophy, as a result of the standard form nature of the insurance policy and the consequential inequality in bargaining power of the parties to the contract, means that a difficulty is encountered when attempting to determine a consensus *ad idem* ideology within the context of insurance. To the individual insured who did not participate in the negotiation or drafting of the contract, the superior position of the insurance company is reinforced by the prevalence of drafting devices such as declaration clauses and basis of contract clauses. Specific terms expressed within the proposal form and/or the policy of insurance may operate as conditions precedent to the conclusion of the contract or, more significantly, the liability of the insured in the case of conditions in proposal forms.

From a practical standpoint, the contract of insurance possesses distinguishing features from other commercial contracts. First, the contract of insurance cannot be secured without the involvement of several different actors or intermediaries: agents, salesmen, brokers and underwriters, along with medical personnel with respect to life insurance. Second, the contract of insurance comprises several distinct documents which collectively constitute the contract: the proposal form, policy and (in motor insurance) cover notes. Third, the insurance industry embraces several different types of insurance contracts each possessing unique characteristics (e.g. Lloyd's contracts, travel insurance and coupon insurance).

3.3   OFFER AND ACCEPTANCE

An offer to enter into a proposed contract may be made by the potential insured by completing a proposal form. This is a standard form, a mass-produced document, drafted by the insurer. The insurer may simply accept the offer or may accept it with qualifications which, in classical contract terms, will amount to a counter-offer.[8] Section 25 of the Barbados Marine Insurance Act[9] provides that a contract of marine insurance is inadmissible in evidence unless it is embodied in a marine policy.

---

7   See further A. S. Burrows, 'The Will of Contract Revived – Freid's "Contract as Promise"' (1985) *Current Legal Problems* 141; M. A. Eisenberg, 'The Responsive Model of Contract Law' [1984] 36 *Stan. L. Rev.* 1107; A. D. Burgess, 'Adhesion Contracts and Unfair Terms; A Critique of Current Theory and Suggestion' (1986) 15 *Anglo-Amer L. Rev.* 255–280; J. Cumberbatch, '"In Freedom's Cause": The Contract to Negotiate' [1992] 12 *Oxford J. of Legal Stud.* 58.

8   Earlier, in *Joseph v First National Insurance Co. Ltd*, TT 1977 CA 40, it was stated that it is clear that the offer may assume the form of a letter. *Bennett v Advantage General Insurance Co. Ltd*, JM 2011 SC 98. From the Supreme Court of Jamaica it has been noted, however, that there is no rule of insurance law that there can be no binding contract of insurance until the premium has been actually paid or the policy has been issued. Once the terms of the insurance have been agreed upon by the parties, there is, *prima facie*, a binding contract of insurance and the assured is obliged to pay a premium as agreed, while the insurers, for their part, must deliver a policy containing the agreed terms (see M. Parkington and N. Legh-Jones, *MacGillivray & Parkington on Insurance Law*, 6th edn (Sweet & Maxwell: 1975), p. 86).

It is duly noted that the form exhibited does bear a signature purporting to be that of the claimant . . . this form was signed by the claimant. I accept as a fact, in all the circumstances, that the proposal form exhibited by the defendant was signed by the claimant and submitted to the defendant for the issuance of a policy of insurance.

9   Cap 292.

Subsequently, in *Perry v B&L Insurance Co. Ltd*,[10] also from Trinidad and Tobago, the court observed *Taylor v Allen*[11] on the question of effecting a contract of insurance:

> It is well established that in order for a binding contract of insurance to arise, there must first be an offer put forward by one party to the contract and the acceptance of it by the other. An offer, it is said, is usually made by the proposer (the proposed assured) who completes a proposal form and sends it to the insurers for their consideration. The insurers would then accept the proposal made leading to an agreement. In some situations, counter-proposals may be made by the insurer so that negotiations may end with the insurer making a final offer for insurance cover to the proposer which is up to the proposer to accept by, for instance, tendering the premium due.

Neatly summarised in *Neita (Executor of Estate of Stephen O.B. Mclean – Deceased) v Life of Jamaica*:[12] 'No policy of insurance was ever issued to the deceased during his lifetime . . . the conclusion is inescapable that the company incurred no liability.' Wright J.A., however, opined:

> there is no rule of insurance law that there can be no binding contract of insurance until the premium has been actually paid or the policy has been issued. Once the terms of the insurance have been agreed upon by the parties, there is, *prima facie*, a binding contract of insurance and the assured is obliged to pay a premium as agreed, while the insurers, for their part, must deliver a policy.[13]

Lord Parker CJ, while conceding that there can be an acceptance of an offer by conduct without communicating with the insurance company, stated:[14]

> Bearing in mind that a valid insurance for the purposes of the section must derive from an enforceable contract, it seems to me that the contract, if any, contained in the temporary cover note must arise by offer and acceptance.

His conduct in driving the vehicle on the road was held not to amount to a sufficient acceptance of the offer in the cover note.

In St Lucia, *Diener et al. v The Caribbean General Insurance Co. Ltd*,[15] relying on British jurisprudence, stated that the policy of insurance issued to the plaintiffs was an 'unvalued' policy, that is the sum specified in the policy as the amount of insurance merely indicated the amount beyond which the liability did not extend.[16] According to Mitchell J:

> The corollary to that statement of Cockburn CJ is that even if an insured person claimed the total amount stated on the policy it is not necessarily incumbent on the insurers to pay that amount but only the amount of actual loss or damage. A policy of insurance is a contract of indemnity. The liability of the insurers, the defendants, to make good the loss under the policy is a liability to do so by a payment in money . . . The contract of insurance was reflected in the policy of insurance.[17]

---

10 TT 1986 HC 49.
11 [1966] 1 QB 304.
12 JM 1988 CA 45.
13 See Parkington and Legh-Jones, supra n. 8, p. 86.
14 Supra n. 11, p. 311 (C).
15 LC 1984 HC 1.
16 It was stated by Cockburn CJ in *Chapman v Pole* (1870) 22 LT 306 at 307.

> You must not run away with the notion that a policy of insurance entitles a man to recover according to the amount represented as insured by the premiums paid . . . He can only recover the real and actual value of his goods.

17 *Rayner v Preston* (1881) 18 Ch 1 CA.

In Jamaica, in *Bennett v Advantage General Insurance Co. Ltd*, the court stated:[18] 'Of course, the policy is usually treated as the document that records the contract between the parties.'[19]

3.4 AGREEMENT ON MATERIAL TERMS

In the Guyanese decision of *American Life Insurance Company v Sumintra*,[20] the contract of insurance has been terminated at the option of the company when it sent the insured a notice described as an

> 'offer to accept late payment' . . . that notice was a business arrangement or practice of the company, and not a term or conditions of the contract of insurance, whereby the company offered to accept late payment from an insured who was in default when the grace period had expired. Such a notice, would be in the ordinary course of business have been posted to the insured about one or two days after the expiration of the grace period. In proof of the sending of such a notice I pause here to explain the company's policy in relation to the late payment of premiums. If a premium is not paid when it falls due under the policy, there is allowed a grace period of 31 days during which payment may be made. If the premium is not paid within the grace period, the company makes an offer by post to the assured to accept payment of the premium within a period extended to 60 days after the due date of the premium, subject to certain terms and conditions.

The House of Lords in *Alliss-Chalmers Co. v Fidelity & Deposit Co. of Maryland*[21] suggests that both parties to the contract must agree on all the terms and conditions of the contract. Essential factors include the amount of premium and the nature and duration of the risk. However, a curious feature of insurance is that the insured may be deemed to have agreed to the usual terms and conditions to be found in an insurance of that type. In *General Accident Insurance Corp. v Cronk*,[22] the proposal form that the insured completed did not correspond to certain terms that were in the policy which the insured subsequently received. The insured refused to pay the premium, arguing that the policy he received amounted to a counter-offer. It was held that the insured was liable for the premium as he was deemed to have applied for the usual form of policy issued by the insurer in respect of the particular type of insurance and having agreed to its terms. Most proposal forms today contain an express clause to the effect that the proposer's offer is subject to the insurer's usual terms and conditions. In *Anderson v North American Life Assurance Company*,[23] a decision from the Supreme Court of British Columbia, the insurer sent

---

18 Supra n. 3.
19 J. W. Stempel, *Law Insurance Contract Disputes*, 2nd edn (California University Press: 1995). In this regard, the learned editors of the text helpfully explain:

> The proposal form, when filled in and signed by the proposed assured and sent to the insurer will contain representations about the risk to the insurer but otherwise, without more, will merely constitute a formal offer by the proposed assured to the insurer to enter into a contract of insurance. Ordinarily, once a policy is issued and accepted in response to a proposal form, it will be a policy that is the contractual document. A mere reference to the proposal as having been made will not have the effect of its being incorporated into the contract. Unless the proposal form or its contents are expressly incorporated into the contract of insurance, the proposal form will not be a contractual document and the statements will have no contractual status unless individually they amounted in law to a warranty. Furthermore, if the proposal form is not incorporated into the contract of insurance, it cannot be referred to for the purpose of construing the policy.

20 GY 1983 CA 2.
21 (1916) 114 LT 433.
22 (1901) 17 TLR 233.
23 [1980] ILR 1-1267.

a premium notice for life assurance to the wrong person. That person paid, and the insurer accepted the premium. The court denied the insurer's liability of the policy since the existence of a contract could not be inferred from the insurer's conduct.

In the event of ambiguity, insurance law depicts an anomaly. In *Rust v Abbey Life Assurance Co.*,[24] Rust, on the advice of the insurers and her own advisors, completed a proposal form and forwarded it to the insurers. The insurers duly dispatched the policy but on terms different from those initially agreed to. The court held that Rust's application was an offer and the insurer's action, in sending out the proposal, amounted to an acceptance of the offer so that a contract existed. However, the court recognised that as the policy differed from the proposal it might be regarded as a counter-offer by the insurer, but since the insured waited seven months before responding, there was an acceptance of the counter-offer. In circumstances of a conflict between the proposal form and the policy, a fair and reasonable construction must be placed on the questions in the proposal form and on the answers which the proposer has given to them. In *Zainool Mohammed v Capital Insurance Co. Ltd and All Trinidad Sugar Estates and Factory Workers' Trade Union*,[25] the plaintiffs sustained personal injuries as a result of a collision between a vehicle owned by the third party and a vehicle owned by the first plaintiff. The St Vincent and the Grenadines High Court awarded damages against the third party. At the trial it was discovered that the third party's policy of insurance and the proposal form differed in respect of who was an authorised driver. The Court applied general rules of construction, finding that if there is a final and direct inconsistency between the proposal form and the express condition of the policy, the terms of the policy must prevail. Further, where clauses of a contract of insurance are in conflict, three rules are applicable to determine which clause shall prevail: (1) the policy shall be construed against the insurers *contra preferentum*; (2) where there are printed, written or typewritten words, greater weight is to be given to typewritten words; and (3) where there is more than one document, greater weight should be given to the later in date. The presumption is the parties intended to vary it. In the oft-cited *Condoginanis v Guardian Assurance Co.*,[26] Lord Shaw of Dunfermline opined –

> In a contract of insurance it is a weighty fact that the questions are framed by the insurer, and that if an answer is obtained to such a question which is upon a fair construction is a true answer, it is not open to the insuring company to maintain that the question was put in a sense different from or more comprehensive than the proponent's answer covered.[27] Where an ambiguity exists, the contract must stand if an answer has been made to the question, on a fair and reasonable construction of that question. Otherwise the ambiguity would be a trap against which the insured would be protected by the Courts of Law. Their Lordships accept that doctrine to the full and no question is made of the soundings of it as set forth in many authorities.

American Life Insurance Company v Sumintra[28] surrounded an appeal against an order of the High Court that the insurance company was estopped from disputing the entitlement of Sumintra, the executive of the estate of the deceased. The policy contained a 'days of grace clause' and an automatic termination provision if the premium remained outstanding during the period. The insurance company issued a policy of insurance to the insured after he paid the first premium to an agent. Premiums were due on the 19th of each month. The agent collected the premium but failed to hand it over to the insurer. The issue of the role and function of the intermediary was discussed and whether he had authority to receive subsequent premiums after the death of the insured. The Court found that the express clause on the reverse side of

---

24 [1979] 2 Lloyd's Rep 334.
25 (1990) 1 Trin LR 43.
26 [1921] 2 AC 125.
27 Ibid. at 130.
28 (1983) 37 WIR 242. See also *Looker v Law Union and Rock Insurance Co. Ltd* [1928] 1 KB 554.

the receipt negated that conclusion: 'not to be construed as a precedent/waiver of any condition of the policy.' Finding that there was no implied and or ostensible authority to do anything which is unusual in the trade or profession, the offer to accept the late payment was construed as a special offer reflecting business convenience or custom and was not a term or condition of the contract. Valid acceptance of the offer could only be effected on payment being received by the company during the lifetime and good health of the insured. In setting out the criteria for pleading estoppel and waiver, Luckhoo J opined that estoppel or waiver must be specially pleaded and should be done with care and particularity, setting out the facts on which the party relied. That representation, whether by words or conduct, must be shown to be with the intention of inducing a course of conduct on the part of the representee.

3.5   COUNTER-OFFER

The insurer may insert a condition that acceptance is subject to the payment or receipt of the first premium: 'No insurance shall be held to be effected until the first premium due thereon shall have been paid.'[29] As seen from the decision of *Administrator General of Jamaica v Life of Jamaica Ltd*,[30] where the policy stipulated that it did not commence until the actual payment of the first premium, and further that premiums were to be paid quarterly and in advance, the court held the insurers not liable where the insured was in breach of the condition and the policy had lapsed. Therefore, if death occurs before the first premium is paid, the insurer will not be liable. This clause operates as a condition precedent to the commencement of the policy and thus the attaching of risk,[31] the effect of which is that the insurer is not at risk until receipt of the premium. It operates to extend or suspend the conclusion period, during which time the insured remains under the duty of utmost good faith.[32] It is a matter of law for the court to decide whether a policy issued subject to such a condition precedent is a fully concluded contract of insurance binding the insurer so that the insurer is obligated to accept the premium. Although the insurer's act may be interpreted as a counter-offer, the insurer is not free to revoke that offer once the risk remains the same. If the risk changes, the insurer is at liberty to reject.

As early as the nineteenth century, the principles were laid down in *Canning v Farquhar*.[33] In *Canning v Farquhar*, Canning effected a proposal on his life. It was made on a form issued by the company which contained certain statements about health and other matters, together with a declaration that the statements were 'true and were to be taken as the basis of contract.' The proposal

---

29   *Sickness & Accident Assurance Association v General Accident Assurance Corp.* (1892) 19 R 977. An insurance company, after paying to a tramway company a sum due under a policy insuring against loss by accident, raised an action in its own name against another insurance company for contribution on the ground that it had insured the same risk.

> In marine insurance a rule which has long been recognised is that when the insured has recovered to the full extent of his loss under one policy, the insurer under that policy can recover from other underwriters who have insured the same interest against the same risks a rateable sum by way of contribution. The foundation of the rule is that a contract of marine insurance is one of indemnity, and that the insured, whatever the amount of his insurance or the number of the underwriters with whom he has contracted, can never recover more than is required to indemnify him. The different policies being all with the same person, and against the same risk, are therefore regarded as truly one insurance, and if one of the underwriters is compelled to meet the whole claim, he is entitled to claim contribution from the other underwriters, just as a surety or cautioner who pays the whole debt is entitled to claim rateable relief against his co-sureties or co-cautioners.

30   Unreported decision, Supreme Court of Jamaica No. 40 of 1982.
31   *Canning v Farquhar* (1885–1886) LR 16 QBD 727; *Harrington v Pearl Life Assurance Co. Ltd* (1914) 30 TLR 613.
32   See Chapter 5.
33   (1885–1886) 16 QBD 727.

was accepted at a specified premium, but upon terms that no insurance should take effect until the premium was paid. Before the premium was tendered there was a material alteration in the state of health of the proposer, and the company refused to accept the premium or to issue a policy. It was held that since the nature of the risk had been altered at the time the premium was tendered, there was no contract binding the insurer to issue a policy. Lord Esher MR stated that the real ground for the decision is that negotiations before the time when the policy is effected are mere statements of intention, and that until the insurance company accepts the premium they have a right to decline to accept the risk. The point is that the presence of delaying words extends the commencement period, logically expanding the period of disclosure. Prior to the payment of the premium, there was a material alteration of the risk. The decision of *Roberts v Security Co. Ltd*[34] also illustrates that where the policy contains a statement to the effect that the premium has been paid, the insurer is estopped from denying that there is a binding contract.

In a case originating from Dominica, *Barrington Pond v Netherland Antilles General Insurance Corp. NV*,[35] the claimant owned a truck insured with the defendant company. The policy of insurance was for the period 31 October 1991 to 29 October 1992. The claimant did not pay the entire annual premium, which was paid only after the accident. On the issue of waiver, the fact that the claimant was assisted in completing the claim form was not evidence that the insurer considered the policy to be still in force. According to the Court, this argument ignores the reality that it is common practice for insurance companies

> in this part of the world to assist persons in completing the claim forms. The assistance cannot be considered any indication by the insurer that they accepted the policy remained in force or, that they concede any liability to indemnify the claimant for losses covered under the policy.

The Court continues:

> I think it more likely that the claimant waited until he had the funds to pay the balance of the premium before he made a claim. In effect it was only after the occurrence of the peril that the claimant sought to regularize his insurance policy.

Absent such payment the policy stood cancelled. The legal effect has been clear since the end of the nineteenth century. Justice Cottle, citing the decision *Canning v Farquhar*,[36] accepted the general rule that an insured is not covered while the premium remains unpaid.

3.6   ACCEPTANCE

Any positive act of an intention to create a contract may be sufficient acceptance, for example receipt of a premium without object or qualification. There can be no concluded contract unless there is an express or implied agreement in respect of the amount of the premium and mode of its payment. The High Court of the British Virgin Islands had an opportunity to review the issue of acceptance in the decision of *Tuky Air Transport Inc. v The Liquidators of Edinburgh Insurance Co. Ltd*.[37] The court stated that there is no authority for the bald proposition that once a premium is paid and accepted there is a binding contract of insurance. *Tuky* surrounded an action for $150,000 and damages for breach of contract, the affiliated company and insured with the defendant company for one of its aircrafts totally lost in a crash at sea. The plaintiff

---

34   [1897] 1 QR 111.
35   Unreported decision, High Court of Dominica No. 10530 998 of 1998.
36   (1866) 16 QBD 727.
37   [1988–1989] *Carib. Comm. L. Rev.* 263.

insured two aircraft. The defendants contended, *inter alia*, that the plaintiff could not claim for the value of the policy since the plaintiff did not meet certain conditions, namely (1) failure to pay the full premium, (2) nondisclosure *vis-à-vis* other insurance contracts, (3) the full slate of binder who will be operating the aircraft and (4) defaults in piling notification and proof of loss of the aircraft. The court ruled that it violated the policy of insurance that was in existence at the time of the loss of the aircraft. The defendant insurance company issued the policy after accepting a cheque for the plaintiff in part payment of the premium. With the defendant's full knowledge, the plaintiff arranged for a credit line. The defendants could not revert to the previous legal position. Applying the decision of *Lickiss v Milestone Motor Policies*,[38] where Lord Denning MR stated:

> if one party by his conduct leads another to believe that the strict rights arising under the contract will not be insisted on, intending that the other should act on that belief, and he acts on it, then the first party will not afterwards be allowed to insist on the straight rights where it would be inequitable for him so to do.

Here it was ruled that a valid policy was in existence at the time of loss and that the corporation was required to pay the remainder of the premium. The plaintiff was entitled to recover the value of the policy minus 10 percent deductible under the terms of the policy in addition to special damages which were awarded to the plaintiff for loss of profits resulting from the frustration of the contract under which the plaintiff had leased the aircraft to another air cargo company. Interesting observations can be made on the nature and status of the proposal form in the conclusion of the contract of insurance. In *Tuky*, the plaintiff filled out a blank proposal form for the issuance of the policy in the presence of a broker/agent. At the time of the trial, although the form had been completed in blue ink, red and black ink, in addition to the blue ink was evident. The High Court of the British Virgin Islands ruled, a valid contract was in existence at the time of loss.[39]

3.7   USUAL TERMS AND CONDITIONS

The universal practice in fire, burglary and accident risks is to insure for a year and in the absence of anything to indicate the contrary that may possibly be taken as an implied term of the contract. MacGillivray[40] provides:

> There is no rule of insurance law that there can be no binding contract of insurance until the premium has actually been paid or the policy has been issued. Once the terms of the insurance have been agreed upon by the parties, there is a binding contract of insurance . . . In fire, burglary and motor insurance the practice is to give temporary cover pending the insurer's consideration of the proposal, and, so far as temporary cover is concerned, there is no presumption whatsoever against an informal contract that is immediately binding – in fact rather the reverse.

The rationale for this principle was stated in the American decision of *Hawke v Niagara District Mutual Fire Insurance Co.*,[41] where Proudfoot VC stated:

> It would be unreasonable to hold that by giving an interim receipt the company meant to insure a larger liability than they were subject to on a policy, they must be understood as contracting for an insurance of the 'ordinary kind.'[42]

---

38   [1966] 2 All ER 972.
39   *Ashcroft v Butterworth*, 136 Mass. 511, 514; *Smith v Gowdy*, 8 Allen 566; *Lincoln v Erie Preserving Co.* 132 Mass. 129; *Edge Moor Bridge Works v Bristol*, 170 Mass. 528; *Moulton v Kershaw*, 59 Wis. 316; *Spencer v Harding*, LR 5 CP 561; *Canning v Farquhar*, 16 QBD 727, 732.
40   Parkington and Legh-Jones, supra n. 8, pp. 203, 204.
41   (1876) 23 Gr. 139.
42   Ibid., 1148.

In *Solomon Ghany Oil & Engineering Ltd v N.E.M. (West Indies) Insurance Ltd*,[43] before Justice Moosai, the plaintiff claimed $952,635 being the loss suffered as a result of fire. The issue was whether or not the plaintiff was guilty of misrepresentation for failure to apprise the defendant of material facts, and whether the questions on the proposal form formed the basis of contract. The proposal form was filled out in the agent's presence. The Court of Appeal from a perusal of the proposal form concluded that the area designated for the signature of the agent was left blank.

> It is difficult to imagine an agent, if he were present, not appending his signature to such an important document. Although the receipt refers to a specific policy and the commencement date of risk, this is not an indication as to the contractual period, but it would seem to me that the reference by the defendant to a specific policy and a date of commencement of the risk would at least seem to suggest that the defendant intended to provide to the plaintiff coverage from 29 April 1986 for a one-year period . . . the court took note of the fact that: If there is no express stipulation in a cover note that is issued subject to the conditions contained in the insurer's policies, the insurance is subject to the conditions usually inserted in policies relating to the particular class of risk in question.[44]

3.8 CONDITIONS PRECEDENT

The usual declaration at the foot of the proposal form, that the answers are true and that they are to be the basis of the proposed contract of insurance, makes the truth of the answers a condition precedent, and the proposed assured, by signing it, signifies agreement thereto. Where the truth of the statements is made the basis of the contract, it is unnecessary to consider whether the fact inaccurately stated is material or not, or whether the assured knew or did not know the truth. In *Solomon Ghany*, the court found that given the experience and insurance history of the plaintiff (he was a sophisticated plaintiff who knew the meaning and importance of the basis clause in a contract of insurance and thus could not claim that the information required in the proposal form) was unimportant.

3.9 PREMIUM

A premium can be described as the consideration given by the insured in return for the insurer undertaking to cover the risks insured against the policy of insurance. In accordance with *Lewis v Norwich Union Fire Insurance Co.*,[45] the premium is the consideration given by the insured in return for the insurer's undertaking to cover the risk insured against in the policy of insurance. Payment must be to the insurer or to an agent with actual or apparent authority to receive payment or premium for the insurer. In today's current environment, several ancillary issues arise with respect to the payment of premiums. Is this an unconditional/conditional payment of a premium? Is acceptance conditional upon the cheque being honoured? If it is conditional and the cheque is dishonoured, then the position is the same as if no payment had been made. There is little common law on point. In *Kunti v Demerara Mutual Life Assurance Co.*,[46] the issue was whether premium notices amounted to estoppel by the insurance company, thereby precluding their denial of a policy of insurance. Finding estoppel was

---

43   TT 2000 HC 93.
44   E. R. Hardy Ivamy, *General Principles of Insurance Law*, 4th edn (Butterworths: 1979), p. 181; p. 182 sets out the effect of a basis clause.
45   [1916] AC 509.
46   (1981) 30 IR 173 CA.

not established, the Court reinforced the cardinal principle that the continued existence of a life policy was the regular payment of premiums as they became due. As to payment by third parties (e.g. bankers' standing orders), *Lakhan v United Life Assurance*[47] is noteworthy. Here the bank defaulted in remitting monthly payments so that the failure of the bank was tantamount to a failure of the insured resulting lapse. Despite expressing sympathy, the issue is whether the default by the person responsible for paying the premium renders the policy liable to forfeiture by the insurance company for non-payment. This is dependent on whether the person paying the premium is to be regarded as the agent of the assured or the agent of the insurance company. In *Fordyce v American Life Insurance Co. & Transport*,[48] the assured assigned his policy to his employer, the second defendant, who agreed to pay premiums annually under the policy and to recover by way of monthly deductions. The second defendant failed to pay the premiums on the due date or outside the grace period. It was held that the conduct of the insurer amounted to waiver.[49]

3.10   RETURN OF PREMIUM

An insured has no right to a return of premium unless the insurer has wrongfully repudiated the contract or induced the contract by misrepresentation or non-disclosure. In *Tyrie v Fletcher*,[50] Lord Mansfield stated:

> If the risk of that contract of indemnity has once commenced, there shall be no appropriate or return of premium afterwards. For though the premium is estimated, and the risk depends upon the nature and length of the voyage; yet if it has commenced, though it may be for 24 hours or fewer, the risk is run; the contract is for the whole entire risk, and no part of the consideration shall be returned.

The exceptions to this rule are contract terms and if the risk is divisible. In many cases the insured will receive nothing tangible for the consideration paid, since the event which triggers the insurer's liability may never occur.

3.11   WHEN WILL A PREMIUM BE RETURNED?

The general rule is that if the insurers have never been on risk, they have not earned the premium and ought therefore to return it. 'Equity implies a condition that the insurer shall not receive the price of running a risk if he runs none.'[51] A premium will be returned:

1   Where the policy is void as being made under a mistake of fact (not law).
2   Where the assured rescinds the contract before the contract is concluded before any risk attaches. This is not generally available, but according to Section 145 Industrial

---

47   [1988–1989] 1 Car 290.
48   High Court of Guyana 25 No. 2571 of 1970.
49   In *Hypolite v Demerara Mutual Life Assurance Society Ltd*, there was sufficient evidence of an express waiver of the obligation of the appellant to perform certain conditions of the policy of insurance, namely, the condition to pay arrears on the policy. The respondent had voluntarily granted concession to the appellant by not insisting on his payment of the arrears of the premiums for the insurance monies after he was already in breach of his obligation to pay. The appellant provided consideration for the waiver by discharging the respondent from all claims he had against them and discontinuing the pending legal proceedings.
50   (1777) 2 Cowp. 666.
51   Lord Mansfield, *Stevenson & Snow* (1761) 3 Burr. 1237, 1240.

Life Policies in Trinidad and Tobago: 'a holder has a right to withdraw at any time within 28 days after delivery of the policy.'

3   In case of breach of a warranty relating to the statement as to the insured's health prior to the conclusion of the contract.

4   In case misrepresentation or fraudulent/material non-disclosure render the contract void *ab initio*.

5   In case of inducement (i.e. where the insurer fraudulently misrepresented that the insured had insurable interest).

3.12   DAYS GRACE

Policies of insurance may contain a days of grace clause to the effect that

> one month, not fewer than 30 days, will be allowed for the payment of any premium on this policy other than the first. Notwithstanding default in payment of the premium when due, the policy shall continue in force during the period of grace.[52]

A days of grace clause operates as a concession by the insurer to the insured. The question as to whether the insured's estate will recover in the event of death occurring during the period of grace is dependent upon the construction of the policy. In *Lakhan v United Security Life Insurance Co. Ltd*,[53] non-payment of a premium terminates the contract of insurance. On the death of the assured, the two policies had already lapsed. The term 'days of grace' refers to the additional time period granted by the insurer to the insured within which the premium is to be paid. In a life contract, the effect is usually that the contract remains in force during the days of grace, although the premium has not been paid on time. Time is not of the essence until the days of grace period has expired. If a person dies during the days of grace in accordance with *Stuart v Freeman*,[54] there is cover.

3.13   ROLE OF INTERMEDIARIES

The case of *Tuky* reveals the relevance of the principles of agency: (1) the filling out of the proposal form and (2) the payment of premiums. With respect to the filling out of the proposal form, Bertrand J held that the agent was not a dual agent but was the agent of the insurance company. A critical issue in *Tuky* was the perennial problem of whose agent was the agent with respect to the filling out of the proposal form and whether the agent's knowledge was to be imputed onto the principal. One mechanism which may assist the insured is the days of grace clause, and it is a matter of construction of the policy in the context of the specific facts as to whether the policy is still in existence. Clauses of this nature represent a concession by the insurer. In the Trinidad and Tobago decision of *Lakhan v United Security Life Insurance Co. Ltd*,[55] a 'days of grace clause' provided a grace period of one month for the payment of every premium after the first.

> On the death of the assured the two policies had already lapsed. There can be no agency or relationship of principal and agent in regard to an act unless the alleged principal actually or

---

52   Standard policy term.
53   TT HC No. 2294 [1989] *Carib. Comm. L. Rev.* 290.
54   [1903] 1 KB 47.
55   [1988–1989] 1 *Carib. Comm. L. Rev.* 290.

ostensibly authorised or appointed the alleged agent to perform the act for or on behalf of the alleged principal or unless the alleged principal subsequently ratified the act purported to have been performed on his behalf.

The principle that there can be no agency without consent of the principal was succinctly expressed by Lord Person in the House of Lords decision of *Garnac Grain Co. Inc. v H.M.F. Faure & Fairclough Ltd*:[56]

> The relationship of principal and agent can only be established by the consent of the principal and agent. They will be held to have consented if they have agreed to what amounts in law to such a relationship, even if they do not recognise it themselves and even if they have professed to disclaim it.

In a situation where there is no agency relationship, any person acting without authority of an alleged disclosed or undisclosed principal who performs or purports to perform an act for or on behalf of an alleged principal, represents and warrants that he has the alleged principal's authority to do so. In *Starkey v Bank of England*,[57] the House of Lords held that a broker who applied to the Bank of England for a power of attorney, wrongly believing himself to have been instructed by the stockholder, was liable to indemnify the bank against the claim of the stockholder on the ground that he must have been taken to have given an implied warranty that he had authority. The agent's liability is strict, is not fault based and is not dependent on negligence.

3.14   STATUTE

Caribbean statutes abrogate the common law and render the agent the agent of the insured for the purposes of the receipt of premium. Moreover, statute imposes personal liability on the agent if he fails to pay over premium within a stipulated period.[58] The agent may be also rendered personally liable to the insured for unauthorised contracts in the same manner as if he were the insurer. Section 79 of the St Lucia Insurance Act provides that

> an insurance agent, an insurance broker or an insurance salesman is guilty of an offence where he received money from a client for an account of an insurer and fails to pay over the same less any commission and other deduction within 30 days after demand for payment is made in writing.

Section 90 of the Barbados Insurance Act states that a

> sub agent, broker, salesman shall for the purpose of receiving a premium for a contract of insurance be deemed to be the agent of the insurer and notwithstanding any conditions or stipulations to the contrary, the registered insurer shall be deemed to have received any premium received by the agent, sub agent broker or salesman.

3.15   ADDITIONAL REQUIREMENTS

A premium can be described as the consideration given by the insured in return for the insurer undertaking to cover the risks insured against the policy of insurance.[59] In *British Workmans and General Assurance v Cunliffe*,[60] the insurer or agent's conduct is important where an agent of

---

56   [1968] AC 1130.
57   [1903] AC 114.
58   Section 94, Barbados Insurance Act, Cap 310.
59   *Lewis v Norwich Union Fire Insurance Co.* [1916] AC 509.
60   (1902) 18 TLR 425 CA.

insurers induced the insured to effect insurance on brother in law's life in which he had no interest, the Court of Appeal allowed the insured to recover the premiums paid.[61]

3.16 CAPACITY

Authorised body corporates, registered under the Insurance Act, have contractual capacity. In this regard, regional company legislation constitutes a residual regulatory base for insurance companies.[62] With respect to the insured, regional insurance legislation slightly modifies the rule on capacity, enabling minors to contract.[63] Section 111 of the Barbados Insurance Act, for instance, enables a minor between the ages of 10 and 16, with the written consent of his parent or someone in *loco parentis*, to effect a policy upon his own life or upon another life in which the minor has insurable interest. Section 95 of the Jamaica Insurance Act enables a minor who has attained the age of 16 to effect a policy upon his own life or upon another life in which he has an insurable interest or take an assignment of a policy.

3.17 IMPORTANCE OF DETERMINING THE DATE THE CONTRACT WAS EFFECTED

It is important to determine when a contract of insurance has been concluded for the purposes of the liability of the insurer and the fundamental duty of *uberrimae fides*, which operates up until the contract has been concluded. There is a presumption that a life contract is an 'entire contract' existing until death of the life assured or the specified death unless the policy lapses, in which case the duty emerges once again. In indemnity insurance, the insured enters into a new contract at the expiration of the defined period. An insurer cannot allege non-disclosure of material facts which happen after the contract is concluded. This duty will arise again on renewal after lapse. Renewal constitutes an entire new contract.

3.18 SPECIAL CONTRACTS OF LLOYD'S

Lloyd's was formed in a coffee shop in the eighteenth century and is distinctive. Prior to the events at the end of the twentieth century it was not an insurance company. Formed in 1688 when Edward Lloyd first opened his coffee house for merchants to conduct their business, which often included underwriting of marine insurance risks, his successors (now known as the Corporation of Lloyd's) then evolved to a constituted society of underwriters. This society comprises 'names' (private individuals trading with unlimited liability) and corporate members (which trade with limited liability). The broker, acting on behalf of the insured, completes a 'slip,' setting out the details of the risk, and then it is taken to underwriters in order to receive the best 'quote.' Once the best acceptable quote is achieved, he gets the chosen underwriter to indicate on the slip what share of the total risk he is willing to accept. He is in effect 'leading' the underwriting, and the broker then proceeds to get similar agreements from other underwriters on the same basis. Risk

---

61 *Harse v Pearl Life Assurance* [1903] 2 KB 822.
62 Barbados Companies Act, Cap 308; Jamaica Companies Act No. 26 of 2004; Trinidad and Tobago Companies Act No. 81:01 of 1995.
63 St Lucia Insurance Act No. 6 of 2013; Section 111, Barbados Insurance Act 1996: 'a minor between the age of 10 and 16 may with written consent of his parent or someone in *loco parentis* effect a policy upon his own life or upon another life in which the minor has insurable interest.'

pooling takes place. In the 1980s and 1990s, Lloyd's suffered a series of losses of enormous pro-portion. In total, over £7 billion had to be paid by its members, many of whom then sued their underwriting agents alleging that their affairs had been handled negligently. Cases of fraud had also been alleged earlier. The crisis which all this provoked in the market led to sweeping reforms. The main one was the introduction of limited liability capital (that is, from corporate members). As well as this break with tradition, Lloyd's overhauled virtually every aspect of the way in which it conducted business. These reforms began in earnest with the publication of Lloyd's first cen-tral business plan in April 1993. This ushered in a far more direct and centralised management process to ensure the market's survival without past mistakes being repeated.[64]

Each party completes a binding contract for the percentage of any loss that becomes pay-able. Often no policy is issued, hence the slip assumes greater significance. The legal conun-drum[65] inheres in the point at which the Lloyd's contract concludes. The Court of Appeal[66] has authoritatively decided that the underwriter is bound from the moment he initials the slip, even though a later underwriter may decline the offer or amend its terms. Undoubtedly this decision can produce odd results, as it appears that the insured may have separate contracts with different underwriters.[67] On 29 March 2017, the United Kingdom formally triggered Arti-cle 50, beginning the divorce proceedings from the European Union as a result of the Brexit referendum. This compels the United Kingdom to renegotiate all trade agreements to which it was a signatory as a member of the European Union (EU), while the economic partnership agreement (EPA)[68] is likely to be affected. The implications for Lloyd's are significant.

Focus on the twenty-first century indicates change in the Lloyd's market, punctuated (or rather driven) by significant technological advancements. Since the eighteenth and nineteenth centuries, change punctuated by drones, Uber,[69] self-driving cars, surveillance,[70] terrorism and kidnapping insurance. Brexit means that Lloyd's has to shop for underwriting facilities. This 'progress'/transition has implications for both the insurer and the insured. At outset, advances in technology question the availability of liability insurance and has implications for the insured with respect to disclosure.

3.19   TEMPORARY COVER AND COVER NOTES

Temporary cover and cover notes are features of motor vehicle insurance. Because the contract is renewed annually, motor insurance, like other indemnity contracts, cannot be considered an 'entire' contract such as life insurance. This option to renew annually perhaps is why life insurance can be regarded as 'a locked-in product,' whereas the insured generally does not shop around for insurance at the end of each year. Perhaps it is also the reason why life insurers are more dominant in the regional capital market. The sanctuary afforded to life products is absent

---

64   A. M. Best Co., *Understanding the Insurance Industry*, 2016 edn.
65   J. Birds, *Modern Insurance Law*, 6th edn (Sweet & Maxwell: 2014), p. 81.
66   *General Reinsurance Corp. v Forsakringsaktiebolaget Patria* [1983] QB 856.
67   This is an economic partnership between the Caribbean and the European Union.
68   This is an economic partnership between the Caribbean and the European Union.
69   There is an Uber insurance gap. While driving for Uber, the app is switched on and coverage is attached. The danger lies when the app is turned off. Once the insurance companies find out that the driver works for Uber or Lyft, they're stuck with no personal auto coverage.
70   Greyball is part of a broader program called VTOS, short for 'violation of terms of service,' which Uber created to root out people it thought were using or targeting its service improperly. The VTOS program, including the Greyball tool, began as early as 2014 and remains in use today, predominantly outside the United States. Greyball was approved by Uber's legal team.

combined with the likelihood of greater claims. Resources within general insurance are not as with life insurance; the insurer's profit margin is arguably smaller.

A binding temporary cover can be achieved via a cover note, which is generally given by an insurance company to the insured who has effected a policy. It acts as an interim certificate of insurance until the full policy is issued and operates as the Certificate of Insurance. There is considerable regional case law on the viability and status of cover notes. In the unreported decision of *Hypolite v Demerara Mutual Life Assurance Society Ltd*[71] from St Vincent and the Grenadines, the appellant engaged the respondent as an insurance consultant agent and/or broker to secure insurance coverage for certain contract works. The respondent issued to the appellant a cover slip purporting to provide the said insurance coverage. The cover slip was alleged to contain the following statement. 'Principal: To be advised as required by contract.' There was no principal in existence for whom the defendant acted. The statement of claim alleged that during the currency of the cover slip, the appellant's property was damaged by flood, causing special damages of over $700,000. In disputing liability, the defendant insurers contended, *inter alia*, that the premium had not been paid and disputed the degree of damage alleged to have been suffered. On the issue of whether the defendant, as a mere broker, could be sued successfully for losses as if he were a principal insurer, the court held that the respondent can be sued for breach of warranty that he had authority to make the contract.[72] The court held the defendant, as a broker, could be sued as an agent for an undisclosed or non-existent principal for the breach of warranty that there was a principal, and is equally liable where an undisclosed principal has not consented or authorised the contract to be made on his behalf. On the issue of whether, in the absence of a claim in negligence or fraudulent or negligent misrepresentation or breach of warranty of authority, the plaintiff has any cause of action against the defendant, it found that the agent's liability is strict and does not depend on negligence or fraud. The authority to conclude a binding cover note will invariably rest in an insurance agent. The law of agency will be discussed in Chapter 10, but in *Hypolite v Demerara Mutual Life Assurance Society Ltd*[73] there was apparently no principal for whom the agent acted. The fact that an agent is entrusted with blank cover notes will be sufficient to confer upon the agent implied actual or apparent authority. In *Mackie v European Assurance Society*,[74] the actions of the principal in supplying the agent with cover notes conferred authority on him to bind the principal. Illustrating the agent is pivotal to the conclusion of an insurance contract. This point is witnessed in *Mossiah v Regent Insurance Co. Ltd et al. Motor Insurance Policy*.[75] In this case, a 30-day cover note was issued by the first defendant's agent. A vehicular accident occurred, to which the first defendant resisted the claim. An issue was whether the cover note was valid at the date of the accident. The Supreme Court of Belize found that the defendants were not permitted to rely on the fact that the assured was not the owner of the vehicle since the agent of the first defendant was aware of that fact. Judgment found for the plaintiff. The uniqueness of insurance contracts is displayed in *Khan v Trans-Nemwil Insurance (Grenada) Ltd*.[76] Here the Court affirmed that the contract of insurance is not confined strictly to a policy but embraces a cover note, proposal form and the

---

71   St Vincent and the Grenadines Civil Appeal No. 25 of 1993.
72   *Starkey v Bank of England* [1903] AC 114 HL. The Earl of Halsbury L.C. set out the notion that it was necessary to establish a contract between the purported principal and the plaintiff as illogical, and confusing the question whether the facts established a contractual warranty between plaintiff and defendant, with the question as to whether a contract follows in consequence of a representation. He said: 'that which does enforce the liability is this – that under the circumstances of this document being presented to the Bank for the purpose of being acted upon.'
73   Supra n. 71.
74   (1869) 17 WR 987.
75   Supreme Court of Belize BZ 2000 SC 6.
76   GD 2001 HC 12.

accompanying documents. The plaintiff is bound by the terms and conditions. The issue was whether there was a breach of disclosure and whether the insurance contract consisted of the cover note. The plaintiff failed to supply all relevant information reasonably required. Finding that plaintiff was in breach of obligations in refusing to supply same. It is ruled in favour of the defendant. Applying *United General Insurance Co. Ltd v Hutchinson*,[77] the cover note is the same as the Certificate of Insurance – *Roberts v Security Co. Ltd.*[78]

3.20   ORAL CONTRACTS

Although it is rare, as with other contracts an insurance contract need not be in writing. There is *dicta* to the effect that an informal agreement by word of mouth can indeed support a contract of insurance for a line of insurance to protect the risk in the meantime, if made by an authorised agent of the insurer which will be liable in the case of loss.[79] In the case of *Edgar v Demerara Mutual Life Assurance Society Ltd*[80] arising from the jurisdiction of St Lucia, insurance was secured to cover a 20-year loan from a finance company. The insurance company initially granted a ten-year policy. After the expiration of the first policy, the insurance company sent a letter to the plaintiff informing him that they would not grant him further coverage. Despite this, the plaintiff paid two yearly premiums which were accepted and subsequently signed a proposal form for a second policy. The issue before the court was whether there was a valid insurance policy in operation and whether the agent had indicated that after the expiration of the first policy the company would insure him for a consecutive ten-year period. The court held that the plaintiff's offer had been rejected in a letter sent by the insurance company stating that the company could not grant him insurance coverage. The existence of an oral contract could not be established as the essentials of the agreement (i.e. amount of coverage, the nature of the risks and the rate of premium) were not agreed upon, and further that the defendant's agent had no authority to enter into such an agreement. The fact that there was prior insurance history between the parties cannot be discounted but, if the particulars of the agreement are established with sufficient specificity, an oral contract of insurance is possible. In *Murfitt v Royal Insurance Co.*[81] an agent was held to have implied actual authority to enter into temporary oral contracts of fire insurance. The facts were special because the agent in question had been giving such cover orally for two years with the full knowledge and consent of the company.[82] Marine insurance contracts are required, however, to be in writing. Section 25 of the Barbados Marine Insurance Act provides that a contract of marine insurance is inadmissible in evidence unless it is embodied in a marine policy.

3.21   RENEWAL VERSUS EXTENSION

The *Oxford English Dictionary* defines 'renewal' as the action of extending the period of validity of a license, subscription or contract. An 'extension,' on the other hand, is a part added to something to enlarge or prolong it; a continuation. The distinction between renewal of a policy

---

77   Vol. 25, para. 402.
78   Supra n. 34.
79   *Mayne Nickless Ltd v Pegler* (1974) 1 NSWLR 228.
80   Unreported decision, St Lucia Suit No. 160 of 1989.
81   (1922) 38 TLR 334, KBD.
82   In *Mayne Nickless Ltd v Pegler*, an Australian case, the insured purchased a car and the vendor immediately arranged for insurance over the telephone. A binding contract of insurance occurred before the issue of the cover note and before the policy was issued.

and extension of a policy is imperceptible to say the least. A definition was outlined by Mayo J in *Re Kerr*:[83] 'strictly, a "renewal" is descriptive of a repetition of the whole arrangements by substituting the like agreement in place of that previously subsisting, to be operative over a new period.' See illustrations of this discussion and its ambit in *Mutual Holdings (Bermuda) Ltd v American Patriot Insurance Agency Inc. et al.* and *American Patriot Insurance Agency Inc. v Mutual Indemnity (Bermuda) Ltd et al.*;[84] see also *Coakley v Home Insurance Co.*[85]

Renewal is 'at the option of the Company only.' The clause defining 'grace period' imposes on the defendant company the obligation to give 30 days' notice of its intention not to renew – a period which in the normal course of events would allow alternative cover to be negotiated. In that regard the policy is somewhat more favourable to the insured than are the usual terms described in *MacGillivray & Parkington on Insurance Law*,[86] where mere non-acceptance of a premium tendered is enough to terminate the risk.

The effect of the definition of the 'grace period' upon the renewal clause seems to me to result in a situation in which the failure by the insurer to issue a notice of intention not to renew within 30 days of the premium due date can be treated by the insured as an offer to renew the policy for an additional term. The insured would then have the right to tender the premium within the 30 days prescribed as the grace period. Once this sum was tendered, the insurer, not having responded within the grace period with notice of intention not to renew, is obliged to accept the premium, extending cover for that additional term; whereas 'an "extension" betokens a prolongation of the subsisting contract by the exercise of a power reserved thereby to varying one of its provisions, that is, by enlarging the period.' Upon a renewal similar rights revest. A contract reserving continuous rights of renewal will, if these be exercised, lead to succeeding contract 'in a series, the identity of each contract [being] separate and distinct. On the other hand, the exercise of the right of extension augments the length of time over which the contract operates, without changing its identity.'

Where there is a renewal or extension of an insurance policy, this is a question of construction. The problem occurs when the term renewal is referred to as an extension, both words seemingly being used interchangeably.[87] In *Harding v Bahamas First General Insurance*,[88] the words cover will continue, when read with the words, 'for any subsequent period' are open to meaning one or more successive annual periods without any intervening gaps in coverage. According to the judgment,

> there is also I think room for a contrary view. Mr. McDonald contended for the former. He saw the meaning of 'continue' as decisive of what was intended and as pointing to a steady stream of unbroken coverage so long as the premium asked for was accepted.

Accordingly some observations by Lord Morris in *Wickman Machine Tool Sales Ltd v Schuler A.G.*[89] are apt. He said:

> If it is clear what [the parties] have agreed a court will not be influenced by any suggestion that they would have been wiser to have made a different agreement. If a word employed by the parties in a contract can have only one possible meaning then, unless any question of rectification arises, there will be no problem. If a word either by reason of general acceptance or by reason of judicial construction has come to have a particular meaning then, if used in a business or technical document, it will often be reasonable to suppose that the parties intended to use the word in its accepted sense. But if a word in a contract may have more than one meaning then, in interpreting the contract, a court will have to decide what was the intention of the parties as revealed by or deduced from the terms and subject matter of their contract.

---

83   J. Lowry and P. Rawlins, *Insurance Law: Cases and Materials* (Hart: 2004), p. 346.
84   BM 2010 SC 36.
85   BS 1985 SC 6; see also *Attorney General v CL Financial Ltd et al.*, TT 2017 CA 44.
86   Parkington and Legh-Jones, supra n. 8.
87   C. E. Heath *Underwriting & Insurance (Australia) Pty Ltd v Edwards Dunlop & Co.* [1993] 176 CLR 535 (HC).
88   BS 1998 SC 82.
89   [1974] AC 235 [1973] 2 All ER 39.

Lord Reid, speaking to the same effect, said:

> The fact that a particular construction leads to a very unreasonable result must be a relevant consideration. The more unreasonable the result the more unlikely it is that the parties can have intended it, and if they do intend it the more necessary it is that they shall make that intention abundantly clear.[90]

According to *Harding v Bahamas First General Insurance*, it is renewable by mutual consent and a provision to that effect does not bind the insurer to renew. In *Halsbury's Laws of England*,[91] the learned author states:

> An offer of renewal may come for the insurers, such as where they send out a renewal notice, and then payment of the appropriate premium amounts to acceptance of their offer so as to create a binding contract and there is no room for refusing to take the premium.

Renewal connotes a fresh new contract, as opposed to an extension.

3.22   RULES FOR CONSTRUCTING INSURANCE POLICIES

The general approach is to apply the ordinary natural meaning to the wording of the policy, but perhaps there is a need for more detailed guidance. The rules for construing insurance policies generally are stated to be the same as those applicable to contracts in general. The following abridged list of rules is taken from Ivamy:[92]

> the intention of the parties must prevail; the whole of the policy must be looked at; the policy must be construed in accordance with the ordinary rules of grammar; the ordinary meaning of words will be adopted; the meaning of a particular word may be limited by the context; the words of the policy must be taken to mean what they say; the words of the policy must be construed literally; ion case of ambiguity the reasonable construction is to be preferred; in case ambiguity the reasonable construction is to be preferred; in case of ambiguity the *contra preferentum* rule will be applied. How do the courts decide which rule to apply in any given case? Particular words may give rise to problems, eg: An accident, A loss, A flood, or labeling such as the term A householders' policy or all risks.

3.23   CONCLUSION

Risk pertains to a future event, one that may be possible, probable, contingent, fortunate or unfortunate. The fear of the risk is the *grundnorm*[93] of insurance. It prescribes a current value to the risk and ascribes a cost – an insurance premium – a fee. In insurance, a monetary evaluation takes place. The sharing of risk is achieved via standard form of insurance policy or contract, which consists of several documents. It has been shown that cover notes as interim insurance pending conclusion of the formal policy are subject to the normal principles of contract law. The regional case law illustrates that an agreement may be achieved at once or after protracted negotiation, as is the case of large commercial risk. When negotiations are prolonged, and dispute emerges concerning the existence of a binding contract or its terms, it is then necessary

---

90   [1974] AC 235, p. 251E.
91   Fourth edn (Butterworth: 1989), Vol. 25, p. 270, para. 474.
92   Supra n. 44.
93   Edwin W. Patterson, 'Hans Kelsen and His Pure Theory of Law' (1952) 40 *Calif. L. Rev.* 5.

to review the whole course of the negotiations to determine if there was full agreement on the material of the insurance or, as the case may be, agreement that a particular term was agreed. In carrying out this exercise a tribunal should have regard to subsequent events which bear upon the question at issue.

There is no rule of insurance law that there can be no binding contract of insurance until the premium has been actually paid or the policy has been issued. Once the terms of the insurance have been agreed upon by the parties, there is *prima facie* a binding contract of insurance until the premium has been issued. The assured is obligated to pay the premium as agreed, while the insurers for their part must deliver a policy containing the agreed terms. Regional case law indicates that often discrepancies exist between the cover note and the policy.[94] To say that it is a part of a standard form of contract is insufficient. The challenges confronting the insured are aptly captured by Mitchell, J in *Thomas Al v Ira Archibald Insurance Eit Al*,[95] where he lamented on the challenge confronting the insured:

> [as] much as one may sympathise with the claimants, their obligation was to have carefully studied the terms of their policy. They were then required faithfully to comply with all of its terms, and, in particular, to pay their renewal premium promptly. The claimants cannot so casually enter into an insurance contract, making no enquiries as to their rights and obligations under the contract, as to entitle them, when things go wrong, to claim, in the face of the terms of the policy to the contrary, either that their insurance broker was their principal insurer or that he should be held liable as if he were their principal insurer.

94   *Re Coleman's Depositories Ltd and life and Health Association* [1907] 2 KB 798 CA.
95   AG 2002 HC 45. Indemnity for damage. Claimants purchased a homeowners comprehensive policy from the first defendant, a broker of the second defendant. There was an express term of policy was that it lapsed unless insured had paid the renewal premium. The Claimant paid the renewal premium, however, they did not pay renewal premium to the insurer. Hurricane Luis caused damage to the claimant's house. The insurer rejected a claim for indemnity. As to whether the first defendant could be sued as principal insurer, the judgment was that the first defendant could not be sued as if he were an insurer.

CHAPTER 4

INSURABLE INTEREST IN LIFE INSURANCE

4.1   INTRODUCTION

Regional Insurance Acts have modified the rules governing insurable interest in life, representing an implicit acceptance that intervention is justified in the context of life insurance because of the overall public policy against the temptation for insurance to serve as an incentive/inducement to murder. Indeed it is a fundamental requirement of the contract of insurance that the insured must have an interest in the subject matter being insured. This interest, known as insurable interest, restricts what can be legally insured and distinguishes the contract of insurance from other commercial contracts. Considered one of the great outstanding principles in the formation of an insurance contract, the law 'expressly prohibit[s] (*mala prohibita*) the making of contracts devoid of insurable interest, rendering them null and void.'[1] Prior to legislative intervention, wagering contracts where enforceable, it was common for insurance to be effected where the insured had no interest in the subject matter of the insurance. A series of eighteenth-century legislation designed to eradicate 'mischievous gaming' was introduced, which today still represents the foundation for the law of insurable interest in the Commonwealth Caribbean.[2]

Although insurable interest is required in both life and indemnity insurance, and while Lord Justice Waller tenders an elastic approach blurring the demarcation between life insurance and indemnity in *Feasey v Sun Life Assurance of Canada*, this text adopts for simplicity in understanding the traditional approach to the capacity and function as the relevant rules differ.[3] This chapter deals with insurable interest in life insurance. Insurable interest with respect to indemnity insurance will be considered in Chapter 5.

4.2   INSURABLE INTEREST IN LIFE INSURANCE

The rules governing insurable interest in life policies and policies providing for payment of fixed sums in the event of personal injury can be found in modern regional Insurance Acts. Because these Acts expressly commence with the inclusive statement 'without restricting the meaning of the expression "insurable interest . . .,"[4] they operate in conjunction with the residual Life Assurance Act of 1774 and the common law.

4.3   STATUTE

Prior to legislative intervention, there was no requirement for insurable interest in insurance contracts. The general principle of every contract was simply that a contract was enforceable by the parties irrespective of its subject matter provided it was neither illegal, immoral

---

1   Per Justice Luckhoo, *American Life Insurance v Sumintra* (1983) 37 WIR 242, CA.
2   The Marine Insurance Act 1745, 19 Geo. II, c. 37; the Life Assurance Act 1774, 14 Geo. III, c. 48; the Marine Insurance Act 1788; the Gaming Act 1845, 8 & 9 Vict. c. 109; the Marine Insurance Act 1906, 6 Edw. 7 c. 41; the Marine Insurance (Gambling Policies) Act 1909, 9 Edw. 7 c. 12.
3   In the Court of Appeal decision of *Feasey v Sun Life Assurance of Canada* [2003] ECWA Civ 885 [2003] Lloyd's Rep IR 637, Lord Justice Waller put forward a flexible approach essentially blurring the demarcation between life insurance and indemnity. *See infra*, n. 44 and accompanying text.
4   Cap 310.

or contrary to public policy. Three statutes brought about change: the Life Assurance Act of 1774,[5] the Marine Insurance Act of 1906[6] and the Gaming Act of 1845. By virtue of the Life Assurance Act of 1774,[7] insurable interest is required in contracts of life insurance.

The Life Assurance Act of 1774 applies throughout the Caribbean in the absence of express statutory exclusion and contains only four sections:

(1)   . . . No insurance shall be made by any person or persons, bodies politick or corporate, on the life or lives of any person or persons, or on any other event or events whatsoever, wherein the person or persons for whose use, benefit, or on whose account such a policy or policies shall have not an interest, or by way of gaming or wagering; and that every such assurance made contrary to the true intent and meaning hereof shall be null and void.

(2)   . . . It shall not be lawful to make any policy or policies on the life or lives of any person or persons, or other event or events, without inserting in such policy or policies the person or persons name or names interested therein, or for whose use and benefit or on whose account such policy is so made or underwrote.

(3)   And . . . in all cases where the insured hath interest in such life or lives, event or events no greater sum shall be recovered or received from the insurer or insurers than the amount or value of the interest of the insured in such life or lives, or other event or events.

(4)   . . . Provided always, that nothing herein contained shall extend or be construed as to extend to insurances bona fide made by any person or persons on ships, goods or merchandises, but every such insurance shall be valid and effectual in the law as if this Act had not been made.

4.4   APPLICATION

Either by settlement or statutes expressly incorporating English law as former British colonies, Caribbean territories all received or adopted the Life Assurance Act of 1774 and the principles of the English common law. This is reflected in the judgment delivered by Justice Luckhoo in *American Life Insurance Co. v Sumintra*, arising out of the Guyana Court of Appeal.[8] Discussing the origin, import and nature of the doctrine of insurable interest, Justice Luckhoo states:

Now, it is trite law that one of the three great principles of insurance law is that the insured must have an insurable interest in the subject matter of insurance, i.e. to effect a valid contract of insurance the insured must have something at stake; he must have something to lose by the happening of the peril he seeks to insure against. This is a statutory requirement under the Life Assurance Act, 1774 (UK) a provision which applies in Guyana by virtue of section 13 of the Civil Law of Guyana Act, Cap 6:01. But, generally speaking, any insurance effected by an insured without an insurable interest would be void as gaming or wagering transaction under section 18 of the Gaming Act 1845 (UK).

4.5   RATIONALE FOR INSURABLE INTEREST

The rational for the requirement of insurable interest can be gleaned from the preamble to the Life Assurance Act of 1774, which states, 'Whereas it hath been found by experience that the making insurances on lives or other events wherein the assured shall have no interest has

---

5   14 Geo. III, c. 48.
6   Edw. 7 c. 41, which repealed the Marine Insurance Act of 1745, 19 Geo. II, c. 37.
7   14 Geo. 3, c. 48.
8   (1983) 37 WIR 243.

introduced a mischievous kind of gaming.' Indeed, before the legislature intervened, wagering contracts were not illegal and could be enforced in a court of law. Early English case law series reveal a predilection for insuring lives of well-known personages.[9] This practice attracted the ire of noted seventeenth-century theorists who agonised over the possibility of the insured making a profit out of insurance. According to Blackstone:[10]

> gambling promotes idleness, theft and debauchery among those of the lower class; and among persons of superior ranks, it hath been attended with the sudden ruin and desolation of ancient and opulent families, an abandoned prostitution of every principle of honour and virtue and too often ended in self-murder.

Patterson, expressing similar views, opined: 'A sense of antagonism is aroused in a community of workers against persons who obtain a means of livelihood without participating in the machinery of social or economic production and, or distribution.'[11] Lord Ellenborough CJ refused to countenance a wager, considering it 'injurious to the interests of mankind.'[12] A stark and dramatic example of insurance operating as an incentive for murder can be seen in the US decision *Liberty National Life Insurance Company v Weldon*.[13] In this case, the plaintiff was the father of a little girl called Shirley, who died when she was two and a half years of age from arsenic poisoning. The insurance policies were effected with several insurance companies for various sums. An aunt-in-law of Shirley was charged with murder and subsequently executed in the state of Alabama.

Established in earlier chapters, insurance law often requires consideration of other areas of law: crime, family law, estate planning and taxation and public policy. An insurance policy can be manipulated with the peril occasioning instigated by spite or malice whereby profit rationale can take the form of deprivation of profit. As stated in the Bahamian decision of *Stuart et al. v Colonial Imperial Insurance Ltd*,[14] although the suicide clause was against public policy, the insurance company could not abrogate responsibility under the policy. The policy was held lawful and enforceable. Madame Justice Allen noted further that the public policy rule in the United Kingdom has been gradually modified by the Courts in cases[15] where the Court is given power to modify the public policy rule 'having regard to the conduct of the offender and of the deceased.'

In many Commonwealth countries, the validity of a promise by insurers to pay in the event of suicide is replicated. In Trinidad and Tobago, the rule in *Beresford's Case* has been abrogated. Section 162 and 164 of the Barbados Insurance Act provides that

> A policy shall not be avoided merely on the ground that the person whose life is insured died by his own hand or act, sane, or insane, or suffered capital punishment, *if upon the true construction of the policy, the company thereby agreed to pay the sum insured in the events that have happened*[16]. Thus upon the true construction of the policy where the insurer has agreed to pay the sum assured in the event of suicide, the policy is lawful and enforceable.

Failure on the part of a company to comply with any provision of this Act shall not in any way invalidate any policy issued by the company. It is to be noted that this provision means that if a policy does not include a suicide provision, the common law position still applies and such a life policy would be governed by the rule in *Beresford's Case*. Philips LJ in

9   T. Mortimer, *Every Man His Own Broker* (W.J. & J. Richardson: 1801); *Gilbert v Sykes* (1812) 16 East 150.
10   W. Blackstone, *An Analysis of the Laws of England* (Clarendon Press: 1756).
11   Edwin Patterson, 'Insurable Interest in Life' (1918) 18 *Colum. L. Rev.* 381, 381–382.
12   *Gilbert v Sykes* (1812) 16 East 150.
13   267 Ala. 171, 100 So. 2d 696 (Supreme Court of Alabama, 1957).
14   BS 2007 SC 143.
15   *Hardy v Motor Insurers' Bureau* [1964] 2 QB 745; *Saunders v Edwards* [1987] 1 WLR 1116; and subsequently by the Forfeiture Act 1982.
16   Emphasis added.

Dunbar v Plant[17] held that judges would themselves have modified the rule if the legislature had not done so in the United Kingdom. He added:

> the only logical way of modifying the rule would have been to decline to apply it where the facts of the crime involved such a low degree of culpability, or such a high degree of mitigation, that the sanction of forfeiture, far from giving effect to the public interest, would have been contrary to it.

In *Dawkins v Imperial Life Association Company of Canada*,[18] originating from the Bahamas, a woman 'walked out' (left the house of the deceased to live with another man). Afterwards the insured became depressed. The insured, allegedly motivated by anger, sought a form of the 'Samson option' i.e., while he would not benefit financially he would see that she did not, by ensuring the collapse the life insurance policy. Indeed, a note found 'Bye Bye Baby Hah Hah Husband E. Dawkins.' Although death occurred fewer than three months after the policy took effect, the Court ruled in favour of the insured, there being no discussion on the construction of the policy, considering the failure to settle, unreasonable. It was a term of the policy that the defendant was under no liability if a life assured died by suicide within two years of the policy taking effect. It is clear that profit motive can operate in the positive – a production of a gain or loss, a personal vendetta.

The Judicial Committee of the Privy Council, in *Siu Yin Kwan v Eastern Insurance Co. Ltd, The Osprey*,[19] revisited the issue of profit motive, commenting on the 1774 Act:

> The 1774 Act was passed to prevent gambling by the medium of insurance. Whereby parties used to bet on the arrival or non-arrival of a vessel in which the 'assured' had absolutely no interest. This practice was outlawed by the Marine Insurance Act 1745 and the subsequent Marine Insurance Act of 1906. Gambling then turned to the expected longevity of the rich and famous, odds on whom soon appeared in the newspapers. To prevent this mischievous form of gaming, the Life Assurance Act 1774 prohibited in section 1, insurance on 'life or lives' or on 'other events or events whatsoever,' and section 2, in order to prevent evasion by the fraudulent use of own life policies – provided that the names of all interested parties must be inserted into a policy within the 1774 Act.

Unfortunately, one only has to watch television or social media or read the newspapers to appreciate that motive propelled the introduction of legislative intervention in the eighteenth century. It remains with us today.

4.6   THE STATUTORY MODIFICATION OF THE LAW OF INSURABLE INTEREST

It is against this backdrop that the modification occurred in the Commonwealth Caribbean. The Dominica Insurance Act[20] is straightforward in nature. Section 119 stipulates:

> An insurable interest is deemed to be held by
>
> (a)   a person in his or her own life;
> (b)   a parent of a child who is under 18 years of age, or guardian, in the life of the child;
> (c)   a husband, in the life of his wife;
> (d)   a wife, in the life of her husband;

---

17   [1977] 4 All ER 289 (CA), p. 310.
18   BS 1992 SC 124.
19   [1994] 1 All ER 213.
20   Chapter 78:49.

(e) any person, in the life of another person upon whom he or she is wholly or partly dependent for support or education;

(f) a company or other entity in the life of an officer or employee of the company or other entity; and

(g) any person who has a pecuniary interest in the duration of the life of another person, in the life of that person.

While recognising own-life insurance, an obvious omission is it does not recognise spousal relationships. In addition, the perennial 'For the purposes of this Act, but without restricting the meaning of the expression "insurable interest," an insurable interest shall be deemed to "be had by,"' present in other Acts, is notably absent.

Indeed, Section 127 of the Barbados Insurance Act[21] represents a good example of the CLI-driven reforms and commences at subsection (2). Section 127 provides:

(1) For the purposes of this Act, but without restricting the meaning of the expression 'insurable interest' an insurable interest shall be deemed to 'be had by':

    (a) a parent of a child under the age of 18 years of age, or a person in *loco parentis* of such a child, in the life of the child;

    (b) a spouse, in the life of his or her spouse;

    (c) any person, in the life of another upon whom he is wholly or in part dependent for support or education;

    (d) a company or other person, in the life of an officer or employee thereof; and

    (e) a person who has a pecuniary interest in the duration of the life of another person, in the life of that person.

(2) This section shall apply to policies whether effected before or after the commencement of this Act.

(3) For the purposes of this section, the expression 'child' in relation to any person, includes

    (a) an adopted child;

    (b) a step-child; or

    (c) any other child, living with that person and wholly or mainly maintained by that wholly or in part dependent for support or education.

Section 127 serves as an illustration of regional response. Hitherto the question of insurable interest was resolved by an application of the Life Assurance Act of 1774 and the common law. Among the jurisdictions of Barbados, Guyana,[22] St Lucia,[23] St Vincent and the Grenadines[24] and Trinidad and Tobago, where reform has occurred, subtle differences are discernible. Barbados is the only jurisdiction which recognises the spousal relationship for the purposes of insurable interest.

Section 96, Jamaica Insurance Act

(1) For the purposes of the Act, but without restricting the meaning of the expression, 'insurable interest,' the following persons shall be deemed to have an insurable interest in the life of another person as follows:

    . . .

    (c) a parent or guardian of a child who is under 18 years of age, in the life of the child;

    (d) a husband, in the life of his wife;

---

21 No. 32 of 1996.
22 St Lucia Insurance Act No. 20 of 1998.
23 Section 99, St Vincent and the Grenadines Insurance Act of 1995.
24 Section 106, St Vincent and the Grenadines Insurance Act No. 43 of 2003.

(e)   a wife in the life of her husband;

(f)   a grandparent of a child who is under 18 years of age, in the life of his grandchild;

(g)   any person, in the life of another upon whom he is wholly or partly dependent for support or education;

(h)   a company or other person, in the life of an officer or employee thereof; and

(i)   any person who has a pecuniary interest in the duration of the life of another person, in the life of that person.

(2)   This section applies to policies whether effected before or after the appointed day.

In Jamaica, the presumption of insurable interest has been extended to embrace a grandparent in the life of his grandchild, while Dominica recognises own-life policies.

4.7   NATURE, SCOPE AND AMBIT OF WEST INDIAN MODIFICATION OF THE LAW OF INSURABLE INTEREST

The nature, scope and ambit of the West Indian modification of the law of insurable interest can be determined from an application of the common law construing the underlying Life Assurance Act of 1774.[25]

4.8   THE POINT AT WHICH INSURABLE INTEREST IS REQUIRED

The regional modification into the law of insurable interest provides no indication as to the point at which insurable interest in the life insured is required. Thus the Life Assurance Act of 1774, with its attendant deficiencies, continues to be relevant to discussion. This is because the statute mentioned commences with the inclusive phrase 'without restricting the meaning of the expression, insurable interest.' Applying the 1774 Act, a conflict exists between Section 1 and Section 3 of the Act. Whereas Section 1 indicates that interest is required at the date of effecting the contract, Section 3, by providing that the insured shall recover no greater sum than the amount of the interest of the insured, can be construed as requiring interest at the time of loss.[26] The requirement of interest at the time of loss was applied in the early decision of *Godsall v Boldero*,[27] where a policy effected by a creditor on the life of his debtor was held to be an indemnity policy under Section 3 requiring insurable interest at the time of loss. *Godsall* was subsequently overruled by the landmark decision of *Dalby v India and London Life Assurance Co.*[28] The position therefore in the Commonwealth Caribbean on the authority of *Dalby* is that it is necessary for the insured to have an interest only at the time when the policy as effected, and not at the date of loss.

25   See further R. Merkin, 'Gambling by Insurance – A Study of the Life Assurance Act 1774' [1980] 9 *Anglo-Amer. L. Rev.* 331.

26   Insurable interest seems to have been required at common law both at the date of the contract and at the date of loss. See *Sadler's Co. v Badcock* (1743) 2 Atk. 554.

27   (1854) 15 CB 365.07) 9 East 72, followed in *Henson v Blackwell* (1845) 4 Hare 434.

28   (1854) 15 CB 365.

4.9 NAMING OF PERSONS INTERESTED

Regional Insurance Acts do not expressly require names of persons interested be inserted. By virtue, however, of Section 2 of the Life Assurance Act of 1774 and modern commerce, the names of persons interested must be inserted in the policy. As a result, the attendant difficulties associated with the Section 2 requirement apply. The policy itself is not conclusive evidence that the insurance was made for the use or benefit of the person named therein. In *Shilling v Accidental Death Insurance Co.*,[29] parol evidence was admissible to support the contention that the assured's son who paid the premium, filled out the proposal form and was a beneficiary under the assured's will was indeed entitled to receive the benefit. The term for 'whose use, benefit or on whose account' is given a restrictive definition and does not necessarily accommodate all persons who are ultimately intended to benefit under insurance.[30] A strict application of Section 2 can lead to injustice. In *Evans v Bignold*,[31] a husband effected an insurance policy on his wife's life as security for a loan obtained from trustees. The husband, however, was not named in the policy, so the policy was held to be illegal.

The merit of the requirement for the names of persons interested and any beneficiaries to be inserted is to prevent an evasion of Section 1. But Section 2 can be viewed as superfluous as, once it is established that a person has an insurable interest under Section 1, it is arguably unnecessary that that person be named in the policy (indeed, in *Evans v Bignold*, the husband had an insurable interest in his wife's life). There are several disadvantages with the Section 2 requirement. It represents a nuisance where an employer effects a policy for the benefit of employees. In the United Kingdom, reforms introduced provide that Section 2 does not invalidate a policy for the benefit of unnamed individuals within a class or description if the class or description is stated in the policy and every member is identifiable at any time.[32]

It is important at this juncture to make a distinction between an insertion of the name of persons interested and an assignment,[33] or testamentary disposition. Sections 1 and 2 of the 1774 Act pertain to the former, and are not intended to cover the situation where the object of the insurance is to secure himself, property which he may later dispose of on his demise. In the latter case, there is no requirement to show that the ultimate beneficiaries had any interest in the life of the assured.

4.10 NATURE OF INSURABLE INTEREST

Now, it is trite law that one of the three great principles of insurance law is that the insured must have an insurable interest in the subject matter of the insurance, that is to effect a valid contract of insurance the insured must have something at stake; he must have something to love by the happening of the peril he seeks to insure against. This is a statutory requirement under the Life Assurance Act of 1774 (UK), a provision which applies in Guyana by virtue of Section 13 of the Guyana Civil Law Act, Cap. 6:01. But generally speaking, any insurance affected by an

---

29 (1857) 2 H & N 42.
30 *M'Farlane v Royal London Friendly Society* (1886) 2 TLR 755; *Brewster v National Life Ins Sy* (1892) 8 TLR 648.
31 (1868–1869) LR 4 QB 622.
32 Section 50, Insurance Companies (Amendment) Act 1973 c. 58; see further J. Birds, *Modern Insurance Law*, 6th edn (Sweet & Maxwell: 2014), p. 47.
33 See Chapter 6.

insured without an insurable interest would be void as a gaming or wagering transaction under Section 18 of the Gaming Act of 1845 (UK).

> The interest must be such that if the event insured against does not happen, the party will gain an advantage; if it does happen the party will suffer a loss [See per Blackburn J in *Wilson v Jones* (1867) 2 Ex. 139, at pp. 150, 151]. Any person is deemed to have an insurable interest in his own life [See *Wainewright v Bland* (1835) 1 Moo. & R. 481]. A husband or wife is presumed to have an insurable interest to the extent of the amount insured by the policy in the life or a spouse [*Griffiths v Fleming* (1909) 1 KB 805, CA].

Modern regional insurance statutes do not attempt to define insurable interest but rather deem insurable interest to exist in certain circumstances, administratively discharging the evidential burden on the insured to establish a pecuniary interest in the person whose life is insured. Additionally, persons unable to bring themselves within the defined categories can establish a pecuniary interest in the duration of the life of another person,[34] or by proving that they are wholly or in part dependent for support or education on the person insured.[35] In this regard, the statute uses proof of pecuniary interest as a residual savings mechanism opening the stated categories.

The presumption of insurable interest can be grouped into two groups – family relationships and business relationships – and in that regard it adopts the approach at common law. There are several regional decisions on insurable interest relating to indemnity insurance, for example *Sookdeo & Sookdeo's Motor Supplies Ltd v Trinidad & Tobago Insurance Ltd* and *Advantage General Insurance Co. Ltd v Myrie*.[36]

4.11   FAMILY RELATIONSHIPS

The fundamental principles relating to insurable interest in family relationships are highlighted in the judgment of Justice Luckhoo in American *Life Insurance Co. v Sumintra*, arising out of the Guyana Court of Appeal.[37] Justice Luckhoo, in summing up the common law position, states:

> The interest must be such that if the event insured against does not happen, the party will gain an advantage; if it does happen the party will suffer a loss [See per Blackburn J in *Wilson v Jones* (1867) 2 Ex. 139, at pp. 150, 151]. Any person is deemed to have an insurable interest in his own life [See *Wainewright v Bland* (1835) 1 Moo. & R. 481]. A husband or wife is presumed to have an insurable interest to the extent of the amount insured by the policy in the life of a spouse [*Griffiths v Flemings* (1909) 1 KB 805, CA].

The common law position, as expressed in *American Life Insurance v Sumintra*, represents the law in most Caribbean jurisdictions. However, in Barbados, Jamaica, St Lucia and Trinidad and Tobago, the instances where insurable interest is presumed have been extended.

4.12   OWN LIFE

Regional Insurance Acts refrain from expressly identifying the common law presumption on the insured's own life. Nevertheless, common sense dictates as recognised by common law the

---

34 Section 127(1)(e), Barbados Insurance Act No. 32 of 1996, Cap 310.
35 Section 127(1)(c), Barbados Insurance Act No. 32 of 1996, Cap 310.
36 The plaintiffs held a policy of fire insurance with the defendant. The policy covered losses under three heads. After investigations were conducted, the defendant paid the plaintiffs the following sums: $1,804,350.34 on the building loss; $18,000 on the loss of air conditioning units and an interim payment of $191,734 on the loss of stock.
37 Supra n. 8.

validity of own-life insurance.[38] As noted by Justice Luckhoo in *American Life Insurance Co. v Sumintra*, at common law a person is deemed to have an insurable interest in his own life.[39] Such an interest is unlimited, as it is difficult to place an economic value on life.

4.13 HUSBAND AND WIFE

Regional Insurance Acts preserve the traditional common law recognition of insurable interest of a husband in the life of his wife,[40] and a wife in the life of her husband,[41] to the extent of the amount insured by the policy for, as with own life policies, they are not considered as being within the mischief of the 1774 Act.

4.14 CHILDREN

Statute extends the presumption of insurable interest on a parent or guardian of a child who is under 18 years of age, in the life of the child,[42] and in Jamaica, a grandparent of a child who is under 18 years of age, in the life of his grandchild. 'Child' is broadly defined in the Insurance Act to include step-children and adopted children representing a logical progression from the early reforms of the 1960s embodied in regional Status of Children legislation.[43] In so doing, the Insurance Acts of the region abrogate the common law as expressed in *Halford v Kymer*, to wit: a parent will not normally have such an interest except perhaps to cover funeral expenses.[44] In *Halford*, a father attempted to insure the life of his son. The father claimed that he had a pecuniary interest in that he expected the son to reimburse him for the cost of his education and maintenance at some date. This claim was rejected presumably because there is no legal obligation on the parent. In *Worthington v Curtis*,[45] a father effected a policy in the name of and on the life of his son. Creditors objected to the payment by the insurance company to the father arguing that the money should have gone to the estate instead. This argument was rejected. It was held that as the 1774 Act makes provision for the insurance company to pay the monies where there is no insurable interest, and since this had already taken place, it was not open to the creditors to contest the payment.

With respect to the converse situation, the position is not as clear. Regional insurance legislation is silent on the presumption of insurable interest of a child in the life of the parent. Section 117(1) states that a minor who has attained the age of 10 but not 16 may, with written consent of his or her parent or of a person standing in *loco parentis* to the minor

(a) effect a policy his or her own life or upon another life in which he or she has an insurable interest; or (b) take an assignment of a policy. (2) a minor who has obtained the age of 16 years (a) may effect a policy upon his or her own life or upon another life in which he or she has an

---

38 *Wainwright v Bland* (1835) 1 Moo & R 481.
39 Ibid.
40 *Griffiths v Fleming* (1909) 1 KB 805.
41 *Reed v Royal Exchange Assurance Co.*, Peake, Add Cas 70.
42 Section 127, Barbados Insurance Act No. 32 of 1996; Section 96, Jamaica Insurance Act No. 10 of 2001.
43 Antigua and Barbuda Status of Children Act, Cap 414; Barbados Status of Children Reform Act of 1979, Cap 220; Jamaica Status of Children Act 1976; St Kitts and Nevis Status of Children Act 1983; St Vincent and the Grenadines Status of Children Act, Cap 180 [1990 Rev.]; Trinidad and Tobago Status of Children Act No. 46:07 of 1976.
44 Section 127(1)(a), Barbados Insurance Act No. 32 of 1996, Cap 310.
45 (1875) 1 Ch D 419.

insurable interest; or (b) may take an assignment of a policy; and (c) subject to subsection (3) is competent in all respects and exercise the powers and privileges of a policyholder of full age in relation to a policy of which he or she is holder. (3) a minor who has obtained the age of 16 years may assign or mortgage a policy with the prior consent in writing of his or her parent or other person standing in loco parentis to the minor. (4) this section does not (a) impose on a minor, any liability to which the board this section, he or she would not be subject; (b), confer on a minor any power or capacity that, but for this section, the minor would not have not have; (c) validate a receipt, a discharge for a surrender of, or security over a policy given by a minor, if, but for this section, that receipt, discharge, surrender or security would not be valid; or (d) validate any assignment of the policy that, but for this section, would not be valid.

Applying the common law, a child who is a minor has an insurable interest in the lives of his parents only if they are legally obliged to support him. Available statutory procedures under ancillary family and maintenance legislation may support such an obligation.[46] There is some uncertainty as to whether parents are legally obliged to support the child in the absence of a statutory order. Certainly, an adult child cannot establish insurable interest in the absence of a legal obligation on the part of the parent.[47] In *Harse v Pearl Life Assurance Co. Ltd*,[48] a son insured his mother who lived with him and kept house for him. The insurance was expressed to be for 'funeral expenses.' The Court of Appeal held that the policy was void for lack of insurable interest, there being no legal obligation on the part of the son to bury his mother and no legal obligation on the mother to 'keep house.'

Further, the decision of *Feasey v Sun Life Assurance Corp. of Canada; Steamship Mutual Underwriting Association (Bermuda) Ltd v Feasey*[49] suggests an alternative approach. Although the facts of the decision concerned property insurance, namely, the basis of a sub-contractors' insurable interest, the Court of Appeal treated the Life Assurance Act of 1774 as applying. The result is that the inquiry as to the meaning of insurable interest must now be approached differently. Waller LJ proffered the following summary:

(1) It is from the terms of the policy that the subject of the insurance must be ascertained; (2) It is from all the surrounding circumstances that the nature of the insured's insurable interest must be discovered; (3) There is no hard and fast rule that because the nature of the insurance relates to liability to compensate for loss, that insurable interest could only be covered by a liability policy rather than a policy insuring property or life or indeed properties or lives; (4) The question whether a policy embraces the insurable interest intended to be recovered, is a question of construction. The subject or terms of the policy may be so specific as to force a court to hold that the policy has failed to cover the insurable interest, but a court will be reluctant to so hold; (5) It is not a requirement of property insurance that the insured must have a legal or equitable interest in the property. It is sufficient under section 5 of the Marine Insurance Act 1906 for a person interested in a Marine Adventure to stand in a legal or equitable relation to the adventure. That is intended to be a broad concept; (6) In a policy on life or lives, the court should be searching for the same broad concept. It may be that on an insurance of a specific identified life, it will be difficult to establish a legal or equitable relation without pecuniary liability recognised

---

46   Section 25, Barbados Married Women's Property Act, Cap. 219; Section 12, Jamaica Married Women's Property Act; Section 8, Barbados Child Care Board Act 1981, Cap. 381; C. Denbow, 'Insurance Law Reform in the Commonwealth Caribbean – The Named Beneficiary under Life Policies' [1992] *Caribbean Law Business* 58; Barbados Family Law Act 1981, Cap 214; Guyana Family and Dependant Provisions Act No. 22 of 1990. Section 2(6)(a)(1) of the Trinidad and Tobago Matrimonial Proceedings & Property Act states that 'A "wife" shall include a reference to a single woman living together with a single man in a common law union for seven years immediately preceding the date of his death.' Chapter 45:51 of T&T.

47   *Shilling and Accidental Death Co. Ltd* (1857) 2 H & N 42.

48   [1904] 1 KB 558.

49   [2003] EWCA Civ 885.

by law arising on the death of that particular person. There is, however, no authority which deals with a policy on many lives and over a substantial period and where it can be been that a pecuniary liability will arise by reference to those lives and the intention is to cover that legal liability;

(7) The interest in policies falling within s 1 of the 1774 Act must exist at the time of entry into the policy, and be capable of pecuniary evaluation at that time.

Waller LJ then continued, identifying the following groups:

Group (1) those cases where the court has defined the subject matter as an item of property; where the insurance is to recover the value of that property; and where thus there must be an interest in the property – real or equitable – for the insured to suffer loss which he can recover under the policy.[50]

Group (2) Where the court has recognised an insurable interest in that life of a particular person; and where the insurance is to recover a sum on the death of that particular person.[51]

Group (3) Cases where even though the subject matter may appear to be a particular item of property, properly construed the policy extends beyond the item and embraces such insurable interest as the insured has.[52]

Group (4) Policies in which the court has recognised interests which are not even strictly pecuniary. In relation to life policies there are policies on own life; policies on husband's life and policies on the life of the wife.[53] But even in the case of property something less than a legal or equitable or even simply pecuniary interest has been thought to be sufficient.[54]

It is evident that Waller LJ tenders a far more flexible approach to the question of insurable interest. By blurring the line of demarcation between indemnity insurance and life, the result is that the inquiry as to meaning of insurable interest should now be approached differently (i.e. that the terms of the policy and the subject matter of insurance are relevant but remain relevant), but that there is no hard and fast rule dividing indemnity insurance from life.

4.15   A COMPANY OR OTHER ENTITY IN THE LIFE OF AN OFFICER OR EMPLOYEE OF THE COMPANY OR OTHER ENTITY

This provision appears to be referring to key-person insurance, also commonly called key-man insurance an important form of business insurance. There is no legal definition for 'key-person insurance.' In general, it can be described as a policy taken out by a business to compensate that business for financial losses that would arise from the death or extended incapacity of an important member of the business. To put it simply, key-man insurance is a standard life insurance. The policy's term does not extend beyond the period of the key-person's usefulness, with the aim of compensating the business for losses incurred by the loss of the income generator.

On the death of a key-man, the company is paid money to indemnify loss, whereas in the United States, any business buying key-man insurance for its employee can claim a deduction for the

---

50   *Lucena v Craufurd* (1806) 2 Bros & PNR 269, 127 ER 630; *Anderson v Morice* (1875) LR 10 CP 609, affirmed (1876) 1 App Cas 713; *Macaura v Northern Assurance Co. Ltd* [1925] AC 619.
51   *Law v London Indisputable Life Policy Co.* (1855) 1 K & J 223, 69 ER 439. *Simcock v Scottish Imperial Insurance Co.* (1902) 10 SLT 286; *Harse v Pearl Life Assurance Co.* [1903] 2 KB 92.
52   *Wilson v Jones* (1867) LR 2 Exch 139.
53   *Griffiths v Fleming* [1909] 1 KB 805.
54   *Sharp v Sphere Drake Insurance plc, The Moonace* [1992] 1 Lloyd's Rep 501; *Glengate – K.G. Properties Ltd v Norwich Union Fire Insurance Society* [1996] 2 All ER 487; *Deepak Fertilisers & Petrochemical Ltd Davy McKee (London) Ltd* [1999] 1 All ER (Comm) 69.

premium paid for the policy as a business expense under income tax legislation. This policy can be used as either an extra-super-annuation benefit or an *ex gratia* payment to the key-employee during the service period. If the company receives the proceeds on maturity, then they may be taxable.

In the Caribbean, *Caribbean Atlantic Life Assurance Co. Ltd v Nassief*[55] illustrates that where there is a misrepresentation of tax treatment by the insurer, the premium must be returned. In this case the respondent, having been assured by an agent and by the chairman of the Board of Directors of the company that any premiums paid by him on an insurance policy would be deductible for the purposes of taxation, took out an insurance policy on the life of an employee in the sum of $100,000. The policy in question was a 'key-man' insurance policy. The issue of innocent misrepresentation fell to be decided. Reference was made to *Brown v Rapheal* (1958) 1 CHD 636, where Lord Evershed MR laid down the conditions which must be satisfied if he is to succeed on this ground. He said at page 641:

> In order that he may succeed on such a ground it is, of course, necessary that three things should be established. He must, first, show that the language relied upon does import or contain the representation of some material fact. Second, he must show that the representation is untrue, and, third, he must show that the plaintiff in entering into the contract was induced so to do in reliance upon it. An issue which arises is the distinction between an Executive Flexible Premium Annuity (EFPA) and key-man insurance. The distinction is imperceptible. Beyond the label, there is an obvious correlation with the insured person in both cases. Attributable to key figures tied to an organization, the large single deposits above market rates, arguably are disguised insurance product and defy the characteristics of insurance. Similarly, in *Quarry Products Ltd. v Mcclurg*,[56] a policy was effected by an employer on life of manager. Sometime in 1964, Mr. Cushman, Managing Director of Quarry Products Limited, hereinafter called Quarry, arranged with Mr. Martin, Manager in Barbados of Colonial Life Insurance Company Limited, hereinafter called Colonial, to take out a 'key-man' policy on the life of Thomas Lednor. Quarry wanted to insure itself against the death of Mr. Lednor, its Manager and expert in explosives. The policy was to be in the sum of $20,000 with double indemnity benefit in case of death by accident. Quarry was to pay the premiums and to be beneficiary under the policy. The discussions on the policy in this case originated with Quarry; the deposit, which was treated as the first premium, was paid by Quarry; the premiums were to be paid by Quarry so that if Mr. Lednor had not died the policy would have been maintained by Quarry; both Mr. Cushman and Mr. Martin are quite specific that Quarry was taking the policy and was to be the beneficiary. The purchaser of the policy was on the evidence clearly Quarry and there is nothing to indicate an intention to benefit anyone but Quarry. Manager's estate as beneficiary – Mistake – Whether resulting trust of policy money.

4.16   SHORTCOMINGS OF THE STATUTORY REFORMS

While the instances at common law where insurable interest is presumed have been expanded, several deficiencies are apparent in the statutory reforms introduced. Apart from the obvious limitation in their application to life insurance only, the statutes conveniently refrain from defining what constitutes insurable interest in life. Instead the statutes commence with the phrase 'without restricting the meaning of the expression insurable interest.' This approach neatly sidesteps the issue and more importantly imports the application of the 1774 Act together with the relevant common law. Further, no guidance is provided on when insurable interest in life is required, making it necessary to resort to the common law. More importantly, the effect of a lack of insurable interest and the treatment of premiums (e.g., are premiums to be returned

55   DM 1970 CA 6.
56   Court of Appeal of Dominica No. 1 of 1970.

in the absence of insurable interest?) and the perennial entanglement of insurable interest and subrogation also remains unresolved.[57] In essence, the statutory reforms fail to seize the opportunity to address many of the criticisms levied at the Life Assurance Act of 1774. While circumstances that exist at common law have been expanded upon, noteworthy is fact that only Barbados recognises unions other than marriage for the purposes of insurable interest. Section 2 of the Barbados Insurance Act provides that 'Spouse has the meaning assigned to it by sub-section (3)–(5) of the Succession Act.' The Succession Act defines a spouse as '[a] single man living continuously for a period of five years up until the time of death.'[58] An anomaly exists in that the definition of spouse contained in the Succession Act refers to 'immediately preceding the date of death.' If insurable interest in life insurance is required at the time the contract is concluded, then once the five-year period has been satisfied and a spousal relationship is deemed to exist, the phrase 'immediately before the date of death,' for the purposes of insurable interest, becomes superfluous. Another arguable deficiency is that the reforms introduced, while salutary in their socio-economic relevance, do not capture all unions. Thus, in the case of same-sex unions or the situation of a married man living consistently with a single woman, as was the case in *Asaram v Demerara Life Insurance*,[59] pecuniary interest is still required. In light of the deficiencies as highlighted, it is worthy to consider Section 69 of the 1973 Revised Jamaica Insurance Act,[60] the precursor to Section 96 of the 2001 Act.

Section 69 (1) of the Jamaica Insurance Act[61] provided:

(1) Subject to the provisions of this section at the time when a contract of life insurance is made (being a contract made after the prescribed date) the insured person has no insurable interest in the life of the person whose life is insured under the contract, the contract is void.

(2) For the purposes of subsection (1) but without restricting the meaning of the expression insurable interest) a person shall be deemed to have an insurable interest in his own life and in the life of

    (a) His child or grandchild;

    (b) his spouse;

    (c) any person upon who, he is wholly or in part dependant, or from whom he is receiving, support or education;

    (d) his employees; and

    (e) any person in the duration of whose life he has a pecuniary interest.

(3) Subsection (1) does not apply to contracts of group insurance.

(4) Subsection (1) does not apply to a contract or any provision in a contract where under the liability of the insurer is limited to insuring moneys to be paid for expenses in connection with death or funeral of any person, but every such contract or provision made after the prescribed date shall be void unless it is (and is clearly expressed to be) a contract only to indemnify the insured in respect of expenses actually incurred by him in connection with death or funeral of such person

(5) Where a contract of life insurance is void for lack of insurable interest, all premiums paid thereunder shall be returnable by the insurance company unless it proves that it was not aware of the lack of insurable interest owing to a false representation on the part of the insured person or the person whose life is insured under the contract.'

---

57   *Mark Rowlands Ltd v Berni Inns Ltd* [1985] 3 All ER 473; *Petrofina (UK) Ltd v Magnaload Ltd* [1983] 3 All ER 35.
58   Cap 249.
59   See Chapter 6. The facts of this case surrounded a married man living together with a single woman for more than seven years.
60   [1973 Rev.].
61   Ibid.

(6)   In this section –

    'insured person' in relation to a contract of life insurance, means the person who makes the contract with the insurer;

    'child,' in relation to any person, includes –

    (a)   an adopted child;

    (b)   a step-child; and

    (c)   any other child, whether legitimate or not, wholly or mainly maintained by that person;

    'contract of life insurance' means any contract of insurance upon a life;

    'grandchild' in relation to any person, means a child of any of that person's children;

    'group insurance' means insurance whereby the lives of a number of persons are insured severally under a single contract between an insurance company and an employer or other person.'

Section 69 clarified a number of the weaknesses apparent in the Life Assurance Act.[62] The Act:

(i)   addressed the question of timing stipulating that it was required at 'the time when a contract of life insurance [is] made.'

(ii)   the Act expressly identified the effect of a lack of insurable interest by stipulating that a lack of insurable interest rendered the contract void and also by virtue of subsection

(iii) dealt with the issue premiums, in subsection (5) where a contract of life insurance is void for lack of insurable interest, all premiums paid there under are returnable by the insurance company unless it is proven that it was not aware of the lack of insurable interest owing to a false representation on the part of the insured person or the person whose life is insured under the contract.

(iv)   Moreover, section 69 (2) deemed insurable interest in one's own life;

(v)   the Act seemingly captured the 'spousal' relationship! In that regard, *prima facie*, it appears that Jamaica, which recognised such relationships under the 1973 Insurance Act, has now reverted to the narrow relationship of husband and wife under the 2001 reforms. This seemingly retrograde step cannot be viewed simply as legislative oversight given the fact that the 'spousal relationship' is recognised and applied to the status of the beneficiary under sections 97–106 of the same Act. What therefore can the reason for ignoring this relationship for the purposes of insurable interest? Before one can contend be that the previous Act was 'an Act before its time,' further analysis is necessary.

    (a)   An examination of the Insurance Act, 1969 reveals that section 2 thereof – the definition provision, did not define 'spouse' for the purposes of insurance.

    (b)   Further, a review of the prevailing family and social legislation of the time; the Marriage Act,[63] Matrimonial Causes Act, Succession Act, and Status of Children Act,[64] also all failed to recognise the 'spousal relationship.'

    (c)   Turning to the Oxford Dictionary for assistance, a spouse is defined as 'either a husband or wife.' The obvious implication of the foregoing is that spouse in the previous Act was used in the colloquial, rather than in a technical sense as is used in modern legislation.

It is perhaps this lack of legal certainty which propelled to the subsequent legislative abandonment of the term 'spouse' for the purposes of insurable interest in the 2001 Act. Section 96 of the 2001 Jamaica Insurance Act deems insurable interest to exist in a husband in the life of

---

62   Supra n. 25.
63   Cap 237, No. 48 of 1957.
64   No. 36 of 1976.

his wife, and a wife in the life of her husband, thereby expressly ignoring the concept of spouse. 'Spouse' is defined in Section 2 as a

> single woman who has cohabited with a single man as if she were in law his wife for a period of not less than five years; or (b) a single man who has cohabited with a single woman as if he were in law her husband for a period of not less than five years, and the terms 'single woman' or single man include widow or widower or divorcee.

Therefore anyone falling outside the traditional nucleus of husband and wife must establish a pecuniary interest under Section 96(g) or prove alternatively that he is 'wholly or mainly supported' under Section 96(e). Perhaps instead of abandoning the recognition of the relationship, a better solution would have been to recognise the relationship which is recognised under ancillary social family legislation – status of children,[65] family law[66] and domestic violence[67] –for the purposes of insurable interest.

4.17   SPECIAL RELATIONSHIPS IN LIFE INSURANCE

Regional insurance legislation also recognises business relationships within which the insured must establish that he would suffer financially by the loss of a legal right on the death of the life insured.

4.18   BUSINESS RELATIONSHIPS

As provided for by statute, insurance may be effected by a company or other person in the life of an officer or employee. This is in accordance with the position at common law. At common law, a contract of employment at a salary for the term of years gives the employee an insurable interest in the employer's life during the unexpired portion of the term. This is aptly illustrated in the decision of *Hebdon v West*.[68] Here a bank clerk insured employer's life with two insurers, one policy for £5,000 and the other for £2,500. The clerk had a contract of employment for seven years at a salary of £600 per annum and he owed his employer £4,700. The employer died and the employee received £5,000 from the first insurer. The second insurer refused to pay the sum insured, a position upheld by the court, stating that the employee had an insurable interest to the extent of what he was contractually entitled to under the employment contract. Thus £4,200 was recoverable because he was contractually entitled to this amount and he stood to suffer by loss of a legal right. The fact that the assured was promised that the debt would not be called in was immaterial. There was no consideration, and therefore the promise was not legally enforceable. It follows from the fact that the right to

---

65   Anguilla Matrimonial Proceedings and Property Ordinance 1996; Antigua and Barbuda Divorce Act of 1997; Barbados Family Law Act, Cap 214; Barbados Marriage Act, Cap 106; Guyana Adoption (Amendment) Act of 1997; Guyana Family and Dependent Provisions Act No. 22 of 1990. Section 2(6)(a)(i) of this last Act states that 'a "wife" shall include a single man in a common law union for seven years immediately preceding the date of his death.' See also Jamaica Matrimonial & Causes Act 1989; Trinidad and Tobago Cohabitation Relationships Act of 1998. See also T. Robinson, 'New Directions in Family Law Reform in the Caribbean' (2000) 10 *Carib. L. Rev.* 101; Roberts, 'Developments in Family Law since Emancipation' [1985] *W.I.L.J.* 9; S. Owuso, 'Unions Other Than Marriage under the Barbados Family Law Act, 1981' [1992] 21 *Anglo-Amer. L. Rev.* 53.
66   Barbados Domestic Violence (Protection Orders) Act of 1992.
67   Section 127(1)(d), Barbados Insurance Act.
68   (1863) 3 B & S 579.

a salary is a legal right arising from contract and that such contract being for personal services would expire with the death of either party, that the employer would also have an insurable interest in the life of the employee, bound by a contract for a certain time. In *Simcock v Scottish Imperial Insurance Co.*,[69] an employer insured the life of his employee with two policies of £250 each. A claim under one policy was paid, but the other was defended on the ground of lack of insurable interest. It was held that the limit of insurable interest was the value of services for the 'period of notice.' The employer's interest will only be the value of the services, which he will lose if the employee dies.

The decision of *Hebdon v West*[70] illustrates that with regards to life insurance on business relationships, the effect of Section 3 of the 1774 Act is to measure the insured's loss at the time of the policy is effected. In this regard there is a divergence between theory and practice. In group insurance policies, for instance, the nature and value of the employee has an impact on the premiums paid and the assured sum, as evident from the decisions of *Green v Russell, McCarthy (Third Party)*[71] and *Marcel Beller Ltd v Hayden*.[72] In both of these decisions, the sum insured bore no relationship to the pecuniary interest of the employer.

4.19   DEBTOR AND CREDITOR

A creditor or surety has an insurable interest in the life of the debtor. If the debt is to be paid by two or more persons jointly, it will support a good insurable interest for a policy on the life of each of them, for the whole amount. Despite the decision of *Godsall v Boldero*[73] which held otherwise, it is now immaterial that the debt has been repaid before death. In *Godsall*, the court based its decision on Section 3 of the 1774 Act and held that a policy effected by a creditor on the life of his debtor was a policy of indemnity and the interest was valued at the time of loss (i.e. at the death of the life insured). This decision was overruled by the decision of *Dalby v India and London Life Assurance Co.*,[74] where the phrase 'shall have no interest' in Section 1 was interpreted to mean 'no interest at the time of contract.' Hence, if interest exists at the time of effecting the policy of insurance, the insurance policy is valid. In essence, as the creditor can recover more than the amount of the debt, it can be viewed as the creditor making a profit out of death. *Dalby* was later confirmed by *Law v London Indisputable Life Policy Co.*[75] On the other hand, a debtor has no insurable interest in the life of the creditor, even where there is a promise by the creditor not to require payment of the debt during his life. The rationale for this rule is that there is no consideration. Its absence deprives the relationship of enforcement a deficiency, which means that all the debtor has is an expectation that the debt will not be called in.

4.20   TRUSTEES

Trustees as such do not have an insurable interest in the life of any beneficiary, but they may have an interest arising out of the terms of the trust. In such circumstances, trustees can effect a life policy provided the trust instrument directs or permits the trustee to do so.

69   (1902) 10 SLT 286, OH.
70   Supra n. 68.
71   [1959] 2 QB 226.
72   [1978] 3 All ER 111.
73   (1807) 9 East 72.
74   (1854) 15 CB 364.
75   1 K & J 223.

4.21 MORTGAGEES

Generally, the importance of the mortgage deed in establishing a contractual arrangement between the mortgagor and the mortgagee can be seen in the Trinidad and Tobago decision of *Guichard et al. v Bank of Nova Scotia Co. of Trinidad and Tobago Ltd et al.*[76] In this case, the facts surrounded a comprehensive fire insurance policy effected with the insurers through a bank acting as servant/agent. The premises, situated in San Fernando, Trinidad and Tobago, were destroyed by fire. Prior to the fire, the plaintiff insured received a letter addressed to the bank, purporting to cancel the policy. In finding for the plaintiff, the High Court ruled that plaintiffs were not aware of the cancellation and had not received notification. The court noted:

> When a mortgagee wishes to safeguard his insurable interest . . . he acts as an agent as for the mortgagors. What the mortgagee is doing is protecting its interest in order to satisfy any purported loss, future loss etc. When than right is purportedly exercised by a mortgagee pursuant to the mortgage deed the onus is upon the mortgagee to take all necessary precautions to get the best possible coverage in the circumstances, and to act fairly.

A policy to provide security for a mortgage may be effected by the mortgagor and assigned to the mortgagee. In such circumstances, no question of insurable interest arises. But the mortgagee has an interest in the life of the mortgagor and can effect a policy on the mortgagor's life and pay the premium himself. If he does so, the mortgagee is entitled both to the policy and the mortgage debt. Where the premiums are paid by the borrower or charged him in account, the lender must account to the borrower for any money received under the policy.

4.22 COMPANY AND OFFICER/EMPLOYEES

A company is statutorily deemed to have an insurable interest in the life of a director or manager.[77] At common law, a company has an insurable interest in the life of the director or manager if the death of the insured would result in the loss of special services, resulting in reduced profits.[78] Unless the Insurance Act expressly excludes an application to group life insurances, then the inference is that the provision modifying insurable interest also applies to group. If this is indeed the case, then the difficulties associated with Section 2 of the Life Assurance Act logically apply.[79]

4.23 COMMENT

The law is concerned only to prevent gambling at the inception of the policy. Thus, an ex-wife is entitled to successfully claim on a joint policy on the death of her ex-husband. Although the parties had divorced and remarried, the policy had been maintained by the ex-wife.[80] An employer is entitled to maintain key-man insurance on the life of his employee even after the termination of the employer-employee relationship on the authority of *Dalby*, a decision which itself 'illustrates that a creditor is entitled to insure for the amount of the debt owing when the

---

76 Unreported decision, High Court of Trinidad and Tobago S-601 of 1987.
77 Section 127, Barbados Insurance Act.
78 *Hebdon v West* (1863) 3 B & S 579.
79 Section 127(1)(d), Barbados Insurance Act No. 32 of 1996, Cap 310.
80 *Connecticut Mutual Life Insurance Co. v Shaeffer*, 94 US 457 (1877).

policy is taken out, so that when the debt if fully paid, the policy can be kept up by the credi-tor.'[81] The implication is to allow recovery is a lesser evil than denying it.

4.24　APPLICATION OF THE 1774 ACT TO INSURANCES OTHER THAN LIFE

Despite the title of the Life Assurance Act, question arises as to whether the Act applies to insurances other than life insurance. As expressed in Section 4 of the Act, it clearly has no application to insurance on ships or goods. In *Williams v Baltic Insurance Association*,[82] the owner of a motor car insured in respect of all sums for which the insured 'any licensed friend or rela-tive of the insured while driving the car . . . shall be come liable.' A person was injured by the car driven by the insured's sister. The insurance company denied liability contending that the policy was void under Section 2 of the Life Assurance Act of 1774, as the sister's name was not inserted in the policy. It was held that the policy was an insurance on goods, namely a motor car, within Section 4 of the 1774 Act and only incidentally insured against third party risks. Therefore, being within the proviso of Section 4, it was outside the ambit of the statute.

The issue has arisen as to whether the Act applies to real property. Early *dicta* to the effect that the Act did indeed apply to real property[83] has since been affirmatively rejected by the Judi-cial Committee of the Privy Council in *Siu Yin Kwan v The Eastern Insurance Co. Ltd, The Osprey*.[84] In this case, the insurer defendants argued that the policy under consideration was void under Section 2 of the Life Insurance Act of 1774, and that even if the policy was valid, the owners were not insured parties under the policy, as the name of the owner of the vessel did not appear in the policy. Further, that as the owner was intended to be the insured person, the policy was void and illegal under Section 2 of the 1774 Act. The Privy Council, following the earlier decision of *Mark Rowlands*,[85] held that the 1774 Act did not apply to indemnity policies. They reasoned that a liability policy could not be described as providing insurance against 'events,' and further that it was not possible to describe liability insurance as a 'mischievous form of gaming' in the terms of the preamble of the 1774 Act.

4.25　EFFECT OF LACK OF INSURANCE INTEREST

The incursion into the common law by Insurance Acts of the Commonwealth Caribbean is notably silent on the effect of a lack of insurable interest. Once again, regard must be had to the Life Assurance Act. Section 1 of the 1774 Act states: 'No insurance shall be made on the life or lives of any person/persons for use, benefit or on whose account such policy or policies shall be made, shall have no interest . . . shall be null and void.' In *Harse v Pearl Life Assurance Co.*,[86] it was stated that the lack of insurable interest renders the contract illegal.

Interestingly, the CLI reforms eradicated perhaps one of the most effective statutory solu-tions: Section 69 (1) of Jamaica Insurance Act, the precursor to the 2001 reform,[87] provided

---

81　Supra n. 25, 333.
82　[1924] 2 KB 282.
83　*Re King* [1963] Ch 459, per Lord Denning at 485.
84　[1994] 2 AC 199.
85　[1985] 3 All ER 473.
86　Supra n. 48.
87　Supra n. 60.

that '[where] the insured person has no insurable interest in the life of the person whose life is insured under the contract, the contract is void.' It not only addressed the effect of a lack of insurable interest but also made provision for the return of premiums. Thus, Subsection 5 stated

> Where a contract of life insurance is void for lack of insurable interest, all premiums paid there-under shall be returnable by the insurance company unless it proves that it was not aware of the lack of insurable interest owing to a false representation on the part of the insured person or the person whose life is insured under the contract.

In *Harse v Pearl Life Assurance Co*,[88] the question arose whether premiums paid for a policy that was in breach of the Act could be reclaimed by the proposer. The insurance agent in good faith represented to the plaintiff that he could effect a policy on his mother's life to cover funeral expenses. Some 12 years later, the plaintiff was informed that the policy was void for a lack of insurable interest. The Court of Appeal, in a judgment delivered by Collins MR, refused to order a return of premiums as the agent was not guilty of fraud. In the Caribbean, the statute provides no guidance on either the effect of a lack of insurable interest or on the status of the premiums. On the authority of *Harse v Pearl Life Assurance Co.*, if there has been a total failure of consideration – where it could be shown that one party deceived or oppressed the other party into making the contract by way of fraud duress –a return of premiums would be ordered. Generally, such contracts are void under a mistake of law. To allow recovery of premiums where there is no insurable interest would violate the rule against enforcing illegal contracts. In the House of Lords decision of *Kleinwort Benson Ltd v Lincoln City Council*,[89] it was held that on the basis of unjust enrichment, money paid under a contract void for mistake of law may be recovered by way of a restitutionary claim.[90]

4.26 WAIVER

Insurable interest is a basic requirement of any contract of insurance unless it is lawfully waived. Although a waiver of insurable interest is possible in indemnity insurance, it is not possible in the case of interest on life. Since regional Insurance Acts incorporate the prevailing law at the time of enactment, waiver is not possible in life insurance on the authority of the Life Assurance Act of 1774. The 1774 Act, by stating that a contract without insurance is void, expressly precludes waiver in the case of life insurance.

4.27 CONCLUSION

The present position on the law of insurable interest in the Commonwealth Caribbean can be described as an uneasy mixture of statutory and common law rules. This description is merited. The open-ended language of regional reform imports consideration of the common law and the underlying Life Assurance Act of 1774. In that regard, the reform is disappointing, unfortunately leaving unresolved many of the inherent deficiencies associated with the 1774

---

88 Supra n. 48.
89 [1999] 2 AC 349.
90 See Law Commission Report, *Restitution: Mistakes of Law and Ultra Vires Public Authority Receipts and Payment* (1994) Law Com No. 227, paras 3.1 *et seq.*, which recommends that the mistake of law rule should be abrogated. See also *Woolwich Equitable Building Society v IRC* [1993] AC 70, where Lord Keith of Kinkel expressed the opinion that the mistake of law rule was too deeply imbedded to be uprooted judicially.

Act. Thus, the statute opts not to assist on the question of precisely when insurable interest in life is required or to outline the effects of a lack thereof. Further, it provides no guidance on the return of premiums in instances where there is a lack of insurable interest, all questions which were remarkably addressed in Jamaica by the 1969 Act and which were subsequently removed by the 2001 Act.

The rationale for insurable interest has been established for unquestionably life insurance demands an eradication of 'profit' as incentive. An uneasy mixture of statutory and common law rules a description merited due to the open-ended nature of the Acts and persistent relevance of the historical Life Assurance Act. The disappointing element of the reform is that it leaves unresolved many of the inherent deficiencies associated with the 1774 Act. Thus, reformed statutes opt not to assist on the question of precisely when insurable interest in life is required. Reliance on 'shall have no interest' in Section 1 of the 1774 Act is interpreted to mean 'no interest at the time of contract.' As well, not prescribing the consequences of breach is injurious, certainly for the insured. While waiver and estoppel often arise in the few regional cases on point, insurable interest cannot be waived in life insurance precisely because of our colonial history. As presently constructed, only one Act, the Dominica Insurance Act, recognises insurable interest on one's own life, and only the Barbados Insurance Act recognises spousal relationships; this leaves other relationships like controversial same-sex relationships[91] to be established on the proof of a pecuniary relationship. Perhaps in the future there will be an accommodation of broader acceptance. Apart from addressing family relationship, the Insurance Acts attempt to address business relationships. The situation of creditors and debtors, mortgagees/mortgagors and corporations require application of Section 8 of the Marine Insurance Act. Key-man insurance and EFPAs have proven problematic. One is forced to resort to basics to determine that 'shall have no interest' in Section 1 was interpreted to mean 'no interest at the time of contract.' Hence, if interest exists at the time of effecting the policy of insurance, the insurance policy is valid. Insurable interest must be resolved through a combination of antique legislation, the common law and modern Insurance Acts.

---

91   T. Holness, 'Same-Sex Couples – Comparative Insights on Marriage and Cohabitation: Is It Possible?,' 42 *Comparative Perspectives on Law and Justice* 168–188. Here the subject is described as a fast-moving target. The author states:

> However, human rights advocates are working tirelessly to generate rights legal reform and social tolerance for sexual minorities. LGBTI rights, or lack thereof, is evident in several bodies of law, including but not limited to sodomy law and marriage law. Additionally, a dialogue on LGBTI rights would be incomplete without an honest account of ongoing violence and other manifestations of homophobia and transphobia in the region . . . it shows that heteronormativity in family law is a vestige of British colonialism.

CHAPTER 5

INSURABLE INTEREST IN PROPERTY INSURANCE

5.1   INTRODUCTION

We established in the previous chapter that insurable interest is a fundamental requirement of insurance law. The insured must be in the position susceptible to suffering economic loss as the proximate result of damage to or destruction of property. Regional jurisprudence indicates respect for Commonwealth decisions on insurable interest relating to indemnity insurance. In this regard, *Sookdeo & Sookdeo's Motor Supplies Ltd v Trinidad & Tobago Insurance Ltd*,[1] *Advantage General Insurance Co. Ltd v Myrie*[2] and *Rambally v Barbados Fire & General Insurance Co. Ltd et al.*[3] stand out. They suggest support for this broad approach is the dominant position in the context of modern commerce. This enables an undisclosed principal to benefit from the existence of an insurance contract with property insurance. Historically, guiding principles were extrapolated from the Gaming Act of 1845,[4] Marine Insurance Act of 1906[5] and the relevant common law which constitute the current position.

At common law, the conventional test for insurable interest is the insured's possession of some legal, equitable or contractual interest in the subject matter of the policy. Additionally, the broader factual expectancy test operates (i.e. 'to be interested in the preservation of a thing, is to be so circumscribed with respect to it as to have benefit from its existence, and prejudice from its destruction.'[6]

5.2   ACADEMIC CRITICISM

Before exploring the legal position on insurable interest relating to property, it is important to observe academic criticism of the term 'insurable interest.' It is argued that the term insurable interest is manifestly a misnomer, the proper term being 'insurable relationship,' that factual expectation of damage should be the exclusive test of an insurable relationship.

> To those who cling to strict property delineations in fear of the process of drawing the line between a genuine factual expectation of damage and wager, it can be said not only that judicial wisdom is equal to the task, but that a just line drawn with difficulty exceeds in value a simple line which works disproportionate injustice.[7]

---

1   The plaintiffs held a policy of fire insurance with the defendant. The policy covered losses under three heads. After investigations were conducted, the defendant paid the plaintiffs the following sums: $1,804,350.34 on the building loss; $18,000 on loss of air conditioning units; and an interim payment of $191,734 on loss of stock.
2   JM 2012 SC 10.
3   Unreported decision, High Court of St Lucia No. 1179 of 2000.
4   8 & 9 Vict. c. 109.
5   7 Edw 7. c. 41.
6   *Lucena v Craufurd* (1806) 2 Bros & Pul (NR) 269 per Lawrence J at 302. See *infra*, n. 36 and accompanying text. In *Lucena v Craufurd*, the surrounding legislation provided that Crown Commissioners could take possession and manage the affairs of ships owned by Dutch Nationals but only when such ships were brought into British port. England and France were at war. Holland was neutral but under threat from France. The ships were captured and brought into British port, but losses were incurred before the vessels reached the port. The Court held that the Commissioners had no insurable interest in these vessels.
7   B. Harnett and J. V. Thompson, 'Insurable Interest In Property: a Socio-Economic Re-evaluation of A Legal Concept' (1948) 48 *Colum. L. Rev.* 1162; A. Tarr, 'Insurable Interest' (1986) 60 *Aust. L.J.* 613.

Despite the acknowledged limitations of the term 'insurable interest,'[8] the conventional approach has a constancy of meaning which makes it convenient for the purposes of this text.[9]

5.3 HISTORICAL DEVELOPMENT

The Marine Insurance Act of 1745,[10] Life Assurance Act of 1774,[11] Gaming Act of 1845,[12] Marine Insurance Act of 1906[13] and the Marine Insurance (Gambling Policies) Act of 1909[14] were all collectively designed to stamp out mischievous gaming with respect to indemnity insurance. Section 1 of the Marine Insurance Act of 1745 first introduces 'insurable interest' as a requirement with respect to all British ships and their cargoes; absence of insurable interest renderd the contract null and void. The explanation for the statutory intervention is evident from the preamble to the Act, which provided:[15] 'the institution and laudable design of making assurances, hath been perverted; and that which was intended for the encouragement of trade and navigation, has in many instances, become hurtful of, and destructive to the same.' The 1745 Act was eventually repealed by the Marine Insurance Act of 1906.[16]

5.4 STATUTORY POSITION IN THE COMMONWEALTH CARIBBEAN

To ascertain the rules governing insurable interest in indemnity insurance, attention must be paid to statute, primarily the Marine Insurance Act of 1906,[17] evident in Sections 8 and 9 of the Barbados Marine Insurance Act[18] which, despite its title applies to all contracts of indemnity.[19] The Marine Insurance Act assists in defining insurable interest and the issue of timing, but the difference between insurable interest in life insurance and insurable interest in property is immediately apparent. In life insurance, insurable interest is required at the point of effecting the contract. In contrast, in property insurance, insurable interest is not necessary at the time of effecting the contract but must exist at the time of loss. Moreover, within indemnity insurance a distinction emerges between marine and non-marine insurance. On the authority of *Grover & Grover Ltd v Matthews*,[20] ratification is only effective in non-marine insurance if it takes place

---

8   As observed in *Constitution Insurance Co. of Canada v Kosmopoulos* (1987) 34 DLR (4th) 208:

> how does one own a direct interest in property which is not in existence at the time of the contract? Can next season's crops or fluctuating inventory be insured? Are warehousing and other bailee policies subject to the law as set out in *Macaura* so as to limit the right to insure to the bailee's liability to the bailor?

9   Supra n. 7.
10   19 Geo. II, c. 37.
11   14 Geo. III, c. 48.
12   Supra n. 4.
13   6 Edw. 7 c. 41.
14   9 Edw. 7 c. 12. Section 1(1) provides that a person effecting marine insurance without interest shall be guilty of an offence and shall be liable, on summary conviction, to imprisonment.
15   Supra n. 13.
16   Ibid.
17   9 Edw. 7 c. 12. Section 4 of the Marine Insurance Act of 1906. This Act replaced the two former Marine Insurance Acts of 1745 and 1788.
18   Cap 242.
19   This is evident, for instance, construing the Act as a whole, in Section 10 of the Barbados Marine Insurance Act, Cap 242, which expressly governs insurable interest on goods.
20   [1910] 2 KB 401.

before loss. In *Grover*, Hamilton J refused to extend the marine insurance principle, that ratification can take place after loss, to non-marine insurance. Thus, insurable interest can be attained after loss once the insured is unaware of the loss at the time of his election. The fundamental principle of indemnity operates in all property insurance: the value of the interest is critical; the insured is precluded from recovering more than the value of his loss.[21]

5.5   EARLY STATUTE

In addition to regional marine insurance legislation, the UK Gaming Act of 1845 applies.[22] Given the relative certainty of the instances where the Life Assurance Act and the Marine Insurance Act will be held to apply, the Gaming Act operates residually (i.e. it will apply when the other Acts do not).[23] Section 18 thereof provides:

> All contracts or agreements, whether by parole or in writing, by way of gaming or wagering, shall be null and void; and no suit shall be brought or maintained in any court of law or equity for recovering any sum of money or valuable thing alleged to be won upon any wager, or which shall have been deposited in the hands of any person to abide the event on which any wager shall have been made.

The Gaming Act does not require the interest to exist at any particular time. Therefore, in cases of insurance on goods or merchandise not forming part of a marine adventure, contracts of insurance made with an expectation of acquiring an interest would not necessarily be avoided as a wager in the event of an interest being acquired before loss.

5.6   APPLICATION OF THE 1774 ACT TO INSURANCES OTHER THAN LIFE

An issue which has arisen before the courts is whether the Life Assurance Act of 1774 applies to property insurance. The Life Assurance Act of 1774 provides:

> No insurance shall be made by any person or persons, bodies politick or corporate, on the life or lives of any person or persons, or on any other event or events whatsoever, wherein the person or persons for whose use, benefit, or on whose account such a policy or policies shall have not an interest.

The debate that emerges is whether the 1774 Act, while directed primarily at life insurance, captures insurances other than life. A literal interpretation of the phrase 'other event or events' widens the scope for the Act to apply to real property.[24] The opposing purposive viewpoint restricts its application to life insurance. The matter was considered in the seminal decision of *Mark Rowlands v Berni Inns Ltd*.[25] In this case, the facts surrounded a landlord and tenant relationship where the basement of a building was leased by the plaintiff/landlord the building was destroyed by fire due to the tenant's negligence. The lease provided that the plaintiff would insure the property and that the tenant would contribute approximately one quarter of the premium, thereby relieving him of the covenant to repair in respect of loss or damage caused

---

21 See further *Davjoyda Estates v National Insurance Co. of New Zealand* (1967) 65 SR (NSW) 381.
22 Supra n. 4.
23 See *infra*, n. 72 and accompanying text.
24 *Re King, Robinson v Gray* [1963] Ch 459.
25 [1986] 1 QB 211.

by any insured risk since the tenant was not a party to the contract of insurance. Consequently, the insurer argued that the tenant could not benefit from the insurance, being not named in the policy in accordance with Section 2 of the 1774 Act. Kerr LJ, in finding for the plaintiff, rejected the contrary view as expressed in *Re King*[26] and held that the statute was not intended to apply indemnity insurance, but only to insurances which provide for the payment of a specified sum upon the happening of an insured event; a literal interpretation of Section 2 would 'create havoc in modern insurance law.'

The debate on the application of the 1774 Act was again revisited by the Judicial Committee of the Privy Council in *Siu Yin Kwan v The Eastern Insurance Co. Ltd, The Osprey*,[27] which was cited and applied in the St Lucia decision of *Rambally v Barbados Fire & General Insurance Co. Ltd et al.*[28] The decision of *Siu Yin Kwan v The Eastern Insurance Co. Ltd, The Osprey* settled the dispute as to whether the 1774 Act applied, emphatically stating that by 'no stretch of the imagination could indemnity be described as a mischievous form of gaming in the terms of the preamble of the 1774 Act.'[29] In this case, the owners of the *Osprey* instructed their agent to secure employer's liability insurance for the owners in respect of potential liability to employees working on the vessel moored off the bay of Hong Kong. The agent applied for insurance in his own name and, in the policy subsequently issued, he was cited as the assured. The policy did not refer to the insurers at all. The *Osprey* was later sunk by a typhoon and a number of crew members were either killed or injured. The owners were insolvent and unable to meet the HK$1 million judgment, causing the plaintiff to instigate direct proceedings against the defendants.[30] The insurer defendants had two defences: that the name of the owner of the vessel did not appear in the policy and that, as the owner was intended to be the insured person, the policy was void and illegal under Section 2 of the 1774 Act. The Privy Council followed the decision of *Mark Rowlands*,[31] ruling that the 1774 Act did not apply to indemnity policies since a liability policy could not be described as providing insurance against 'events.' Further, that Section 2 was coloured by the short title and the preamble to Section 1. Both *Mark Rowlands* and *The Osprey* are foundational decisions which have paved the way for recognition of non-disclosed parties. Both were followed and applied in the decision of *Rambally v Barbados Fire & General Insurance Co. Ltd et al.*[32]

In *Rambally*, while there was no express reference to the question whether the 1774 Act applied, the result of the decision (i.e. that there is no legal requirement that a policy covering fire risk must contain the names or identity of all the persons who are able to seek indemnity) is tantamount to a rejection of the 1774 Act. The inevitable conclusion is that the 1774 Act does not apply to property insurance despite reference in the Act to 'other event or events.'

---

26 *Re King, Robinson v Gray* [1963] Ch 459.
27 [1994] 2 AC 199.
28 Supra n. 3.
29 Per Lord Lloyd of Berwick, ibid. See however *Davjoyda Estates Ltd v National Insurance Co. v New Zealand* (1965) NSWR 1257. In this case, Justice Manning's opines that Section 2 only applies when the insured himself has no interest to satisfy Section 1, but is insuring on behalf of another with an interest who must therefore be named. It is arguable that upon a proper construction Section 1 does indeed apply to real property. With regard to Section 3, property insurance is usually a contract of indemnity which ensures that only the value of his loss can be recovered. Hence Section 3, which required that 'no greater sum is recoverable' is unnecessary, nevertheless it represents a confirmation of the indemnity principles.
30 The Third Party Insurance Act of 1930 operated, under which the victim of an insolvent wrongdoer can bring direct proceedings against the wrongdoer's liability insurers provided that the liability of the wrongdoer had first been established.
31 Supra n. 25.
32 Supra n. 3.

5.7 DEFINING INSURABLE INTEREST IN PROPERTY

Before embarking on an examination of insurable interest as it relates to property, it is helpful to understand that the task of determining insurable interest in property insurance is not as clear-cut as it is for life insurance. Such an undertaking is complicated by the nature of 'property itself.' 'Property' refers both to real property[33] and personal property,[34] each embracing several varieties of property compounded by the variables in the type of interest possessed (e.g. absolute or limited). The nature of the policy under consideration often adds to the complexity and accordingly the question becomes one of construction.

The situation is not helped by the fact that legislation, to the extent that it exists, similarly cuts across boundaries. Further, the assisting common law principles are not determinative of the issue, so that it is not simply a question of applying the narrow test, to where there is a clearly identifiable proprietary/contractual interest and the broader test where the interest is incapable of being easily ascertained. Even in the case of property, something less than a legal or equitable or even simply pecuniary interest has been held to be sufficient.[35] There is no hard and fast rule.[36] With regard to insurable interest as it relates to construction projects, for instance, the basis of sub-contractors' insurable interest is not necessarily their potential liability in the event of causing damage to the project, but rather their potential pecuniary loss should the project be damaged. Moreover, since a sub-contractor arguably also has an interest in his own liability, even property insurance is capable of being construed to cover such liability upon the existence of a further 'legal link.'[37] These difficulties relating to insurable interest in property insurance must be resolved by an application of the common law.

5.8 THE COMMON LAW TESTS

The case which has shaped judicial thinking in the Commonwealth Caribbean is the *locus classicus* decision of *Lucena v Craufurd*.[38] Derived from this decision are two common law tests which assist in the determination of insurable interest.[39] The tests formulated are:

1   The insured must have a legal, equitable or contractual interest in the subject matter, otherwise known as the proprietary interest test; and,

2   The insured must be interested in the preservation of the subject matter, otherwise known as the factual expectancy test.

These common law tests appear to be captured in regional marine insurance legislation. Section 8(2) of the Barbados Marine Insurance Act, for instance, provides:[40]

> In particular, a person is interested in a marine adventure where he stands in any legal or equitable relation to the adventure, or to any moveable property at risk therein, in consequence of

---

33   C. Harpum, S. Bridge and M. Dixon, *Megarry & Wade: The Law of Real Property*, 5th edn (Sweet & Maxwell: 1984), pp. 964–971; S. Owusu, *Law of Property in the Commonwealth Caribbean* (Cavendish: 2007).

34   *Williams v Baltic Insurance Association of London Ltd* [1924] 2 KB 242. See however regional road traffic legislation.

35   *Sharp v Sphere Drake Insurance plc, The Moonace* [1992] 1 Lloyd's Rep 501; *Glengate – K.G. Properties Ltd v Norwich Union Fire Insurance Society* [1996] 2 All ER 487; *Deepak Fertilisers & Petrochemical Ltd Davy McKee (London) Ltd* [1999] 1 All ER (Comm) 69.

36   *Feasey v Sun Life Assurance Corp. of Canada; Steamship Mutual Underwriting Association (Bermuda) Ltd v Feasey* [2003] 2 All ER (Comm) 587.

37   Ibid. See further n. 98 and accompanying text.

38   (1806) 2 Bos & Pul (NR) 269.

39   J. Lowry and P. Rawlings, *Insurance Law, Cases and Materials* (Hart: 2004), p. 270.

40   Ibid.

which he may benefit by the safety or due arrival of insurable property or may be prejudiced by its loss, or by damage thereto, or by the detention thereof, or may incur liability in respect thereof.

The foregoing acknowledges both the restrictive legal propriety test and the broader test of factual expectancy.

The legal or proprietary interest test

The legal or proprietary interest test was postulated by Lord Eldon in *Lucena v Craufurd*.[41]

> Since the 19 Geo 2 (Marine Insurance Act), it is clear that the insured must have an interest, whatever we understand by that term. In order to distinguish that intermediate thing between a strict right, or a right derived under a contract, and a mere expectation or hope, which has been termed insurable interest, it has been said in many cases to be that which amounts to a moral certainty. I have in vain endeavoured, however, to find a fit definition of that which is between a certainty and an expectation; nor am I able to point out what is an interest unless it be a right in the property, or right derivable out of some contract about the property, which in either case may be lost upon some contingency affecting the possession or enjoyment of the party.

In *Advantage General Insurance Co. Ltd v Myrie*,[42] the Supreme Court of Jamaica reaffirmed its application referencing *Routh v Thompson*[43] so that an insurable interest arises on possession of a legal or equitable right in property. The English courts have gone on to hold that a bare legal title either to land or goods does not necessarily give the holder an insurable interest. However, mere possession could, since possession in English law is a root of title which is only defeated by a claim from the true owner.

The factual expectancy test

The factual expectancy test was formulated by Lawrence J in *Lucena v Craufurd*,[44] to wit: '[insurable interest] is to be interested in the preservation of a thing, is to be so circumstanced with respect to it as to have benefit from its existence, prejudice from its destruction.'

Application of the common law tests to property insurance

The common law on the application of the tests enunciated in *Lucena v Craufurd*[45] is instructive on the nature, scope and ambit of insurable interest in property insurance. First, Lord Eldon's narrow test of proprietary or contractual interest in the subject matter insured, resulted in the creation of a narrow basis for the determination of insurable interest. Lord Eldon's concern that a broad definition of insurable interest will lead to an increase in insurance, led to its being manipulated as a convenient tool to advance the ancillary but pertinent practice of insurers

---

41   (1806) 2 Bos & Pul (NR) 321.
42   Supra n. 2.
43   (1890) 11 East 428, 433.
44   (2 Bos VP) at 302.
45   Ibid.

seeking to avoid their obligation under the contract of insurance. This sparked considerable judicial unease.[46] In *Stock v Inglis*,[47] Brett MR stated:

> In my opinion it is the duty of a court always to lean in favour of an insurable interest, if possible, for it seems to me that after underwriters have received the premium, the objection that there was no insurable interest is often, as nearly as possible, a technical objection, and one which has no real merit, certainly not as between the assured and the insurer.[48]

Similar sentiments are evident in the dissenting judgment of Ward LJ in *Feasey v Sun Life Assurance Corp. of Canada*.[49] Here, Ward LJ regarded the practice of the insurer raising the lack of insurable interest in order to avoid its obligations as morally reprehensible: 'they raised their clean hands and cried foul. They sought to avoid the obligations they had undertaken to the syndicate by alleging, *inter alia*, the lack of insurable interest.'

Both the narrow proprietary interest test and the broader test of factual expectancy have a role to play in determining the question of insurable interest in the Commonwealth Caribbean. In the *Bernard v N.E.M. West Indies Insurance Ltd*[50] decision in the jurisdiction of Grenada, Patterson J, describing the principle of insurable interest as one of the great outstanding principles of the law of insurance,[51] stated:

> it is important that the insurers know whether the assured is the sole beneficial owner of the vehicle. Persons who might be considered unfit to become parties to the insurance contract by reason of their previous record may procure other persons who possess no interest in the vehicle to enter into the insurance contract on their behalf. The law frowns on these collusive insurances arrangements . . . What is insurable interest? I adopt the following statement . . . Where the assured is so situated that the happening of the event on which the insurance money is to become payable would, as a proximate cause, involve the assured in the loss or diminution of any right recognised by law or any legal liability there is an insurable interest in the happening of that event to the extent of the possible loss or liability.

In *Bernard*, the plaintiff effected motor insurance with the defendant insurers. In 1980, the vehicle experienced mechanical difficulties and eventually the car broke down. The plaintiff locked the vehicle and left it on the side of the road, only to discover it missing on his return. The vehicle was eventually discovered in the sea. The insurers rejected liability alleging that the vehicle was in fact owned by another. The High Court of Grenada upheld the insurer's claim finding that the plaintiff was not the owner of the car. Patterson J, ruling that a mere moral claim affords no insurable interest, opined that

> commonsense and the law dictates therefore that he has no insurable interest in the vehicle. If the so-called assured had no interest at the time of the contract then he would have no interest at the time of the event . . . the plaintiff could not recover anything as he lost nothing.

Accordingly, the nature of the facts under consideration, bear a direct correlation to the test to be applied. Given the particular facts of the *Bernard* decision, the narrow test – the loss or diminution of any right or legal liability recognised by law – was appropriately applied and, as the instances outlined below indicate, this might not always be case.

---

46 *Stock v Inglis* (1884) 12 QBD 564; *Mackenzie v Whitworth* (1875) 10 Exch 142; *Re London County Commercial Reinsurance Office Ltd* [1922] 2 Ch 67; *Cepheus Shipping Corp. v Guardian Royal Exchange Assurance plc (The Capricorn)* [1995] 1 Lloyd's Rep 622.
47 *Stock v Inglis* (1884) 12 QBD 564.
48 Ibid.
49 [2003] EWCA Civ 885; [2003] Lloyd's Rep. IR 637.
50 Grenada High Court No. 113 of 1981.
51 Ibid., p. 2.

Proprietary or contractual interest

The law indicates that a present right to a legal or equitable interest or a right under contract will support an insurable interest. Mere hope, however strong, or sentimental interest of acquiring an interest is not enough,[52] but an expectancy based on legal rights may support an insurable interest.[53] The circumstances giving rise to a legal or equitable interest are varied and embrace the interests of mortgagors and mortgagees,[54] vendors and purchasers, landlords and tenants and trustees and beneficiaries. At common law, a vendor under a contract for the sale of land is regarded as a constructive trustee for the purchaser, pending completion.[55] The personal representative of a deceased's estate has an insurable interest in the property of the deceased.[56] An equitable interest is also sufficient, as a *cestui que trust* has an insurable interest in respect of his equitable interest.[57] As Lord Eldon noted in *Lucena v Craufurd*,[58] a remainder man whose interest is vested has an insurable interest in the subject matter but a person with a contingent interest does not; the rationale being that the contingency may never occur.[59] So a beneficiary under a will does not have an insurable interest in the insured's estate as the testator has testamentary freedom and may change his will at any time before death. Similarly, anyone who by contract is liable to pay money in the case of the loss of the subject matter has an insurable interest in that subject matter, although one cannot insure a thing merely because there is a chance that some collateral benefit may arise should it not be lost.[60] The instances outlined below are not exhaustive but indicate that the nature of the property interest under consideration is relevant to the test applied.

Company/shareholders

Property that is owned by a limited liability company is owned by the company as a separate legal entity and not the shareholders or ordinary creditors of the company. This is as a logical consequence of the salient company law principle established by the House of Lords in *Salomon v Salomon*,[61] whereby a company is a separate legal person distinct from its incorporators. This rule was followed in the decision of *Macaura v Northern Assurance Co. Ltd*[62] which is authority for the proposition that shareholders have neither a legal nor equitable interest in the assets of the company. In this case, the sole shareholder of a limited company, who was also a substantial creditor of the company, insured in his own name timber owned by the company. The timber was subsequently destroyed by fire. The House of Lords held that Macuara had no insurable interest in the assets of the company (the timber) even though as a shareholder he suffered 'loss' by virtue of the diminution in the value of the shares as a result of the destruction of the company's property. Lord Buckmaster opined that if the shareholder were entitled to insure holdings on the shares in the company, each shareholder would equally be so entitled, if the shares were in separate hands:

> Now no shareholder has any right to any item of property owned by the company, for he has no legal or equitable interest therein. He is entitled to a share in the profits while the company

52   E. R. Hardy Ivamy, *General Principles of Insurance Law*, 5th edn (Butterworths: 1986); R. Merkin, *Colinvaux's Law of Insurance*, 7th edn (Sweet & Maxwell: 1997), p. 59.
53   *Cook v Field* (1850) 15 QB 460; Hardy Ivamy, supra n. 52.
54   *Westminster Fire Office v Glasgow Provident Investment Society* (188) 13 App Cas 699.
55   *Lysaght v Edwards* (1876) 2 Ch D 499.
56   *Tidswell v Ankerstein* (1792) Peake 204; *Stirling v Vaughan* (1809) 11 Est 619; *Bailey v Gould* (1840) 4 Y & C 221.
57   *Ex parte Yallop* (1808) 15 Ves 60, 67, 68.
58   (2 Bos VP) at 302.
59   *Farmer's Mutual Insurance Co. v New Holland Turnpike Road Co.*, 122 Pa. 37 (1888).
60   *Routh v Thompson* (1809) 11 East 428.
61   [1897] AC 22.
62   [1925] AC 619.

continues to carry on business and a share in the distribution of the surplus assets when the company is wound up. If he were at liberty to effect an insurance against loss by fire, of any item of the company's property, the extent of his insurable interest could only be measured by determining the extent to which his share in the ultimate distribution would be diminished by the loss of the assets – a calculation almost impossible to make. There is no means by which such an interest can be definitely measured and no standard which can be fixed of the loss against which the contract of insurance could be regarded as indemnity.

Lord Sumner stated:

It is clear that the appellant had no insurable interest in the timber described. It was not his. It belonged to the Irish Canadian Sawmill Co. Ltd of Skibberdeen, County Cork. He had no lien or security over it, and though it lay on his land by his permission, he had no responsibility to its owner for its safety, nor was it there under any contract that enabled him to hold it for his debt. He owned almost all the shares in the company, and the company owed him a great deal of money, but, neither as creditor nor as shareholder, could he insure the company's assets. The debt was not exposed to fire nor were his shares, and the fact that he was virtually the company's only creditor while the timber was the only asset, seems to me to make no difference. He stood in no legal or equitable relation to the timber at all. He had no concern in the subject insured.

It would appear, according to the decision of *Macaura*, that mere possession of property in *simpliciter* is insufficient.[63] Possession accompanied with legal liability will establish insurable interest, thus bailees can insure goods temporarily in their possession, premised on the fact that possession provides a good root of title.[64] The logistical problem identified in *Macaura*, namely, the difficulty in quantifying the precise value of the shareholding given the potential for diffused shareholdings and variables in relation shareholder's rights such as dividends, in proportion to overall corporate assets, compelled the House of Lords to understandably abandon such an inquiry. As far as the Commonwealth Caribbean insurance law is concerned, it is important to appreciate the factual circumstances of the *Macaura* decision. *Macaura* concerned a *de facto* one-man company, although there were seven incorporators as required by the 1862 UK Companies Act.[65] In substance there was a one-man company in existence since the controller ran the show, and the other six incorporators – members of Macuara's family – existed merely to satisfy the statutory requirement.

This decision must be contrasted with the position adopted later in the Canadian decision of *Constitution Insurance Co. of Canada v Kosmopoulos*.[66] Here the Supreme Court of Canada departed from the position adopted in the earlier cases and accepted the broader concept of insurable interest. The facts were similar to those in *Macaura*. Kosmopoulos was the sole shareholder and director of a company that manufactured and sold leather goods. He effected in his own name a fire policy. A fire broke out on adjoining premises which resulted in fire, smoke and water damage to the company. Madame Justice Wilson declined to lift the veil, upholding the principle that the company was a legal entity distinct from Mr Kosmoupolos. On the issue of insurable interest, however, the approach of Lawrence J was preferred to that of Lord Eldon's restrictive requirement of a legally enforceable right. The broader factual expectancy test thereby neatly avoiding the problem of ascertaining that 'intermediate thing between a legal right and a mere expectation:'

if wagering should be the major concern in the context of insurance contracts, the current definition of insurable interest is not an ideal mechanism to combat this ill. The insurer alone

---

63   *Macaura v Northern Assurance Co. Ltd* [1925] AC 619.
64   *Stirling v Vaughan* (1809) 11 East 619.
65   Supra n. 63.
66   (1987) 34 DLR (4th) 208.

can raise the defence of lack of insurable interest; no public watchdog can raise it. The insurer is free not to invoke it for reasons completely extraneous to and perhaps inconsistent with those underlying the definition. The *Macaura* principle is too imperfect a tool to further public policy against wagering. By focusing merely on the type of interest held by the insured, but no pecuniary interest, will be able to receive pure enrichment unrelated to any pecuniary loss whatsoever.

In the *Kosmopoulos* decision, the Supreme Court considered the *Macaura* principle an imperfect tool to further public policy against wagering. The position in the Caribbean is therefore the salient principle as enunciated in *Macaura*. In other cases, a shareholder is entitled to insure his shares against the diminution in the value of his shares due the pursuit by the company of a specific venture.[67] In the Commonwealth Caribbean, however, an important caveat to the general proposition operates. Following Canadian precedent, on the authority of *Kosmopoulos*, if the shareholder is the *sole* shareholder in a *de jure*, one-man company, then *Macaura* is distinguishable on its facts and the *Kosmopoulos* position applies. Most Caribbean territories have adopted the position under the Ontario Business Companies Act[68] and the Canadian Business Corporation Act.[69] Regional company law statutes recognise the existence of one-man companies. Section 4 of the Barbados Companies Act, for instance, provides that 'one or more persons may incorporate a company,' representing a *de jure* recognition of one-man companies. Since the Caribbean Law Institute's (CLI) Companies Bill of 1991 was based on the Barbados Companies Act,[70] an act which adopted the position in Canada, the position is that a sole shareholder, though lacking any property interest in a corporation's assets, nevertheless has an insurable interest in them.[71] Further, as noted in *Kosmopoulos*, the decision of *Macaura* is an odd case as it originally went to the arbitrator on the question of fraud. Although the arbitrator held there was no fraud, it is difficult to reject the inference that, though not provided, the charges of fraud did not influence the court to conclude in the way it did.[72]

Creditors

Macaura v Northern Assurance Co. Ltd[73] indicates a creditor of a company ordinarily has no right to the property charged in the sense of a mortgage or charge over it, or some other proprietary security interest. A creditor, however, may insure against the insolvency of the debtor,[74] and may have a legal proprietary interest in the subject matter insured under statute, in accordance with the authority of *Moran Galloway & Co., Uzeilli*. In this case, the Court held that the plaintiffs, having a right under Section 6 of the Admiralty Court Act of 1840 to enforce their claim for advances, so far as they were in respect of necessaries supplied to the ship, by an action in *rem*,[75] and for that purpose to arrest the ship, had an insurable interest in the ship to the extent of the unsatisfied balance of those advances. According to Walton J, considering that there was

---

67   *Wilson v Jones* (1867) LR 2 Ex 139.
68   RSO, 1990.
69   R.S.C., 1985, c. 44.
70   Cap 308.
71   N. L. Jones, J. Birds and D. Owen, *MacGillivray on Insurance Law*, 10th edn (Sweet & Maxwell: 2002); R. A. Hasson, 'Reform of the Law Relating to Insurable Interest in Property – Some Thoughts on *Chadwick v Gibraltar General Insurance*' (1983–1984) 8 *Can. Bus. L.J.* 114; R. A. Hasson, 'The Supreme Court in Flames, Fire Insurance Decisions after Kosmopoulos' (1995) *Osgood Hall L.J.* 679.
72   R. E. Keeton, *Basic Text on Insurance Law* (West Publishing Co.: 1971), p. 117.
73   [1925] AC 619.
74   *Waterkeyn v Eagle Star Insurance Co.* (1920) 5 LILR 12.
75   *In rem* jurisdiction (Latin, 'power about or against "the thing"') is a legal term describing the power a court may exercise over property (either real or personal) or a 'status' against a person over whom the court does not have *in personam* jurisdiction.

a considerable sum owing independent of their lien upon the freight, they had an insurable interest to an amount equal to the value of the ship in respect of what was owing to them for disbursements, whether secured by a charge or lien on the ship or not, and that such an interest was insured by the policy.

The distinction which emerges at common law therefore is that between an ordinary unsecured creditor and a secured creditor possessing a lien or charge over the subject matter insured. In the case of the former, a creditor has no insurable interest but, if the creditor is a secured creditor then such an interest may be held to exist.

Insurable interest in real property – including joint and limited interest

An absolute owner of real property obviously has an insurable interest in the property. As noted earlier, as is the case with all categories of property, the situation may arise where more than one person has an interest in the property. Where two persons have an interest in the same subject matter, they may insure the property independently without specifying their interests. Both may recover in full from their respective insurers, for there is no double insurance without the insurances covering the same interest. Thus a landlord and a tenant may insure the same building; the tenant is under an obligation to repair, but not to insure. The exception expressed in *Castellain v Preston*[76] applies, where the tenant remains in possession after expiry of the lease. Both a mortgagor and a mortgagee may insure their own interests alone via separate insurances or as bailor and bailee. A mortgagor has legal ownership by virtue of ancillary Law of Property Legislation.[77] He is therefore entitled to insure, at the expense of the mortgagee, against loss, damage or fire.[78] He may insure and recover the whole of the amount of the loss, as he is liable personally for the amount of the mortgage debt.[79] A mortgagee of land by virtue of his equitable ownership has an insurable interest in the mortgage property and may insure if he has covenanted to insure. Recovery may be limited where there is a valued policy (i.e. a policy with a ceiling fixed amount).

Insurable interest in goods

As observed earlier, the term 'goods' relates to personal property as opposed to real property. Guidance on insurable interest as it relates to goods must be gained from an application of the Marine Insurance Act,[80] the Gaming Act[81] and the common law.

Limited ownership of goods

There is a right to insure in a variety of situations beyond simple ownership, risk or possession, in particular where the assured has a certainty of benefit from the preservation of goods and the certainty of loss from their destruction. Absolute ownership of goods will therefore

---

76 (1882–1883) LR 11 QBD 380.
77 United Kingdom, Law of Property Act 15 & 16 Geo. 5 c. 20. A mortgagor's covenant to insure operates as an equitable assignment in favour of the mortgagee. *Clerical Mutual General Insurance Co. Ltd v ANZ Banking Group (New Zealand) Ltd* [1995] 3 All ER 987.
78 *Royal Caribbean Hotels v Bank of Nova Scotia* BB 1992 CA 31.
79 *Castellain v Preston* (1882–1883) LR 11 380 CA.
80 Supra n. 17.
81 Supra n. 4; Barbados Gaming Act, Cap 135.

obviously support insurable interest, but it is not essential. Owners of goods in addition to vendors and purchasers of the goods, all have an insurable interest in the goods.[82] The vendor of goods has an insurable interest in those goods for two reasons. First, because of his legal ownership of those goods, and second, because he will have to suffer any loss or damage caused by any mishap which occurs after conclusion of the agreement to sell, if the purchaser does not carry out his end of the bargain. In such circumstances, the vendor's interest will continue so long as his *lien* for the purchase money continues while the purchaser simultaneously has an insurable interest in goods when either the property or the risk attached to the goods passes to him.

Apart from the situation of vendor and purchaser, commercial practice reveals a host of variables where a party temporarily holds goods on behalf of another. Where goods are held in trust or on commission, the bailees or carriers of the goods have an insurable interest in the goods entrusted to them. Their interest is limited to the extent of their commission or other changes of bailment, but it is clear that they can insure for the whole value of the goods, holding that balance over their own interest for the benefit of the owners of the goods. The proviso, however, is that the policy must provide for this.[83] In *Waters v Monarch Fire*,[84] warehousemen effected two floating policies drafted in general terms, leaving certain particulars to be later defined. One policy was on goods on trust or held in commission, and the second policy was on goods owned or held in commission. A fire destroyed flour owned by the claimant's customers. Some owners were unaware that a policy was effected on the goods and had effected their own policies. The insurers offered to pay only the value of the lien for warehouse charges, arguing that the plaintiffs had no insurable interest in goods not owned by them. The Court found in favour of the claimants, holding that the policy of insurance was valid, it not being tainted by illegality. Commenting on the commercial convenience of floating policies, Lord Campbell CJ stated:

> I cannot doubt that the policy was intended to protect such goods and it would be very inconvenient if wharfingers could not protect such goods by a floating policy . . . And I think that a person entrusted with goods can insure them without orders from the owner.[85]

This case raises an important question on the law of fire insurance. The circumstance that the insurers were ignorant of the contract for sale is immaterial. It is clear that the vendors could have recovered, notwithstanding the contract for sale. That point was decided in *Coilingridge v Royal Exchange Assurance Co.*,[86] where a suggestion was made by the learned judges in such circumstances the vendors might be trustees of the amount recovered for the purchasers. Acting possibly on that suggestion, the purchasers brought the action of *Rayner v Preston*[87] in the Chancery Division. His Lordship then referred to the doubts above referred to and expressed by the judges in that case and continued: 'there is no English authority directly on point, and the question must be decided on principle.' The plaintiffs contend that the contract of insurance is merely a contract of indemnity, and unless they recover in this action the defendants will receive double satisfaction. Undoubtedly it is settled law that a contract of insurance is a contract of indemnity. The principle of subrogation applies to fire insurance, whether the subject matter of the insurance be chattels or buildings annexed to the soil. The law on the subject is ably stated in the judgment of the Master of the Rolls and

---

82   *Castellain v Preston* (1882–1883) LR 11; QBD 380.
83   *Waters v Monarch Fire and Life Assurance Company* (1856) 5 El & Bl 870.
84   (1856) 5 El & Bl 870.
85   (1856) 5 EL & BL 881.
86   LR, 3 QB Div 173.
87   Case Law Rep, 5 Ch Div 569.

of Lord Justice Mellish in the *North British Fire Insurance* and also by Lord Cairns in *Simpson v Thomson*,[88] where he says,

> I know of no foundation for the right of the underwriters, except the well-known principle of law, where one has agreed to indemnify another, he will, on making good the indemnity, be entitled to succeed to all the ways and means by which the person indemnified might have been protected.

This commercially sensible approach, as will be seen in subsequent discussion, was endorsed by the House of Lords in *Hepburn Tomlinson (Hauliers) Ltd v Hepburn*[89] and in the decision of *Glengate-K.G. Properties Ltd v Norwich Union Fire Insurance Society Ltd*.[90] In *North British & Mercantile Insurance Co.*,[91] however, since interest over the goods had already passed to a purchaser, the insured merchants could not recover, the phrase 'interest or on commission' in the policy being restricted by the words 'for which they are responsible.' An important consideration in property insurance arises in respect of the fundamental ancillary right in indemnity insurance: to wit, the right of subrogation. What if the insured declines to sue, thus preventing the third party from recouping his losses? Is the third party entitled to sue? In *Vandepitte v Preferred Accident Insurance Corp. of New York*,[92] the Judicial Committee of the Privy Council denied the third party's claim on the ground of privity of contract. Jean Berry, a minor, was driving a car which was owned by her father. She was involved in an accident with E. J. Vandepitte (Alice's husband) while Alice was in the car and she was injured. It was found that there was money owing to the appellant for her injuries, so E. J. Vandepitte issued an execution to R. E. Berry (Jean's father) for the balance. He refused to pay, so Vandepitte, under the provisions of the Insurance Act, sued the insurance company directly. Vandepitte was successful at the Supreme Court and Court of Appeal of British Columbia but was overturned by the Supreme Court of Canada. Vandepitte appealed to the Judicial Committee of the Privy Council. It was argued that there was no contract between the parties, Vandepitte arguing agency and trust. The argument failed.

To create a trust, there must be clear intention to create a trust.[93] In accordance, however, with *Grover & Grover Ltd v Matthews*,[94] ratification is only effective if it takes place before loss. In *Grover and Grover Ltd*, Hamilton J refused to extend the marine insurance principle that ratification can take place after loss, to non-marine insurance.[95] A barge owned by the appellant sank while chartered to the respondent. The appellant's insurance policy included clauses waiving subrogation and extending coverage to affiliated companies and charterers. The insurers paid the appellant the fixed amount stipulated in the policy for the loss of the barge. The appellant made a further agreement with the insurers to pursue a negligence action against the respondent and to waive any right to the waiver of subrogation clause. The negligence action against the respondent was allowed at trial and dismissed on appeal. At issue was whether a third-party beneficiary can rely on a waiver of subrogation clause to defend against a subrogated action on the basis of a principled exception to the privity of contract doctrine. The appeal was dismissed.

---

88 Law Rep, 3 App Cases 279.
89 [1966] 1 All ER 418.
90 [1996] 2 All ER 487.
91 (1871–1872) LR 7 CP 25, CCP.
92 [1933] AC 70.
93 Supra n. 34.
94 Supra n. 20; Sections 10, 24, 152, 153, 154, British Columbia Insurance Act of 1925.
95 See the case of *Fraser River Pile & Drueedge Ltd v Can-Dive Services Ltd* [1999] 3 SCR 108, 1999 Can LII 654 (SCC). Here the issue was whether charterer was entitled to rely on a waiver of subrogation clause in order to defend against subrogated action initiated by barge owner's insurers on basis of principled exception to the privity of contract doctrine.

As a general rule, the doctrine of privity provides a contract can neither confer rights nor impose obligations on third parties. Consequently, a third-party beneficiary would normally be precluded from relying on the terms of the insurance policy between the barge owner and its insurers.

Given the circumstances, however, a principled exception to the privity doctrine applied. A new exception is dependent upon the intention of the contracting parties. This intention is determined on the basis of 'two critical and cumulative factors':

1   The parties to the contract must intend to extend the benefit to the third party seeking to rely on the contractual provision; and

2   The activities performed by the third party seeking to rely on the contractual provision must be the very activities contemplated as coming within the scope of the contract in general, or the provision in particular, as determined by reference to the intentions of the parties. According to the judgment, the first condition was satisfied as the waiver of subrogation clause expressly included the respondent within the class of intended beneficiaries. That clause was not conditional on the appellant's initiative in favour of any particular third-party beneficiary and can be enforced by the respondent acting independently.

Sound policy reasons exist for relaxing the doctrine of privity in these circumstances. Such an exception establishes a default rule that closely corresponds to commercial reality. When sophisticated commercial parties enter into a contract of insurance which expressly extends the benefit of a waiver of subrogation clause to an ascertainable class of third-party beneficiaries, any conditions purporting to limit the extent of the benefit must be clearly expressed. Relaxing the doctrine of privity here would not introduce significant change to the law which would be better left to the legislature. The factors supporting the incremental nature of the exception were present. The appellant's concerns regarding the potential for double recovery were unfounded, as the respondent cannot rely on any provision in the policy to establish a separate claim. Iacobucci J observed this appeal concerns the application of the doctrine of privity of contract and a waiver of subrogation clause in a contract of insurance.

Warren J next considered Can-Dive's submission that, notwithstanding its status as a third party to the contract, the insurers were bound by the waiver of subrogation clause contained therein, as the doctrine of privity of contract does not apply in circumstances where a third-party beneficiary relies on the waiver to defend against an action initiated by the insurers. Having reviewed the existing jurisprudence purporting to deal with privity of contract in this context, and relying in particular on the decision of the Privy Council in *Vandepitte v Preferred Accident Insurance Corp. of New York*,[96] Warren J concluded that the doctrine was still applicable except to the extent it was incrementally abrogated through the creation of specific judicial exceptions, or more substantively, through legislative reform, as has generally been the case with automobile insurance legislation. He held that the Court's decision in *London Drugs Ltd v Kuehne & Nagel International Ltd*[97] was controlling on this issue: a waiver of subrogation clause, as with any other contractual provision, is subject to the doctrine of privity unless a traditional exception applies or sufficient reason exists to relax the doctrine in the given circumstances. Warren J held that relaxing the doctrine of privity of contract in the present circumstances would alter the doctrine in excess of the incremental changes contemplated by the reasoning in *London Drugs*.[98]

---

96   Supra n. 92; [1932] 3 WWR 573.
97   1992 Can LII 41 (SCC) [1992] 3 SCR 299.
98   *Kuehne & Nagel* were storing a transformer owned by London Drugs valued at $32,000. The agreement between the parties included a limitation of liability clause which limited liability for damage to the transformer to $40. Two employees were moving the transformer with a forklift and negligently dropped it. London Drugs sued the two employees on the basis that they owed a separate duty of care and could not seek protection under the contract.

Factual expectancy in modern commerce

General

Modern commerce depicts a growing trend towards an acceptance of the broader factual expectancy test as laid down by Lawrence J in *Lucena v Caufurd*.[99] This trend is evident in the decision of *Mark Rowlands Ltd v Berni Inns Ltd*,[100] where the Court of Appeal adopted Lawrence J's open-textured approach. It is also discernible in a series of building contract cases in which the main issue was the exercise of subrogation rights by insurers. In these cases the courts utilise the jurisprudence of the so-called bailee cases as a means of buttressing the shift from the narrow proprietary interest test towards finding that sub-contractors possess a persuasive interest in the whole construction project.[101]

The St Lucia decision of *Rambally v Barbados Fire & General Insurance Co. Ltd et al.*[102] is indicative of this approach. In *Rambally*, the facts are unimportant; the *dicta* reveals the utilisation of the broader factual expectancy test and the importance of the so-called bailee in resolving the dispute on the status of the undisclosed principal's insurable interest. Observing 'that there is no legal requirement that a policy covering fire risk must contain the names or identity the interests of all the persons who are able to seek indemnity,' the Court applied the Privy Council decision of *Sui v Eastern Insurance*[103] approving *Mark Rowlands Ltd v Berni Inns*:[104] 'That, although evidence of intention is clearly not admissible in aid of construing the insurance contract, such evidence become relevant when insurable interest is in question.' An obvious hurdle to recovery in *Rambally*, an obstacle which the Court sought to overcome, is the principle of privity of contract. In circumventing the privity of contract law principle that only a person who is a party to a contract can sue on the contract, the Court relied, *inter alia*, on the judgment of Lord Wright in *Vandepitte v Preferred Accident Insurance Corp of New York*[105] and recognised that there were many cases in which commercial convenience permitted an assured with limited interest to insure the 'whole property in the goods and to recover the whole of the money, holding the balance in trust for those whose loss it represents.' The Court concluded by accepting that 'the law that an undisclosed principal can take the benefit of a contract[106] only where the insurers are aware that the person entering into the contract is a mere agent, or is likely to be insuring other interests as well as his own.'[107] This statement, albeit *obiter*, is a clear indication that a lack of proprietary interest is not fatal to the establishment of insurable interest in the Caribbean, the foundation having been laid by the broader factual expectancy test and its application to bailees.

Bailee

A bailee has an insurable interest in the goods entrusted to him. The *locus classicus* decision is *Waters v Monarch Fire and Life Assurance Co.*,[108] which is authority for the principle that a bailee can insure merely his own loss or his personal liability to the owner of the goods, but if he chooses

---

99 Supra n. 58.
100 Supra n. 25.
101 *Petrofina (UK) Ltd v Mangnaload* [1983] 2 Lloyds Rep at 91.
102 Supra n. 3.
103 [1994] 1 All ER 213.
104 [1985] 3 All ER 473.
105 [1933] AC 71.
106 Supra n. 104.
107 *Boston Fruit Co. v British & Foreign Marine Insurance Co. Ltd* [1906] AC 336.
108 [1834–1860] All ER Rep 654.

to insure for the full value of goods entrusted to him, although he can recover the full value of the goods he is required in law to account to the owner for the surplus. This decision stands in contrast to the decision of *North British & Mercantile Insurance Co. v Moffat*.[109] In *North British*, since the property insured had already passed to the purchasers at the time a fire occurred, destroying tea chests stored in the insured's premises, the insured had no interest in the tea chests and could not recover in respect of the loss. Here the words 'for which they are responsible' qualified the words 'in trust' and 'on commission.'[110] Another important and influential decision on Caribbean jurisprudence is the House of Lords decision of *Hepburn v A. Tomlinson (Hauliers) Ltd v Hepburn*.[111] In this case, a consignment of cigarettes which the claimants had contracted with the manufacturer to transport was stolen without any fault on the part of the plaintiff claimants. The insurers repudiated the claim on the basis that the claimants had no liability, as there was no loss in respect of which they required indemnification. The resolution of the issue was dependent on the true construction of the policy. The policy under consideration was not simply a policy covering the carrier's potential legal liability, but was a 'goods in transit policy' providing coverage while the goods were being transported from one place to another. The owners of the goods were expressly named in the policy. The House of Lords concluded that the position *vis-à-vis* bailees having been accurately stated in the earlier decision of *Waters v Monarch Fire & Life Assurance Co.*,[112] the carriers had an insurable interest in the goods because of their potential legal liability if they were negligent. The law pertaining to the insurable interest of bailees in goods temporarily in their possession has led the way for recognition of the interests of other parties, both embraced by the policy.

Undisclosed principals

The commercial utility of the broader factual expectancy test and its extension to non-disclosed interests can be seen in *Petrofina (UK) Ltd v Magnaload Ltd*,[113] which applied the earlier decisions of *Waters v Monarch*[114] and *Hepburn v Tomlinson (Hauliers) Ltd*.[115] In *Petrofina*, the main contractors on a site effected an 'all-risks insurance' policy to include damage to property. The insureds were defined as including the main contractors, sub-contractors, owners and lessees of the site. Serious damage was caused by a sub-contractor's negligence. The owners were compensated under the policy and the insurers sought to subrogate against the negligent party, who in their defence argued that they were insureds under the policy. If the defendants were not sub-contractors, the insurers would have a complete defence. If they were insured, however, the insurer under the policy would be prevented from exercising subrogation rights against the sub-contractors in respect of damage to the project, which had resulted in the death of two workers, allegedly caused by their negligence. The Court viewing the bailee's right to insure the full value of goods as highly convenient, held that the phrase 'the insured' covered the owners, main contractors and each and every sub-contractor, resulting in the disallowance of the right of subrogation.[116] While the so-called *Petrofina* principle,[117] which recognises that various parties involved in a construction project have a persuasive interest in the whole

---

109 (1871) LR 7 CP 25.
110 See *Ramco (UK) Ltd v International Insurance Co. of Hannover Ltd* [2004] EWCA Civ 675.
111 Supra n. 89.
112 Supra n. 84.
113 [1983] 2 Lloyd's Rep 91.
114 Supra n. 84.
115 [1966] AC 451.
116 [1983] *JBL* 497.
117 J. Birds, *Modern Insurance Law*, 6th edn (Sweet & Maxwell: 2014), p. 63.

project,[118] was subsequently endorsed in *Co-operative Retail Services Ltd v Taylor Partnership Ltd*,[119] it was severely critised in the leading decision of *Deepak Fertilisers & Petrochemical Corp. v Davy McKee (London) Ltd & ICI Chemicals & Polymers Ltd*.[120]

Before examining the impact of *Deepak* on insurable interest in property insurance, it is useful to consider the earlier decision of *Glengate-K.G. Properties Ltd v Norwich Union Fire Insurance Society*.[121] In *Glengate* the claimants, who were redeveloping a defunct department store when a fire occurred damaging the building and destroying the architect's plans, claimed under a consequential loss policy. The issue that arose was whether they had an insurable interest in the drawings which were owned by the architect under the consequential loss policy. Copies of the plans and drawings were not kept, the plans and drawings were not separately insured and reproduction would be at a considerable expense. In construing the phrase 'the interest of the insured' in the consequential loss policy, despite the insured's lack of proprietary interest in the plans as understood by Lord Eldon in *Lucena v Craufurd*, the Court of Appeal held that they had an insurable interest in the drawings so as to cover consequential loss. In applying the broad factual expectancy test, Auld LJ stated:

> Although the term insurable interest may have a constancy of meaning in the broad sense stated by Mr Justice Lawrence in *Lucena v Craufurd*, the nature of insurable interest in each case must depend on the type of cover in issue. In the case of insurance against cost of repair or reinstatement of damaged property, to qualify as an insurable interest, must normally be of a proprietary or contractual nature. *Mark Rowlands Ltd v Berni Inns Ltd* is an example of both proprietary and contractual relationship, and as Lord Kerr's reliance on the broad proposition of Mr Justice Lawrence in *Lucena v Craufurd* was necessary on the facts of the case. Bailees are long established and special example of a possessory insurable interest. But not every contractual interest in property creates an insurable interest in it for the purposes of material damage cover. The authorities do not suggest that contractual licensees have such an interest as a rule. However a contractual licensee, or even one at will, may have it if he is on joint occupation of property with the licensor . . . I say that insurable interest for material damage must 'normally' be proprietary or contractual because the Courts have acknowledged the presence of an insurable interest in other circumstances.

The decision has been the subject of intense criticism. In *Deepak Fertilisers & Petrochemical Corp. v Davy McKee (London) Ltd & ICI Chemicals & Polymers Ltd*,[122] although the Court of Appeal applied the factual expectancy test, a limit was placed on this broader concept of insurable interest. The result is that the answer to the question of insurable interest in property insurance must now be approached differently. Pure risk of potential liability for causing damage to property will not, by itself, create an insurable interest in the property. But if there is a further link, that interest may be embraced within the subject of insurance. In *Deepak Fertilisers*,[123] a methanol plant constructed for the plaintiff exploded shortly after it was commissioned. On the liability of the sub-contractors, a firm of engineers who were co-insured under the policy, the Court agreed that the sub-contractor in the building contract has an insurable interest in the entire works during construction, but ruled that once the work was completed such an interest came to an end. Thus the engineers did not have an insurable interest in the plant at the time of the

---

118 *Stone Vickers Ltd v Appledore Ferguson Shipbuilders Ltd* [1991] 2 Lloyd's Rep 288, was subsequently overturned by the Court of Appeal on the question of construction of the policy [1992] 2 Lloyd's Rep 578; *National Oilwell (UK) Ltd v Davy Offshore (UK) Ltd* [1993] 2 Lloyd's Rep 582.
119 [2000] 2 All ER 865.
120 [1999] 1 Lloyd's Rep 387.
121 Supra n. 90.
122 Supra n. 120.
123 Ibid.

explosion. According to the Court of Appeal, an 'all-risks policy' on a building project is treated as property insurance.[124] Once construction is completed the contractors no longer possess a proprietary interest in the property. Instead, it is up to the contractors to effect a separate policy to cover any potential liability for negligence or breach of contract.

The decision of *Deepak* exhibits the first signs of a more flexible approach to the issue of insurable interest. Later, in *Feasey v Sun Life Assurance Corp. of Canada; Steamship Mutual Underwriting Association (Bermuda) Ltd v Feasey*,[125] the Court of Appeal reviewed insurable interest as it relates to construction projects and considered that the basis of sub-contractors' insurable interest was not their potential liability in the event of causing damage to the project but rather their potential pecuniary loss should the project be damaged; moreover, that the sub-contractors also had an interest in their own liability so that even property insurance could be construed to cover such liability. Waller J opined that if a further legal link existed, that interest may also be embraced within the subject of the insurance. Accordingly the question becomes one of construction. Although it may be more usual to cover liability with liability insurance, there was no hard and fast rule, so that if the policy as construed leads to such a construction, there was no reason not so to construe it. '[Deepak] is not authority for any broader proposition such as it being impossible to cover the insurable interest of liability by virtue of a policy on property if the terms of the policy embrace the insurable interest.' Waller LJ then identified the following groups.

> Group (1) are those cases where the court has defined the subject matter as an item of property; where the insurance is to recover the value of that property; and where thus there must be an interest in the property – real or equitable – for the insured to suffer loss which he can recover under the policy.[126] Group (2) where the court has recognised an insurable interest in that life of a particular person; and where the insurance is to recover a sum on the death of that particular person.[127] Group (3), cases where even though the subject matter may appear to be a particular item of property, properly construed, the policy extends beyond the item and embraces such insurable interest as the insured has.[128] Group (4) policies in which the court has recognised interests which are not even strictly pecuniary. In relation to life policies there are policies on own life; policies on husband's life and policies on the life of the wife.[129] But even in the case of property, something less than a legal or equitable or even simply pecuniary interest has been thought to be sufficient.[130]

Waiver of insurable interest

In the case of life insurance, insurable interest cannot be waived. With respect to indemnity insurance, however, the position is not so clear.[131] The Marine Insurance Act and the Gaming

---

124 On the construction of 'all-risks' policies, see the decision of *British & Foreign Marine Insurance Co. v Gaunt* [1921] 2 AC 41, where it was held that the term covers all loss to property insured as occurs through accidental cause, but not such damage as is inevitable from ordinary wear and tear and inevitable depreciation. The insured need only establish that the loss was accidental and need not prove the exact nature of the accident or casualty which occasioned the loss.

125 [2003] 2 All ER (Comm) 587.

126 *Lucena v Craufurd* (1806) 2 Bros & PNR 269, 127 ER 630. *Anderson v Morice* (1875) LR 10 CP 609, affirmed (1876) 1 App Cas 713; and *Macaura v Northern Assurance Co. Ltd* [1925] AC 619.

127 *Law v London Indisputable Life Policy Co.* (1855) 1 K & J 223, 69 ER 439; *Simcock v Scottish Imperial Insurance Co.* (1902) 10 SLT 286; *Harse v Pearl Life Assurance Co.* [1903] 2 KB 92.

128 Supra n. 67.

129 *Griffiths v Fleming* [1909] 1 KB 805.

130 *Sharp v Sphere Drake Insurance plc, The Moonace* [1992] 1 Lloyd's Rep 501; *Glengate – K.G. Properties Ltd v Norwich Union Fire Insurance Society* [1996] 2 All ER 487; *Deepak Fertilisers & Petrochemical Ltd Davy McKee (London) Ltd* [1999] 1 All ER (Comm) 69.

131 M. A. Clarke, *The Law of Insurance Contracts* (Informa Law from Routledge: 2009), para. 4.1.D.

Act, which apply to indemnity insurance, are silent on the effect of a lack of insurable interest.[132] If insurable interest is a contractual requirement, then arguably it should be capable of being waived or dispensed with. If the public policy ground argument against such a construction is valid, then regardless of the type of insurance, insurable interest cannot be waived. In *Prudential Staff Union v Hall*,[133] the contractual undertaking by the insurer to pay the association waived the requirement of insurable interest,[134] in this case, an association of employees that insured with Lloyd's against any loss suffered by any of its members or money held by them as agents or collectors of their employer. Despite the lack of insurable interest, it was nevertheless held that the policy was enforceable. Morris J utilised the trust device circumventing the element of wagering, stating:

> In my judgment, the alleged loss is one in relation to which the union would regard themselves as trustees for the particular members of any amount recovered, so that those members could pay such amount in settlement of any claims made on them by their employers for money received or held on their behalf.

Assignment of policy

Assignment involves the transfer of an interest or benefit from one person to another. However the 'burden,' or obligations, under a contract cannot be transferred. In the context of a building contract, the employer may assign its right to have the works constructed, and its right to sue the contractor in the event that the works are defective he assumes no obligation to pay for the works, the contractor may assign its right to payment of the contract sum – but not its obligation to construct the works in accordance with the building contract or its obligation to meet any valid claims, for example for defects.

After assignment, the assignee is entitled to the benefit of the contract and to bring proceedings against the other contracting party to enforce its rights. The assignor still owes obligations to the other contracting party and will remain liable to perform any part of the contract that still has to be fulfilled since the burden cannot be assigned. In practice, what usually happens is that the assignee takes over the performance of the contract with effect from assignment and the assignor will generally ask to be indemnified against any breach or failure to perform by the assignee. The assignor will remain liable for any past liabilities incurred before the assignment.

In construction contracts, the issue of assignment often arises in looking at whether collateral warranties granted to parties outside of the main construction contract can be assigned. Financiers may require the developer to assign contractual rights against the contractor and the design team as security to the funder, and the developer may assign such rights to the purchaser either during or after completion of the construction phase.

Contractual assignment provisions

Many contracts exclude or qualify the right to assignment, and the courts have confirmed that a clause which provides that a party to a contract may not assign the benefit of that contract without the consent of the other party is legally effective and will extend to all rights and benefits

---

132 *Beard v American Agency Life Ins. Co.* 550 A.2d 677 (Md. 1988); *Farm Bureau Mutual Insurance Co. v Glover*, 616 S.W.2d 755 (1981).
133 [1947] KB 685.
134 See also *Thomas v National Farmers' Union Mutual Insurance Society* [1961] 1 WLR 386.

arising under the contract, including the right to any remedies. Other common qualifications on the right to assign include:

- A restriction on assignment without the consent of the other party, whether or not such consent is not to be unreasonably withheld or delayed; only one of the parties may assign;
- Only certain rights may be assigned. For example, warranties and indemnities may be excluded; a limit on the number of assignments is generally in the case in respect of collateral warranties; a right to assign only to a named assignee or class of assignee.

Note that in some agreements where there is a prohibition on assignment, it is sometimes possible to find the reservation of specific rights to create a trust or establish security over the subject matter of the agreement instead.

Legal and equitable assignment

The Law of Property Act creates the ability to legally assign a debt or any other chose in action where the debtor, trustee or other relevant person is notified in writing. If the assignment complied with the formalities in the Act it is a legal assignment; otherwise it will be an equitable assignment.

Some transfers can only take effect as an equitable assignment, for example:

- An oral assignment;
- An assignment by way of charge;
- An assignment of only part of the chosen in action;
- An assignment of which notice has not been given to the debtor;
- An agreement to assign.

If the assignment is equitable rather than legal, the assignor cannot enforce the assigned property in its own name and to do so must join the assignee in any action. This is designed to protect the debtor from later proceedings brought by the assignor or another assignee from enforcing the action without notice of the earlier assignment.

Security assignments

Using assignment as a way of taking security requires special care, as follows:

- If the assignment is by way of charge, the assignor retains the right to sue for any loss it suffers caused by a breach of the other contract party;
- If there is an outright assignment coupled with an entitlement to a re-assignment back once the secured obligation has been performed, it is an assignment by way of legal mortgage.

There are different types of assignments. Modern commerce dictates invariably that life insurance policies are assigned in order to secure loan facility. The decision of *Brodie and Rayner Ltd v British Guiana and Trinidad Mutual Fire Insurance Co.*[135] illustrates the assignment of the policy as security. The assignment was enforceable in equity. An assignment of rights under a contract

---

135 9 WIR 253.

is normally restricted to the benefit of the contract. Where a party wishes to transfer both the benefit and burden of the contract, this generally needs to be done by way of a novation. The distinction between assignment and novation was addressed in *Davies v Jones*, whereby the court considered whether a deed of assignment of the rights under a contract could in addition transfer an affirmative contractual obligation – the obligation to pay. Both assignment and novation are common within the construction industry of relevance to indemnity insurance. Assignments are frequently used in relation to collateral warranties, whereby the benefit of a contract is transferred to a third party. Likewise, an assignment of rights to a third party with an interest in a project may be suitable when the employer still needs to fulfil certain obligations under the contract, for example, where works are still in progress. A novation is appropriate where the original contracting party wants the obligations under the contract to rest with a third party.[136]

Assignment of the subject matter

At common law, a vendor under a contract for the sale of land has always been regarded as a constructive trustee for the purchaser pending completion.[137] In the situation of property sold or otherwise disposed of by the insured, the matter at issue is the status of the insurance. The assignment of the subject matter of an insurance policy cannot simultaneously assign the insurance to which the subject matter is subject. Once contracts for the sale of land are exchanged, the purchaser obtains an equitable interest in the property, although the vendor retains legal title. On completion of the purchase, or where the title to the land is registered, upon registration of the purchaser as proprietor, the legal estate vests in the purchaser and the vendor ceases to have an insurable interest.[138] If between contract and completion the purchaser does not insure, the issue is whether, in the absence of an assignment of the benefit of the policy, the purchaser can claim under the policy of insurance. Undoubtedly, the vendor is entitled to recover since he still has an insurable interest to the extent of the unpaid interest in the property. Uncertainty, however, surrounds whether the vendor holds any insurance monies that he might receive for the benefit of the purchaser as constructive trust.[139] In *Rayner v Preston*,[140] before the sale was completed, fire destroyed the property that was the subject matter of an insurance policy.

> Preston received the full agreed purchase price from Rayner. An action was brought by Rayner claiming that the assignment of the property to him operated also to assign the benefit of the insurance. Rayner argued that following the contract of sale Preston held the land and the insurance contract on trust for him. The Court of Appeal by a majority denied Rayner's claim holding the insurance contract was merely collateral to the main contract and that the relationship between vendor and purchaser of land was not generally that of trustee and beneficiary.

The absence of an express assignment of the insurance policy or monies was not in issue. In effect the vendor was unjustly enriched, being paid twice for the property. Subsequently in *Castellain v Preston*,[141] Preston was liable to repay the insurance monies. This principle also applies to

---

136 This is commonly seen in a design and build scenario, whereby the employer novates the consultants' contracts to the contractor, so that the benefit and burden of the appointments are transferred, and the employer benefits from a single point of responsibility in the form of the contractor.
137 Supra n. 55.
138 *Ecclesiastical Commissioner v Royal Exchange Assurance Corp.* (1895) 11 TLR 476.
139 *Collingridge v Royal Exchange Assurance Corp.* (1877) 3 QBD 173.
140 (1881) 18 Ch D 1.
141 (1883) 11 QBD 380.

insurance on goods.[142] Where a specific good is being sold, the conveyance itself may operate as a conveyance of the property, in which case the vendor will be able to insure only if he retains actual possession. If the sale has been completed, the vendor no longer has an insurable interest in the subject matter and his policy will lapse automatically. It is against this background that Section 47 of the Law Property Act must be examined.

Relevance of the Law of Property Act 1925

As with the Life Assurance Act of 1774, Married Women's Property Act of 1882, Marine Insurance Act of 1906,[143] Marine Insurance (Gambling Policies) Act of 1909[144] and Gaming Act of 1845,[145] the UK's Law of Property Act of 1925[146] was similarly received in the Commonwealth Caribbean.[147] This Act, which is relevant to all contracts of indemnity, provides the foundation for an understanding of insurable interest and assignment.

While an assignment of the subject matter does of itself assign the benefits under the insurance policy, the benefit can be expressly assigned. Benefit relates not to the policy itself but to the right to recover any benefits as a chose in action. The benefit under an insurance policy is an intangible piece of property which can be assigned either at law under Section 136 or in equity.[148] In order to bind the insurer, making him directly liable to pay the assignee, the law demands that notice must be provided. Failure to provide the insurer with notice will restrict the assignee to suing the assignor to compel him to claim from the insurer. Such an assignment can take place before or after loss,[149] and the consent of the insurer is irrelevant.[150] This has enabled the development of viatical settlements.[151] A viatical settlement, also called a life settlement, is an agreement in which a life policyholder assigns ownership of the policy.[152] In the Caribbean, since viatical settlements are essentially collective investment schemes, reform of securities legislation is currently being undertaken to broaden its scope to accommodate this. The assignee's right to the policy proceeds mirrors the assignor's rights so that the assignee's rights will be hampered by any rights the insurer possesses to avoid the policy for non-disclosure or breach of warranty.

Statutory assignment

The Law of Property Act of 1925 (UK) Sections 205(1) and 47(1)[153] provides:

> where after the date of any contract for the sale or exchange of property, money becomes payable under any policy of insurance maintained by the vendor in respect of any damage to or destruction of property included in the contract, the money shall, on completion of the contract,

---

142 *Rogerson v Scottish Automobile & General Insurance Co. Ltd* (1931) 48 TLR 17; *Tattersall v Drysdale* [1935] 2 KB 174.
143 Supra n. 13.
144 9 Edw. 7 c. 12.
145 Supra n. 4.
146 15 & 16 Geo. 5 c. 20.
147 Owusu, supra n. 33.
148 A mortgagor's covenant to insure operates as an equitable assignment in favour of the mortgagee. *Clerical Mutual General Insurance Co. Ltd v ANZ Banking Group (New Zealand) Ltd* [1995] 3 All ER 987.
149 *Tailby v Official Receiver* (1888) 13 App Cas 523; *Peters v General Accident Fire & Life Assurance Corp. Ltd* [1937] 4 All ER 628.
150 *Re Turcan* (1888) 40 Ch D 5.
151 In the United States, several states have introduced legislation regulating viatical settlements. See Pennsylvania Viatical Settlements Act 2003.
152 See www.insurance.state.pa.us.
153 Section 136.

be held by or receivable by the vendor on behalf of the purchaser and paid by the vendor to the purchaser on completion of the sale or exchange, or as soon thereafter as the same shall be received by the vendor.

By virtue of Subsection (2), once (a) there are no stipulations to the contrary in the contract; (b) the consent of the insurers, if required, is obtained; and (c) payment by the purchaser of the proportionate part of the premium is made,[154] the policy may contain a condition giving its benefit to any purchaser rendering the consent of the insurers unnecessary.[155] Section 47 of the Law of Property Act of 1925 overruled the decision of *Rayner v Preston*.[156] The statute removed the need for express assignment where the parties are vendor and purchaser of property, whether land or goods. Section 47 was cited and applied in the decision of *Rambally v Barbados Fire & General Insurance Co. Ltd et al.*[157] arising out of the jurisdiction of St Lucia. Here the High Court recognised that a party to a contract can constitute himself as trustee for a third party, under Article 916A of the Civil Code.[158] This article provides that implied, constructive and resulting trusts shall arise under the law of St Lucia in the same circumstances as they arise under the law of England

> . . . (3) Subject to the provisions of this code or of any other statute the law of England for the time being in force governing the right, powers and duties of trustees and beneficiaries under a trust shall extend to and apply in . . . St Lucia. (4) Whenever by the law of England a beneficiary of trust is entitled to a right in equity, a beneficiary shall be entitled to a like right under this Code.

In construing Section 47 of the Law of Property Act, the limitations of the statute were ignored. The section does not give the purchaser any direct rights against the insurer as he does have where there has been an express assignment under Section 136. The mechanics of Section 47 consider whether statutory assignment pertains to the contract of insurance itself or whether it merely pertains to benefits payable thereunder. On a literal interpretation, 'monies payable' imports that the provision applies to the money payable under the policy rather than an assignment of the policy itself. This brings to the fore the dispute surrounding the construction of Subsection (2) and the requirement of consent. The effect of *Rayner v Preston* may be mitigated by an assignment of the benefit, but it may not be possible where the insurer has refused consent. Persuasive authorities dispel the assumption that 'any requisite consents' means any consent actually required in the policy. The requirement seems to refer to the specific need for express consent of the insurer. Most insurance policies do contain a clause giving the purchaser the benefit of insurance. This clause additionally will have the effect of disallowing the insurer from exercising subrogation rights in the vendor's name against the purchaser.[159]

Novation

You have to novate the burden of a contract as well as the benefits under it. Like assignment, novation transfers the benefits under a contract, but unlike assignment, novation transfers the burden under a contract as well.

In a novation, the original contract is extinguished and is replaced by a new one in which a third party takes up rights and obligations which duplicate those of one of the original parties

---

154 Section 47(2)(a)(2); Section 47(2)(c).
155 Section 47(2)(b), (3).
156 Supra n. 140.
157 Supra n. 3.
158 St Lucia, Cap 242.
159 M. Parkington and N. Legh-Jones, *MacGillivray & Parkington on Insurance Law*, 6th edn (Sweet & Maxwell: 1975), p. 917, para. 20.

to the contract. Novation does not cancel past rights and obligations under the original contract, although the parties can agree to novate these as well.

Novation is only possible with the consent of the original contracting parties as well as the new party. Consideration (the 'price' paid, whether financial or otherwise, by the new party in return for the contract being novated to it) must be provided for this new contract unless the novation is documented in a deed signed by all three parties.

Conclusion

The position in the Commonwealth Caribbean is that although guidance is attained by regional Marine Insurance Acts – replicas of the 1906 Marine Insurance Act – little common law exists. The question of insurable interest in indemnity insurance is recognised in the St Lucia decision of *Rambally*, which commented on the common law tests postulated in the *locus classicus* decision *Lucena v Craufurd*. It is from the terms of the policy in light of the nature of the subject matter that determines the test of insurable interest. There is no rigid rule that because the nature of an insurable interest relates to liability it should be contained in a liability insurance policy. The question whether the policy embraces the insurable interest intended to be covered remains a question of construction. As it currently stands, the law pertaining to insurable interest in property insurance appears to be in a state of flux. Within the several identifiable categories of insurable interest in property insurance, the type of interest cuts across boundaries, compounding the difficulty. There is no solid rule as to approach. Typically, the proprietary or contractual interest will operate. But insurable interest has been held to exist in circumstances considered not strictly pecuniary, and the broader factual expectancy test, while useful, is similarly not coherently determinative of the issue as demonstrable from the seminal decisions of *Deepak Fertilisers & Petrochemical Corp. v Davy McKee (London) Ltd & ICI Chemicals & Polymers Ltd*, criticised in the decision of *Feasey v Sun Life Assurance Corp. of Canada; Steamship Mutual Underwriting Association Bermuda) Ltd v Feasey*, which both display different approaches to the question of insurable interest. Also, as Birds reminds us, the earlier House of Lords decisions still stand. Inextricably intertwined with indemnity insurance is the availability of assignment. This especially occurs in the case of construction projects. If the assignment is equitable rather than legal, the assignor cannot enforce the assigned property in its own name and to do so must join the assignee in any action. This is designed to protect the debtor from later proceedings brought by the assignor or another assignee from enforcing the action without notice of the earlier assignment. In a novation, the original contract is extinguished and is replaced by a new one in which a third party takes up rights and obligations which duplicate those of one of the original parties to the contract. Novation does not cancel past rights and obligations under the original contract, although the parties can agree to novate these as well.

CHAPTER 6

THE STATUS OF THE BENEFICIARY
IN LIFE INSURANCE

6.1   INTRODUCTION

Twenty-first-century legislation introduced distinct categories of beneficiaries: revocable and irrevocable. This reform replaced an inadequate framework highlighted in the recent Caribbean Court of Justice decision *Katrina Smith v Selby*[1] which highlighted Caribbean societal family dynamics; inadequacies of the Succession Act, Married Women's Property Acts; and the common law:[2]

> The Act was social legislation to address one of the realities of Caribbean society that had not been reflected in the common law or statute law inherited or adopted from England. Persons living together as man and wife but who were not married to each other and their children had not been recognized in the colonial legal and juridical regime, with unfair results.[3]

Status of the beneficiary in life insurance logically falls into three distinct periods. The first reflects British colonial control, with the beneficiary's status governed by eighteenth- and nineteenth-century UK legislation. In this dispensation the beneficiary was forced to circumvent the vagaries of trust, succession and contract law. This prevailed until the twentieth century, identified here as the second phase (nationalistic or formative) which recognised significant elements of Caribbean family structure (the actual relationships) that normally provide the objectives governing the need for life insurance. The third phrase results partly from crises: marketplace disruption, insolvency of insurance giants bearing household names and major failures of corporate governance. These events became the catalysts both for Jamaica at the end of the twentieth century and the Organisation of Eastern Caribbean States (OECS) and Trinidad and Tobago in the first decade of the twenty-first century.

6.2   SUMMARY

Historically, life insurance policies contain room – a blank slot – requiring the insured 'fill in' the space by inserting the name(s) of the beneficiary: spouse, child, family member or personal representative. During this era, however, the law remained unclear and uncertain with respect to the nature and effect of that insertion or declaration. Indeed, it has been convincingly argued that for the Commonwealth Caribbean,

> this is probably the most controversial topic in the mainstream of life insurance law and at the same time one which produces, in terms of advice-work, the most activity for lawyers and the most anguish for policyholders, their friends and family.[4]

The rights of beneficiaries to claim under a life insurance policy are determined by the common law and statute. The beneficiary's interest in the common law ultimately depends on the

---

1   *Katrina Smith v Albert Anthony Peter Selby*, CCJ BB Civil Appeal No. 14 of 2010; *Re Osborne Hall v Bleasdille* (1991) 2 OECS Law Rep at 215.
2   An unmarried woman with whom the deceased was cohabiting up until his death.
3   Supra n. 1.
4   C. H. Denbow, *Life Insurance Law in the Commonwealth Caribbean* (Butterworths: 1984).

existence of a trust. Thus, the insured must have clearly alienated the policy proceeds in favour of the beneficiary.[5] With respect to statute, residually the Life Assurance Act of 1774[6] requires the insertion of the 'name for whose use and benefit the policy is effected,' while more importantly the Married Women's Property Act of 1882[7] creates a statutory trust in favour of the beneficiary in defined circumstances. This nineteenth-century legislation represented the law in most Caribbean jurisdictions. The result is that two distinct groups emerge. At one end of the spectrum are jurisdictions where radical reform has been conducted, driven by the Caribbean Law Institute's (CLI) recommendations – broad sweeping reform introducing the clearly defined categories of beneficiaries of revocable and irrevocable designations. The result is that irrevocable beneficiaries are empowered to the extent that the common law doctrine of privity of contract virtually ceases to exist.[8] At the other end of the spectrum are those jurisdictions which have not adopted the CLI's reforms, like Belize, so the law can only be understood by reference to the common law, the Life Insurance Act of 1774 and the Married Women's Property Act of 1883. Between these two extremes is the jurisdiction of Trinidad and Tobago, where hybrid reform has been introduced relaxing the narrow requirements of the Married Women's Property legislation, but not to the extent of the CLI recommendations.

6.3   RELEVANCE OF THE LIFE ASSURANCE ACT OF 1774

Section 2 of the Life Assurance Act of 1774[9] stipulates that persons for whose 'use, benefit, or on whose account' a policy is effected must be inserted. A failure to observe this requirement renders the contract 'unlawful.'[10] While the rationale for this provision is to counteract an avoidance of Section 1, discussed in Chapter 4, the relationship between Sections 1 and 2 is uncertain. The common law reveals that the term for 'whose use, benefit or on whose account' is given somewhat of a restrictive definition and it does not necessarily include all persons who are ultimately intended to benefit under insurance.[11] The fact that some person paid the premium is not conclusive to show that the policy was effected on behalf of that person even if that person in fact obtained the benefit of the policy. In *Wainwright v Bland*,[12] although Miss Abercromby 'paid' the premiums on a policy effected on her own life, the policy was held to be illegal since, on the evidence, she could not afford the premiums on her own without the assistance of her brother-in-law, who the court suspected had brought about her demise. In *Shilling v Accidental Death Insurance Co.*,[13] a father effected a policy on his own life. Parol evidence was admissible to support the contention that the assured's son, who paid the premiums, filled out the proposal form and who was a beneficiary under the assured's will, was indeed entitled to receive the benefit. Since the son lacked insurable interest in the life of the father, the policy

---

5   *Collett v Morrison* (1851) 9 Hare 162.
6   14 Geo. III, c. 48.
7   45 & 46 Vict. c. 75; the Bahamas Married Women's Property Act Chapter 115; Barbados Married Persons Act, Cap 219; Guyana Married Person's (Property) Act Chapter 45:04; Jamaica Married Women's Property Act, Cap 239; Law Reform Married Women's and Tortfeasor's Act 1935; Section 19, Married Women's Property Act of St Kitts and Nevis, Cap 12.11.
8   Section 120, Barbados Insurance Act of 1996, Cap 310 abrogates the contract law principle and expressly states that the 'beneficiary may enforce for his own benefit even though there is no privity of contract.' See also Section 139, Guyana Insurance Act No. 20 of 1998; Section 105, Jamaica Insurance Act No. 10 of 2001.
9   Supra n. 6.
10 J. Birds, *Modern Insurance Law*, 6th edn (Sweet & Maxwell: 2014), p. 81; *Wainwright v Bland* (1835) 1 Moo & R 481; *Shilling v Accidental Death Insurance Co.* (1857) 2 H & N 42.
11 *Mc Farlane v Royal London Friendly Society* (1886) 2 TLR 755.
12 (1835) 1 Moo & R 481.
13 (1858) 1 F & F 116.

was not upheld.[14] Thus, the circumstances must be considered against the totality of evidence. The 1774 Act demands that a distinction be made between an insertion of the name of persons interested, and assignment or testamentary disposition. Sections 1 and 2 of the 1774 Act pertain to the former and are not intended to cover the situation where the object of the insurance is to secure himself property which he may later dispose of on his demise. In the latter case, discussed further below, there is no requirement to show that the ultimate beneficiary had any interest in the life of the assured.

6.4 APPLICATION OF MARRIED WOMEN'S PROPERTY ACT OF 1882

Historically, prior to the implementation of regional reform, the simplest way to create a trust was under regional Married Women's Property legislation.[15] The origin of regional Married Women's Property legislation can be traced to the UK Married Women's Property Act of 1882[16] (MWPA). The MWPA creates a statutory trust of life policies in cases where, apart from the Act, they would not be created. Section 11 provides:

> A policy of assurance effected by a man on his own life, and expressed to be for the benefit of his wife, or of his children, or of his wife and children, or any of them, or by any woman on her own life, and expressed to be for the benefit of her husband, or of her children, or any of them, shall create a trust in favour of the objects therein named, and the moneys payable under any such policy shall not, so long as any object of the trust remains unperformed, form part of the estate of the insured or be subject to his or her debts.
>
> Provided that if it shall be proved that the policy was effected and the premium paid with intent to defraud the creditors of the insured, they shall be entitled to receive, out of money payable under the policy, a sum equal to the premiums so paid.

The UK Married Women's Property legislation operates throughout the Commonwealth Caribbean, as is reflected, for instance, in Section 2 of the Jamaica Married Women's Property Act,[17] which provides, *inter alia*:

> a married woman shall:
>
> (a) be capable of acquiring, holding and disposing of any property; and
>
> (b) be capable of rendering herself, and being rendered liable in respect of tort, contract, debt, or obligation; and

---

14 See also *Wainwright v Bland* (1835) 1 Moo & R 481.

15 The Bahamas Married Women's Property Act Chapter 115; Barbados Married Persons Act, Cap 219; Guyana Married Person's (Property) Act Chapter 45:04; Jamaica Married Women's Property Act, Cap 239; UK Law Reform Married Women and Tortfeasor's Act 1935; Section 19 of the St Kitts and Nevis Married Women's Property Act, Cap 12.11 allows married women to retain property owned at the time of the marriage and during the marriage as separate property. It provides that 'In any question between husband and wife as to the title to or possession of property,' either of them can apply to the Court for an order and the judge 'may make such order with respect to the property in dispute . . . as he thinks fit.' This confers on the court a jurisdiction to determine ownership of the property of the parties to the marriage. The MWPA does not give the court power to vary existing titles and no wider power to transfer or create interest in property than it would have in any other type of proceedings. See further *Pettit v Pettit* [1970] AC 777; *Tittle v Tittle* (1976) 23 WIR 174. Therefore the court will simply declare the parties' interest based on common law principles of the law of trust and property.

16 Supra n. 7.

17 Cap 239.

(c) be capable of suing and being sued, either in tort or in contract or otherwise; and

(d) be subject to the law relating to bankruptcy and to enforcement of judgments and order,

in all respects as if she were a *femme sole*.

This legislation operates as the ground for recognition of the rights of beneficiary in insurance law. As outlined in *Matheson v Matheson*,[18] referring to the MWPA, Pompey J states:

> Now this Section speaks of 'wife' of the assured and there is nothing in the Act to indicate that the word 'wife' is not used in the strict legal sense, as it is quite well established that wife means legal wife of the person insured. This policy was originally taken out to benefit his estate on maturity, at a time when he was legally married to the applicant who was not expressly for benefit of his reputed wife.

It was impossible to bring the benefit of the Act, as she was never married to the insured person but merely a 'common law' wife. As such, though the intention of the assured was to benefit the respondent on his death, the law does not create a trust in her favour in view of her peculiar position. But if the Act does not create a trust, it is difficult to see how such trust can be created otherwise. Several English cases *Re: Clay's Policy of Assurance, Clay v Earnshaw* [1937] 2 All E.R. 548; *Re: Sinclair's Policy* [1939] 2 All E.R. 125 . . . were referred to applying Section 11 of the *Married Person's Property Act*[19] (identical to Section 11 of the *Married Woman's Property Act*, 1882 of England) The English authorities arising thereunder are worthy of careful consideration.: – "Having considered the authorities which I found very persuasive and the evidence, I have regretfully come to the conclusion that although there has been an assignment by the Insurance Company this was executed without regard being paid to Section 11 of Cap. 45:04 and finally that there had been no gift in law or trust created in favour of the respondent."[20]

The significance of the implementation of the Married Women's Property legislation can be understood by a brief examination of the socioeconomic climate of the nineteenth century.[21] Previously the common law treated married women as having no capacity to hold property in their own right. Any property held by a woman at her marriage became the property of her husband. She could take comfort in the fact that under the common law, if she survived him, she became entitled to a proportion of his property as 'dower.' As Hancombe observes:

> The common law regarded a woman's husband as her guardian, under whose 'wing' protection and cover she lived, moved and had no legal being. But equity, generally considered to be the guardian of the weak and unprotected, such as married women, infants and lunatics, tend to view a woman's husband as the 'enemy' and against his exorbitant common law rights the Court of Chancery waged constant war.[22]

During this period, the assumption at common law that married women needed protection was being gradually eroded due, *inter alia*, to the breakdown of the doctrines and power of

---

18 GY 1980 HC 17.
19 Chapter 45:04.
20 Pompey J states that:

> it follows therefore that I must find that the policy money lodged in court, that is, $13,590.16 must be paid to the Estate of James Horita Matheson, deceased, under provisions of the Deceased Persons' Estates Administration Act Chapter 12:01 less an amount representing 24 payments of $40.41 which should be paid to the respondent Claudette Crawford. Funeral and other legitimate expenses incurred by on behalf of the estate should be paid by the legal representative out of the said estate according to law. And the court so orders.

21 See further S. Ingham and K. Inwood, 'Property Ownership by Married Women in Victorian Ontario,' (1997) *Dalhousie L.J.* 406.
22 L. Hancombe, *Wives and Property* (University of Toronto Press: 1983), pp. 37–42.

the established Church and the rise of the Reformation movement. Changes in landholding patterns accompanied the emergence of a bourgeois class whose wealth derived from commerce and industry, in part facilitating ascendency of the women's rights movement. These combined to influence a change in society's attitude towards women. Thus, MWPA legislation allowed women to retain property owned both at the time of and during marriage, as separate property, bestowing contractual capacity on married women as *femme sole*, enabling a married woman to effect a policy upon her own life or the life of her husband for her own benefit.[23]

6.5 ANALYSIS

The predominant limitation of the MWPA concerns its application. Only a restricted class of beneficiaries can claim entitlement applying narrowly to 'own-life' policies. Further, by referring to the traditional family unit of 'husband and wife,' 'other unions' such as common law unions fall outside the parameters of the statute.[24] With respect to children, prior to the introduction of Status of Children legislation in the region, a child born outside of marriage was unable to be benefit under the trust.[25]

The MWPA creates a statutory trust, insulating the policy proceeds from claims on the estate by creditors and as a trustee, the insured, is subject to the duties imposed on trustees to act in the best interests of the beneficiaries. In order to resolve whether or not a beneficiary is entitled to the policy proceeds, the policy of insurance must be construed in light of the language of the MWPA. The question of the beneficiary's entitlement to the policy proceeds is answered in part by the Bahamian decision of *Imperial Life Assurance Co. v Adderley*,[26] which is instructive on the approach to be adopted. In this case, the husband's own-life policy named his wife as beneficiary with the provision that if she predeceased him, the insurance money would be payable to him (if living) and to his estate (if he had died). The policy further allowed the granting of loans on security of the policy, provided for an automatic premium loan whereby any unpaid premium could be satisfied, and provided for payment of net value and the exercise of paid-up policy options. It was contended that these powers, the exercise of which rested with the policyholder, were inconsistent with the existence of a trust originating from the insurance of the policy. In rejecting this contention, Georges CJ, finding in favour of a trust, opined:

> The terms of the policy are therefore important in determining the circumstances under which the beneficiary becomes entitled to the sum payable under the trust or circumstances under which the objects of the trust have been performed or are no longer capable of being performed. Whether or not there is a trust depends entirely on whether the policy is one which falls within the terms of s. 7 of the Act. Should Mrs Stirrup predecease Mr Stirrup . . . the trusts would end because in the language of the Act, the object of the trust could no longer be performed. The trust lasts only as long as any object of it remains unperformed.

---

23 St Kitts and Nevis Married Women's Property Act, Cap 328; Belize Married Women's Property Act Chapter 142.
24 See for instance Section 127, Barbados Insurance Act, Cap 310; Section 96, Jamaica Insurance Act No. 26 of 2001.
25 Anguilla Law Reform (Illegitimate) Ordinance 1982; Antigua and Barbuda Status of Children Act 1986; Barbados Status of Children (Reform) Act 1979; Belize Families and Children Act 1998; Grenada Status of Children Act 1991; Guyana Children Born of Wedlock (Removal of Discrimination) Act 1983.
26 Unreported decision, Supreme Court of the Bahamas No. 169 of 1987.

The MWPA recognises that where the objects of the trust are incapable of being fulfilled, the policy monies will revert to the estate on a resulting trust.[27] As the case law reveals, the problem confronting the beneficiary lies in the limited scope of the MWPA, a limitation which propelled some Caribbean jurisdictions to embrace the CLI's approach so that the Married Women's Property Legislation, more particularly the Section 11 equivalent, has been repealed.[28]

6.6   POSITION AT COMMON LAW

In jurisdictions where the beneficiary is forced to rely substantially on the common law, he or she is confronted with several difficulties. First, there is overall an onerous evidential burden to prove the existence of a trust. Unless a trust is clearly established, the beneficiary's entitlement can only be described as vulnerable, as his 'entitlement' is subject to modification or destruction by the insured. Further, at common law, the doctrine of privity of contract operates precluding the beneficiary, as a third party, from enforcing the contract and enjoying the policy proceeds. Also, considerable uncertainty exists at common law as to whether a designation under an insurance policy must satisfy the formalities required under the Wills Act[29] and Succession Act. In accordance with Section 9 of the Wills Act the testator must attest and sign the will or acknowledge his signature in the presence of the witness. They must do so after the testator has signed or acknowledged it. It is not essential that they sign in each other's presence.

A failure to adhere to requirements under Succession of Wills legislation thus may render the designation void,[30] so that the common law 'suffers from an undue emphasis on the testamentary or not testamentary nature of nominations with the consequential conclusion of the applicability of the Wills Act and hence the validity or invalidity of the designation.'[31]

6.7   THE DIFFICULTY IN ESTABLISHING
THE EXISTENCE OF A TRUST

It has been stated that the courts' 'discovery of an actual trust would appear, in practice, to be restricted to that created by legislative means.'[32] As stated earlier, in the past the easiest way to constitute a trust was under the Married Women's Property Act of 1882.[33] As far as common law is concerned, the case law illustrates the difficulty of establishing entitlement. Apart from statute, there must be a clear intention to create a trust. The phrase 'for the benefit of' a third party will not of itself be sufficient to give that third party any right of property or interest in it. If on the other hand the third party is a husband, wife or child, the words 'for the benefit of,' as

---

27   *Cleaver v Mutual Reserve Fund Life Association* [1892] 1 QB 147.
28   *Re Fleetwood* [1926] 1 Ch 48; *Re Cooks Settlement Trusts* [1965] Ch 902; *Swain v Law Society* [1983] AC 598; *Re Webb, Barclays Bank Ltd v Webb* [1941] All ER 321; *Vandepitte v Preferred Accident Insurance Corp. of New York* [1932] All ER 527; *Re Schebsman, Exp, The Official Receiver* [1943] 2 All ER 768.
29   Barbados Wills Act, Cap 251, wherein the testator and first witness signed without the presence of the second. In Section 9 of the Wills Act, anyone who wishes to make a will must have attained the age of 18 or be married. The Succession Act states that for a will to be valid it must be written, signed by the testator or by a representative of the testator in his presence, and the signing attested to by two or more witnesses. This raises the presumption of due execution and the presumption is a strong one.
30   Barbados Succession Act, Cap 249.
31   Anderson, 'Policies of Life Assurance' [1996] *Anglo-Amer. L. Rev.* 221.
32   Ibid., 232.
33   Supra n. 7.

used in the Act, will suffice, but if the third party is not a husband, wife or child, then there must be clear intention by stating that the policy is effected as 'trustee.' Where a policy is effected for the benefit of a named wife or child, the identity of the beneficiary is clear. But where there is reference to a relationship only, it is necessary to construe the policy so as to ascertain who are in fact to be beneficiaries. It must also be noted that the legal right to sue upon a contract must be distinguished from the equitable right to enforce an obligation under trust.

Clearly an effective trust may be constituted outside the Act, if a clear intention can be deduced from the construction of the trust instrument. A trust is said to be completely constituted when the trust property has been vested in trustees for the benefit of beneficiaries either by conveyance to trustees or by declaration. An imperfect conveyance to the trustees will be treated as a contract to convey and the courts will see that it is perfected. However, there is no equity to perfect an imperfect voluntary trust.[34] The burden of establishing a trust at common law, and the emphasis placed by the courts on the form, often result in the expectation of the insured not being met so that in most cases, the policy proceeds fall to the estate. The common law is replete with examples of the considerable difficulty confronting the beneficiary.[35] At common law, three certainties are required to establish a trust: certainty of words,[36] certainty of subject matter[37] and certainty of objects.[38] The absence of any one of these is fatal: the courts require cogent evidence that the nominator intended to alienate his property and impose upon himself the onerous duties of trustee. In *Re Englebach's Estate*,[39] it was held that an endowment policy taken out by the insured in his own name for the benefit of his daughter, to mature on her attaining a specified age, created no legal estate in the daughter and thus she could not sue on the contract. By simply using the term 'for his daughter' as opposed to 'on behalf of his daughter of the policy monies payable thereunder,' the assured had not properly constituted himself as trustee, so that if the assured died before the policy matured, the policy money fell to the assured's estate upon a resulting trust. The court held that the policy belonged to the executors of the father. Similarly, in the decision of *Re Sinclair Life Policy*,[40] where an own-life policy was expressed to be 'for the benefit of his god-child,' who was described as the 'nominee,' the circumstances were held to be insufficient to prove any trust in favour of the nominee.[41]

The difficulty in ascertaining whether a trust exists is compounded when the beneficiary is unnamed in the insurance policy. In such circumstances it is necessary to construe the policy to ascertain precisely who the beneficiary is. The insured may have remarried several times since the policy was effected, making it necessary for the court to construe the policy to ascertain if the policy proceeds are intended for the present wife, the second wife, third wife or widow (as the case may be). This issue arose in *Re Griffith's Policy*.[42] Here the policy was expressed to be for the benefit of his wife, 'or if she be dead between his children in equal proportions.' The wife died, leaving eight children, and the assured remarried. On the assured's death, the court held that the presence of the words 'If she be dead' indicated that the wife living at the time the policy was effected was intended to benefit. In *Wood v James*,[43] the policy contained a clause 'for

34 E. H. T. Snell, R. Megarry and P. V. Baker, *Snell's Principles of Equity*, 24th edn (Sweet & Maxwell: 1954), pp. 105–110, 114–117.
35 Supra n. 27; *Re Schebsman* [1943] 2 All ER 768; *Re Osbourne* (1991) 2 OECS Law Rep 215; *Ramnarine v Kowsilia* (unreported decision, Supreme Court of Guyana No. 3033 of 1971).
36 *Re Kayford* [1975] 1 WLR 279.
37 *Re Golays WT* [1965] 2 All ER 660.
38 *Mc Phall v Doulton* [1971] AC 424.
39 [1924] 2 Ch 348.
40 [1938] Ch 799.
41 Ibid.
42 [1903] 1 Ch 739.
43 (1954) 92 CLR 142.

the absolute benefit of the wife of the assured, should the amount of the assurance become payable during her life time, failing which, for the absolute benefit of such children of the assured as shall survive the assured.' The wife died and the husband remarried. The husband then died, leaving his second wife and three children of the first marriage. The policy was held to benefit the wife existing at the time the policy was effected. Consequently, the policy monies went to the children. This can be contrasted with the decision of *Re Parker's Policies*.[44] Here, the assured effected a policy on his life and made the policy monies payable to the 'widow and children.' The first wife died and the assured appointed his second wife as beneficiary under the policy. It was held that on the death of the assured, the second wife who became his widow was entitled to the policy proceeds. The decision of *Re Browne's Policy*[45] illustrates that where it is impossible to glean upon a construction of the policy the intention of the assured, overwhelming policy considerations will prevail. In this decision, the words used in the policy were 'for the benefit of his wife and children.' The wife living at the date of the policy died; the assured was survived by the second wife and all the children from both marriages. It was held that the second wife and all the children benefitted from the policy proceeds as a matter of principle. This decision appears to be in conflict with the earlier decision of *Wood v James*,[46] which arose out of the Australian High Court. In *Wood*, the court stated that the 'wife in contemplation was more likely to be the existing wife than some hypothetical future wife.' The decision of *Re Browne's Policy* can however be understood as an example of judicial focus on the wife's interest being abandoned for that of the family unit, because of the language used in the policy.

An insurance policy effected by a husband or wife and expressed to be for the wife or husband creates in that beneficiary a vested or contingent interest.[47] Where the marriage comes to an end, the question as to the disposition of the beneficiary's interest arises as divorce does not automatically terminate the trust created by the policy. An application for an order varying the trust must be made under ancillary Matrimonial Proceedings legislation. Section 26(1)(c) of the Matrimonial Proceedings and Property Act[48] provides for an order varying the benefit of the parties to the marriage and of the children of the family or either or any of them any ante-nuptial or post-nuptial settlement (including such a settlement made by will or codicil) made on the parties to the marriage. In *Gunner v Gunner and Stirling*,[49] the husband successfully applied to the court for an order, varying the policy as a settlement. Similarly, in the Trinidad and Tobago decision of *Gulbenkian v Gulbenkian*,[50] the husband successfully requested an order varying the trusts resulting in the Court striking out the name of the wife on the insurance policy. It is clear that insurance policies will be treated as post-nuptial settlements within the language of ancillary matrimonial legislation.[51]

Another consideration that arises is where the interest of the beneficiary is not for whole extent of the policy monies but is limited by the use of appropriate words. Such an example may be seen in *Re Fleetwood's Policy*,[52] where a husband effected a policy on his wife if she be

---

44   [1906] 1 Ch 526.
45   Supra n. 42.
46   Supra n. 43.
47   Supra n. 4, pp. 116 *et seq.*
48   Trinidad and Tobago Matrimonial Proceedings and Property Act Chapter 45:51.
49   [1949] p. 77.
50   [1927] p. 237.
51   *Gulbenkian v Gulbenkian* [1927] p. 237; *Gunner v Gunner and Stirling* [1949] p. 77; *Lori-Williams v Lori-Williams* [1951] p. 395; see further Denbow, supra n. 4, p. 130.
52   [1926] Ch 48.

living at his death but otherwise to his executors. The policy reserved to him various options as trustee, one of which he exercised. The court held that he had exercised his option as trustee and that the trusts attached to the resulting benefit. The policy was expressed to be for the benefit of the wife in a certain event only, but the fact that her interest was of a limited contingent character did not prevent the policy from being a policy within the Act. In *Re Ioakimidis' Policy Trusts, Ioakimidis v Hartcup*,[53] a husband effected an endowment assurance expressed to be for the benefit of his wife only in the event of his death before a stipulated date. The assured died prior to the date stipulated and the creditors claimed the monies. The Court found that the policy fell within the scope of the Act; a valid trust was created since the condition had been satisfied. This case lends further to the principle that the beneficiary's interest may be made contingent on the occurrence of a particular event.

Where the policy refers to for the benefit of his wife and children, the wife and children take as joint tenants.[54] Where the beneficiary is the child only, it is now irrelevant that the child is adopted or born outside of marriage.[55] Their interest may be made contingent on attaining the age of 21 or on surviving the assured. Generally the children who are entitled are those living at the time when the fund comes into existence.[56] If a trust is affirmatively established, the policy proceeds are automatically vested in the beneficiary. The policyholder is no longer free to assign or surrender of the policy proceeds and is prevented from withdrawing dividends or using the policy as security for a loan unless those powers are expressly reserved at the time of designation. An express reservation enables the insured to enjoy dividends and enjoy rights under the policy. This can be seen from the Trinidad and Tobago decision of *Etta Verselles v New York Life Assurance Co.*[57] Here, the assured effected policies on his own life for the benefit of his daughter. The sums assured were stated to be payable 'less any indebtedness thereto due to the insurance company.' Further, the assured expressly reserved the right to exercise 'every right and enjoy every privilege conferred by the insurance company, on security of the policies, without consent of the beneficiary.' It was held that on the death of the assured, loans effected by the insured on security of the policy, were deductible. Thus, the decision illustrates that the statutory trust created by the Married Women's Property legislation can be restricted by the assured, once those rights were expressly reserved at the time the trust was created. Further, the MWPA does not prohibit the assured from surrendering the policy without the consent of the beneficiary.[58] However, if the insured surrenders the policy, as a trustee of the policy proceeds he holds the proceeds as trustee and he is not permitted to use the sums exclusively for his personal use.

If the objects of the trust fail or are incapable of performance, the trust property reverts to the ownership and control of the person who established the trust, on a resulting trust. This arises from a construction of Section 11 of the MWPA which provides 'so long as any object remains unperformed.' Hence if no object remains to be performed, the policy monies form

---

53   [1925] 1 Ch 403.
54   *Re Griffiths' Policy* [1903] 1 Ch 739.
55   Belize Status of Children Ordinance No. 32 of 1980; Barbados Status of Children (Reform) Act No. 32 of 1979; Jamaica Status of Children Act No. 36 of 1976; Trinidad and Tobago Legitimation Act, Cap 46:04; Status of Children Act No. 17 of 1981; St Vincent and the Grenadines Status of Children Act No. 18 of 1980.
56   *Re Seyton, Seyton v Satterthwaite* (1887) 34 Ch D 511.
57   (1919–1922) TLR 161.
58   See *Mutual Life Insurance Co. of New York v Pechotsch* (1905) 2 CLR 823; *Gibb v Australian Mutual Provident Society* (1922) 23 SR (NSW) 19.

part of the estate. The rigidity of the trust under the MWPA is apparent from the common law so that once a perfect trust is created, not even death and divorce disturb the sanctity of the contract.

6.8   PRIVITY OF CONTRACT

The doctrine of privity of contract operates as a significant obstacle to the beneficiary's entitlement to the policy proceeds.[59] In accordance with the authoritative decision of *Tweddle v Atkinson*,[60] the doctrine of privity of contract establishes that only the parties to the contract can sue and be sued on the contract. Further, that there cannot be a conferral of rights or the imposition of liabilities on non-contracting parties or 'strangers,' so that third parties have no right to sue for recovery of policy proceeds on the death of the insured.

Commonwealth Caribbean courts in the absence of express statutory intervention will resort to established exceptions to the doctrine of privity of contract in order to find in favour of the beneficiary. This can be seen in the decision of *Asaram v North American Life Insurance Co.*,[61] arising out of the jurisdiction of Guyana, where the Supreme Court exhaustively reviewed the doctrine of privity of contract as it relates to policies of insurance and the status of the beneficiary. Here, the plaintiff was the reputed wife of the deceased insured, having lived together for several years. They had three children who were aged 17, 11 and 7 at the time of the proceedings. On his death, no doubt the insurance company would have had little difficulty in paying the sum insured to the plaintiff (as she was the named beneficiary in the policy), had not the lawful wife of the deceased wife evinced an interest in the money and the estate, claiming that the reputed wife was a stranger to the contract. A married man living with a woman who was not his lawful wife clearly does not satisfy the definition found in the Family and Dependents Provision Act of 1990.[62] Under this Act, a 'wife' is defined as a single (i.e. unmarried, widowed or divorced woman) living together with a single man for more than seven years before the date of death. 'Husband' is defined as including a single man living together with single woman for more than seven years before the date of death. In the absence of statutory incursion into the doctrine privity of contract, the Court was forced to apply the common law.[63] Chancellor Bishop, in finding for the reputed wife, arguably dispensed 'social equity,' but perhaps more accurately resorted to the established exceptions to the doctrine of privity of contract since on the facts, the payment by the plaintiff of the insurance premiums amounted to a collateral contract.[64] The husband of the plaintiff had, with full and actual knowledge of his power and right to choose, deliberately and specifically identified the plaintiff as the named beneficiary, contemporaneously accepted her offer to pay the monthly premiums and made a distinct

---

59   *Dunlop Pneumatic Tyre Co. Ltd v Selfridge* [1914–1915] All ER 333; but see the Law Commission Consultation Paper No. 121, *Privity of Contract: Contracts For the Benefit of Third Parties* (1991); Lord Denning's judgment in *Smith & Another v River Douglas Catchment Board* [1949] 2 All ER 179; *Northern Regional Health Authority v Derek Crouch Construction Co. Ltd* [1984] 2 All ER 175; *Norwich County Council v Harvey* [1989] 1 All ER 1180.
60   [1861–1873] All ER 369.
61   Supreme Court of Guyana No. 2366 of 1993.
62   Ibid.
63   *Re Cook's Settlement Trusts* [1965] Ch 902; *Swain v Law Society* [1983] AC 598; *Re Webb, Barclays Bank Ltd v Webb* [1941] All ER 321; *Vandepitte v Preferred Accident Insurance Corp. of New York* [1932] All ER 527; *Re Schebsman, Exp, The Official. Receiver* [1943] 2 All ER 768.
64   *Peyman v Sanjani* [1984] 3 All ER 703; *Alli-Shaw v Walloo* [1967] 11 WIR 357.

election in her favour at the expense of his estate. This constituted a legally binding collateral agreement supported by consideration.[65]

Earlier, in *Rajkumar v First Federation Life Insurance Co.*,[66] a case that preceded the legislative intervention of 1980 in Trinidad and Tobago, Rees J – in a judgment which has been described as illustrative of the functional usefulness of law as an instrument of social justice and an expression of judicial will bearing the semblance of 'judicial rationality' – found in favour of the named beneficiary despite privity of contract doctrine. The plaintiff and Dolly Rajkumar, the insured, were married according to Hindu religious rites. The marriage was never registered under the provisions of the Hindu Marriage Ordinance.[67] It followed that the parties were not legally married as husband and wife according to the law of Trinidad and Tobago. Subsequently, a policy of insurance was issued by the defendant insurance company in favour of Dolly Rajkumar, who stated in the proposal form that the premiums were to be paid by her husband and named the plaintiff as her beneficiary. The plaintiff paid the premiums and on her death, the plaintiff claimed the policy proceeds. The insurers contested liability, claiming that the plaintiff was merely a third party. It was held that the contract of insurance impliedly created a trust in favour of the plaintiff so that the action to enforce payment was upheld. Hon. Mr Justice Fraser opined:

> Perhaps the time is ripe for Law Reform Commissioners in the English-speaking Caribbean to consider legislation which would effectively revive the former common law that if a promise in a simple contract were made expressly for the benefit of a third party and intended to be enforceable by him, then he could enforce the contract although he was not a party to it.[68]

It is clear that despite the rigours of privity of contract doctrine at common law, regional courts have circumvented privity of contract where necessary. Accordingly, the inability of the named beneficiary at common law to sue on the policy has never been recognised in Commonwealth Caribbean jurisdictions notwithstanding common law rules. Social equity emerged from the prevalence of Canadian Life Insurance Companies which introduced Canadian[69] and American law.[70]

6.9   SUCCESSION LAW AT COMMON LAW

Beneficiaries in jurisdictions where there has been little or no reform are plagued with the perennial difficulty at common law of the potential that a nomination in an insurance policy is a testamentary disposition requiring compliance with succession law. This danger arises because of the free revocability of the nomination under an insurance policy and its dependence upon the death of the nominator for its vigour and effect.

Three crucial questions are triggered:

1   Whether nominations constitute testamentary dispositions, requiring as a condition of their validity attestation in accordance with the statutory requirements for the execution of wills;

---

65   *Shanklin Pier v Detel Products Ltd* [1951] 2 KB 854; *Esso Petroleum Ltd v Customs & Excise Commissioners* [1976] 1 All ER 117; *Helibut Symons & Co. v Buckleton* [1913] AC 30.
66   (1970) 16 WIR 447.
67   Chapter 45:03.
68   Hon. Mr Justice Aubrey Fraser, J.A.
69   Section 172, RSO 1980 Chapter 218. Under Section 174, in the case of an irrevocable designation, consent is required.
70   Supra n. 4, p. 117.

2   Whether a designation under an insurance policy insulates the proceeds from the residual claims of the insured's estate; and

3   Whether the designation takes priority over a subsequent disposition of the policy proceeds in a will.

The case law reveals the dichotomy. On the one hand lies the decision of *Re Danish Bacon Co. Ltd Staff Pension Fund*[71] and the Privy Council decision of *Baird v Baird*[72] arising from the jurisdiction of Trinidad and Tobago, to the effect that an insurance designation is not testamentary in character, hence does not require compliance with ancillary will and succession legislation. On the other lies the Barbadian decision of *Norris v Norris*,[73] applying the Canadian decision of *Re MacInnes*,[74] which suggests that compliance with wills and succession legislation is necessary.

The answer to the first question (i.e. whether nominations are testamentary dispositions) resides in the bifurcation made at common law between the terms of the members' policy or scheme – the member possessing absolute entitlement – and the condition of limited entitlement. In the former case, authority suggests no need for the designation to conform with formal requirements of the Wills and Succession Act. For the latter category however, such compliance is necessary. This distinction is evident in *Re Danish Bacon Co. Ltd Staff Pension Fund*.[75] Here it was held that nominations under a pension scheme were not testamentary so that a nomination under the rules of a company's staff pension fund did not have to satisfy the Wills Act of 1837. Although the nominations had certain testamentary characteristics they were not sufficient to make the 'paper on which it is written a testamentary paper.'[76] This decision must be contrasted with the Barbadian decision of *Norris v Norris*.[77] In this case, a nomination was made under a group insurance policy effected by an employer for the benefit of his employees. The employee concerned had, during his marriage to the first defendant, designated her as beneficiary, but before his death he had divorced her and remarried to the plaintiff. On his death, the plaintiff as administratrix of his estate claimed entitlement. Williams J rejected any claim by the first defendant to the policy proceeds because, *inter alia*, the nomination in her favour did not satisfy the requirements under the Wills Act, in that it was not attested to by two witnesses.[78] Williams J, commenting on the testamentary character of the designation, stated:

> The deceased had the right under the policies to change his beneficiary at any time and in the document of designation he in fact reserved this right. All his interest in the policies remained vested in him while he lived and the beneficiary only became entitled to an interest on the death of the deceased. Thus, the acts of the deceased were testamentary in character and invalid by the reason of their being in breach of the requirement of the Wills Act.[79]

The decision of *Norris v Norris*[80] was subsequently applied in *Rochester v Arthur*,[81] where only one witness had attested to the designation. In the absence of statutory clarification, the nature of the designation must be construed in light of the terms of the policy.

---

71   [1971] 1 All ER 436.
72   [1990] 2 All ER 300.
73   (1977) 29 WIR 22.
74   [1935] 1 DLR 401.
75   Supra n. 71.
76   W. F. Nunan, 'The Application of the Wills Act to Nominations of Beneficiaries Under Superannuation of Pensions Schemes and Insurance Policies' (1966) 40 *Aust. L.J.* 13; Chappenden, 'Non-Statutory Nominations' [1972] *LBL* 20.
77   Supra n. 73.
78   Cap 251.
79   See, however, *Guyana Credit Corp. v Brittlebank* [1967] Law Reports of Guyana 405.
80   BB 1977 HC 19.
81   *Rochester v Arthur* (1989) (unreported decision, High Court of Barbados No. 1279 of 1987).

With respect to the second question, whether a designation under an insurance policy insulates the policy proceeds from the residual claims on the insured's estate, the answer depends on whether a trust has been validly constituted in favor of the beneficiary. A mere designation of a beneficiary under a life insurance policy does not suffice to create a trust in favour of that person. If, however, the designation amounts to a trust under the MWPA for instance, then the subject matter of the trust has been completely constituted on the designation and the third question is answered. The policyholder is precluded from subsequently disposing of the policy proceeds by way of will. Simply put, an affirmative answer to the second question answers the third.

The issue of the requirement for conformity with the law of succession arose for consideration by the Judicial Committee of the Privy Council in *Baird v Baird*,[82] on appeal from the jurisdiction of Trinidad and Tobago. Here their Lordships ruled that the question turned on the nature of the members' rights, under the relevant scheme or policy. Where the member has an absolute entitlement, it is accompanied by a concomitant freedom to nominate, revoke and reappoint beneficiaries, as was the case in *Re MacInnes*,[83] thus disposition under an insurance policy would amount to a disposition under a will and require an attestation clause. On the other hand, where the nominator had only a limited, non-assignable power of disposition, a nomination was not testamentary in character but operated merely by the force of the operation of the relevant scheme. In *Baird*, the nomination concerned a contributory pension scheme organised by a Trinidad oil company for its employees. The consent of the management committee of the scheme was critical and the rights of the members were of a 'very limited order.'[84] The Privy Council expressed doubts as to whether *Norris v Norris* was correctly decided and commented on the 'absence of clear indications' that the policy before Williams J was within the deceased's control during his lifetime.[85] Accordingly the Privy Council ruled that the nominations made under the contributory pension scheme did not have to satisfy succession law. Since the nominators had an inhibited power of disposition, the nomination was not testamentary in character but operated merely by force of the operation of the scheme.

An interest under a trust overrides a contrary disposition in valid will. In the Bahamian decision of *Rose v Rose & Crown Life Insurance Co.*,[86] the insured effected a policy of life insurance naming her husband as the sole beneficiary. The parties later separated, and the insured sought to effect a change of beneficiary to her four children. In her will the insured expressed a 'desire' that all monies from her insurance policies be put in trust for the children. At no time, however, before the death of the insured did her husband relinquish his right. The issue before the Court was the determination of the beneficiary's interest. The husband argued that the provisions of the Act and the policy provided him with a vested interest which could only be altered by consent. The Supreme Court of the Bahamas agreed and held that under the MWPA, the husband's interest in the policy vested from its inception, so that the wife could not remove him as beneficiary or add beneficiaries without his consent. Therefore, the declaration in the will purporting to create a trust for the children was of no effect. Justice Strachant stated: 'The inescapable result in this case may well invite legislative reappraisal of the law.'

The common law is replete with examples where the designation under an insurance policy failed. In *Re Osborne, Hall v Bleasdille*,[87] the High Court of Grenada was provided an opportunity

---

82   Supra n. 72.
83   Ibid.
84   Ibid., 304.
85   Ibid.
86   Supreme Court of the Bahamas Suit No. 1558 of 1990.
87   (1991) 2 OECS Law Rep 215.

to explore the issue. Osborne died in 1970, leaving an insurance policy which named his common law wife, with whom he lived for six years, as beneficiary. His testamentary requests could only be met if the policy fell to estate. St Bernard J decided that the policy proceeds should be paid to the executrix for the benefit of the estate. The named beneficiary was not entitled because (1) there had been no valid bequest to her in a will; (2) the contract of insurance had not created a trust in her favour; (3) there had been no valid assignment of the benefit of the policy to her; and (4) she did not fall within the category of persons in relation to whom the designation gave rise to a presumption of advancement. The common law wife was a mere nominee (i.e. a person to whom the company could pay the policy proceeds under contract to enable it to get a good discharge), but she was precluded from suing under a policy by privity of contract[88] doctrine.

The equitable concepts raised by the decision merit further thought. In *Re Osborne*,[89] the High Court ruled that as a common law wife, the beneficiary did not fall into a category of persons to whom the presumption of advancement applies. The presumption of advancement is an equitable doctrine of necessity which operates where a person purchases property in the name of another. The general rule regarding the transfer of title dictates that the person who supplies the money is presumed to be a beneficiary, while the person in whose name the property was purchased holds the legal title. The separation of legal and equitable title is trumped, however, by the operation of the presumption of advancement. This equitable rule applies in special relationships of husband and wife and parent and child. In the case of husband and wife, where the husband purchases an insurance policy, for instance, the husband is presumed to be making a gift to the wife who is thus presumed to hold both the legal and equitable title. Equity intervenes to presume that the wife is to benefit from the gift, taking both legal and equitable interest. At the core of this principle is the general law governing acquisition of property by gift or contract. A transfer of property by gift is essentially a trust. Equity follows the law, thus if a person purchases property it follows that consideration is required.

The position at common law appears to rest on the rules of the particular scheme or policy. There remains uncertainty, however, as to the degree of limitation required to take the nomination outside the realm of succession law. At further issue are the implications for employer's pension schemes. In new law jurisdictions, the CLI's reforms apply to designations under life insurance policies, and in some cases the statute expressly applies to group life. It is imperative that the particular pension legislation[90] together with the particulars of the relevant scheme be carefully scrutinised to ensure that the designation is not in danger of being characterised as being a testamentary disposition. Concomitantly, it is vital to discover whether the residual Insurance Act applies to the relevant scheme and whether the rights of the nominators are significantly curtailed to permit nomination without adhering to the Wills Act.

6.10   CARIBBEAN LAW INSTITUTE'S INSURANCE BILL

The reforms implemented in the Commonwealth Caribbean are attributable to the Caribbean Law Institute's Insurance Bill.[91] The CLI, desirous to abolish the dichotomy between beneficiaries under the common law and beneficiaries under the statute and motivated by the need

---

88   According to Anderson this case 'provides clear, even if unwelcome, confirmation that English doctrine of privity of contract governs assurance policies in the Commonwealth Caribbean' (Anderson, 'Designation under Policies of Life Assurance' [1993] 2 *Anglo-American Law Rev* 2, 221–222.

89   Supra n. 87.

90   See for instance Barbados Occupational and Benefits Legislation Act of 2003, Cap 350B.

91   CLI Insurance Bill of 1993 (IAC) (2000 Rev.).

to inject a greater degree of flexibility and certainty into the law, drafted the Insurance Bill of 1992 based on the Canadian Ontario Insurance Act.[92] The aims of the CLI were threefold: (1) there should be a statutory provision conferring a right of action on the named beneficiary to recover the proceeds of a life policy effected in his favour; (2) the statutory framework should reflect a policy that, if he so desires, the insured could irrevocably designate a person as beneficiary and render the policy immune of his creditors and unilateral action altering the designation; and (3) the new framework should recognise that beneficiaries other than what is called the irrevocable beneficiary could be changed at any time during the lifetime of the policyholder in order to give flexibility to designations.

6.11 NEW LAW JURISDICTIONS

The new law jurisdictions[93] have introduced reforms premised on the Caribbean Law Institute's Insurance Bill. The CLI's reform divides beneficiaries into discernible categories: irrevocable and revocable beneficiaries. With respect to the former, a statutory trust can be irrevocably created in favour of a spouse and/or a child, while a revocable nomination can be made in favour of a wider class of beneficiaries. The centerpiece of the legislation is the statutory rights bestowed on irrevocable beneficiaries to enforce the payment of a policy effected for their benefit, thereby effectively dislodging the privity of contract principle. Moreover, *inter alia*, it puts to rest debate surrounding whether a designation under an insurance policy is testamentary in character, by stating that a designation under the policy takes precedence over a will. Additionally, the reforms embrace group life policies, although with respect to employer's pension schemes the particulars of the schemes must be examined.[94]

6.12 IRREVOCABLE BENEFICIARIES

An irrevocable beneficiary can only be created in favour of a spouse or child.[95] The effect of such a designation is profound, making it imperative that the insured be made aware of its implications, a fact underscored by the statutory stipulation of sufficient evidence that the irrevocable nature of the designation has been explained to the policyholder. By creating such a designation, the insured automatically relinquishes all control over the policy proceeds. He is prohibited from altering or revoking the designation, or assigning or exercising rights thereunder without the beneficiary's consent. The beneficiary's consent is also required to encash any units accruing to or surrender or otherwise deal with the insurance policy. The import of an irrevocable designation is clear – the insured's power being effectively reduced to a peripheral one – entitlement to dividends and bonuses.

---

92 Sections 167–178, Ontario Insurance Act RSO 1980 Chapter 218. This jurisdiction also provides for revocable and irrevocable beneficiaries.
93 Barbados Insurance Act, Cap 310. In Jamaica, prior to comprehensive reform in 2001, Section 73A of the Insurance (Amendment) Act of 1995 similarly reflected the CLI's position with respect to the status of the beneficiary. This Act has since been repealed by the Jamaica Insurance Act No. 26 of 2001; Guyana Insurance Act No. 20 of 1998; St Vincent and the Grenadines Insurance Act No. 45 of 2003; Bahamas Insurance Bill of 2002.
94 Section 112, Barbados Insurance Act; Section 106, Jamaica Insurance Act.
95 Section 135(4), Guyana Insurance Act; Section 100, Jamaica Insurance Act; Section 147 of the Guyana Insurance Act provides: 'the policy-holder is entitled while living, to the dividends or bonuses declared on a contract, unless the contract otherwise provides.'

Simultaneously, the beneficiary has been elevated from the status of a 'stranger' to that of an integral party to the insurance contract, as in addition to his consent being required, statute plainly bestows on the beneficiary a right to enforce payment of monies payable under a policy even though no privity of contract exists. A segregated fund is created so that the insured and/or his creditors have no control over the policy proceeds forming no part of the insured's estate.[96]

An impressive trait of the legislation is its elasticity. Should the marriage or spousal common law relationship comes to an end, the beneficiary's consent is no longer required. In such circumstances, the policy monies immediately revert to the insured's dominion and control. This neatly avoids the acrimony normally associated with the requirement of consent in post-nuptial proceedings so graphically portrayed in *Campbell v Colonial Life Insurance Co.*[97] In this case, as their relationship deteriorated during divorce proceedings, the couple then residing in Trinidad and Tobago decided to travel to Barbados on the instigation of the husband, intending to discuss the wife's designation under the husband's insurance policy. The husband threatened that if the wife did not sign over to him two insurance policies 'she would not get one red cent.' The wife signed the document. The Court ruled that the wife, by signing the document, had effectively relinquished her right to the policy proceeds and held that she was not entitled to the policy proceeds on the husband's death. The result is unfortunate, bearing in mind that the wife most probably was in an emotionally disturbed state and no doubt felt 'compelled' to sign. Regardless, the fundamental principle in contract applied.

Additionally, the primacy of the irrevocable beneficiary is predicated on the beneficiary being alive. Should the beneficiary predecease the insured, preferred status automatically ends/ceases. In such cases, the hierarchy under succession law operates residually, ranking entitlement where no express provision has been made in the contract. The statute also fortuitously prescribes rules regarding simultaneous death,[98] and resolves the situation where the beneficiary predeceases the insured.[99] This approach abrogates the common law position highlighted in *Cousins and Sun Life Assurance Society*,[100] where despite the fact that the wife predeceased her husband, her interest nevertheless persisted, going to her legal personal representatives. Now, under the modern position, policy proceeds immediately revert to the policyholder.

Another significant feature of the reforms is that the difficulties associated with the relationship of insurance contract and succession laws have been resolved. First, the designation process has been simplified. Whereas at common law there is a danger that a designation under a will would be treated as being testamentary in character requiring compliance with relevant succession legislation, the current statutory position effectively eradicates this likelihood. The insured may, at the time the policy is effected or at any time thereafter, either effect or revoke a designation by a simple designation in writing. Moreover, the insured's freedom to make a contrary disposition under a will has been overturned, as the statute expressly provides that a 'designation under a will does not affect a designation under the policy.'[101]

Since reform, the statutory trust can be created only in favour of a spouse or child.[102] This change expands the narrow platform of 'husband and wife' that existed under the previous

---

96 Section 105, Jamaica Insurance Act; Section 139, Guyana Insurance Act.
97 Unreported decision, High Court of Trinidad and Tobago CA No. Cv 3517 of 1990.
98 Section 119, Barbados Insurance Act, Cap 310.
99 Section 118.
100 [1933] 1 Ch 126.
101 Section 116, Barbados Insurance Act, Cap 310; Section 107(3), St Vincent and the Grenadines Insurance Act No. 45 of 2003.
102 See Section 115(4).

regime. In order for a union to be accorded recognition 'as a union other than marriage,' a five- or seven-year living requirement is needed depending on the jurisdiction.[103] Section 2 of the Barbados Insurance Act states that a spouse has the meaning ascribed to it by Subsections (3)–(5) of Section 2 of the Succession Act, which defines a spouse as a single man living together with a single woman for a period of five years.[104] Modern Insurance Acts in the region have responded to the Caribbean family relationships long ago identified by sociologists. The controversial statement by the Hon. Justice Anderson on the socio-economic relevance of law warrants attention:

> It has been stated that the statutory and common law rules do not always respond to the emergent social, and in particular, the indigenous patterns of family relations comprising society. In English society, the present rules work reasonably well in the protection of members of the nuclear family designated as beneficiaries under life assurance policies. Transposed into the context of the West Indies, however, these rules have shown themselves unresponsive to the reality of daily lives of large sections of the populace. The extreme case is that of partners in a stable homosexual common law union of over 20 years having no special relief against the harsh effects of the privity rule or the strictness of the law of succession. On the assumption that this so-called 'alternative lifestyle' (actually practised by a comfortable majority of West Indians) has now attained authenticity, if only on the basis of social reality, the challenge to the legislative process must be its incorporation into the mainstream protection given to more Euro-centric views of family arrangement. Some progress is being made on this front, with the agitation for statutory reform being carried on by the CLI but the acid test of passage into law is yet to be confronted.

In the absence of statistics to support the allegation that an alternative lifestyle is indeed practised by 'a comfortable majority of West Indians' and considering that the 'acid test of passage into law' has since taken place in the jurisdictions of Barbados, Guyana and Jamaica, several observations can be made. Legislation expressly outlaws same-sex relations in several territories.[105] 'Sentencing in many cases, is severe and the language of "comfort" belies the statement of affording comfort and security.'

The statutory recognition, while broader than the nuclear family previously recognised under the MWPA, still excludes same-sex partners and married persons so that the factual circumstances of *Asaram v North American Life Insurance Co.*[106] remain outside the ambit of the reform. It is contended, however, that the selective nature of this category is justified when one examines the degree of insularity that comes with an irrevocable designation. As seen, this category shields the policy proceeds from the actions of both the insured and creditors, abrogating the privity of contract principle. Section 120 of the Barbados Insurance Act[107] abrogates the contract law principle and expressly states that the 'beneficiary may enforce for his own benefit even though there is no privity of contract.' Not only does the legislation expressly upend the privity of contract principle, but rather than being a stranger to the contract he is an effective party to the contract to the extent that he can enforce the contract, and his consent is required

---

103 See Section 115(2). In Guyana, the requirement is six years.
104 Cap 249. Family relationships typical of the Commonwealth Caribbean possess features specifically derived from societal imperatives of 'New World' slavery. See Edith Clarke, *My Mother Who Fathered Me: A Study of the Families in Three Selected Communities of Jamaica* (The Press, University of the West Indies: 1999[1957]). Edith Clarke took her title from George Lamming's *In the Castle of My Skin* (Michael Joseph: 1953); and Fernando Henriques, *Family and Colour in Jamaica* (Eyre and Spottiswoode: 1953).
105 Section 13, Trinidad and Tobago Sexual Offences Act Chapter 11:28; Section 12, Antigua and Barbuda Sexual Offences Act.
106 Supreme Court of Guyana No. 2366 of 1996.
107 Cap 310.

before he can be removed. As a precautionary measure, statute requires that the designation cannot be construed as irrevocable unless the words creating the designation are clear and unequivocal, prominently displayed on the proposal form and signed by the policyholder.

6.13   REVOCABLE BENEFICIARIES

The revocable beneficiary is an open-ended category available to 'other' beneficiaries unable to satisfy the conditions required for an irrevocable designation. Thus the main advantage, at least as far as the insured is concerned, resides in its flexibility. The insured remains free to assign, exercise rights under, surrender or otherwise deal with the policy.[108] As a revocable designation necessarily captures all persons excluded from the irrevocable designation, it stands to reason that it is available to 'other unions.' Their 'rights,' however, are not secure, as an insurer can terminate such a designation at any time.[109]

Given its vulnerable status, it is reasonable to conclude that a revocable designation is subject to a contrary disposition under a will. This appears to be the case in Barbados. However the position is not so clear in St Vincent and the Grenadines. Section 107(3) of the Insurance Act expressly states that a 'designation by a will does not affect a designation made under a policy.' The problem is, construing the statute contextually, this statement is contained in the same section that creates revocable designations. Further, the term 'designation' is unadorned, suggesting that the priority of insurance over wills extends to revocable designations.

6.14   THE MODERATE POSITION

The moderate position is exemplified in Section 139 of the Trinidad and Tobago Insurance Act.[110] The description 'moderate' is warranted, for although some reform has taken place, it is not to the extent displayed in other jurisdictions which have embraced the CLI model. Thus, Section 139 of the Trinidad and Tobago Insurance Act provides:

(1)   Notwithstanding any rule of law to the contrary where a policy of insurance is effected by a person on his own life and is expressed to be for the benefit of a named beneficiary, the money payable under such a policy shall not, on the death of the policy-holder, form part of his estate, but shall be paid to the person named as the beneficiary.

(2)   The provisions of subsection (1) shall apply to a policy effected before or after the commencement of this Act.

In light of the previous discussion, the limitations of the insurance legislation are immediately apparent. Its scope is restricted, as it applies, as does the MWPA, to own-life policies only. The question that arises is whether the Act successfully avoids the difficulties that confronted the beneficiary at common law. The provision commences: 'Notwithstanding any other law.' Thus there is no express revocation of the common law or the Married Women's Property legislation. Another weakness is that the designation is subject to the debate surrounding the relevance of the succession law, and since the section is dependent on the death of the insured for its vigour and effect, the beneficiary's rights continue to be subject to modification and destruction. Also,

108 Section 97(2), Jamaica Insurance Act No. 26 of 2001.
109 Section 114(2), Barbados Insurance Act, Cap 310.
110 Cap 242.

by simply using the word 'beneficiaries,' no distinction is made between irrevocable and revocable designations. Further the Act, *prima facie*, has no application to group life polices or pension schemes. The inevitable conclusion of the foregoing, construing the hybrid legislation operating in the jurisdictions of Trinidad and Tobago and St Lucia, is that the legislation does not resolve the uncertainties that exist under the MWPA or at common law.

6.15   SECURING IMMUNITY

An insurer faced with competing claims between the insured's estate and the named beneficiary is often in a quandary: to whom are insurance monies payable? In some cases the insurer will pay the proceeds to the estate, uneasy as to the named beneficiaries' claim. If the insurer honors the contract and pays policy proceeds to the third party, the insurer is discharged from any further obligation.[111] The personal representatives of the assured under such circumstances have no right to intervene to stop the payment to the beneficiary. An option is available under statute for the insurance company to apply to the court on originating summons for directions as to the person entitled to the money it holds.[112] In the absence of creation of a trust, the beneficiary has no right to sue for policy proceeds or to intervene and stop the assured from modifying or destroying his interest, but if the beneficiary receives such payment, he is entitled to retain and keep those proceeds. Given the considerable uncertainty as to the status of the beneficiary, it is important to consider that insurance companies can avoid the maelstrom by obtaining immunity by paying the monies to the Regulator.[113]

Regional insurance legislation provides that where a company makes a payment, the company shall be discharged from all further liability with respect to (1) the money paid to the Commissioner of Inland Revenue and (2) the application of the money paid under any policy issued by it. For instance, Section 115(1) of the St Lucia Insurance Act[114] enables the insurance company to pay to the Registrar any money payable by it in respect of a policy for which, in the opinion of the company, no sufficient discharge can otherwise be obtained. The receipt of the Registrar for any money paid under Subsection (1) shall be good and valid discharge to the company for the money so paid, and the money shall be dealt with according to an order made by the court. Also in accordance with Section 103 of the Barbados Insurance Act, the insurer is not bound to see the application of monies paid by it, but if the insurance company has notice of any contemplated breach of trust, it is under a duty to withhold payment.[115]

Conclusion

The law pertaining to the status of the beneficiary is located primarily in the modern Commonwealth Caribbean. The Caribbean has implemented significant reform regarding the status of the beneficiary in life insurance. This reform collectively circumvents the challenges associated with trust law, insurance statutes which have abrogated the Married Women's Property

111 *Re Schebsman* [1944] 1 Ch 83.
112 Section 13, Guyana Civil Law Act Chapter 6:01.
113 Section 140, Trinidad and Tobago Insurance Act 1980; Section 143, Trinidad and Tobago Insurance Act of 1980 Chapter 45.
114 See Chapter 12.08.
115 *Mutual Life Ins Co. v Pechotsch* [1905] 2 CLR 823.

legislation,[116] the recent CCJ decision of *Katrina Smith v Albert Anthony Peter Selby* and the common law. In jurisdictions without such assistance, reliance must continue to be placed on this nineteenth-century legislation. At one end of the spectrum are the jurisdictions where radical reform has been conducted, driven by the Caribbean Law Institute's recommendations: broad, sweeping reform, introducing the clearly defined categories of beneficiaries of revocable and irrevocable designations, results in the irrevocable beneficiary being empowered to the extent that the common law doctrine of privity of contract virtually ceases to exist.[117] At the other end of the spectrum are those jurisdictions which have not adopted the CLI's reforms so that the law can only be understood by reference to the common law, the Life Insurance Act of 1774 and the Married Women's Property Act of 1883. Between these two extremes is Trinidad and Tobago, where hybrid reform has been introduced relaxing the narrow requirements of the Married Women's Property legislation, but not to the extent of the CLI recommendations. The result is that reform propelled by the Caribbean Law Institute was directed at strengthening the regulatory regime and simultaneously achieved a 'necessary byproduct.'

Assignment of life insurance policies

Introduction

The benefit under a life insurance policy can be used as security, sold or otherwise disposed of. This is because of the fundamental underlying property feature of an insurance contract, a feature that is enhanced by the fact that insurable interest is required at the date of the commencement of the policy so that once a valid insurance contract is effected, the benefit can be disposed of. Generally, there are three types of assignment in law: (1) assignment of subject matter of insurance; (2) assignment of the benefit of insurance policy;[118] and (3) statutory assignment.[119]

Assignment in life insurance

A life insurance policy as property is a chose of action which can be assigned or used as security for a loan. Assignments of insurance policies can be made in equity under the Policies of Assurance Act of 1867 or by way of Section 136 of the Law of Property Act of 1925. Under the 1867 Act, assignment may be made either by endorsement on the policy or by a separate document incorporating the wording as set out in the schedule to the Act. It is sometimes necessary to construe the substance of the transaction to determine whether the transaction is an absolute assignment or is in fact a mortgage.[120] Where the insured assigns the benefit of a life insurance policy as security for a debt, the insured is entitled to redeem the mortgage on repayment of the debt and recover his policy, notwithstanding any provision to the contrary. In

---

116 N. M. Forde, 'Family Inheritance Provisions in the Barbados Succession Act – Redefining "the Family"' in K. Nunez-Tesheira, ed., *Commonwealth Caribbean Family Law: Husband, Wife and Cohabitant* (Routledge: 2012), pp. 65–68.
117 Section 120 of the Barbados Insurance Act of 1996, Cap 310 abrogates the contract law principle and expressly states that the 'beneficiary may enforce for his own benefit even though there is no privity of contract.' See also Section 139, Guyana Insurance Act No. 20 of 1998; Section 105, Jamaica Insurance Act No. 10 of 2001.
118 Section 136, Law of Property Act of 1925, 15 & 16 Geo. 5 c. 20.
119 Section 47, Law of Property Act of 1925, 15 & 16 Geo. 5 c. 20.
120 *Murphy v Taylor* (1850) 1 Ir Ch R 92.

accordance with the general law on mortgages, clogs or fetters on the equity of redemption or the equitable right to redeem are void.[121] In *Salt v Marquess of Northampton*,[122] the transaction was held to be in substance a mortgage, despite the agreement to the contrary. In this case, sums were borrowed from the insurer and secured by a charge on his reversionary interest in certain property. He also agreed to pay the premiums on a policy for £34,000, taken out by the insurers against the possibility of the interest not vesting. It was agreed that if he paid off the loan before the interest was vested, the policy would be assigned to him, but if he died before repayment and vesting, the policy would belong to the insurers. In fact, he died before the stipulated time.

Modern commerce dictates that a degree of flexibility be awarded to the recognition of the assignment of life policies. Frequently, a mortgagee requires the mortgagor to effect life insurance to cover the amount of the loan in case the mortgagor dies before the loan is repaid. In such cases the insurance policy is assigned to the mortgagee. The emergence of viatical settlements lends further support to the fact that life insurance is one of the most recognised forms of investment: self-compelled savings. 'So far as reasonable safety permits, it is deny the right to sell except to persons having such an interest is to diminish appreciable the value of the contract in the owner's hands.'[123]

Statutory assignment

Where the Insurance Act is silent on the availability of assignment, reliance must be placed on the Policies of Assurance Act of 1867 and the Law of Property Act which was received in all Caribbean territories. Assignment of life polices was permitted in equity, but the assignees could only sue to enforce the policy by joining the assignor in the action and an insurer could not obtain a good discharge against payment from the assignee alone. The Policies of Assurance Act of 1867[124] enabled life polices to be legally assigned. The assignee of the life policy, once the criteria of the Act are satisfied,[125] may enforce the policy in his own name. Since life insurance is an intangible form of property,[126] an alternative procedure for assignment is available under Section 136 of the Law of Property Act.[127] The procedure under the 1867 Act differs from that under the Law of Property Act, in that a valid assignment can be created over the assignor's whole interest in the policy or of merely a part of it, by way of mortgage. In the Section 136 assignment under the Law of Property Act, however, an assignment must be absolute, embracing the whole of the assignor's interest. However, unlike the formalities pertaining to assignments under the 1867 Act, which must be in a prescribed form, under the Law of Property Act assignment must simply be in writing. Notice must be given to the debtor. The consent of the insurers is not necessary in either case, but a condition in the policy to the effect that it is non-assignable is effective to prevent a legal assignment, although an equitable assignment remains effective.[128] An equitable assignment may arise, for instance, where the assignor simply deposits the policy with the assignor as a security and fails to provide the insurer with notice.[129] Equitable assignment ranks in order of creation. In areas of doubt as to priority where there are competing claims, the insurer can opt to pay the monies into the court.

---

121 C. Harpum, S. Bridge and M. Dixon, *Megarry & Wade: The Law of Real Property*, 5th edn (Sweet & Maxwell: 1984), pp. 964–971.
122 [1892] AC 1.
123 *Grigsby v Russell*, 222 US 149 (1911), per Mr Justice Holmes.
124 30 & 31 Vict. c. 144.
125 See Section 5.
126 *Re Moore* (1878) 8 Ch D 519.
127 15 & 16 Geo. 5 c. 20.
128 *Re Turcan* (1888) 40 Ch D 5.
129 *Williams v Thorp* (1828) 2 Sim 257.

Assignment under the Insurance Act

In some territories, the Insurance Act expressly preserves the right of the insured to assign the benefit under an insurance policy. This can be seen, for instance, in the Insurance Acts of Guyana and St Vincent and the Grenadines. Assignment is available whether or not the policy has been designated revocable or irrevocable, but in the case of a policy subject to an irrevocable designation, the written consent of the beneficiary must first be obtained. In order for the assignment to be binding on the insurer it must comply with the prescribed formalities. In accordance with the Act, the assignee has priority of interest as against other assignees and beneficiaries, other than the irrevocable beneficiary.[130] Section 141 of the Guyana Insurance Act[131] provides:

(1) Where a beneficiary is not designated irrevocably, the policyholder may assign, exercise rights under or in respect of, surrender or otherwise deal with the contract as provided therein ir in this part or as may be agreed upon with the insurer.

(2) Where a beneficiary is designated irrevocably the policy-holder may not assign the policy, use the policy as a security, surrender it or otherwise deal with it without the consent in writing of the designated beneficiary.

Section 143 states:

An assignee of a contract who gives notice in writing of the assignment to the head office of the insurer his priority of interest as against –

(a) any assignee other than the one who gave notice earlier in like manner; and

(b) a beneficiary other than one designated irrevocably as provided in section 135 prior to the time the assignee gave notice to the insurer of the assignment in the manner prescribed in this subsection.

(3) Where a contract is assigned absolutely, the assignee has all the rights and interests given to the policy-holder by the contract and by this Part and shall be deemed to be the policy-holder.

(4) A provision in a contract to the effect that the rights or interests of the policyholder, or, in the case of group insurance, the group life insured, are not assignable is valid.

---

130 Section 116(1), St Vincent and the Grenadines Insurance Act No. 45 of 2003.
131 Guyana Insurance Act No. 20 of 1998.

CHAPTER 7

UTMOST GOOD FAITH, FRAUD, MISREPRESENTATION AND NON-DISCLOSURE

7.1 INTRODUCTION

Utmost good faith, fraud, misrepresentation and the duty to disclose, like no other area of insurance, has received substantial attention from insured(s), insurers, lawyers and the judiciary. Indeed, a large percentage of regional legal reporting is devoted to this issue.[1] The considerable case law explains and determines the range and reach of the duty, influenced by extra-regional common law.[2] As far as statute is concerned, early twentieth-century Marine Insurance Acts continue as the foundation of insurance, assisted by consumer legislation, replacing early Misrepresentation Acts in the jurisdictions of Antigua and Barbuda[3] and Trinidad and Tobago.[4] A noteworthy development is Rehabilitation of Offenders legislation,[5] alleviating the burden of *uberrimae fidei* with respect to 'spent' convictions as it pertains to the moral hazard. Insurance contracts require utmost good faith *uberrimae fidei* – the duty is mutual – imposed on both the insurer and the insured. Originating from early marine insurance legislation, notwithstanding the title of the statute, the concept applies to all types of insurance,[6] there being no difference between marine and non-marine insurance in this respect.[7] The rationale is explained in the Guyana case *Prasad v Demerara Mutual Life Assurance Society Ltd*:[8]

> As is well known, insurance is a contract *uberrimae fidei* and requires full disclosure of such material facts as are known to the assured. As the underwriter knows nothing and the man who comes to him to ask to insure knows everything, it is the duty of the assured, the man who desires to have a policy, to make a full disclosure to the underwriter without being asked of all the material circumstances, because the underwriter knows nothing and the assured knows everything. This is expressed by saying that it is a contract of the utmost good faith per Scrutton LJ in *Rozanes v*

---

1   See CARILAW; OECS Law Reports; Jamaica Law Reports: *Roberts v Colonial Life Insurance Co.* GY 1980 HC 23.
2   The three headings are treated as one by practitioners.
3   Misrepresentation Act No. 7 of 1992.
4   Misrepresentation Act No. 12 of 1983.
5   The Bahamas Rehabilitation of Offenders Act No. 11 of 1991; Barbados Criminal Records (Rehabilitation of Offenders) Act No. 6 of 1997; Cayman Islands Rehabilitation of Offenders Law No. 20 of 1985; Guyana Rehabilitation of Offenders Act No. 6 of 1994.
6   *Lindenau v Desborough* (1828) 8 Barn & C 586.
7   *PCW Syndicates v PCW Reinsurers* [1996] 1 WLR 1136.
8   GY 1978 HC 6. See also *Hilton v Barbados Fire & Commercial Insurance Ltd LC*, 2005 HC 48, according Shanks J It is important to note the limits of this doctrine, however:

> In a business context the assured's duty of disclosure is not confined to his actual knowledge; it also extends to those material facts which, in the ordinary course of business, he ought to know. But a person effecting insurance cover as a private individual must disclose only material facts known to him and he is not to have ascribed to him any form of deemed or constructive knowledge.

See *Halsbury's Laws of England*, 5th edn (LexisNexis: 2017), Vol. 16, para. 44 and *Economides v Commercial Union* [1997] 3 All ER 636. It is also sufficient if facts which are disclosed put insurers on inquiry and their inquiry would in the normal course elicit such further facts as may be material. See *Halsbury's Laws of England* (2017), para. 37 and *Anglo-African Merchants v Bayley* [1969] 2 All ER. An entirely innocent misrepresentation may entitle the insurer to avoid the insurance, but where the representation is qualified and stated to be to the best of an assured's knowledge and belief, then provided the assured is honest in making the representation, the insurer is not entitled to avoid the insurance even if it is in fact inaccurate.

Bowen.[9] The assured therefore must disclose everything known to him that is material in fact even though he does not appreciate its materiality and even though a reasonably prudent man would not do so.

7.2 FRAUD

Fraud can occur at any stage of the insurance relationship. At this juncture, however, the focus is on fraudulent conduct at the time the contract is being effected (i.e. conduct inducing the other party to enter into the contract), as opposed to the operation of fraud at the point of loss, where the insured allegedly brings about the insured peril through fraudulent conduct as exemplified in the decisions of *Derrick St Ville v Netherlands Antilles General Insurance Corp.*[10] and *Soloman Ghany Oil & Engineering Ltd v N.E.M. (West Indies) Insurance Ltd.*[11] It is noted that there is Caribbean authority which highlights the mutuality of the duty to disclose: *Charles v The New India Assurance Co.*:[12]

> After all, the duty to disclose material facts in insurance agreements is mutual, so that the insurer too must come clean and cannot hope to avoid a contract by less than a frank and full explanation to the customer of the terms of the proposed policy.

In *Merchants Insurance Co. v Hunt*,[13] the plaintiff knew that the answers he made on the proposal form were incorrect and 'this fact should immediately distinguish that case from the instant matter where I have found that what's on the proposal form did not represent accurately the information the plaintiff supplied.' So although it is the plaintiff's document in that he signed it, yet because the plaintiff relied for the wording of the answers on the expertise of the Company's servant, I would consider that on the married equitable I hold therefore that the construction to be placed on the words in the instant proposal form should not conform with the construction placed on the words in the Hunt ease. There it was held that the affirmative unqualified negative 'No' could not be qualified to mean 'No, to the best of my knowledge and belief,' and understandably because the plaintiff knew that the information was false. The instant matter is very different and should be given a different interpretation because there was no misrepresentation by the plaintiff and no failure to disclose any material fact.

It has been said that 'fraud is a thing apart . . . reflect[ing] an old legal rule that fraud unravels all: *fraus omnia corrumpit*. It reflects the practical basis of commercial intercourse. Proof of fraud, vitiates judgment, contracts and all transactions whatsoever.' The leading authority on fraud and a decision which has been consistently applied in the Caribbean is *Derry v Peek*[14] – to wit – the insured is guilty of fraudulent misrepresentation if he knowingly makes a statement that is false without belief in its truth or recklessly disregards whether it be true or false. *Derry v Peek* was followed and applied for instance in *Dalkan v Colonial Life Insurance Co. Ltd*,[15] where

---

9   *(1928)* 32 Ll LR 98 at 102.
10 High Court of Dominica Suit No. 100 of 1997; DM 1982 HC 7.
11 High Court of Trinidad and Tobago No. S 3114 of 1986.
12 DM 1982 HC 7.
13 (1940) 4 All ER 205.
14 [1889] UKHL 1.
15 (1965) 12 WIR 133. In this case, the appellant had insured his house and its contents with the respondent insurance company against loss by fire. He did not disclose that he had taken out insurance with another company against similar loss, and in his declaration, he misrepresented the value of the property to the respondent. The house was destroyed by fire and the appellant claimed $23,000 from the respondent. In its defence, the respondent pleaded breach of certain conditions of the policy. They identified the failure to disclose the existence of another policy of insurance and the false declaration of the value of the house ($27,000) when the appellant knew that is worth no more than $14,000.

the failure to disclose the existence of another policy of insurance led the Court of Appeal of Trinidad and Tobago to find that there was fraudulent misrepresentation: 'There was no question here of mere exaggeration based on the appellant's honest opinion of the value of the insured property, but that this is a case of wilful misrepresentation made with full knowledge of its actual value.' Similarly, in *Dass v Maritime Life Caribbean Ltd*,[16] the High Court of Trinidad and Tobago found that there was evidence of fraudulent misrepresentation. In this case the insured was asked, 'Have you ever been treated or ever known to have chest pain, palpitation, high blood pressure, diabetes, thyroid; are you under observation or taking treatment?' The deceased, who replied in the negative, in fact had an 11-year history of diabetes, elevated blood pressure and unstable angina. The defendant insurer was held to be entitled to avoid the policy. Applying the decision of *Derry v Peek*, the court restated the salient principle that, fraud is proved when it is shown that there is a false representation made knowingly or without belief in its truth or recklessly, careless as to whether it be true of false. This decision highlights the burden of proof necessary to establish fraud and its relevance to the issue of fraudulent misrepresentation. In order to sustain an action of deceit there must be proof of fraud, nothing short thereof will suffice.[17] The *onus probandi* is upon he who alleges; those who allege fraud must clearly and distinctly prove the fraud alleged.

In *Derrick St Ville v Netherlands Antilles General Insurance Corp.*,[18] reference was made to false or fraudulent claims, citing the decision of *Hosein & Co. Ltd*. The standard of proof by which the insurer has to discharge this burden is the ordinary civil standard – proof on a balance of probabilities that the assured wilfully caused the loss, or that the claim was dishonest and/or fraudulent. The degree of probability varies with the determined extent of criminality or fraud alleged. 'It does not, require proof which reaches the criminal standard – proof beyond a reasonable doubt.'

The application of fraud to misrepresentation can also be seen in the Barbadian Court of Appeal decision of *Matthew Joseph v CLICO International General Insurance Co. Ltd*.[19] In this case, the insured, a professional musician and entertainer, kept his musical instruments and electronic equipment in the house used by members of his band. After the destruction of the house and contents by fire in January 2000 while the insured was on St Lucia, it was discovered that the house had already been insured with another insurer, British American, for $35,000. Kentish J, in the lower court, ruled that the insurer was entitled to avoid the policy because on the proposal form, a pre-existing mortgage on the house was not disclosed and further, that the insured had failed to disclose that he had already insured with another insurance company. Finding that the insured was fraudulent, the insurer was held to be entitled to avoid a claim for payment under the insurance policy, a position upheld by the Court of Appeal. Chief Justice Simmons in the Court of Appeal, citing with approval the earlier decision of *Dalkhan*, which in his words 'reeked of fraud,' stated:

> It was for the trial judge to determine as a question of fact whether his claim was fraudulent within the meaning adumbrated in *Derry v Peek* (1889) 14 App Ca 357 (i.e. whether it contained false statements made recklessly, not caring whether the statements were true or false). His duty to act with the utmost good faith extended beyond the contractual date of the policy.

The Caribbean jurisprudence on point illustrates the utility of fraud in establishing fraudulent misrepresentation.

---

16   High Court of Trinidad and Tobago No. 2456 of 1998.
17   Ibid.
18   *Derrick St Ville v Netherlands Antilles General Insurance Corp.*, High Court of Dominica. See per Phillips J.A., supra n. 16., 138; High Court of Trinidad and Tobago No. 2456 of 1998.
19   Court of Appeal of Barbados Civil Appeal No. 2 of 2003.

7.3   MISREPRESENTATION

Misrepresentation is used to describe situations in which the wrong or misleading answer is supplied in response to a question posed to the insured, usually in the proposal form, whereas non-disclosure is used to describe the condition of the insured having failed to volunteer material information, perhaps because no specific question was posed. Despite this distinction, the line between misrepresentation and non-disclosure is imperceptible.

Historically, misrepresentation was of little importance to insurance contracts. The concept applies to statements made prior to the conclusion of the contract of insurance and by virtue of the wide scale use of basis of contract clauses incorporating representations made in the proposal form in the terms of the contract, the need for misrepresentation was reduced. Also, the broad scope and effectiveness of the duty to disclose has meant that the duty of *uberrimae fides* has effectively consumed the development of the law of misrepresentation. This is compounded by the fact that the case law fails to distinguish between the two defences, aided by the approach of insurers who often plead both defences – a trend entrenched by the decision of *Pan Atlantic Insurance Co. Ltd v Pine Top Insurance Co. Ltd*,[20] which, to use the words of Lord Justice Mustill, has muddied the waters by introducing inducement into the law of non-disclosure, blurring the distinction between non-disclosure and misrepresentation. The ease with which non-disclosure can be applied seems to have been tightened by the decision of *Economides v Commercial Union Assurance Co. plc*,[21] which suggests that the courts will no longer permit the defence of non-disclosure to succeed when the assured has allegedly merely made an innocent misrepresentation, so that misrepresentation may now be more relevant than it has been in the past.[22] Given the distinction between innocent misrepresentation where the insured knows the truth, and innocent non-disclosure where the insured knows the truth and does not think it important,[23] perhaps misrepresentation does have a distinct place in insurance law.[24] Regional marine insurance legislation outlines the parameters of an action for misrepresentation.

7.4   STATUTE MARINE INSURANCE LEGISLATION

Section 23 of the Barbados Marine Insurance Act[25] establishes that if misrepresentation is evident, in accordance with the Act, the party induced is entitled to avoid the contract 'if he establishes that he was induced to enter into the contract by a misrepresentation of fact made

---

20   [1994] 3 All ER 736.
21   [1998] QB 587.
22   H. Brooke, 'Materiality in Insurance Contracts' [1985] *LMCLQ* 437; J. Birds and N. J. Hird, 'Misrepresentation and Non-disclosure in Insurance Law-Identical Twins or Separate Issues' (1996) 59 *MLR* 285; N. J. Hird, 'Pan Atlantic – Yet More To Disclose' [1995] *JBL* 608; see further H. N. Bennett, 'Statements of Fact and Statements of Opinion in Insurance Contract Law and General Contract Law' (1998) 61 *MLR* 886; H. Bennett, 'The Duty to Disclose in Insurance Law' (1993) *LQR* 513; Clarke, 'Failure to Disclose and Failure to Legislate: Is It Material? – II' [1988] *JBL* 298; A. Diamond, 'The Law of Marine Insurance – Has It a Future?' [1986] *LMCLQ* 25; Hudson (1969) 85 *LQR* 524; Steyn J, 'The Role of Good Faith and Fair Dealing in Contract Law: A Hairshirt Philosophy?' [1991] *Denning L.J.* 131, 138–140.
23   J. Birds, *Modern Insurance Law*, 6th edn (Sweet & Maxwell: 2014), p. 101.
24   H. N. Bennett, supra n. 22; Hird [1998] *JBL* 279.
25   Cap 292.

by another that was false in a material particular.'[26] Since the Act simply provides that 'if the representation is untrue,' the innocent party is entitled to avoid the contract, it appears to be immaterial whether the falsehood was fraudulent, negligent or innocent.[27]

In addition to the Marine Insurance Act, misrepresentation legislation operates in some jurisdictions, restricting an insurer's right to avoid the contract for misrepresentation.

7.5   MISREPRESENTATION LEGISLATION

Misrepresentation legislation[28] operated in Antigua and Barbuda and Trinidad and Tobago. Section 2(2) of this Act vested discretion to award damages in lieu of rescission or avoidance. The relevance of the Court's discretionary power was questioned, *obiter dicta*, in the decision of *Highlands Insurance Co. v Continental Insurance Co.*,[29] which suggests that the discretion would never be used in respect of commercial contracts. Subsequently in the decision of *Economides v Commercial Union Assurance Co. plc*,[30] where the insurer pleaded non-disclosure, as well as misrepresentation, although the defence was unsuccessful, it appears that the discretion to award damages under Section 2(2) may still be relevant.

Misrepresentation legislation applied in only a few jurisdictions and its focus was on the remedial aspect of misrepresentation and in that sense only of marginal assistance. It is thus towards the Marine Insurance Act and the common law that regard must be had in order to ascertain the essential principles.

7.6   CONSUMER GUARANTEE LEGISLATION[31]

The introduction of consumer legislation may put an end to the age-old debate as to whether the standard exception dealing with 'liability assumed by agreement' excludes liability to an insured in the event of the insured warranting goods sold and delivered, irrespective of fault on its part. The legislation extends liability attaching to the insured 'notwithstanding such agreement' with a third party. Therefore, liability also assumed by the agreement may very well be covered.

---

26 Section 23, Barbados Marine Insurance Act, Cap 242; see also Anguilla Marine Insurance Act RSA 2000 CM 25; British Virgin Islands Marine Insurance Ordinance, Cap 257 [1961 Rev.]; Cayman Islands Marine Insurance Act 1959, Cap 711; Marine Insurance Act 1959, Cap 711 [1961 Rev.]; Grenada Marine Insurance Act No. 5 of 1990, Cap 182; St Kitts and Nevis Marine Insurance Act 1959, Cap 711; St Lucia Marine Insurance Act 1959, Cap 711; St Vincent and the Grenadines Marine Insurance Act, Cap 105 [1990 Rev.]; Trinidad and Tobago Marine Insurance Act, Cap 45:01 [1980 Rev.]; Turks and Caicos Marine Insurance Act 1959, Cap 711.
27 Section 23(4), Barbados Marine Insurance Act, Cap 292.
28 Misrepresentation Acts No. 7 of 1992 and No. 12 of 1983. This operated in Antigua and Barbuda. Section 2(2) of the Act vests in the court the discretion to award damages in lieu of rescission or avoidance.
29 [1987] 1 Lloyd's Rep 109.
30 Here, the assured effected a household contents insurance policy with the defendant insurers. He completed and signed a proposal form, which among other things stated the value of the contents of his flat as being £12,000. To the best of my knowledge and belief. It contained a basis of contract clause. The statements were true at the time. In 1990 the insured's parent came to England from Cyprus and took up residence in the flat. They brought with them same jewelry and silverware worth £300,000. The insured took little interest in the items but increased the sum assured. The insured's denied liability on the basis that of non-disclosure and misrepresentation. The court followed earlier cases finding that Section 20 of the Marine Insurance Act laid down the law on misrepresentation for all insurances. Held in favour of the insured. He had honest belief. Note that Gibson LJ found that the insured did have reasonable grounds for belief.
31 Barbados, Cap 326 E.

7.7   COMMON LAW

In order for an action for misrepresentation to be successful, the statement must be one of fact, not opinion or law. It must be a statement of present fact and it must have induced the innocent party into making the insurance contract on the terms on which it was made. The statement must be untrue or inaccurate. If there is no basis of contract clause, the statement must be material to the making of the insurance contract and the questions posed are not exhaustive.

As Shanks J stated in *Hilton v Barbados Fire and Commercial Insurance Ltd*:[32]

> it is important to note the limits of this doctrine in a business context the assured's duty of disclosure is not confined to his actual knowledge; it also extends to those material facts which, in the ordinary course of business, he ought to know. But a person effecting insurance cover as a private individual must disclose only material facts known to him and he is not to have ascribed to him any form of deemed or constructive knowledge.[33]

It is also sufficient if facts which are disclosed put insurers on inquiry and their inquiry would in the normal course elicit such further facts as may be material.[34] An entirely innocent misrepresentation may entitle the insurer to avoid the insurance, but where the representation is qualified and stated to be to the best of an assured's knowledge and belief, then provided the assured is honest in making the representation the insurer is not entitled to avoid the insurance even if it is in fact inaccurate.[35]

Misrepresentation is available to either the insured or the insurer and is relevant, outside of insurance law, to both the law of tort and contract law. A distinction emerges however between its application in general contract/tort law and that in insurance law. While it appears to be immaterial whether the falsehood in insurance law was fraudulent, negligent or innocent,[36] in the case of fraudulent misrepresentation, the innocent party has an additional cause of action at common law, under the tort of deceit.[37] Traditionally at common law, negligent misrepresentation has a distinct identity. This approach is, however, uncertain as it relates to insurance law.[38]

Misrepresentation has assumed greater relevance as a result of the decision of *Economides v Commercial Union Assurance Co. plc*. There is distinction between innocent misrepresentation where the insured knows the truth and innocent non-disclosure where the insured knows the truth and does not think it important.[39]

Misrepresentation is available to both insured and insurer. With respect to the insured there is Commonwealth Caribbean jurisprudence, where the insurer has been held to have misrepresented material facts by incorrectly asserting that the insured had an insurable interest or that the policy had certain tax benefits. An example is *Caribbean Atlantic Life Assurance Co. Ltd*

32   LC 2005 HC 48.
33   See *Halsbury's of England*, supra n. 8, para. 44 and *Economides v Commercial Union* [1997] 3 All ER 636.
34   See *Halsbury's of England*, supra n. 8, para. 37 and *Anglo-African Merchants v Bayley* [1969] 2 All ER.
35   See *Halsbury's of England*, supra n. 8, para. 47.
36   Supra n. 27.
37   *Derry v Peek* (1889) 14 App Cas 337.
38   Supra n. 22.
39   Supra n. 23.

v Nassief[40] arising from the jurisdiction of Dominica. In this case, the insured alleged that the insurer and its agent incorrectly informed the insured that if he purchased the policy, premiums were tax deductible. The Court of Appeal, in finding for the insured that misrepresentation was established, held that the premiums were recoverable. It is important to observe that the insurer's argument – that the contract was no longer executory as the insurer was already at risk so that the insured was not entitled to a return of his premiums – failed. Thus, in the case of innocent misrepresentation by the insurer, the insured is entitled to rescind the contract and claim return of premiums at any time.[41]

The burden of proof required to establish fraudulent misrepresentation is understandably much higher. In *Baptiste v British American Insurance Co. & White*,[42] another decision arising out of Dominica, the insured's claim that the insurer misrepresented the nature of the insurance contract failed. In *Baptiste*, an illiterate plaintiff effected an accident and sickness policy with the defendants paying $1.40 cents per week. It was alleged that the agent, who spoke in both English and Patois,[43] induced the insured to enter into the contract – a 20-year endowment policy and not an accident and sickness policy as the insured thought. Mr Justice Barridge stated:

> My conception of the law is that a misrepresentation is fraudulent when a person makes it knowing it to be false or without belief in its truth, or recklessly, without caring whether it is true or false and, it is sufficient if a person has knowingly assisted in inducing another to enter into a contract by leading him to believe that which the former knows to be false, he knowing that if that other person had not been thus misled he would not have entered into the contract.[44] . . .
> Be that as it may, however, I believe the defendant, White, when he says what he outlined to and offered the plaintiff was a 20 year endowment policy.

A misrepresentation is fraudulent when a person makes it knowing it to be false or without belief in its truth, or recklessly, without caring whether it is true or false. In the seminal decision of *Economides v Commercial Union Assurance Co. plc*,[45] the insurer pleaded both misrepresentation and non-disclosure; the Court found that Section 20 of the Marine Insurance Act (the equivalent to Section 23(5) of the Barbados Marine Insurance Act) laid down the law on misrepresentation for all insurances. Finding in favour of the insured, they concluded that a representation as to a matter of expectation or belief is true if it is made in good faith. On the facts, the insured had acted in good faith when he stated the value of the contents of his flat as £12,000 – statements which were true at the time the policy was effected but which were inaccurate in 1990, when the insured's parents came to England from Cyprus and took up residence in the flat, bringing with them some jewelry and silverware worth £300,000. The insured took little interest in the items but increased the sum assured. In response to the claim by the insurers that a requirement of reasonable grounds was to be implied into Section 20(5), the Court of Appeal refused to stretch statutory interpretation to unacceptable levels, finding that honesty was all that was required.

---

40 Court of Appeal of Dominica No. 1 of 1970.
41 In *British Workman's and General Assurance Co. v Cunliffe* (1902) 18 TLR 502, the insured effected a contract through an agent of the insurers who represented that the policy would be valid and effective. In fact, the insured did not have insurable interest to effect the insurance and the insured successfully claimed a return of premiums. The Court of Appeal found that the misrepresentation, although innocent, was made by a man skilled in insurance matters to a person ignorant of the law.
42 Supreme Court of Dominica No. 120 of 1966.
43 The *Oxford English Dictionary* defines 'patois' as 'the speech or dialect peculiar to one part of the country, differing from standard or written English.'
44 *Lee v Jones* (1864) 34 LLCP 131, per Blackburn J at 140.
45 Supra n. 21.

A critical element of an action for misrepresentation is materiality, that is if it would 'influence the judgment of a prudent insurer in fixing the premium, or determining whether he will take the risk.' Materiality in an action for misrepresentation is the same as that for non-disclosure. In the Grenada decision of *Bernard v N.E.M. West Indies Insurance Ltd*,[46] the plaintiff deliberately misstated that he was the owner of a motor vehicle which in fact was owned by his brother. Patterson J, regarding utmost good faith as the second great principle of insurance law, observed on the issue of materiality that during negotiations the assured must make full and frank disclosure of all such material facts which he must know or ought to know any prudent insurer would want to discover.[47] Stating that materiality is always a question to be determined by the court and is a question of fact in each case, he concluded:[48]

> Applying the facts of this case to this principle, it is pellucidly clear that there was a deliberate misstatement of a material fact by the plaintiff that he, was the owner of the vehicle. This duty to disclose material information also exists when a claim is made.

While the facts suggest fraudulent misrepresentation, such a determination is unclear from the judgment. Instead, the High Court focused on the plaintiff's breach of the duty of *uberrimae fides*.

7.8 NON-DISCLOSURE

There is no class of documents to which the strictest good faith is more rigidly required in the courts of law than policies of insurance.[49] The duty to disclose originates from the Marine Insurance Act. This provides that a contract of 'marine insurance is a contract based upon the utmost good faith and if the utmost good faith be not observed by either party, the contract may be avoided by the other party.'[50] The assured's duty to disclose continues up until the contract of insurance is concluded.[51] In the event of a continuing duty, the insurer specifically, by way of a warranty, for example information regarding alteration in the risk or a change in circumstances, places upon the insured an additional continuous obligation to disclose which operates to extend the duty to disclose. In practice, this is likely to occur in commercial contracts. Generally, unlike the position with misrepresentation, the law itself does not distinguish between fraudulent, negligent or innocent non-disclosure.

Lord Mansfield appears to have considered a difference between the concealment which the good faith prohibited and mere silence. Sometimes the policy itself can distinguish between fraudulent and innocent non-disclosure. In *Arab Bank plc v Zurich Insurance Co.*,[52] the policy itself excluded the insurer's right to avoid for non-disclosure or misrepresentation where the assured could establish that the alleged non-disclosure, misrepresentation, was innocent and free of any 'fraudulent conduct or intent to deceive.' In the absence of express language, no distinction between possible causes of non-disclosure operates.

---

46 High Court of Grenada No. 113 of 1981.
47 *Glicksman v Lancashire and General Assurance Co. Ltd* [1925] 2. KB 593, 1927 AC 139 at 143; see also *Locker & Wolf Ltd v Western Australian Insurance Co.* [1936] 1 KB 408.
48 *Zurich Insurance Co. v Morrison* [1942] 1 All ER 529 at 542.
49 Per James VC, *Mackenkie v Coulson* (1869) LR 8 Eq 368; see further H. Y. Yeo, 'Of Reciprocity and Remedies: Duty of Disclosure in Insurance Contracts' [1991] *LS* 131; Kelly, 'The Insured's Rights in Relation to the Provision of Information by the Insurer' [1989] *Insurance L.J.* 45.
50 Section 20, Barbados Marine Insurance Act, Cap 292.
51 Section 21(1), Barbados Marine Insurance Act, Cap 292.
52 [1999] 1 Lloyd's Rep 262.

7.9 RATIONALE FOR THE DUTY TO DISCLOSE

The rationale for duty to disclose is the assumption that the underwriter knows nothing about the risk while the insurer knows everything.[53] It is generally accepted as having originated from a judgment of Lord Mansfield as long ago as 1766 in the *locus classicus* decision of *Carter v Boehm*,[54] where he states 'insurance is a contract upon speculation. The special facts upon which the contingent chance is to be computed, lie more commonly within the knowledge of the insured only.' This statement has been consistently applied to justify the principle of non-disclosure in insurance contracts. There exists academic discourse, however, which holds that the court's application of the duty to disclose misinterprets Lord Mansfield's judgment, creating an entirely different doctrine than that intended by Lord Mansfield himself.[55]

7.10 BASIS OF THE DUTY TO DISCLOSE

Differences surrounding the basis of the duty to disclose[56] may be associated with three schools of thought. Earlier authorities saw the duty to disclose as contractual – an implied term of the contract. In the Barbadian decision of *Matthew Joseph v CLICO International General Insurance Co. Ltd*,[57] Chief Justice Simmons opined that

> In a contract for fire insurance, in addition to the express terms constituted through the answers to the specific questions in the proposal form, there is an implied term of the contract that the person seeking insurance must communicate to the insurer all matters within his knowledge which are in fact material to the question of insurance and not merely those which he believes to be material.

This statement seemingly supports the viewpoint that disclosure is an implied term of the contract. However, given that Section 21(1) of the Barbados Marine Insurance Act provides that the 'assured must disclose to the insurer, before the contract is concluded,' how therefore can the requirement of *uberrimae fidei* be an implied term of the contract? Another approach perhaps is to view the duty not as an implied duty but as a condition precedent to the conclusion of the contract of insurance.[58] A third school of thought suggests that the nature of the duty is fiduciary.[59] There is *dicta* supporting the latter view. In *Joel v Law Union and Crown Insurance Co. (No. 2)*,[60] Flecture-Moulton LJ stated that the requirement of the insurer to establish that the insured consented to the accuracy of his statement is merely 'the fulfilment of a duty – it is not contractual.' Whatever the basis of the duty to disclose – whether contractual duty implied into the terms of the contract, a condition precedent to the conclusion of the contract or a duty which is fiduciary in nature – it is beyond doubt that the duty of *uberrimae fidei* is an essential requirement of the contract of insurance.

---

53 See further P. Matthews, '*Uberrimae Fides* in Modern Insurance Law,' in F. D. Rose, ed., *New Foundations in Insurance Law, Current Legal Problems* (Stevens & Son: 1987); J. Fleming, 'Insurers' Breach of Good Faith – A New Tort?' (1992) *LQR* 357.
54 (1766) 3 Burr 1905.
55 R. A. Hasson, 'The Doctrine of *Uberrimae Fides* in Insurance Law – A Critical Evaluation' (1969) *MLR* 615.
56 R. W. Hodgin, 'The Early Development and Rationale of Utmost Good Faith in Insurance Law,' in David Feldman and Franklin Meisel, eds, *Corporate and Commercial Law: Modern Developments* (LLP: 1996).
57 Civil Appeal No. 2 of 2003.
58 Supra n. 48.
59 *Merchants & Manufacturers Insurance Co. v John Hunt* [1941] 1 KB 863.
60 [1908] 2 KB 863.

7.11   CONSEQUENCES OF A BREACH OF *UBERRIMAE FIDEI*

In accordance with Section 20 of the Barbados Marine Insurance Act, 'if utmost good faith is not observed by either party, the contract may be avoided by the other party.'[61] The operative word is 'may,' so that non-disclosure does not automatically avoid a contract of insurance; it merely makes it voidable. The permissive language bestows on the insurer the right to elect by either affirming or avoiding, the act of avoidance making the contract no longer binding on the insurer who is entitled to refuse to uphold its end of the bargain. The right to avoid a contract on the grounds of undisclosed or misrepresented circumstances arises only if the undisclosed or misrepresented circumstances are material.

Another important observation, the House of Lords decision in *Banque Financièr de la Cité SA v Westgate Insurance Co. Ltd,*[62] reveals the imbalance with respect to the remedies available to the insurer and those available to the insured. Not only is the duty imposed on the insurer framed in far narrower terms than that imposed on the insured, but whereas the insured's breach of duty entitles the insurer to avoid the contract *ab initio*, in contrast, on the insurer's breach, the insured is entitled only to rescind the contract. Damages are not available to the insured who is confined to the remedy of return of premiums only.[63]

7.12   MATERIALITY

An essential component of the duty to disclose is the question of materiality. In the words of Hamel-Smith in the decision of *Hosein & Co. v Goodwill Life & General Insurance Co. Ltd,*[64] non-disclosure does not exist in isolation. 'The crucial qualification [on the duty of *uberrimae fidei*] is the right to avoid a contract on the basis of non-disclosure hinges on materiality.' The insured must disclose to the insurer, before the contract is concluded, every material circumstance. Section 21(2) of the Barbados Marine Insurance Act stipulates: 'Every circumstance is material that *would influence the judgment of a prudent insurer*[65] in fixing the premium, or determining whether he will take the risk.'[66]

The section does not provide guidance on the degree of influence required. The standard is the objective test of the prudent insurer that is determined by the court from objective evidence. The difficulty courts face is that while the test to be applied in order to determine whether or not a non-disclosed fact is material is a question of law, the actual determination of the issue in any particular case involves the resolution of a question of fact. As such, 'it is generally a question solely for the trial judge or arbitrator and not subject to appeal, and, furthermore, strictly no decision is actually binding in a latter case under the doctrine of precedent.'[67] Moreover in construing the section, the critical question for the courts is what test of materiality

---

61   Section 17, Barbados Marine Insurance Act of 1906.
62   [1991] 2 AC 249.
63   W. Anderson, *Banque Financièr de la Cité SA v Westgate Insurance Co. Ltd*, Caribbean Law Reports, *Anglo-Amer. L. Rev.* 140; Yeo, supra n. 23; Kelly, supra n. 23; J. Birds [1990] *JBL* 512.
64   [1990] 3 Carib. Comm Law Rep 163.
65   Emphasis added.
66   Section 18(2), Marine Insurance Act of 1906.
67   Supra n. 23.

applies. Uncertainty arises because the courts are faced with two possible interpretations: (1) the narrow test, that the circumstance of non-disclosure must have had a decisive influence on the judgment of the prudent or reasonable insurer[68] or (2) the wide test, that the circumstance is one of which the insured 'would have wished to know.'[69]

The narrow test

A narrow interpretation of the phrase 'would influence the judgment of a prudent insurer' equates the meaning of the term 'judgment' with the final decision, that is, 'would have a decisive influence in the determination of the premium.' The narrow approach has now, however, been rendered virtually obsolete as a result of the House of Lords decision of *Pan Atlantic Insurance Co. Ltd v Pine Top Insurance Co.*,[70] which endorsed the broad approach pronounced in *Container Transport International Inc. v Oceanus Mutual Underwriting Association (Bermuda) Ltd.*[71] Prior to *CTI* and *Pan Atlantic*, the more stringent approach – equating affecting the mind with those considerations which will ultimately determine whether or not the insurer will accept insurance and, if so, at what premium and on what condition – was evident in the decisions of *Lambert v Co-operative Insurance Society Ltd*,[72] *Barclays Holdings (Australia) Pty Ltd v British National Insurance Co. Ltd & Anor*[73] and the High Court of Trinidad and Tobago decision of *Hosein & Co. v Goodwill Life & General Insurance Co. Ltd.*[74] In *Hosein*, the issue for consideration was whether the failure by the plaintiff to disclose his previous claims experience amounted to a material non-disclosure. The plaintiff, an attorney at law, was issued with an insurance policy covering office furniture, equipment, fixtures and fittings and law books. After a fire broke out, the insurance company refuted the claim, alleging that the fire was caused by the plaintiff's deliberate act and material non-disclosure in his proposal, leading to the conclusion of the formation of the policy. The court found that there was material non-disclosure of the previous cancellation, that the majority of the law books claimed were never in the office and that the claim was fraudulent. The dilemma as to the interpretation of the rubric 'would influence the judgment of a prudent insurer' was succinctly captured in the judgment of Hamel-Smith J:

> A contract of insurance cannot be avoided simply on the grounds of non-disclosure. The non-disclosure does not exist in isolation. The crucial qualification is that the right to avoid a contact of insurance on the grounds of non-disclosure arises only if the undisclosed circumstances are material to the risk. What is material fact has been defined over the years by authority and although generally accepted, the implementation of the rule is not always an easy task. The rule that: 'It is the duty of the insured to communicate all facts within his knowledge which would affect the mind of the underwriter at the time the policy is made, either as to taking the contract of insurance, or as to the premium on which he would take it.' The materiality of the facts depends upon whether or not a prudent underwriter would take the fact into consideration in estimating the premium, or in underwriting the policy. It is the interpretation or application

---

68   *Barclays Holdings v British National Ins. Co. Ltd* (1987) 8 NSWLR 514; *Hosein & Co. v Goodwill Life Insurance & General Insurance Co. Ltd* (High Court of Trinidad and Tobago Suit No. 6603 of 1988).
69   *Containers Transport International Inc. v The Oceanus Mutual Underwriting Association (Bermuda)* [1984] 1 Lloyds Rep 476.
70   [1995] 1 AC 501.
71   [1984] 1 Lloyd's Rep 476.
72   Ibid.
73   (1987) 4 ANZ Ins Cases 60–770.
74   Supra n. 64.

of the test which is the cause of some difficulty. Some judges interpret it in a broad way, others in a much more restricted way. The words 'would affect the mind of the underwriter' is therefore not without ambiguity.

The narrower the interpretation of the phrase 'would influence the judgment of a prudent insurer,' the better the situation is for the insured. In *Hosein*, although the court applied the more stringent decisive influence test, this was nevertheless satisfied given the circumstances of the case. Citing with approval the judgment of Justice Kerr in *Barclays Holdings (Australia) Pty Ltd v British National Insurance Co. Ltd & Anor*,[75] Justice Hamel-Smith reasoned that the preference for the more stringent test over the less stringent approach was that the latter sought to impose too onerous an obligation on the insured

> to disclose virtually endless material about the insured's past leaving it open, to the insurer to deny indemnity claiming that this or that fact would have been taken into account, even though the insurer was unable positively to assert that such fact would ultimately have been determinative in the critical decisions of acceptance or rejection of insurance.

Hamel-Smith J, clearly motivated by a desire to ease the burden placed on the insured, stated:

> It appears that in every case, notwithstanding what was said in *CTI*, the decision of whether a fact is material such that it ought to have been disclosed is a question that can only be answered by looking at the whole of the facts and coming to a judgment as to whether the fact which was not disclosed would reasonably have affected the prudent insurer. I am prepared to follow the more stringent test as laid down in *Barclays*. It is accepted there that the burden imposed on the insured to declare material which would reasonably affect the mind of a prudent insurer is already a heavy one. It involves an element of fiction, so to speak, that the insured will have some appreciation of the operation of the mind of a prudent insurer and some foresight as to what matters will 'affect' that mind. It would be unreasonable to expect an insured to know, in any detail, the kinds of considerations which would affect the business decisions of the insurer . . . The more stringent the test at least goes some way in protecting the insured against a *variety of prudent insurers*.

Despite the valiant attempt by Justice Hamel-Smith to advance the cause of the poor insured, there is evidence that the Commonwealth Caribbean has rejected the narrow stringent approach and embraced the broad test of materiality as postulated in *Container Transport International Inc. v Oceanus Mutual Underwriting Association (Bermuda) Ltd*[76] and reaffirmed in *Pan Atlantic Insurance Co. v Pine Top Insurance Co. Ltd*.[77]

The broad test

The broad test of materiality posits that the phrase 'would influence the judgment' in Section 21 of the Barbados Marine Insurance Act should be construed broadly to mean the 'formation of an opinion' rather than as having a decisive influence on the outcome. The wealth of Commonwealth Caribbean common law embracing *CTI* and *Pan Atlantic* leads to the inevitable conclusion that it is now virtually impossible to resurrect a narrow construction of the phrase 'would influence the judgment.'

---

75 Supra n. 73.
76 Supra n. 71.
77 [1994] 3 All ER 581.

But before exploring the Caribbean decisions of *Bowe v British Fidelity Assurance Ltd*[78] and *Solomon Ghany Oil & Engineering Ltd v N.E.M. (West Indies) Insurance Ltd*,[79] it is useful to examine the English jurisprudence which has so heavily influenced regional courts.[80]

The landmark House of Lords decision *Pan Atlantic Insurance Co. v Pine Top Insurance Co. Ltd*[81] has understandably shaped judicial thinking on the duty of disclosure removing any doubt as to which test applies. This decision may be considered important on several fronts: (1) by adopting the actual inducement test, so that the effect of the disclosure is defined by the expression 'influence the judgment of a prudent insurer,' an assimilation of the law of non-disclosure and that of misrepresentation occurs, so that non-disclosure of a material fact must *induce* the underwriter to enter into a contract; (2) proof of materiality now leads to a presumption of inducement in favor of the insurer; and (3) the broad test of materiality as postulated in *CTI* has been reaffirmed. Construing the term 'would' as opposed to 'might' in the Marine Insurance Act,[82] the legislature looked to the consequence which, within the area of uncertainty created by the civil standard of proof, is definite rather than speculative. According to Lord Mustill, the legislature might have said 'decisive influence' or 'conclusive influence' or 'determine the decision,' but instead left 'influence' unadorned. Consequently, the phrase bore its ordinary meaning: the effect on the thought processes of the insurer in weighing the risk. The result is that the test of materiality accords with the duty of the assured to disclose all matters which would be taken into account by the underwriter when assessing the risk. In essence, the *Pan Atlantic* decision promotes exactly what Justice Hamil-Smith in *Hosein* warned against.

7.13   ANALYSIS AND WEAKNESSES

Although there is an abundance of Caribbean case law endorsing the *Pan Atlantic* approach, closer analysis reveals that regional courts have, by wholesale adoption of the decisions of *Pan Atlantic* and *St Paul's Fire*, neatly sidestepped an analytical deliberation on the nature of the duty of *uberrimae fidei*.[83] The relevance of the *Pan Atlantic* decision to Caribbean jurisprudence can be gleaned, for example, from the decision of *Matthew Joseph v CLICO International General Insurance Co. Ltd*,[84] arising from the Court of Appeal of Barbados.[85] Here Chief Justice Simmons opined:

> It is elementary law that a contract of insurance is one of utmost good faith (*uberrimae fidei*) and as such, that requirement of good faith must be observed by both the insured and the insurer throughout the existence of the contract. In practice, the requirement of *uberrimae fides* means simply that an applicant for insurance has a duty to disclose to the insurer all material facts

---

78   Supreme Court of the Bahamas No. 372 of 1997.
79   High Court of Trinidad and Tobago No. S3114 of 1986.
80   *Solomon Ghany Oil & Engineering Ltd v N.E.M. (West Indies) Insurance Ltd* (unreported decision, Trinidad and Tobago HCA No. S3114); *Bowe v British Fidelity Assurance Ltd* (unreported decision, High Court of the Bahamas No. 372 of 1997); *Zainool Mohammed v Capital Insurance Co. Ltd & All Trinidad Sugar Estates & Factory Workers' Trade Union* (1990) 1 TLR 43.
81   Supra n. 77.
82   (i) The final decision of a prudent insurer would have been decisively influenced by the fact misrepresented or not disclosed; (ii) the fact was one which would have been of interest to a prudent insurer; and (iii) the House of Lords voted by a 3–2 majority, the decisive infuence test was rejected and the CTI test favoured.
83   Brooke, supra n. 22; Diamond, supra n. 22; Steyn J, supra n. 22; H. Bennett, 'The Duty to Disclose in Insurance Law,' (1993) *LQR* 513.
84   Unreported decision, Court of Appeal of Barbados Civil Appeal No. 2 of 2003.
85   Civil Appeal No. 2 of 2003.

within the applicant's knowledge which the insurer does not know. There is a duty of disclosure and a duty not to misrepresent facts. The test of materiality was settled by the House of Lords in *Pan Atlantic Co. Ltd v Pine Top Co. Ltd* [1994] 3 All ER 581 on a 3:2 majority. Lords Mustill, Goff and Stynn, approving in part *Container Transport International Inc. v Oceanus Mutual Underwriting Association (Bermuda) Ltd.* [1984] 1 Lloyd's Rep 476, held that, for the purposes of marine and non-marine insurance a circumstance is material if it would have had an effect on the mind of a prudent insurer in weighing up the risk. This test accorded with the duty of an insurer when assessing the risk. The House also held that, for an insurer to be entitled to avoid a policy for misrepresentation or non-disclosure, the alleged misrepresentation or non-disclosure must be material and must have induced the making of the policy. Lord Mustill at 617.

Recently, in *Drake Insurance v Provident Insurance*, the English Court of Appeal held that inducement must be proved by the insurer.[86] It is therefore a question of fact. Whether non-disclosure or misrepresentation of a fact is deemed material, the insurer has a right to repudiate the contract of insurance as a principle of ordinary law of contract.

Another Caribbean decision in which the *Pan Atlantic* approach applied is *Bowe v British Fidelity Assurance Ltd*, arising from the jurisdiction of the Bahamas.[87] The plaintiff, the beneficiary of the deceased's estate, claimed under a life insurance policy effected by the deceased with the defendant insurers. The insurers rejected the claim on the basis that the insured deliberately withheld information regarding his excessive use of alcohol amounting to a material non-disclosure. The proposal form asked several questions: 'Have any of the persons listed . . . (g) Ever been treated or counseled or joined an organization because of alcoholism or drug abuse?' To this the deceased answered 'no.' However, when subsequently examined by a medical examiner appointed by the defendant insurance company, in response to a medical examiner's report ('Have you ever been treated for or ever had any known indication of excessive use of alcohol, tobacco or any habit-forming drugs?'), the deceased insured answered 'yes.' Further details were given. 'Beers weekends x 2.' The Court of Appeal, Justice Lyons, in finding for the insurer, observed that the law on

> these insurance matters is that the contracts are governed by the principles of utmost good faith (*uberrimae fidei*). It is well settled that material facts must be disclosed, if not the contract is voidable in accordance with Lord Mansfield's statement in *Carter v Boehm*.[88]

Determining whether the statement made by the insured was fraudulent, it has been acknowledged that the insured normally possesses superior knowledge and greater means of discovering material facts connected to the proposed risk.

It is incumbent upon the insured to provide accurate disclosure of sufficient facts such that the underwriter may fairly assess the risk.

> A fraudulent statement is one that is made without an honest belief in the truth by the maker but nevertheless that the recipient should act upon it (see *Derry v Peak* [1889] 14 App. Cas. 337) . . . whole thing together, was there false representation? I do not care by what means it is conveyed – by what trick or device or ambiguous language: all those are expedients by which fraudulent people seem to think they can escape from the real substance of the transaction. If by a number of statements you intentionally give a false impression and induce a person to act upon it, it is not the less false although if one takes each statement by itself there may be a difficulty in chewing that any specific statement is untrue . . . Applying the above to the facts of this case,

---

86   [2004] Lloyd's Reports IR 277.
87   Ibid.
88   Supra n. 54, 1909–1910.

it is inescapable, in my opinion, that the insured set up a pattern of false answers so as to avoid having to reveal the full extent of his alcoholism. Of itself, the answer 'beers weekends x 2' is somewhat innocuous. However when placed against the other answers where the insured has denied medical treatment and even hospitalization which, in one way or another, seemed to be associated with his alcoholism, that answer takes on a more sinister complexion. It appears to me that the answer given was deliberately ambiguous so as to not alert the insurance company . . . To do this he had to avoid telling the insurance company the precise magnitude of his problem. He did this by giving false and misleading answers to those questions posed by the agent when filling out the life insurance proposal, and to the medical officer. I do not think it good enough for the insured to give a general disclosure which points in a certain direction. In my view he has to put before the insurance company all of the information in his possession.

Justice Lyon, quoting Fletcher Moulton LJ's judgment in *Joel v Law Union and Crown Insurance*,[89] and the Court of Appeal of *Pan Atlantic Co. v Pinetop Insurance Co.* held that the fraudulent representations were material and were such that the presumption applied that the insurer was influenced by the fraudulent representation. Had full disclosure been made, a reasonable insurer would have been alerted to the fact that the insured's alcohol problem was such that 'it impacted not only on his general health but also on the very thing that the life insurance policy was concerned with – the preservation of the insured's life.'

Caribbean courts clearly recognise *Pan Atlantic* as having settled the test of materiality as that established in *CTI* and inducement as a requirement of the duty of utmost good faith. The decisions also indicate that inducement is presumed in favour of the insurer. In the case of *Bowe*, the insured's chronic alcoholism clearly supported the presumption in that case it is. In both *Matthew Joseph* and *Bowe*, no attempt is made to distinguish fraudulent misrepresentation from non-disclosure, an approach understandable in light of earlier discussion, and while *Matthew Joseph* cites the subsequent decision of *Drake*, there is no definitive discussion on the parameters of the duty of utmost good faith or as to how the presumption will operate. In this regard it is important to appreciate Lord Lloyd's powerful dissenting judgment in *Pan Atlantic*. Lord Lloyd was of the view that the presumption of inducement was a 'myth long exploded.' He reasoned that for the purposes of Section 18 of the Marine Insurance Act, the phrase 'influence' should be determined by the question whether or not the influence had a decisive effect in moving the underwriter to accept the risk. Admittedly the dissenting judgment was not the view of the majority of the House of Lords. Essentially the House of Lords rejected the narrow test because it required reading more into the equivalent to Section 23 of the Barbados Marine Insurance Act than was apparent on its face. But surely the majority, by concluding 'that there is to be implied in the Act of 1906 a requirement that a material misrepresentation will only entitle the insurer to avoid the policy *if it induced the making of the contract*,'[90] amounts to the same offence since there is no mention of 'inducement' in Section 23.[91] Unfortunately it is no longer open to contest the insertion of the requirement of inducement into the requirement of good faith. Moreover, to those who hold fast to the view that by attaching inducement to the requirement of *uberrimae fidei*, an additional burden is placed on the insurer ultimately enuring for the benefit of the insured, this is no longer supportable given the ease with which inducement, it being presumed, can be found. In *Matthew Joseph*, the court separated the prudent insurer from the actual insurer, enabling the actual insurer to state that regardless of the fact that the undisclosed material may not have induced the prudent insurer into the contract, it

89   Supra n. 60, 883, 884.
90   Per Lord Goff.
91   Supra n. 22.

nevertheless induced him, the actual insurer. The Court of Appeal in the subsequent decision of *St Paul Fire & Marine Insurance Co. (UK) Ltd v McConnell Dowell Constructors Ltd*[92] discussed at length the reasoning in *Pan Atlantic* and regarded it as having settled the uncertainty as to the test of materiality. In *St Paul Fire*, an 'all risk insurance' was procured by the defendant for a major construction project. The insurance was placed on the basis that piled foundations would be used. Various preliminary reports provided differing views on the suitability of the founda-tions. In fact, the foundations were inadequate and subsidence occurred. The insurers pleaded misrepresentation although it was accepted that there had been no intention to mislead them. On the presumption of inducement, the Court of Appeal endorsed the approach adopted by Lord Mustill, finding that the correct view was that the insurer was entitled to rely upon the presumption of inducement – the test being satisfied where the insurer could show that he was influenced in whole or in part by the assured's misleading presentation of the risk.

While marine insurance legislation suggests the necessary causal link between the undis-closed facts/misrepresentation and the insurer's right to rescind, its focus is on the objective 'prudent insurer' rather than on the actual underwriter. The problem explained is 'the current court's insistence on separating the prudent insurer from the actual insurer, is what is causing the problem, and this insistence is both unnecessary, and unfair.' To introduce the actual insurer into the equation places an additional burden onto the insured. It opens the door for an insurer to claim that regardless of the fact that the undisclosed material may not have induced the prudent insurer into the contract, it nevertheless induced him, the actual insurer, with all of his 'particular idiosyncrasies.'[93] *St Paul* effectively makes many of the potential safeguards of the House of Lords in *Pan Atlantic* redundant.[94] An insurer can simply rely on the presumption of inducement, that the misrepresented or undisclosed fact was *an* inducement, not necessarily *the* inducement.

The nature and import of the requirement of inducement thus remains unclear. In *Marc Rich & Co. AG v Portman*,[95] Longmore J stated that the presumption of inducement can only operate where the actual underwriter cannot, for very good reason, give evidence and there is no reason to suppose that he acted other than prudently; at the end of the day it is for the insurer to establish inducement. Effectively *Marc Rich* narrowed the scope of inducement so that it would only be triggered where the insurers were unable, with good reason, to give evidence, a position upheld by the Court of Appeal without any clarification of the issue.[96] It is important to appreciate that *Marc Rich* was decided before *St Paul Fire*, but nevertheless the subsequent decision of *Assicurazoni Generali SpA v Arab Insurance Group (BSC)*[97] utilised this bifur-cation. In *Assicurazoni*, Clarke LJ drew a sharp distinction between materiality on the one hand and inducement on the other. The court stressed that materiality was based on an objective test, whereas non-disclosure was clearly a subjective issue.

Clarke LJ laid out the following guidelines:

(i) In order to be entitled to avoid a contract of insurance or reinsurance, an insurer or rein-surer must prove on the balance of probabilities that he was induced to enter into the contract by a material non-disclosure or misrepresentation;

(ii) There is no presumption of law that an insurer or reinsurer is induced to enter in the con-tract by a material non-disclosure or misrepresentation;

---

92 [1996] 1 AER 96.
93 Supra n. 22.
94 Ibid.
95 [1996] 1 Lloyd's Rep 430.
96 Ibid.
97 [2003] 1 WLR 577.

(iii)   The facts may however be such, that it is to be inferred that the particular insurer or reinsurer was so induced, even in the absence from evidence from him;

(iv)   In order to prove inducement, the insurer or reinsurer must show that the non-disclosure
or misrepresentation was an effective cause of his entering into the contract on the terms
on which he did. He must therefore show at least that, but for the relevant non-disclosure
or misrepresentation, he would not have entered into the contract on those terms. On the
other hand, he does not have to show that it was the sole effective cause of his doing so.

Endorsing the point that the non-disclosed or misrepresented fact need not be the sole inducement but simply an effective cause of the particular insurer or reinsurer in entering into the
contract, if the insurer would have entered into the contract on the same terms in any event, the
representation or non-disclosure will not, however material, be an effective cause of the making
of the contract and the insurer or reinsurer will not be entitled to avoid the contract.

In *Insurance Corp. of the Channel Islands v Royal Hotel Ltd*,[98] the falsification of the hotel's occu-
pancy rates to inflate the sums payable under a business interruption policy easily amounted to
inducement. But in *Drake Insurance plc v Provident Insurance plc*,[99] a case cited with approval in the
Barbadian decision of *Matthew Joseph*, inducement was not established. It is necessary to recite
with some particularity the facts of *Drake Insurance*. In *Drake*, a case of motor insurance, B was
seriously injured as a result of a car accident. The car was driven by K and the car belonged
to K's husband. Both the husband and the wife had separate insurance. The appellant company, Drake, covered the wife whilst she was driving any vehicle with the owner's consent. The
respondent company, Provident, covered the husband. B commenced proceedings against K,
and Drake settled the claim. Drake then sought a 50% contribution from Provident. It was
common ground that the non-disclosure was objectively material due to an elaborate point
system, and thus Provident's case hinged on the inducement issue. Provident denied liability
alleging, *inter alia*, that there was a pre-contractual non-disclosure by S of a speeding conviction
incurred by K, which the insurers said was both material and which induced them to enter into
the contract. The Court of Appeal held that the insurer had no right to avoid the policy as it
had not been induced to enter into the contract by reason of the speeding conviction. Had
the fact been disclosed on renewal, the insurer would have charged a higher premium. It is
clear that *Drake* must be understood in light of its special facts, but collectively, the decisions of
Drake and *Asucorozoni* confirm not only that the onus lies on he who alleges but that further, the
insured may assert that a non-disclosure of a material fact would have made no difference to
the insurer. Thus uncertainty exists as to the context in which *Drake* was cited and applied in the
decision of *Matthew Joseph*, since on the facts *Matthew Joseph* is distinguishable as the insured's
previous claims history would indeed have made a difference to the action.

7.14   DURATION AND SCOPE OF NON-DISCLOSURE

Duration

It is obvious from the Marine Insurance Act that the duty to disclose continues up until the
contract is concluded. Thus if there is a change of circumstance prior to the conclusion of
the contract, the insured is under a duty to disclose.[100] In the absence of an express term to the

---

98   [1998] Lloyd's Rep IR 151.
99   [2003] EWCA Civ 1834; [2003] 1 All ER (D) 02.
100   *Looker v Law Union and Rock Insurance Co. Ltd* [1928] 1 KB 554; *Mayne Nickless Ltd v Pegler* [1974] 1 NSWLR 228.

contrary, there is no corresponding duty during the currency of the policy,[101] and a clause which purports to extend this duty other than in clear and express language will fail.[102]

Scope of duty to disclose

Marine insurance legislation, together with Lord Mansfield's statement in *Carter v Boehm*, clearly indicates that the duty to disclose is a mutual one imposed on both insurer and insured. However, the House of Lords decision in *Banque Financièr de la Cité SA v Westgate Insurance Co. Ltd*[103] indicates that the duty imposed on the insurer is framed in far narrower terms. Moreover, whereas the insured's breach of duty entitles the insurer to avoid the contract *ab initio*, on the insurer's breach, the insured is entitled to rescind the contract. Damages are not available to the insured who is confined to the remedy of a return of premiums only.[104]

7.15   SCOPE OF MATERIALITY

Once the test of materiality to be applied has been determined, it is necessary to ascertain whether, on the facts, the failure to disclose is material. Material facts fall into two categories: those relating to the physical hazards (i.e. statements relating to the property, life or liability of the insured) and those relating to the insured's moral hazard (e.g. claims history or previous convictions). With respect to previous convictions, despite the presence of Rehabilitation of Offenders legislation in some territories, the court may still permit evidence of 'spent' convictions if justice so requires. Also the duty to disclose previous convictions seemingly embraces allegations or rumours of criminal activity.

7.16   PHYSICAL HAZARD

Marine insurance legislation requires disclosure of all facts which are known or presumed to be known by the insured about the life, property or liability of the insured.[105] There is no requirement to disclose that which is not known. There are several decisions highlighting the application of this principle in life insurance. In *Joel v Law Union and Crown Insurance Co.*,[106] the insured was asked if she had any mental illness. She answered in the negative, unaware that she had been treated for acute mania. She later committed suicide. The Court refused the jury's finding and held that the insurers were liable on the policy. In the words of Fletcher-Moulton LJ, 'The duty is to disclose and you cannot disclose what you do not know.' Similarly, in the House of Lords decision of *Cook v Financial Insurance Co. Ltd*,[107] the insured effected disability

---

101 *Pim v Reid* (1843) 6 M & G 1.
102 In *Kausar v Eagle Star Insurance Co. Ltd* [2000] Lloyd's Rep 154, a clause in a policy stated 'you must tell us of any change in circumstances after the start of the insurance which increases the risk of injury or damage.' Saville LJ restrictively interpreted this phrase so as to avoid an imposition of continuing duty to disclose.
103 Supra n. 62.
104 Supra n. 63.
105 Section 18, Marine Insurance Act 1906.
106 *Joel v Law Union & Crown Insurance Co.* [1908] 2 KB 863.
107 [1998] 1 WLR 1765.

insurance with the defendant insurers on 15 October 1992. The policy contained an exclusion clause which provided:

> No benefit will be payable for disability resulting from (a) any sickness, disease, condition or injury for which an insured person received advice, treatment or counseling from any registered medical practitioner during the 12 months preceding the commencement date.

The insured, who regularly went running, collapsed in July 1992 while on a training run. He saw his GP, who could find nothing wrong. On 4 September, the insured again went to the GP complaining of breathlessness and chest pain. Although she thought he was suffering from a viral infection, the GP nevertheless referred him to a cardiologist to exclude the possibility of angina. On 16 October the cardiologist diagnosed him with angina. In December, he was advised to give up work due to angina. The insurers refused payment relying on the exclusion clause. Deciding, *inter alia*, on the issue of whether the insured received advice or treatment prior to 15 October, the House of Lords found in favour of the insured, stating that in order for the exemption clause to operate, some knowledge on the part of the doctor of the disease which he is treating is required, and that on the facts the earliest date on which the insured received advice for angina was 16 October 1992.

Conversely, where the insured is aware of an ailment he is under a positive duty to disclose. In *Marks v First Federation Life Insurance Co. Ltd*,[108] Question 18 in the proposal form, which the plaintiff signed, inquired whether he had ever had any of the diseases mentioned in a long list of diseases and whether he had within the past five years received medical attention for any reason whatsoever; if so, he was to give details. He answered 'No.' Under Question 10, he was also asked whether he was in good health and he gave the answer 'Yes.' In fact, the insured failed to disclose that within the period of five years prior to the effective date of the policies he had received medical attention after suffering an attack of amoebic hepatitis and had spent a period of time in hospital, during which time he received treatment for this disease. Although there was no connection between the attack of hepatitis which produced the jaundiced condition and the coronary insufficiency or angina pectoris which came upon the plaintiff seven months after the effective date of the policies, the insurer was held to be entitled to repudiate the policies, as the non-disclosure of a material fact by the insured rendered the policy of insurance null and void. Applying the decision of *Locker & Woolf Ltd v Western Australian Insurance Co. Ltd*,[109] the court ruled that even if disclosure was made to an agent who withheld information from the insurer, the agent's knowledge is not to be imputed to the insurer, and the insurer was free to repudiate his liability under the contract.

It is well settled that insurance is a contract *uberrimae fidei* and requires full disclosure of such material facts as are known to the assured. The assured must disclose everything known to him that is material in fact, even though he does not appreciate its materiality and even though a reasonably prudent man would not do so.[110]

Another regional decision which illustrates the extent of the insured's duty to disclose is the decision in *Walter Pillay v Guyana & Trinidad Mutual Life Assurance Co. Ltd*.[111] In *Walter Pillay*, the deceased, who held a pilot student's licence, effected an insurance policy with the defendant insurers. The insured failed to disclose that he was a student pilot and had actually flown as a

---

108 (1963) 6 WIR 185.
109 [1936] 1 KB 408.
110 *London Assurance v Mansel* (1879), 11 Ch D 363.
111 (1972) 18 WIR 220.

pupil. Chief Justice Bollers in the Supreme Court, pronouncing that the principles of English law relating to fire and life insurance prevail in Guyana, found that the deceased's flying activity was a material fact to the issuing of the policy and that further, the basis of contract clause, where the assured warrants the answers in the proposal form as true, did not limit the proposer's common law duty to disclose all material facts within this knowledge. The importance of basis of contract clauses will be considered later, but it is clear that questions in the proposal form are not to be construed as exhaustive; silence or failure to acknowledge or question a particular habit on the part of the insurer will not amount to waiver of the common law duty to disclose.[112]

The construction of the proposal form was also integral in the decision of *Alleyne v Colonial Fire & General Insurance Co. Ltd & Agostini Insurance Brokers Ltd*,[113] on appeal against the judgment of Justice Ventour granting a declaration in favour of Colonial Fire and its entitlement to avoid a policy of motor insurance under Section 10(3) of the Motor Vehicles Insurance Act, on the ground that the policy was obtained by the non-disclosure of a material fact and/or misrepresentation. There, in response to a question in the proposal form as to whether the proposer suffered from defective vision or hearing or from any disease or physical infirmity, the proposer replied 'No.' In fact, the appellant was blind in his left eye. Justice Mendonca stated:

> the contract of insurance is based on utmost good faith and the duty of disclosure is an integral part of the duty to act with the utmost good faith. The insured is under a duty to disclose, before the contract is concluded; every material circumstance that is known to him. It is immaterial whether the omission to communicate the material facts arises from indifference or mistake or because it was not present in the mind of the insured that the fact was one which was material to be made known or that the insured did not think material.

In this case, the court followed the English decision of *Zurich General Accident and Liability Insurance Ltd v Morrison*[114] and *Pan Atlantic Insurance Co. Ltd v Pine Top Insurance Co. Ltd*,[115] embracing the broad test of materiality and concluding that the test sought to determine whether it induced creation of the contract upon appropriate terms.

Justice Ventour, relying on Scrutton LJ's judgment in *Glicksman v Lancashire & General Assurance Co.*,[116] ruled that the loss of an eye fell into the category of cases where the materiality was so obvious that it was unnecessary to call expert evidence to establish its materiality. Further, concluding that the non-disclosure or misrepresentation induced the making of the policy, the judgment of a prudent insurer ought not to be influenced by the fact that the authority responsible for issuing driving permits under Section 48 of the Motor Vehicles and Road Traffic Act[117] had in fact issued a permit to a person with one eye and imposed a restriction that he must wear corrective lenses,[118] stating that they were unable to accept, without more, that where someone has lost an eye, use of a corrective lens on the existing eye can compensate for the missing eye and fully restore his capacity to assess speed and distances. In the absence of expert evidence on the effectiveness of corrective lenses, the statement of the appellant that 'he can see as well as a two eyed man with corrective lenses' is of no weight and of no probative value, so that the respondent was entitled to avoid the policy on the basis of non-disclosure of a material fact.

---

112 In *WISE Underwriting Agency Ltd v Grupo Nacional Provincial SA* [2004] EWCA Civ 962 [2004] 2 All ER (Com) 613, Longmore LJ recognised that where the assured has failed to disclose material facts, there is relatively little scope for an argument that the insurers are to be taken to have waived disclosure.
113 Unreported decision, Trinidad and Tobago Court of Appeal No. 58 of 2004.
114 [1942] 2 KB 53.
115 Supra n. 77.
116 [1935] 2 KB 593.
117 Chapter 48:50.
118 See further *Facer v Vehicle and General Insurance Co.* (1965) 1 Lloyd's Rep 113.

The decision of *Alleyne*, while expressly endorsing the *Pan Atlantic* approach (a position also reflected in the decision of *Somati-Ali v Hand-in-Hand Mutual Fire & Life Insurance Co. Ltd*,[119] arising out of the Guyana jurisdiction), reveals the scope of the duty to disclose as it relates to the physical hazard. In *Somati-Ali*, the issue that arose for consideration was whether plaintiff's bankruptcy, which was subsequently discharged a little over one year later, was material to the contract of insurance. Bernard CJ correctly distinguished the decision of *Galle Gowns Ltd v Licences and General Insurance Ltd*,[120] where the 'hectic financial past' of the director of the company amounted to an obvious financial instability, leading the court to conclude that material facts were concealed. In *Somati-Ali*, on the other hand, the insurer was precluded from denying liability. The refusal of the court to extend the physical hazard to the insured's discharged bankruptcy reveals a limitation on the scope of the duty to disclose.

Another example of the duty to disclose circumstances relating to the physical hazard can be seen in the decision of *Green's Wholesale v American Home Assurance Co. Ltd*.[121] Here the plaintiff's claim for indemnity was defeated by his non-disclosure of all material facts, in that he crossed out 'sports car' on the form and put instead 'two-door,' committing a false representation of fact. The High Court held that the insured was guilty of wilful concealment of a material fact and of positively asserting a fact which he knew to be false. Justice Singh clarified the position in the following manner:

> The law is very clear that this type of contract where one party is in a strong position to know material facts and where the other party is in a very weak position to discover them, the former is under a duty not only to abstain from making false representations of material facts but also to disclose in the utmost good faith, such material facts as are within his knowledge to the other party. These contracts are commonly described as '*uberrimae fidei*.'

7.17   MORAL HAZARD

Moral hazard cases fall into three defined categories: (1) matters relating to nationality of origin,[122] (2) information on criminal convictions and (3) information of previous claims history.[123] Disclosure of matters relating to nationality or origin can be quickly dispensed with, as the written constitutions of most Commonwealth Caribbean territories expressly protect the rights of citizens against discrimination on the basis of race, colour or creed, similar in nature[124] to Section 23(1) of the Barbados Constitution.[125]

In accordance with express this constitutional provision, there is no moral hazard for failure to disclose one's race or nationality.

---

119 (2001) 65 WIR 186. See also the decisions of *Solomon Ghany Oil & Engineering Ltd v N.E.M (West Indies) Insurance Ltd* and *Zainool Mohammed v Capital Insurance Co. Ltd and All Trinidad Sugar Estates and Factory Workers' Trade Union*.
120 (1933) L1 LR 186.
121 Unreported decision, High Court of Dominica No. 191 of 1983.
122 *Horne v Poland* [1922] 2 KB 364.
123 *Glicksman v Lancashire & General Assurance Co. Ltd* [1927] AC 139; *Tuky Air Transport Inc. v The Liquidator of Edinburgh Insurance Co. Ltd (In Liquidation)*, British Virgin Islands High Court Suit No. 3 of 1984.
124 Section 14, Antigua and Barbuda Constitution No. 1106 of 1981; the Bahamas Constitution No. 1080 of 1973; Belize Constitution 1981, Cap 4; Dominica Constitution No. 1027 of 1978; Section 24, Jamaica (Constitution) Order in Council 1962 LN 50/1979; Section 15, St Kitts and Nevis Constitution Order No. 881 of 1983; Section 13, St Lucia Constitution Order No. 1901 of 1978.
125 1966[Rev.].

7.18   INFORMATION ON PREVIOUS CONVICTIONS

Statute. Rehabilitation of Offenders legislation

Several jurisdictions have enacted Rehabilitation of Offenders legislation, removing the burden placed on the insured to disclose prior convictions which have become 'spent' under the statute. In so doing, the legislation acts as a fetter on the insurer's right to avoid a contract on the basis of a failure to disclose a previous conviction. In accordance with Section 4 of the Cayman Islands Rehabilitation of Offenders Act, the effect of such legislation is that the person is treated as having been rehabilitated – as having 'not committed, been charged with, prosecuted for, convicted of, or sentenced for the offence which was the subject of that conviction.'[126] Section 23(4) of the Barbados Criminal (Rehabilitation of Offences) Act 'prohibits any insurance company from knowingly attempting to avoid a policy of insurance on the basis of non-disclosure of a spent or expunged conviction is guilty of an offence' and Section 24 of the Act 'fixes the penalty for breach at $10,000, or to imprisonment for a term of two years.' Thus an applicant for insurance is never bound to disclose a conviction which has become spent under the terms of the Act, and the insurer is similarly prohibited from avoiding cover on the basis of a spent conviction.

The legislation operating in the Commonwealth Caribbean is similar in nature to that of the UK Rehabilitation of Offenders Act 1974.[127] It prescribes varying periods of rehabilitation which correlate to the seriousness of the sentence imposed. It does not apply to certain excluded offences, such as a sentence imposed for life, a sentence of imprisonment for a term exceeding 30 months or a sentence of detention during the government's pleasure.

A notable feature of the regime is that the Act bestows discretion upon the court to permit evidence of previous convictions. For insurance law the difficulty that arises is the degree of impact on the issue of disclosure. Section 7(d) of the Barbados Criminal Records (Rehabilitation of Offenders) Act[128] bestows on the court the discretion to admit spent convictions if the court is satisfied that justice cannot be done in the case except by admitting it: 'any civil or criminal proceedings where justice cannot be done without admitting or requiring evidence relating to a person's spent convictions.' This provision is on all fours with Section 7(3) UK

---

126 See Section 23(1) of the Barbados Constitution:

> Subject to the provisions of this section (a) No law shall make any provision that is discriminatory either of itself or in its effect; and (b) no person shall be treated in a discriminatory manner by any person acting by virtue of any written law or in the performance of the functions of any public office or any public authority. (2) In this section the expression 'discriminatory' by means affording different treatment to different attributable wholly or mainly to their respective description by race, place of origin, political opinions, colour or creed whereby persons of one such description are subjected to disabilities or restrictions to which persons of another such descriptions are subjected to disabilities or restrictions to which persons of another such description are not made subject or are accorded privileges or advantages which are not afforded to persons of another such description.

127 A schedule of rehabilitated offences is prescribed in the first schedule to the Act. For a sentence of imprisonment for a term not exceeding one year – seven years.

> A sentence of imprisonment for a term between 1 and 3 years – 10 years; and for a non-custodial sentence, the rehabilitation period is 5 years. A person, under the age of 16, who committed a crime and who has not been convicted of any other offence since that time up until the age of 23 shall be treated as a rehabilitated person under section 3(4). In accordance with section 6 thereof, no evidence shall be admissible in any proceedings before any judicial authority and a person shall not in any such proceedings, be asked, and if asked, shall not be required to answer any questions relating to his past which cannot be answered without acknowledging or referring to the spent conviction.

128 Barbados Criminal Records (Rehabilitation of Offenders) Act No. 6 of 1997.

Rehabilitation of Offenders Act,[129] and the implications thereof remain a mystery. The issue arose for consideration in *Reynolds v Phoenix Assurance Co.*[130] In this case the issue was whether the insured's conviction in 1961 for receiving stolen goods was a material fact which should have been disclosed under Section 7 of the Rehabilitation of Offenders Act. The offence came to light only after the case commenced and the insurers sought to amend their pleadings to allege its non-disclosure. The Act did not apply when the plaintiff applied for insurance in 1972, but it did apply when the matter came to trial. The Court of Appeal held that the pleadings should be amended on the ground that no prejudice would be caused to the plaintiff. Whether or not evidence of the conviction should be admitted then became a matter for the trial judge. Forbes J considered that there were only two factors which required consideration: first, the extent of the dishonesty and second, the age of the conviction. Justice Forbes found that the defendant insurers failed to prove that the particular conviction some 11 years previously was a material fact which would have affected the judgment of a reasonable or prudent insurer in fixing the premium or determining whether to cover the risk. Stating *obiter* on the application of the Rehabilitation of Offenders legislation, the discretion to allow evidence of the spent conviction will not be exercised unless justice could not be done except by admitting evidence of the spent conviction. The implication of the foregoing is that the mere presence of Rehabilitation legislation is not necessarily the end of the matter. First, the Act operates in accordance with stipulated criteria. Second, the Court has the discretion to admit evidence of spent convictions. In this regard the import of regional legislation has yet to be tested. *Reynolds* remains instructive on the exercise of discretion, so that it appears that despite the presence of such legislation, if it is established that the circumstance is material there is no real injustice to the insured by admitting such evidence given that they obtained insurance which ordinarily they would not have secured.

7.19   COMMON LAW

In the absence of statutory incursion by way of Rehabilitation of Offenders legislation, the law reveals that the courts take an extremely broad view when determining the materiality of previous convictions and are prepared to consider outstanding criminal charges and acquittals.[131] The danger is that groundless allegations, circumstances which raise suspicion of involvement in criminal activity but which are subsequently proven false, and circumstances which contain some element to truth which would affect the risk all go to moral hazard. In *Strive Shipping Corp. v Hellenic Mutual War Risks Association (Bermuda) Ltd (The Grecia Express)*,[132] Colman J explained that the attribute of materiality of a given circumstance has to be tested at the time of the placing of the risk and by reference to the impact which it would then have on the mind of a prudent insurer. Three types of circumstances were identified, providing some insight as to the extent of the duty:

(1) allegations of criminality or misconduct going to moral hazard which had been made by the authorities or third persons against the proposer and are known to him to be groundless;

(2) circumstances involving the proposer or his property or affairs which may to all out-ward appearances raise suspicion that he has been involved in criminal activity or misconduct going to moral hazard but which he knows not to be the case;

129 C. 53; S4(3)(a).
130 [1978] 2 Lloyd's Rep 22.
131 *Inversiones Manria SA v Sphere Drake Insurance Co. plc, The Dora* [1989] 1 Lloyd's Rep 69; *Brotherton v Aseguradoa Colseguros SA* [2003] EWCA Civ 705.
132 [2002] 2 Lloyd's Rep 88.

(3)   circumstances involving him or his business or his property which reasonably suggest that the magnitude of the proposed risk may be greater than what it would have been without such circumstances.

Accordingly, the fact an allegation is unfounded cannot divest the circumstance of allegation of the attribute of materiality. However it is not necessary for the assured to evaluate perfectly innocent facts in order to see whether they might or might not be misconstrued by an under-writer. Justice Colman considered that the duty to disclose did not involve such a rigorous approach. Further, if the assured knows of facts which, when viewed objectively, suggest that facts might exist ('the suggested facts') which would increase the magnitude of the risk and the known facts would have influenced the judgment of a prudent insurer, the known facts do not cease to be material because it may ultimately be demonstrated that the suggested facts did not exist. The procedural and evidential consequences which flow from these conclusions were summed up as follows:

(1)   In the field of moral hazard, a failure by the assured to disclose an existing allegation against him of dishonesty or relevant criminal conduct or a criminal charge will normally be non-disclosure of a material fact which *prima facie* entitles the insurer to avoid the policy;

(2)   If, in proceedings in which the insurer seeks to avoid the policy for such non-disclosure the assured proves that the allegation or charge was unfounded and that there has been no dishonesty or criminal conduct on his part, the insurers will not normally be entitled to avoid the policy . . .;

(3)   If I am wrong in concluding that an assured is under no duty to disclose faces merely because they are objectively suspicious as to his wrong-doing when he knows that the suggested facts do not exist, it must by parity of reasoning be open to the assured to displace the underwriters' entitlement to avoid for non-disclosure of circumstances because they are objectively suspicious by proving that the suspicion was misplaced and that the facts of the existence of which there was suspicious never in truth existed;

(4)   If the facts objectively raise suspicion going to the magnitude of the risk, the assured is under a duty to disclose them but if at the trial he establishes that there was in truth no basis for those suspicions it is not open to the insurers to invoke the Court's equitable jurisdiction to avoid the policy.

How far are the courts prepared to go? In *Strive Shipping*, Colman J followed *March Cabaret Club and Casino v London Assurance*[133] regarding outstanding criminal charges and acquittals as relevant. In *Solomon Ghany*, decided before *Grecia* and *Brotherton*, a threat to 'burn the place down' was considered material. In *Brotherton v Aseguradoa Colseguros SA*,[134] media reports of allegations of the Colombian reinsureds were also treated as relevant. Here, Mance LJ drew a distinction between material intelligence that might ultimately be demonstrated as unfounded but which should nevertheless be disclosed by an insured and immaterial, idle rumours which need not be disclosed.[135] It can be argued that media reports may support manifest knowledge within the language of Section 21(3)(b) of the Barbados Marine Insurance Act,[136] as a circumstance that is known, 'matters of common notoriety or knowledge.'

---

133   [1997] 1 Lloyds Rep 169.
134   [2003] EWCA Civ 705.
135   *Lynch v Hamilton* (1810) 3 Taunt 15.
136   Section 18(3)(b), Marine Insurance Act of 1906.

But surely this is a dangerous development which further exacerbates the plight of the insured. To the extent that Colman J's judgment provides a guide, in *Brotherton*, Mance LJ disagreed with Colman J's analysis in the *Grecia Express* that avoidance is an equitable remedy that is, therefore, discretionary. Colman J in *Grecia* was of the view that where the insurers who have avoided a policy subsequently learn that the non-disclosed fact was not actually material, they may be held to be in breach of their own duty of utmost good faith on the basis of their inequitable behaviour. The Court of Appeal in *Brotherton* contended that the right to avoid was a self-help remedy that could be exercised without the court's authorisation, that is avoidance which can be justified at the time the remedy was exercised cannot subsequently be challenged.

Undoubtedly, the duty to disclose is not confined to facts within the insured's actual knowledge.[137] In *Schoolman v Hall*,[138] the criminal record of the proposer was held to amount to a material fact which ought to have been disclosed. In *Roselodge v Castle*,[139] where the insureds, diamond merchants, effected an 'all-risks' policy. The proposal form did not ask, and the insureds did not disclose, whether any of their employees had previous convictions. In fact one of the employees had been found guilty of bribing a police officer 18 years earlier, and another one had been convicted of smuggling diamonds into the United States eight years earlier. The insurers refused a claim on the theft of the diamonds. The court found in favour of the insurer. It was held that the bribery conviction some 20 years earlier fell short of the test laid down in *Joel's* case and need not have been disclosed, but that the smuggling conviction for which a prison sentence was imposed should have been disclosed.[140] It is important to appreciate that none of the questions in the proposal form required disclosure of previous convictions. *Lambert v Co-operative Insurance Society*[141] is another harsh decision. In April 1963, the insured effected an 'all-risks' policy covering her jewelry and her husband's jewelry. At the time she did not disclose the fact that her husband had been convicted some years earlier for receiving stolen cigarettes, for which he was fined £25,000. The policy contained a condition which provided that it would be *ipso facto* void if there was non-disclosure of a material fact. The questions in the proposal form were silent on the occurrence of previous convictions. The policy was renewed in December 1971, after which time the husband was again convicted for offences relating to dishonesty and was sentenced to a prison term. This fact was not disclosed at the next renewal. In April 1972, the insured's claim for £311 was rejected by the insurers who claimed misrepresentation and non-disclosure. Lord Justice Mackenna in the Court of Appeal, finding for the insurers, commented on the unsatisfactory state of the law and observed that the insured was not an underwriter and presumably has no experience in these matters. 'The defendant company would act decently if, having established the point of principle, they were to pay her. It might be thought a heartless thing if they did not but that is their business.'[142] The case law illustrates that the duty of disclosure is onerous and extends beyond the insured to connected persons.

---

137 *Glasgow Assurance Corp. v Symondson* (1911) 16 Com Cas 109; *Glicksman v Lancashire & General Assurance Co.* [1927] AC 139; *Locker & Woolf v Western Australian Insurance Co.* [1936] 1 KB 408; *Co-operative General v Alberta Human Rights Commission* (1992) 2 CCLI (2d) 176.
138 [1951] 1 Lloyd's Rep 139.
139 [1966] 2 Lloyd's Rep 105.
140 [1975] 2 Lloyd's Rep 485.
141 Ibid.
142 Ibid.

7.20　INSURANCE HISTORY: CLAIMS HISTORY AND CANCELLATIONS

A failure by the insured to disclose a previous denial of coverage or claims history goes to the insured's moral integrity.[143] In such circumstances the insured will be viewed as an undesirable person with whom to have contractual relations. In *Locker & Woolf Ltd v Western Australian Insurance Co. Ltd*,[144] a failure to disclose a previous denial of cover was held as material, and there is *dicta* suggesting that a refusal in motor insurance may be regarded as material to a fire insurance policy.[145] This decision can be contrasted with *Tuky Air Transport Inc. v The Liquidator of Edinburgh Insurance Co. Ltd (In Liquidation)*,[146] a case originating from the British Virgin Islands. In *Tuky*, the insurers unsuccessfully alleged, *inter alia*, the non-disclosure of certain facts relating to other insurance coverage and past claim payments made by other insurers.[147]

A distinction must be made between moral hazard as it relates to previous claims history and/or cancellation and instances where the insured fails to disclose an existing insurance policy. There have been several cases in the Commonwealth Caribbean which, while not based strictly on previous claims history and/or cancellation, are based on the insured's failure to disclose a co-existing policy. In such circumstances the question becomes not simply one of materiality, non-disclosure or misrepresentation but one of breach of an express term.[148]

In the Court of Appeal of Trinidad and Tobago decision *Dalkhan v Colonial Life Insurance Co. Ltd*,[149] the appellant insured his house and its contents with the respondent insurance company against loss by fire. He failed to disclose, however, that he had effected insurance with another company against similar loss and further misrepresented the value of the property. The house was destroyed by fire and the appellant's claim for $23,000 was denied. Although the factual circumstances of the case surround moral hazard, the presence of an express condition negated discussion on the question of materiality. The express term made it irrelevant. Accordingly, the issue is not merely one of non-disclosure or innocent misrepresentation of the fact but one of alleged breach of express condition of the policy.

7.21　NATURE OF THE PROPOSAL FORM

Enshrined within the discussion on utmost good faith, misrepresentation and non-disclosure is the nature and import of the proposal form. The proposal form precedes the issuance of the insurance policy and is the document which assists the insurer in making an informed decision as to whether or not to accept the proposer's risk. It is well settled that the proposer must be honest and truthful with the insurer; similarly, it is the duty of the insurer to be fair in its dealings with the insured.[150] As stated by Chancellor Crane in *New India Assurance Co. Ltd v Asseran Jumai &*

143　Per Slesser LJ, *Locker & Woolf Ltd v Western Australian Insurance Co. Ltd* [1936] 1 KB 408.
144　Supra n. 109.
145　*Locker & Woolf Ltd v Western Australian Insurance Co. Ltd* [1936] 1 KB 408.
146　British Virgin Islands High Court Suit No. 3 of 1984.
147　The High Court found, *inter alia*, that the legal relationship between the insurer and the insured had been affected by waiver so that the defendant insurer no longer relied strictly on the provisions in the contract of insurance, and further, that neither in law nor on the evidence did the plaintiff conceal or misrepresent any material fact or circumstance concerning the proposal for insurance coverage.
148　*Matthew Joseph v CLICO International General Insurance Co. Ltd.* (unreported decision, Court of Appeal of Barbados Civil Appeal No. 2 of 2003).
149　(1967) 12 WIR 133.
150　*Condogianis v Guardian Assurance Co.* [1921] 2 AC 125.

Chooraman Gangasarran,[151] a respondent cannot urge in his favour that the insurers are liable to indemnify him regardless of whether he chooses to speak the truth or not in his proposal: 'it would make a nonsense of the basis clause on which the company's liability is founded.'

Invariably, the proposal form contains a 'basis of contract' clause. As acknowledged by Chief Justice Simmons in *Matthew Joseph v CLICO International General Insurance Co. Ltd,*[152] the declaration at the foot of the proposal form that the statements are true and the declaration shall form 'the basis of the contract' of insurance makes the truth of the statements a condition precedent to the liability of the insurer. By incorporating the insured's answers provided in a proposal form into the insurance policy as truthful and correct, it defines the duty of disclosure and prescribes the manner in which that duty is to be performed.[153] The performance of the duty outlined in the proposal form by virtue of the presence of a basis of contract clause is contractual, however, and if it is not performed, there is a breach of the contract of insurance rather than a breach of a duty to disclose. The decision of *Walter Pillay v Guyana & Trinidad Mutual Life Assurance Co. Ltd*[154] reveals the importance of the basis of contract clause to the question of disclosure. Such a clause is invariably contained in the proposal form, a document central to the conclusion of the contract of insurance. Representing a potential trap for the unaware insured, the breadth of the duty to disclose is often not confined to facts within the insured's actual knowledge and extends to all material facts which he ought to have known.[155]

7.22 THE BASIS OF CONTRACT CLAUSE AND THE ISSUE OF MATERIALITY

Generally, the basis of contract clause will read: 'I declare that the statements hereby made by me, the insured, are true and shall be the basis of contract between the insured and the company.' Such a clause represents a trap for the unwary insured. Its effect is to incorporate the insured's answers into the insurance policy as truthful and correct. In the event of an untruthful answer, it is immaterial whether the insured acted in good faith to the best of his knowledge and belief. Further, it obviates the need for the court to embark upon an investigation into the materiality of the omission, which is a question of law.[156] The House of Lords decision in *Anderson v Fitzgerald*[157] held that the presence of a basis of contract clause removed any question of materiality from consideration. Similarly in *Thomson v Weems,*[158] the policy of insurance asked (1) Are you temperate in your habits? (2) And have you always been strictly so? The insured responded (1) 'temperate' and (2) 'yes.' The House of Lords, after admitting that there was untruth without any moral guilt, held that the insurer was entitled to avoid the contract. In *Dawsons Ltd v Bonnin,*[159] an incorrect statement as to where a van was garaged (the van was subsequently destroyed by fire) entitled the insurer to avoid the contract. The word 'basis,' being construed as more than merely 'pleonastic,' hence the misstatement about where the lorry was garaged, was found to be contractually material.

---

151 (1980) 28 WIR 231.
152 Unreported decision, Barbados Civil Appeal No. 2 of 2003.
153 See Chapter 5.
154 Supra n. 111. See further Anderson, 'The Duty To Disclose Material Information Not Solicited in the Proposal Form,' (1991) 3 *Carib. Comm. L.J.* 1, 45.
155 *Schoolman v Hall* [1951] 1 Lloyd's Rep. 139.
156 *Anderson v Fitzgerald* (1853) 4 HLC 483.
157 (1853) 4 HL Cas 584.
158 (1883–1884) LR 9 App Cas 671.
159 [1922] 2 AC 413.

The presence of such a clause relieves the court from the burdensome, laborious task of determining whether a particular fact is material or not. It represents a breach of an express stipulation defining the duty of disclosure and prescribing the manner in which it is to be performed. The performance of the duty outlined in the proposal form in the basis of contract clause is therefore contractual, and if it is not performed there is a breach of contract of insurance rather than a breach of a duty to disclose. In effect it extends the duty of disclosure not only in relation to the accuracy of the statement, but the general obligation at common law remains.

The mere fact that the insurer has asked a specific question also does not relieve the insured of his general obligation at common law to disclose any material fact which might affect the risk. This principle also applies where the questions posed demand a specific time period for recollection. In *Somati-Ali v Hand-in-Hand Mutual Fire & Life Insurance Co. Ltd*,[160] arising out of the jurisdiction of Guyana, the proposal form did not elicit responses from the proposer about his bankruptcy. The court noted that the training manual for agents was of little assistance as it did not advise agents to request such information from prospective proposers, and further, that textbooks were silent on whether in a case of fire insurance the past bankruptcy of the assured is a material fact. In finding for the insured, the court relied on the decisions of *Reynolds v Phoenix Assurance Co. Ltd*[161] and *Quinby Enterprises Ltd (In Liquidation) v General Accident Fire & Life Assurance Corp. plc.*[162]

In *Quinby*, the manager of the plaintiff company completed a questionnaire which was silent on previous criminal convictions, finances or any other matters affecting the risk not stated in the questionnaire. It was held, *inter alia*, that an insured has a duty to disclose material facts to an insurer even in the absence of specific questions in the insurance proposal:

> The duty of disclosure exists independently of any that, that [*sic*] may be spelt out in the policy documents. This is a positive duty so that it is no answer to an allegation of non-disclosure in a proposal that there was no question specifically directed to the particular point.

This, of course, is in keeping with the general principle stated earlier that contracts of insurance are contracts involving the utmost good faith and necessitating full disclosure of all facts likely to have an effect on the mind of a prudent insurer estimating risk. However, in *Quinby* other pertinent considerations arose. Apart from the criminal convictions of the managing director of the plaintiff company, the company was in poor financial circumstances with allegations of dishonesty, and the trial judge, although conceding that it is not usual for an insured's finances to be disclosed to an insurer when fire cover is sought (except where there is loss of profits' cover), felt that cumulatively there should have been disclosure to the insurers of the plaintiff's precarious financial position. In *Quinby*, the judge did not regard as material for disclosure alleged income tax matters and bounced cheques issued by the plaintiffs. In *Somati-Ali*, restating the viewpoint of *Quinby*, the insurers' evidence will not prove materiality from the point of view of a prudent underwriter:

> the previous bankruptcy of an insured may be a fact which a prudent insurer would want to be informed about in keeping with the utmost good faith which must attend all contracts of insurance. However, it must be shown that it influences the moral hazard assumed by the defendants who issued the policy. Was the cover exposed to the risk of the plaintiff's dishonesty or deceptive

---

160 (2001) 65 WIR 186; see also the decisions of *Solomon Ghany Oil & Engineering Ltd v N.E.M (West Indies) Insurance Ltd* and *Zainool Mohammed v Capital Insurance Co. Ltd and All Trinidad Sugar Estates and Factory Workers' Trade Union*.
161 [1978] 2 Lloyd's Rep 440.
162 [1994] 1 NZLR 736.

conduct? No allegation of dishonesty or criminality has been alleged against the plaintiff, and in addition it has not been shown that the defendants were induced by the non-disclosure to issue the policy, as was held in *Pan Atlantic Insurance Co. Ltd v Pine Top Insurance Co. Ltd*.[163]

In the frequently cited decision of *Schoolman v Hall*,[164] the proposal form, which contained a basis of contract clause, asked no fewer than 15 questions, a least seven of which were confined to a five-year period. The proposal form did not contain any questions on the insured's criminal history. Nevertheless, the Court rejected the argument that the insurer's failure to solicit information on criminal history amounted to waiver, finding that the questions did not relieve the insured of his general obligation at common law to disclose any material which might alter the risk being covered.[165]

7.23   WAIVER

Section 21(3) of the Barbados Marine Insurance Act provides: 'In the absence of inquiry the following circumstances need not be disclosed . . . (c) Any circumstance as to which information is waived by the insurer.'[166] Where an insurance is effected for the assured by an agent, Section 22 of the Act places an obligation on the agent to disclose to the insurer every material circumstance that is known to himself, and an agent is presumed to know every circumstance that ought to be known by him or which have been communicated to him.[167] The issue which arises in the context of proposal forms is whether the insurer can be taken as having waived the right to information by virtue of the manner in which the questions were framed. Suppose a question asked, 'Have you consulted a doctor in the past five years?' In such a case, the insurer is viewed as having waived disclosure of consultations falling outside the five-year period, notwithstanding that such claims would satisfy the test of materiality. Whether or not waiver is present depends on the construction of the policy. It is an objective standard: 'would a reasonable man, reading the proposal form be justified in thinking that the insurer has restricted his right to receive all material information?'[168] In *WISE Underwriting Agency Ltd v Grupo Nacional Provincial SA*[169] it was recognised that where the assured has failed to disclose material facts, there is relatively little scope for an argument that the insurers are to be taken to have waived disclosure.

Another issue is whether the failure of an insurer to stop collecting premiums under a direct debit mandate, after avoidance is sought for non-disclosure, amounts to waiver. In *Drake Insurance plc v Provident Insurance plc*,[170] the insured failed to disclose a speeding conviction when renewing his motor policy. Moore-Brick J held that the defendant insurer was induced to renew and therefore entitled to avoid the policy. On the issue of waiver, the judge considered that the automatic collection of premiums was insufficient evidence of any intent to waive avoidance.[171]

---

163   [1994] 2 Lloyd's Rep 427.
164   Supra n. 155.
165   *New Hampshire Insurance Co. v Oil Refineries Ltd* [2002] Lloyd's Rep 462.
166   Section 21, Barbados Marine Insurance Act, Cap 292.
167   Section 22, Barbados Marine Insurance Act, Cap 292.
168   Per Woolf J, *Hair v Prudential Assurance Co.* [1983] Lloyd's Rep 667.
169   [2004] 2 All ER (Com) 613.
170   [2003] All ER (D) 02.
171   *Phoenix Life Assurance Co. v Raddin*, 120 US 183 (1886); *Schoolman v Hall* [1951] 1 Lloyd's Rep 139; *Hair v Prudential Assurance Co.* [1983] Lloyd's Rep 667; *HIH Casualty & General Insurance Ltd v Chase Manhattan Bank* [2001] Lloyd's Rep IR 703.

7.24   CONTRACTING OUT OF THE DUTY TO DISCLOSE

An important issue that has recently come before the courts is the extent to which the parties can exclude or vary the duty of utmost good faith. In *HIH Casualty & General Insurance Ltd v Chase Manhattan Bank*,[172] the policies in question related to high-risk film finance insurance, containing complex exclusion clauses termed 'truth of statement' clauses. The issues before the Court of Appeal were whether the fraudulent, reckless or negligent non-disclosures by the brokers entitled the insurers to avoid the policies despite the truth of statement clauses and further, whether the insurers were entitled to damages. Rix LJ held, *inter alia*, that non-disclosure could not support an action for damages. He opined that where non-disclosure is concerned, the law does not distinguish, unlike with misrepresentation, between innocent, negligent and fraudulent non-disclosure. Even where the non-disclosure can be described as fraudulent, no remedy of breach of duty of care is available; the only remedy available is avoidance. This case confirms that with respect to non-disclosure, the law does not distinguish among innocent, negligent and fraudulent non-disclosure and that non-disclosure does not give rise to any corresponding duty of care in tort. Later, the House of Lords was asked to decide on a series of preliminary issues on the nature of the 'truth of statement' clauses in *HIH Casualty & General Insurance Ltd v Chase Manhattan Bank*.[173] In this case, since no allegations of non-disclosure or of misrepresentation were made against Chase, the question *inter alia* was whether and to what extent was Chase liable for the misrepresentation of Heath. Lord Bingham construed the clauses in the policy against the general law and declared that Chase, as insured, although expressly relieved of liability of any obligation to make any representation, was not relieved of liability for any misrepresentation which it may voluntarily choose to make. Further, since Chase was expressly relieved of any duty or obligation to make disclosures of any nature and since no attempt had been made to relieve Heath of any liability. The waiver did not extend to the broker who was not relieved of his duty to disclose. Citing *Canada Steamship Lines Ltd v King*,[174] the House of Lords stated:

> There can be no doubting the general authority of these principles, which have been applied in many cases, and the approach indicated is sound. The Courts should not ordinarily infer that a contracting party has given up rights which the law confers upon him to an extent greater than the contract terms indicate he has chosen to do; and, if the contract terms can take legal and practical effect without denying him the rights, he would ordinarily enjoy if the other party is negligent, they will be read as not denying him those rights unless they are so expressed as to make clear that they do. . . . the passage does not provide a litmus test which applied to the terms of the contract, yield a certain and predictable result. The Court's task of ascertaining what the particular parties intended, in their particular commercial context, remains.

Lord Bingham explained that where the non-disclosure or misrepresentation was other than innocent, the insurer might have rights additional to that of avoidance: the right to damages given by Section 2(1) of the Misrepresentation Act 1967 to the victim of the negligent misrepresentation; and the right to recover damages for deceit given by the common law to the victim of fraudulent misrepresentation. Applying this *dicta* to the Commonwealth Caribbean, in the jurisdictions of where misrepresentation legislation exists, the right to damages is now permissible.

---

172 [2001] Lloyd's Rep IR 703.
173 [2003] Lloyd's Rep 61.
174 [1952] AC 192.

7.25 WHAT NEED NOT BE DISCLOSED?

Regional marine insurance legislation clearly outlines the circumstances which need not be disclosed. Section 21(3) of the Barbados Marine Insurance Act[175] provides that in the absence of inquiry, the following need not be disclosed:

(a) any circumstance which diminishes the risk;

(b) any circumstance that is known or presumed to be known to the insurer and the insurer is presumed to know matters of common notoriety or knowledge, and matters that an insurer in the ordinary course of business, as such ought to know;

(c) any circumstance in respect of which information is waived by the insurer; and

(d) any circumstance that is superfluous to disclose by reason of any express or implied warranty.

Subsection (4) states that whether any particular circumstance that is not disclosed is material or not is, in each case, a question of fact. Subsection (5) defines circumstance as including any communication made to or information received by the assured.

7.26 MISCELLANEOUS PROVISIONS UNDER THE INSURANCE ACT

Regional Insurance Acts all contain general provisions regarding misstatements of age. In such circumstances, an insurance policy is not avoided by reason only of a misstatement of age of the person whose life is insured.[176] Instead, the solution adopted is to simply make provision for an adjustment of premiums rather than render the contract void/voidable. In some jurisdictions the Insurance Act goes beyond the position adopted in other jurisdictions and addresses incorrect statements other than age.

Section 122(4) of the Trinidad and Tobago Insurance Act[177] provides that a policy shall not be avoided unless the statement was:

(i) fraudulently untrue, or

(ii) material in relation to the risk of the company under the policy and was within the period of three years immediately proceedings the date on which the policy is sought to be avoided or the date of the death of the life insured, whichever is the earlier.

Similarly, Section 94 of the Jamaica Insurance Act provides:

Nothing in any term or condition of a life insurance policy . . . shall operate to exempt an insurance company from liability under the policy or to reduce the liability of the company under the policy on the ground of any matter relating to the state of health of the person whose life is insured, other than the ground specified in subsection (2)

(2) The ground referred to in subsection (1) is that the proposer when making the contract –

(a) made an untrue statement of his knowledge and belief as regards the matter; or

(b) failed to disclose to the company something known by him as regards that matter.

---

175 Cap 292.
176 Section 109, Barbados Insurance Act No. 32 of 1996, Cap 310; Section 100, Belize Insurance Act No. 15 of 1976, Cap 208; Section 132, Guyana Insurance Act No. 20 of 1998; Section 93, Jamaica Insurance Act No. 10 of 2001; Section 97, St Lucia Insurance Act No. 6 of 1995.
177 Chapter 84:01.

These provisions, in the absence of statements of insurance practice or codes of conduct assist the insured and restrict the instances where the insured is entitled to avoid the contract. It is important to appreciate that the statement must be fraudulently untrue.

7.27   CO-INSURANCE, MISREPRESENTATION AND NON-DISCLOSURE

As we saw in Chapter 5, it is not uncommon for one insurance policy to cover the separate interests of parties especially with respect to modern commerce. Several recent construction cases reveal the practice in modern commerce for one composite policy to be effected to cover various interests; mortgagor and mortgagee and the sub-contractors.[178] The issue that arises is whether the non-disclosure or misrepresentation on the part of one co-insured will entitle the insurer to avoid the contract as against all parties. The answer lies in whether the policy is construed as a single policy or as a series of separate contracts. In *Arab Bank plc v Zurich Insurance Co.*[179] Justice Rix identified three interlinked questions: (1) the construction of the policy, (2) the conceptual analysis of the attributes of composite insurance and (3) the question of attribution. On the construction of the policy, Justice Rix reasoned that composite policies should be viewed, *prima facie*, as a bundle of separate contracts between the insurers and the co-insureds so that dishonesty by one co-insured did not permit the insurers to avoid the policy against other parties.[180] In this case, the policy specifically stipulated that dishonesty of one insured will not be held against another insured who is not complicit. In the absence of Caribbean authority on point, it seems clear that with composite policies, the dishonesty by one co-insured will not entitle the insurer to avoid the policy against other innocent parties.

7.28   CONCLUSION

The preceding discussion reveals that regional marine insurance legislation is largely ignored by Caribbean courts to resolve questions of fraud, misrepresentation and the duty of utmost good faith. Rather, considerable reliance is instead placed on UK jurisprudence. The case law also indicates – admittedly assisted by the manner in which the actions where framed – a marked co-mingling of the defences of fraud, misrepresentation and utmost good faith with no clear distinction in judicial approach. Despite the fact that the wide-ranging duty of disclosure that operates today bears little resemblance to the duty as postulated by Lord Mansfield,[181] the result is that the duty of utmost good faith has effectively enveloped the law pertaining to fraudulent misrepresentation. This development has significant implications for the insured. His opinion of what is material is irrelevant, and although the phrase 'would affect the mind of the underwriter' in Section 18 is not without ambiguity, on the authority of *Container Transport International Inc. v Oceanus Mutual Underwriting Association*, reinforced by the landmark decision of *Pan Atlantic Insurance Co. v Pine Top Insurance Co. Ltd,*[182] the test of materiality is what a reasonably prudent

---

178 See further *Samuel & Co. Ltd v Dumas* [1924] AC 431; *Hastings v Westchester Fire Insurance Co.* 73 NY 141 (1878); *Fisher v Guardian Insurance Co. of Canada* [1995] 123 DLR (4th) 336; *New Hampshire Insurance Co. v MGN Ltd* [1997] LRLR 24.
179 Supra n. 52.
180 For a criticism on this approach see Birds [1999] *JBL* 151; for an acceptance of this approach, see *FNCB Ltd v Barnet Devanney (Harrow) Ltd* [1999] Lloyd's Rep IR 459.
181 Supra n. 55.
182 [1994] 3 All ER.

insurer would wish to know. The more lenient test, as far as the insured is concerned, which briefly made an appearance in the decision of *Hosein*, has now been overruled. This broad test of materiality has since received additional assistance with the introduction of the concept of presumed inducement – an inducement which need not necessarily be the inducement and an approach which is followed by regional authorities. While regional misrepresentation legislation operates in the jurisdictions of Antigua and Barbuda[183] and Trinidad and Tobago,[184] and Rehabilitation of Offenders legislation[185] modifies the duty of *uberrimae fidei* with respect to 'spent' convictions.

Undoubtedly, the upshot of the discussion is that the insured, the law of non-disclosure and materiality are formidable hurdles which have the potential to deprive the insured of the right to recover for genuine loss by perils insured against, even if the misrepresentation or non-disclosure had no bearing on the risk. As noted, 'such injustices as there are must now be dealt with by Parliament, if they are to be got rid of at all.'[186] Unfortunately, unlike the position elsewhere,[187] insurance law reform in the Commonwealth Caribbean has taken place without any considered analysis on the law of misrepresentation as it pertains to insurance and the duty *uberrimae fides* its attendant presumption of inducement, and/or its relevance to Rehabilitation legislation.

183 Supra n. 3.
184 Supra n. 4.
185 Supra n. 5.
186 Per Lord Justice Lawton in *Lambert v Co-operative Insurance Society Ltd* [1975] 2 Lloyd's Rep 485.
187 Law Commission Report, *Insurance Law: Non-disclosure and Breach of Warranty* (1980) Cmnd 8064, Law Comm No. 104; Australia Insurance Contracts Act 1984; The Australian Law Reform Commission Report No. 20, Insurance Contracts (1982): Chapter 6, Non-disclosure and Misrepresentation. Association of British Insurers, *Statements of General Insurance Practice* (ABI: 1986 [1977]); Association of British Insurers, *Statements of Long Term Insurance Practice* (ABI, 1997). Sir Andrew Longmore (Lord Justice of Appeal), 'An Insurance Contracts Act for a New Century?' [2001] *Lloyd's Maritime & Commercial Law Quarterly* 356.

CHAPTER 8

CONTRACTUAL TERMS

8.1   INTRODUCTION

Not all terms in an insurance policy are of equal importance. The basic classification of terms that exist in general contract law of warranties and conditions applies to contracts of insurance. There is, however, a distinction between general contracts and contracts of insurance. According to general contract law, a condition is a fundamental term, the breach of which entitles the innocent party to repudiate the contract, while with respect to a breach of a warranty, the contract continues to exist but the innocent party is entitled to sue for damages. This is not the case with respect to contracts of insurance, in which the position is reversed. Thus a warranty, as opposed to a condition, is considered a fundamental term of the insurance contract, the breach of which automatically discharges the insurer from liability.[1] This distinction between general contract law and insurance law extends beyond the form – the label describing the term – to consequences that flow.

Permeating insurance law, there exists a noticeable, indeed a manifest tension between general commercial contracts and contracts of insurance. An overabundance of regional jurisprudence as displayed, reveals the tension readily apparent from the prevalence with which courts have resorted to the import of contractual terms in deliberations on contentious matters. In the House of Lords decision *Bank of Nova Scotia v Hellenic Mutual War Risks Association (Bermuda) Ltd, The Good Luck*,[2] Lord Goff made reference to the Court of Appeal's confusion between conditions as fundamental terms of a contract and conditions precedent, referring to the 'inveterate practice in marine insurance of using the term "warranty" as signifying a condition precedent.' The imperceptible line between general contracts and those of insurance is exacerbated by insurance law's utilisation of general contract principles to resolve problems within insurance law. Thus for example, where the strict categorisation between warranties and conditions is inappropriate, the concept of innominate terms has emerged in insurance law as a hybrid term.[3] Under general contract law, a breach of a fundamental term entitles the innocent party to elect to repudiate the contract.[4] This position held and was applied in insurance law to breaches of warranties until the decision in *Bank of Nova Scotia v Hellenic Mutual War Risks Association (Bermuda) Ltd, The Good Luck*.[5] Thereafter the term 'repudiation' ceased to be considered appropriate. It became settled law that a breach of a warranty automatically discharged the insurer's liability.[6] At the core of the difficulty for insurance law in the Commonwealth Caribbean sits the ongoing debate on whether recently enacted consumer legislation in the region

---

1   Prior to 1992, the prevailing thought was that a breach of a warranty entitled the insurer to repudiate the contract. Since the House of Lords decision of *Bank of Nova Scotia v Hellenic Mutual War Risks Association (Bermuda) Ltd, The Good Luck* [1992] 1 AC 233, it is settled that a breach of a warranty automatically discharges the insurer from liability.
2   [1991] 2 WLR 1279.
3   *Hong Kong Fire Shipping Co. Ltd* [1962] 2 QB 26; J. Davey, 'Insurance Claims Notification Clause: Innominate Terms and Utmost Good Faith' [2001] *JBL* 179.
4   [1989] *JBL* 348; J. Birds (1991) 107 *LQR* 540; Bennett [1991] *JBL* 598; Clarke [1991] *LMCLQ* 437.
5   Supra n. 2.
6   Supra n. 1.

applies to insurance law. In this regard, to ascertain the nature of contractual terms, the Marine Insurance Act and the common law provide the best source of guidance. Marine insurance legislation has now assumed larger significance for contemplation of contractual terms than it had in the past as a result of the House of Lords decision *Bank of Nova Scotia v Hellenic Mutual War Risks Association (Bermuda) Ltd, The Good Luck.*

8.2   REGIONAL AUTHORITY[7]

There is considerable regional authority. In Antigua and Barbuda, *De Castro v Edinburgh Insurance Co. Ltd*[8] considered whether the plaintiff had breached a warranty of seaworthiness. According to the insured, who loved the boat 'more than he loved his wife,' the express warranty was breached, the ship being sent out in an unworthy state, so the insurer was not liable. In *Royal Caribbean Hotels v Barbados Fire & General,*[9] we see conditions must be strictly complied with. The difference between conditions and exemption clauses is displayed in *Mallalieu v Excess Insurance Co. Ltd,*[10] arising from St Kitts and Nevis.[11] Citing *Bond Air Services Ltd v Hill,*[12] the difference between a condition and an exception is that the former places some duty or responsibility on the assured, while the latter restricts the scope of the policy. In *Charles v The New India Assurance Co.,*[13] an insurer sought to avoid the insured's claim on the grounds that there was a misrepresentation of the age of the driver – whether 25 was a term in the contract – since the policy merely asked for the driver's age and it being a written contract could not be varied except in writing. Parnell J stated the true position seems to be that during the currency of the insurance policy there is no implied condition that the risk may not be materially altered. Wiles J put the matter clearly nearly 120 years ago:[14]

> In effect, there being no violation of the law and no fraud on the part of the assured, an increase of risk, to the subject matter of insurance, its identity remaining, though such increased risk is caused by the assured, if it is not prohibited by the policy, does not avoid the insurance.[15]

Condition subsequent to liability

An example can be found in *Smith v Motor Owners Mutual Insurance Association Ltd.*[16] Here, clause 19 provided: 'In no case whatever shall the Association be liable for any loss or damage after the expiration of twelve months from the happening of the loss or damage unless the claim is the subject of pending action or arbitration.'

A fire took place in 1976 and the action was filed in 1978. It was argued that the contract was voidable at the defendant's instance. As to whether the institution of proceedings within a

---

7   *Hetu v Trinidad & Tobago Insurance Ltd*, BB 1985 HC 36.
8   VG 1977 HC 8.
9   BB 1992 CA 31.
10   KN 1971 HC 1.
11   The question involved the construction of the terms of the insurance policy. The damage to the vehicle was caused by flood, and it was a term of the contract that the company would not be liable for the damage in those circumstances.
12   [1955] 2 All ER 479.
13   DM 1982 HC 7.
14   *Thompson v Hopper* [1858] EB & E 1038 at 1049.
15   Ibid.
16   BS 1983 SC 21.

period of 12 months was a condition precedent to the enforcement of any claim, reference was made to *Halsbury's Laws of England* (4th edn), para. 426, which states:

> A condition subsequent affecting recovery under a policy is a condition dealing with the situation where a claim has arisen, or is alleged to have arisen, and prescribing the duties which have to be fulfilled if the claim is to be enforced. A condition of this kind has to be performed before a claim can be ascertained or before the enforcement of a claim in a particular manner can be obtained.

Such a condition is often described as a condition precedent to the maintenance or enforcement of a claim,

> but in the strict sense it is not a condition precedent as it relates to something to be done subsequent to the commencement of the policy's effective life, and failure to comply with such a condition does not affect the essential validity of the policy itself.

Ambiguity

In *Reynolds v State Insurance Corp.*,[17] the High Court of Antigua and Barbuda applied the case of *Canada Steamship Lines Ltd v The King*,[18] where the Privy Council enunciated the following principles regarding the duty of the Court in approaching the consideration of a clause excluding liability for negligence:

(1) If the clause contains language which expressly exempts the person in whose favour it is made (the proferens) from the consequence of the negligence of his own servants, effect must be given to that provision.

(2) If there is no express reference to negligence, the court must consider whether the words used are wide enough, in their ordinary meaning, to cover negligence on the part of the proferens. If a doubt exists on this point it must be resolved against the proferens, that is, the contra proferentum rule applies.

(3) If the words used are wide enough in their ordinary meaning to cover negligence on the part of the proferens the court must then consider whether the head of damage may be based on some ground other than that of negligence. The existence of a possible head of damage other than that of negligence is fatal to the proferens even if the words used are prima facie wide enough to cover negligence on the part of his servants.

Sookdeo & Sookdeo's Motor Supplies Ltd v Trinidad & Tobago Insurance Ltd[19] emphatically stated:

> the insured shall also at all times at his own expense produce, procure and give to the Company all such further particulars, plans, specifications, books, vouchers, invoices, documents, proofs and information with respect to the claim and . . . any matter touching the liability or the amount of the liability of the company (the defendant) together with a declaration . . . of the truth of the claim . . . No claim under this policy shall be payable unless the terms of this condition have been complied with.

In the case *Colfire v John Chung*,[20] the Privy Council in an appeal from Trinidad and Tobago considered the same clause and stated:

> a failure to provide documents and proofs in respect of any head of the claim, constitutes a breach of the condition precedent contained in the final sentence of the clause and disentitles the insured from recovering any part of his loss from the insurer.

---

17   AG 2010 CA 3.
18   [1952] AC 192.
19   TT 2008 HC 232.
20   PC 57 of 1999.

The extent of the duty to comply with this clause was discussed by Lord Steyn in the Privy Council decision *Superchem Products Ltd v Algico*[21] (on appeal from Trinidad and Tobago). At para. 29, he considered the same clause as this one, and he accepted the following *dicta*:

> It is not to be supposed that the condition in the policy required of the insured by way of information more than he had or could practically ascertain . . . The particulars required necessarily vary according to the nature of the insurance. They must be furnished with such details as are reasonably practicable. Whether the details given are sufficient or not is a question of degree, depending partly upon the materials available which particularly in the case of a fire, may be scanty, and partly upon the time within which they have to be furnished. In any case the assured has not performed his duty adequately unless he has furnished the best particulars which the circumstances permit.

8.3   WARRANTY

A warranty is recognised under the Marine Insurance Act as a fundamental term of the contract of insurance. The Act identifies differences in the type of warranty. The Barbados Marine Insurance Act, for instance,[22] provides:

> Section 37(1) A warranty . . . means a promissory warranty, that is to say, a warranty by which the assured undertakes that some particular thing will or will not be done, or that some condition will be fulfilled, or where he affirms or negatives the existence of a particular state of facts.

> (2)   A warranty may be expressed or implied.

> (3)   A warranty as defined in subsection (1), is a condition that must be exactly complied with, whether it is material to the contract or not; and if it is not so complied with, then, subject to any express provisions in the policy, the insurer is discharged from liability as from the date of the breach of warranty, but without prejudice to any liability incurred by him before that date.

> Section 38(1) Non compliance with a warranty is excused when, by reason of a change of circumstances the warranty ceases to be applicable to the circumstances of the contract or when compliance with the warranty is rendered unlawful by an subsequent law.

> (2)   where a warranty is broken, the assured cannot avail himself of the defence that the breach has been remedied, and the warranty complied with before loss.

> (3)   A breach of warranty may be waived by the insurer.

> Section 39(1) An express warranty may be in any form of words from which the intention to warrant is to be inferred.

> (2)   An express warranty must be included in, or written upon he policy, or must be contained in some document incorporated by reference into the policy.

> (3)   An express warranty does not include an implied warranty, unless it is inconsistent there with.

8.4   CLASSIFICATION OF WARRANTIES

In accordance with the Marine Insurance Act, a warranty in insurance law is a statement, description or undertaking on the part of the insured contractually relating to the risk insured

---

21   PC 68 of 2002.
22   Cap 292.

against.[23] Essentially the promise undertaken by the insured to do or not to do something relates to the risk insured against. The promise exemplified in the statement, description or undertaking may be embodied in the policy itself or be incorporated into the policy via a 'basis of contract' clause usually found in the proposal form. Warranties fall loosely into three broad categories:

1   An affirmative warranty – warranty as to some past or existing state of affairs;

2   A promissory warranty – warranty as to some future state of affairs;[24]

3   Warranties of opinion – an opinion by the insured as to the truth of a fact.

8.5   AFFIRMATIVE WARRANTIES

Generally an affirmative warranty arises out of information supplied in the proposal form and made the basis of contract. It asserts the existence of a fact at the time the policy was effected.[25] The insurer remains liable if the answer was correct (true) when given but which subsequently became false due to a change in circumstances. This principle is predicated on the absence of a continuing obligation placed on the insured to notify the insurer of changes to the risk. There is no magic formula regarding the wording necessary to create a warranty. Section 39(1) of the Barbados Marine Insurance Act stipulates that an express warranty may be in any form of words from which the intention to warrant is to be inferred. Accordingly, the word 'warranty' is not necessarily conclusive that the term under consideration is in fact a warranty.[26] Similarly the practice of advocates referring to the consequences of breach as 'void or voidable' is also inconclusive.

    The difficulty which arises is that the terms 'warranties' and 'conditions precedent' are often used interchangeably. Judges have used the description 'condition' when actually referring to statements that in substance conform to the requirements of a 'warranty,' and as Birds observes, 'even terms that are similar in nature have attracted different appellations and different legal consequences in decided cases.'[27] The blurring of the lines occurs as a warranty may refer to a promise relating to the risk stipulating that 'performance of the condition is precedent' to the liability of the insurer.[28] Indeed, this can be seen in the Barbados decision of *Matthew Joseph v CLICO International General Insurance Co. Ltd*,[29] where Chief Justice Simmons referred to the basis of contract clause as a condition precedent to the liability of the insurer. But as the case law indicates, a general declaration making the terms condition precedent to the validity of the policy is not sufficient to create a warranty or fundamental term. Regard must be taken of the particular policy being construed.[30]

---

23   Section 37(1), Barbados Marine Insurance Act, Cap 292.
24   *Dawsons Ltd v Bonnin* [1922] 2 AC 413.
25   *Reid v Hardware Mutual Insurance Co.* 2562 SC 339.
26   *De Maurier (Jewels) Ltd v Bastion Insurance Co.* [1967] 2 Lloyd's Rep 550.
27   J. Birds, *Modern Insurance Law*, 6th edn (Sweet & Maxwell: 2014), p. 151. See for instance *Conn v Westminister Motor Insurance Association* [1966] 1 Lloyd's Rep 407.
28   See further Lord Goff's judgment in *Bank of Nova Scotia v Hellenic Mutual War Risks Association (Bermuda) Ltd, The Good Luck* [1991] 2 WLR 1279.
29   Court of Appeal of Barbados Civil Appeal No. 2 of 2003.
30   *De Castro v Edinburgh Insurance Co. Ltd* (St Vincent High Court), in which evidence revealed that the plaintiff whose boat sunk made seaworthiness a warranty; *Insurance Co. of the West Indies Ltd v Graham*, JM 2010 SC 92.

8.6   THE BASIS OF CONTRACT CLAUSE

Perhaps the most effective way to create a warranty in non-marine insurance is through the use of a basis of contract clause. The basis of contract clause, incorporating statements made in the proposal form into the policy whereby the insured warrants the truth of those statements, is extremely effective in clothing the insurer with a defence to an action on the policy, wider than that existing under the duty of disclosure.[31] Apart from incorporating the insured's answers provided in a proposal form into the insurance policy as truthful and correct, it further defines the duty of disclosure and prescribes the manner in which that duty is to be performed.[32] Nevertheless, despite its implications for the duty of disclosure, performance of the duty is contractual and, if it is not performed, there is a breach of the contract of insurance rather than a breach of a duty to disclose. Another important aspect to the basis of contract clause is its impact on the issue of materiality. According to the Marine Insurance Act, it is immaterial whether the warrant is material to the contract or not,[33] so that, in the event of an untruthful answer, it is irrelevant whether the insured acted in good faith to the best of his knowledge and belief. The practice of the insurer in relying on the basis of contract clause has come under intense criticism.[34] This clause first made its appearance in *Duckett v Williams*[35] and was later entrenched by *Thomson v Weems*,[36] a decision repeatedly cited and followed in the Commonwealth Caribbean.[37] In *Thomson v Weems*, a policy of insurance asked (1) Are you temperate in your habits? (2) And have you always been strictly so? The insured responded (1) 'temperate' and (2) 'yes.' The House of Lords, after admitting that there was untruth without any moral guilt, held that the insurer was entitled to avoid the contract. This decision illustrates the strictness with which such clauses will be interpreted. Although the conclusion is supportable on the basis of non-disclosure, it cannot be so limited since rather than restricting their findings to bad faith, Lord Blackburn went out of his way to state that insurers have the right, if they please, to take a warranty against disease, whether latent or not, and that 'it has very long been the course of business to insert a warranty to that effect.' The effectiveness of basis of contract clause in elevating what might be considered peripheral matters to the status of warranties can also be seen in *Dawsons Ltd v Bonnin*,[38] a decision followed in *Matthew Joseph*. In *Dawsons Ltd v Bonnin*, an incorrect statement about where a lorry was garaged (the van was subsequently destroyed by fire) entitled the insurer to avoid the contract. The word 'basis' was held not to be construed as merely 'pleonastic,' so that the misstatement of the lorry's garaged location was found to be contractually material.

Just because a statement or promise appears to be 'warranted' in an insurance policy does not invest it with the properties of a warranty. The insurance policy must express its intention

---

31   Ibid.
32   See Chapter 5.
33   Section 37(3), Barbados Marine Insurance Act, Cap 292. *Anderson v Fitzgerald* (1853) 4 HLC 483; *Condogianis v Guardian Assurance Co.* [1921] 2 AC 125.
34   For a criticism of this practice see R. A. Hasson, 'The Basis of Contract Clause in Insurance Law' (1971) *MLR* 29; J. Birds, 'Warranties in Insurance Proposal Forms' [1977] *JBL* 231; Adams, 'Basis of Contract Clauses and the Consumer' [2000] *JBL* 203; Law Reform Committee Fifth Report, *Conditions and Exceptions in Insurance Policies* (1957), Cmnd 62; Law Commission Report No. 104, *Insurance Law – Non-disclosure and Breach of Warranty* (1980), Cmnd 8064.
35   (1834) 2 C & M 348.
36   (1884) 9 App Cas 671.
37   (1883–1884) LR 9 App Cas 671.
38   [1922] 2 AC 413. According to Hasson, supra n. 34, the Court misinterpreted the tense of the questions posed in the proposal form which were questions relating to the insured's opinion. 'The Basis of Contract Clause in Insurance Law' (1971) *MLR* 29.

in clear and unambiguous words. Thus, in *Roberts v Anglo-Saxon Insurance Association Ltd*,[39] while the insured's car was carrying passengers on a pleasure trip it caught fire and was destroyed, the insurers attempting to repudiate the claim on the basis that the insured had warranted that the vehicle would be used only for 'commercial traveling.' The court, finding the phrase ambiguous, found in favour of the insured.[40]

Statements of insurance practice and/or statute guiding or operating in Commonwealth Caribbean insurance practice attempt to reduce reliance on the basis of contract clause of ordinary contract law to that of the contract of insurance basis of contract clauses. This continues to be a critical element in the formation of insurance contracts and prove an effective defence to an action on the policy wider than exists under the duty of disclosure.[41] It is indisputable that the basis of contract clause is a powerful drafting device representing a formidable hurdle for the insured's recovery, swinging the pendulum in favour of the insurer.

8.7   PROMISSORY OR CONTINUING WARRANTIES

A promissory or continuing warranty places an obligation on the insured to keep the insurer informed of material facts which may affect the risk during the continuance of the policy. It is an absolute undertaking by the insured that certain facts or conditions pertaining to the risk shall continue, or that certain things will be done or not done.[42] Wherever the promissory warranty is expressed (i.e. in the body of the policy itself or in the proposal form and incorporated into the policy by way of a basis of contract clause), the language used must clearly refer to the future. The insurer cannot draft a warranty in the present tense and then attempt to argue that it was a continuing warranty.[43] While this appears simple enough, in practice it has been and still often is difficult to distinguish between an affirmative and a promissory warranty, as we saw earlier in *Dawsons Ltd v Bonnin*.[44] In this case, the appellants, removal contractors, insured a lorry against damage by fire and third party risks. The policy stated that the proposal should be the basis of contract and incorporated into the policy. The policy was stipulated to be subject to the conditions set out. The fourth condition provided that a 'material misstatement or concealment of any circumstance by the insured material to assessing the premium herein, or in connection with any claim, shall render the policy void.' In response to the question in the proposal form, 'state full address at which the vehicle will usually be garaged,' 'the insured inadvertently answered: Above address' (i.e. the insured's place of business, Glasgow). In fact, the lorry was garaged at a farm on the outskirts of Glasgow. The lorry was subsequently destroyed by fire. The House of Lords, finding for the insurer, held that the insurer was entitled to repudiate liability, stating that compliance with a warranty bearing on the risk is a condition precedent to the attaching of risk, and when the answers are declared to be the 'basis of contract,' exact

39   (1926) Ll L Rep 154.
40   *Provincial Insurance Co. Ltd v Morgan* [1933] AC 240; *Wood v Hartford Fire Insurance Co.* 13 Conn 533, 35 Am Dec 92 (1840); *Unipac (Scotland) Ltd v Aegon Insurance Co. (UK) Ltd*, Lloyd's Rep IR 502; *Dawsons v Bonnin* [1922] 2 AC 413.
41   Supra n. 24; see further *Matthew Joseph v CLICO International General Insurance Co. Ltd*, Court of Appeal of Barbados Civil Appeal No. 2 of 2003.
42   Supra n. 25; *Woolfall & Rimmer v Moyle* [1942] 1 KB 66; *Kennedy v Smith* 1976 SLT 110; *Kirkbride v Donner* [1974] 1 Lloyd's Rep 549.
43   *Woolfall & Rimmer v Moyle* [1942] 1 KB 66; *Kennedy v Smith* 1976 SLT 110; *Sweeney v Kennedy* [1950] Ir R 85; *Kirkbride v Donner* [1974] 1 Lloyd's Rep. 549.
44   30 [1922] 2 AC 413.

fulfilment is foundational to its enforceability.[45] *Dawsons* stands for the proposition that a basis of contract clause converts statements made in the proposal form into warranties.[46] The decision illustrates the fundamental difficulty of drawing a clear line between an affirmative and a promissory warranty. The language of the warranty, while embracing existing fact and truth may, and generally often does, point to the continuance of prescribed facts into the future.

Whether or not a promise will be construed as a promissory warranty depends on the ordinary rules of construction applied to the words the parties used in the light shed by their context. Where, as has been noted, the words are capable of more than one meaning, the Courts will select the meaning which seems more closely to correspond with the prescribed intention of the parties. If a provision can only be construed as referring to the future, then it will be construed as continuing.[47] In the event of ambiguity, the *contra proferentem* rule will apply, construing the phrase against the insurer who formulated the policy in favour of the insured. A warranty must be 'strictly though reasonably construed.'[48] This in effect operates to mitigate the harshness of the law. In the House of Lords decision of *Provincial Insurance Co. v Morgan*,[49] the policy contained a clause which requested: state (1) the purpose in full for which the vehicle will be used and (b) the nature of the goods to be carried. The insured responded (1) 'delivery of coal' and (2) 'coal.' The lorry carrying coal was involved in an accident. At the time of the accident, timber which the lorry had been carrying in addition to the coal had already been unloaded. The House of Lords rejected the insurer's argument that there was a breach of a continuing warranty, finding there was no warrant that the lorry would only exclusively carry coal.

Sometimes the nature of the insurance policy effected may influence the interpretation of the term, providing some indication as to its tense. Thus in *Hales v Reliance Fire & Accident*,[50] a seemingly present tense warranty regarding the nature of goods in a shop was read as a continuing promissory warranty given the nature of the insurance – a commercial fire policy. According to the Court, to hold otherwise would mean that the insurance would have little or no value. The persuasive strength of the *Hales* decision has subsequently been reduced by the decisions of *Hair v Prudential Assurance Co. Ltd*[51] and *Hussain v Brown*.[52] In the latter case, the Court of Appeal rejected the view that answers in a proposal form were to be read, *prima facie*, as importing promises about the future; that according to ordinary principles of construction,

---

45   Ibid., per Viscount Haldane.

> It is clear that the answer was textually inaccurate. I think that the words employed in the body of the policy can only be properly construed as having made its accuracy a condition. The result may be technical and harsh, but if the parties have so stipulated, we have no alternative, sitting as a Court of justice, but to give effect to the words agreed on. Hard cases must not be allowed to make bad law . . . It was a specific insurance, based on a statement which is made of foundational if the parties have chosen, however carelessly, to stipulate that it should be so. Both on principle and in the light of authorities such as those I have already cited, it appears to me that when the answers, including that in question, are declared to be the basis of the contract this can only mean that their truth is made a condition exact fulfillment of which is rendered by stipulation foundational to its enforceability.
>
> (Viscount Finlay dissenting)

46   *Unipac (Scotland) Ltd v Aegon Insurance Co. (UK) Ltd* [1999] Lloyd's Rep IR 502.
47   *Beauchamp v National Mutual Indemnity Insurance Co.* [1937] 3 All ER 19. In *Beauchamp*, the plaintiff, a builder, effected insurance to cover the demolition of a mill. He had never done demolition work and he warranted that he did not use explosives in the business. This was true at the time but the insured later used explosives. It was held that his subsequent use of explosives amounted to a breach of warranty. Presumably, since the plaintiff had never used explosives in the business, the statement could only be inferred as referring to the future.
48   *Provincial Insurance Co. v Morgan* [1933] AC 240, per Lord Wright at 253–254.
49   [1933] AC 240.
50   [1960] 2 Lloyd's Rep 391.
51   [1983] 2 Lloyd's Rep 667.
52   [1996] 1 Lloyd's Rep 627.

the question posed was in the present tense. Nevertheless, current practice and tendencies suggest there is more latitude to stretch a present tense warranty to cover the future, particularly in the area of commercial insurance.

The result is that the insured must exercise extreme caution and diligence when responding to questions in a proposal form. Particular attention must be paid to the context of the warranty to determine whether the warranty is affirmative as to the existence of present facts or promissory as to the continuance of a particular state throughout the duration of the policy. What to the layman may be considered a minor discrepancy may have significant connotations on the insured's ultimate recovery of the sum insured.

8.8   WARRANTIES OF OPINION

Warranties of opinion are common in consumer policies. They operate as a proviso into the contract that the insured merely warrants that the answers are true to the best of his knowledge and belief. A warranty of opinion will be breached if the insured, in supplying answers to questions in the proposal form, was dishonest or reckless.[53] In practice, since such a declaration is usually accompanied by a basis of contract clause incorporating the answers supplied as warranties, their relevance to insurance law is reduced.

8.9   NATURE AND EFFECT OF WARRANTIES

It is well settled law that a warranty must be in strict compliance.[54] In accordance with Section 37(1) of the Barbados Marine Insurance Act,[55] a condition must be exactly complied with, whether it is material to the contract or not. Under general contract law, a breach of a condition entitles the innocent party to elect to repudiate the contract. Previously it was thought,[56] until *Bank of Nova Scotia v Hellenic Mutual War Risks Association (Bermuda) Ltd, The Good Luck*,[57] that a breach of a warranty similarly entitled the innocent party to repudiate the contract. This is no longer the case. A literal interpretation was applied to the UK equivalent to Section 37(3) of the Barbados Marine Insurance Act, which provides: 'the insurer is discharged from liability as from the date of the breach of warranty, but without prejudice to any liability incurred by him before that date.' The result is a repudiation of liability rather than an outright repudiation of the policy. In *The Good Luck*, the House of Lords viewed the language of the Marine Insurance Act as clear and unambiguous, so that the correct term is 'automatic cancellation of cover.'[58] In this case, the insured ship owner breached a warranty by taking the ship into a prohibited area – the Persian Gulf during the Iran-Iraq conflict. The benefit of the insurance had been assigned to a bank, the mortgagee of the ship.

Notwithstanding the insurer's undertaking to advise the mortgagee promptly 'if the ship ceases to be insured,' the insurer failed to advise the mortgagee until several weeks after the breach of the warranty was discovered and the ship was lost. In the interim, the mortgagee had made a further advance to the insured. The mortgagee's claim for damages was upheld by the House of

---

53   *Huddlestone v RACV Insurance Party Ltd* [1975] VR 683; *cf. Mammone v RACV Insurance Pty Ltd* [1976] VR 617; *Macphee v Royal Insurance Co.*, 1979 SLT 54.
54   *De Hahn v Hartley* (1786) 1 TR 343; *Pawson v Watson* (1778) 2 Cowp. 785.
55   Cap 292.
56   Supra n. 4.
57   Supra n. 2.
58   *Kumar v AGF Insurance* [1999] Lloyd's Rep IR 147.

Lords, which considered the Court of Appeal as having confused the distinction between conditions as fundamental terms of a contract and conditions precedent. Lord Goff[59] stated:

> Section 33 (3) of the 1906 Act reflects what has been described . . . as the inveterate practice in marine insurance of using the term 'warranty,' as signifying a condition precedent . . . Once it is appreciated, it becomes readily understandable that, if a promissory warranty is not complied with, the insurer is discharged from liability as from the date of the breach of warranty, for the simple reason that fulfilment of the warranty is a condition precedent to the liability or further liability of the insurer. This moreover reflects the fact that the rationale for warranties in insurance law is that the insurer only accepts the risk provided the warranty is fulfilled. This is entirely understandable, and it follows that the immediate effect of a breach of a promissory warranty is to discharge the insurer from liability as from the date of the breach. In the case of conditions precedent, the word 'condition' is being used in its classical sense in English law, under which the coming into existence of (for example) an obligation, or the duty or further duty to perform an obligation, is dependent upon the fulfilment of the specified condition. Here, where we are concerned with a promissory warranty i.e., a promissory condition precedent, contained in an existing contract of insurance, non-fulfilment of the condition does not prevent the contract from coming into existence, what it does (as section 33 (3) makes plain) is to discharge the insurer from liability as from the date of the breach.

Lord Goff's *dicta* is not confined to marine insurance,[60] and it is viewed by Birds as logical reasoning to make the warranty more like an exception to the risk than a condition in the usual contractual sense. This derives from the fact that operation of an exception clause operates independently of insurer.[61] The result is that the insured's obligations, for example, to pay a premium will survive despite the breach.

The decision of *The Good Luck* is not without controversy. Reconciliation with the earlier decision of *West v National Motor and Accident Insurance Union*[62] is difficult. In this case, the insured was alleged to be in breach of a warranty regarding the value of property insured. The insurers purported to reject the claim while relying upon a term of the policy to enforce arbitration. It was held that, by relying on the term of the policy to enforce arbitration, the insurers had waived their right to avoid the policy, which was the only right they had.[63] This decision has been criticised as being contrary to general contract principles[64] and inconsistent with 'insurance law principles as well.'[65] The decision appears to be at odds with one's understanding of waiver.

Lord Wright's speech in *Ross T. Smyth & Co. Ltd v T. D. Bailey Son & Co.* [(1940) 3 All E.R. 60, 70] is generally quoted on the meaning of the term 'waiver':

> it is a vague term used in many senses. It is always necessary to ascertain in what sense and with what restrictions it is used in any particular case. It is sometimes used in the sense of election as where a person decides between two mutually exclusive rights. It is also used where a party expressly or impliedly gives up a right to enforce a condition or rely on a right to rescind a contract, or prevents performance, or announces that he will refuse performance, or loses an equitable right by laches. The use of so vague a term without further precision is to be deprecated.

---

59   Ibid., per Lord Goff of Chievely, p. 1294.
60   Birds, supra n. 27, p. 142.
61   Ibid., p. 145. It could be argued that the effect of a breach of a condition in contract of sale of goods is similar.
62   *West v. National Motor and Accident Insurance Union, Ltd.* [1955] 1 Lloyd's Rep. 207.
63   This result seems odd, considering that the warranty was not a continuing warranty and warranties in a proposal form are not implied indefinitely into renewals if the contract. Winn LJ, *Magee v Pennine Insurance Co.* [1969] 02 QB 507 at 517.
64   Law Commission Report, *Non-disclosure and Breach of Warranty* (1980) Law Com No. 104, Cmnd 8064.
65   Birds, *Modern Insurance Law*, 6th edn (Sweet & Maxwell: 2014), p. 147.

What is waived or abandoned is a right. Isaacs J described 'waiver' in *Craine v Colonial Mutual Fire Insurance Co. Ltd*[66] as 'a doctrine of some arbitrariness introduced by the law to prevent a man in certain circumstances from taking up two inconsistence positions.' In the present appeal it would mean a waiver of a right, a giving up of a right, under the terms of the contract of insurance. The question is, did the company give up its right to enforce the condition of the contract of insurance by which the contract had terminated and the expiration of the grace period ending on 19 November 1977, when the insured was in default of making payment to the company of the premium due on 19 October 1977? Or, it may be expressed in this form: did the company decide, on the insured's repudiatory breach of the contract of insurance, between two mutually exclusive rights, namely, the right to terminate and the right to affirm the contract? There is no evidence from which it could be ascertained. If a waiver is a circumstance in which an insurer may lose the right to rely upon a breach of warranty, or put another way, the insurer who has the right to avoid a liability may elect not to do so provided that he has knowledge of the breach. If the insured's breach simply discharged the insurers from liability, but did not necessarily affect the contract as a whole, then the reliance on the arbitration clause by itself could not have been a waiver.[67] The common law indicates that no particular form of words is required to create a warranty. Simply describing a term as a 'warranty' is not conclusive evidence that the term is a warranty. The language of the policy must unequivocally point to the intention of the parties to create a fundamental term. Section 37(3) of the Barbados Marine Insurance[68] provides some indication of the nature of a warranty: it is a 'condition that must be exactly complied.' Two issues emerge from this statement. The first is that the terms 'warranty' and 'condition' are used interchangeably. Certainly the *dicta* of Lord Blackburn in *Thomson v Weems*[69] illustrates that judges adopt the term 'condition precedent' to describe a warranty that relates to the risk which is precedent to the insurer's liability: 'Any statement of fact bearing upon the risk . . . [is] to be construed as a warranty, and *prima facie*, at least that compliance with that warranty is a condition precedent to the attaching of the risk.' The blurring of the distinction between a condition and a warranty creates confusion. The second aspect relates to the effect of breach. If the warranty is not so complied with, whether it is material to the contract or not, the insurer is discharged from liability from the date of the breach of warranty by the words 'without prejudice to any liability incurred by him before that date.' The strict application of the breach of warranty can produce harsh results. In *De Hahn v Hartley*,[70] a case of marine insurance covering a ship and its cargo from Africa to its port of discharge in the West Indies, the insured warranted that the ship sailed from Liverpool with 50 hands on board. In fact it sailed with only 46 hands, but it took on a further six hands on its journey. The insurer was held entitled to avoid the policy on the basis of breach of warranty, even though the breach had no connection with the loss that subsequently occurred. Ashurst J stated: 'the very meaning of a warranty is to preclude all questions whether it has been substantially complied with; it must be literally so.' Despite the harshness of the decision, it is supported upon a reading of Section 38(2) that 'where a warranty is broken, the assured cannot avail himself of the defence that the breach has been remedied, and the warranty complied with before loss.' *Codogianis v Guardian Assurance*,[71] a decision often cited and applied in the Commonwealth Caribbean,

---

66   (1920) 28 CLR 305 at 327.
67   *Duckett v Williams* (1834) 2 Cromp & M 348; *Thompson v Weems* (1884) 9 App Cas 671; *Sparenborg v Edinburgh Life Assurance Co.* [1912] 1 KB 195; *Kumar v Life Assurance Corp. of India* [1974] 1 Lloyd's Rep 147; and *Stebbing v Liverpool & London & Globe Insurance Co.* [1917] 2 KB 433, which upheld an arbitration clause.
68   Cap 292; Section 33(3), UK Marine Insurance Act 1906.
69   [1884] 9 App Cas 671.
70   (1786) 1 TR 343.
71   [1921] 1 AC 125.

depicts the application of marine insurance rules to other insurance, where a failure to disclose previous claims history was fatal to recovery on the policy. Similarly, Lord Eldon L.C. remarked in *Newcastle Fire Insurance Co. v Macmorran & Co.*:[72]

> It is a first principle in the law of insurance, on all occasions, that where a representation is material it must be complied with – if immaterial, that immateriality may be enquired into and shown; but if there is a warranty it is part of the contract that the matter is such as it is represented to be. Therefore the materiality or immateriality signifies nothing. The only question is as to the mere fact.

Although there is a legal distinction between a warranty and a condition precedent to a particular liability, the problem is that the policy may describe a warranty as a condition precedent to liability by imposing a promise relating to the risk.

8.10 WARRANTIES IN A MULTI-SECTION POLICY

In some cases it may be necessary to consider whether a stipulated warranty in a policy embraces all the sections in the policy or whether it is to be restricted to the specific section. There is a dearth of Caribbean jurisprudence on point, but it is a matter of construction whether a seamless instrument exists. The issue arose in *Printpak v AGF Insurance Ltd*.[73] Here, the insured, a printing finishing business, effected a commercial inclusive policy which contained a number of sections each covering different risks. Section A of the policy covered the insured's stock and other goods against damage by fire. Shortly after the insurance commenced, the insured claimed for fire damage. The defendants repudiated liability on the basis of breach of warranty. Under warranty number P17 in Section B, the insured had warranted that a burglar alarm had been installed on the premises and was fully operational. At the time of the fire, the alarm had been switched off. The issue was whether the warranty in Section B, P17 applied to each and every section of the policy so that the policy was to be construed as a single instrument or whether the condition applied only to the theft section. The court found upon a construction of the policy that it was based upon a division into sections so that the warranty was only operative in relation to a claim under section B, theft, which it is noteworthy specifically excludes loss or damage caused by fire or explosion.'[74] In the absence of Caribbean authority on point, common sense dictates that a reasonable construction be applied, construing the policy as a whole. The fact that the policy is a single commercial document does not necessarily preclude its being viewed as comprising several distinct contracts.

8.11 CLAUSES DESCRIPTIVE OF RISK: SUSPENSIVE CONDITIONS

A policy of insurance may contain a clause which initially appears to be a warranty but which is in fact a clause descriptive of the risk.[75] Generally, a clause descriptive of the risk is a promise

72 (1815) 3 Dow 262.
73 [1999] Lloyd's Rep IR 542.
74 *Bank of Nova Scotia v Hellenic Mutual War Risks Association (Bermuda) Ltd, The Good Luck. See also HIH Casualty and General Insurance Ltd v Chase Manhattan Bank* [2001] Lloyd's Rep IR 703 (CA).
75 The issue is confused by the reference to a clause describing the risk as a warranty describing the risk. See for instance *De Maurier (Jewels) Ltd v Bastion Insurance Co.* [1967] 2 Lloyd's Rep 550. See also *Kler Knitwear Ltd v Lombard General Insurance Co. Ltd* [2000] Lloyd's Rep IR 47.

relating to the property insured. A term in the policy that describes or limits the risk merely suspends the insurer's liability during the period in which the insured is in breach.[76] It is a suspensive condition so that non-compliance therewith will not necessarily discharge the insurer from all liability, as the risk simply reattaches when the term is complied with.[77] It has a similar effect of an exception to the risk. The insurer is not at risk while the term is not complied with. The Jamaica Court of Appeal in *Swaby v Prudential Assurance Co. Ltd*[78] considered such a clause. Here a fire policy contained a clause descriptive of the risk, suspending the insurer's liability 'if the building insured . . . become unoccupied and so remain for a period of more than 30 days.' The Court, construing the policy, ruled that the phrase 'become unoccupied' implied a change of status, and when applied to a dwelling house it connotes the occupier has ceased to dwell in it, ruling that such a change does not occur when absence is merely temporary where there is a manifest intention to return and assume control of the building or where adequate arrangements for its protection was maintained.[79] Similarly in *Dhanpatiya Herman v New India Assurance Co. (Trinidad and Tobago) Ltd*,[80] the insured's claim for loss under a fire insurance policy in which occupation of premises three nights per week satisfied 'occupation' as required by the policy. These decisions can be contrasted with the Privy Council decision of *Marzouca v Atlantic and British Commercial Insurance Co.*,[81] on appeal from the jurisdiction of Jamaica. In this case, the exact clause in a fire insurance policy was considered. Lord Hodson commented, ruling in favour of the insurers, that for the occupation to be effectual it must be actual, not constructive, involving the regular daily presence of someone in the building.[82]

Further, as with warranties and conditions, there is no need for the insurer to prove a causal link between the 'breach' of such a term and the loss. In *Farr v Motor Trader's Mutual Insurance Society*,[83] the plaintiff insured two taxicabs. In answer to the question on the proposal form: 'State whether the vehicles are driven in one or more shifts per 24 hours,' he answered 'just one.' While one of the taxicabs was undergoing repairs, the other was driven in two shifts for a short period. An accident occurred later on, when both cabs were on the road and no cab was used in more than one shift per day. It was held that the insurers were liable in respect of this accident. The statement was not a continuing warranty, for breach of which they could repudiate, that each cab would only ever be driven in one shift per day. It was merely descriptive of the risk. Had the accident occurred at the time when only one cab was in use, the insurers would not have been liable. In *De Maurier (Jewels) Ltd v Bastion Insurance Co.*,[84] an 'all-risk' insurance effected by jewellers contained a clause to the effect: 'warranted road vehicles fitted with locks and alarm systems approved by underwriters and in operation.' The insured suffered two losses. At the time of the first, the locks on the car in question were not of the required sort; at the time of the second, there were no faults. At first the insurers repudiated the policy and liability for both losses on the ground that a continuing warranty had been broken before the first loss. Subsequently, however, they admitted liability for the second loss. It was held that the insurers were not liable for the first loss, as the risk suspended because the locks were not approved. The term was not a warranty in the true sense; it was a warranty descriptive of the risk. In both of

---

76 *CTN Cash & Carry Ltd v General Accident Fire & Life Assurance Corp. plc* [1989] 1 Lloyd's Rep 299; *Kler Knitwear Ltd v Lombard General Insurance Co. Ltd* [2000] Lloyd's Rep IR 47.
77 *Provincial Insurance v Morgan* [1933] AC 240.
78 (1964) 6 WIR 246.
79 Per Lewis J.A. at 254.
80 HCA No. 1780 of 1993.
81 [1971] 1 Lloyd's Rep 449 (PC Jamaica).
82 Ibid., 453–454.
83 [1920] 3 KB 669.
84 [1967] 2 Lloyd's Rep 550.

these cases the term in question was construed as a statement descriptive of the risk since the language did not sufficiently refer to the future.

The determination of the nature of a particular clause is a matter of construction taking into account the language used in the policy. The label attached to a particular clause is influential but not decisive. Where the question is left at large, it is for the Court to determine after examining all the terms of the policy.[85] Justice Sawyers in *M.P.R. Ltd v Bahamas First General Insurance Co. Ltd*[86] cautioned that both warranties and conditions must be strictly complied with.[87] It has been held that two front tyres being in a 'deplorable state' amounts to a breach of the condition to maintain a vehicle in 'a road worthy condition.'[88] Presumably clauses descriptive of the risk were designed to protect the insured from the draconian effects of a breach of a warranty. It has evolved, however, into a device which offers significant protection to the insurer.[89]

8.12 CONDITIONS

Generally, it may be stated that conditions are collateral promises or stipulations and are not regarded in insurance law as fundamental terms of the policy. Conditions fall loosely into two main groups of mere conditions and conditions precedent. A further categorisation can be made within conditions precedent into those pertaining to commencement of the policy and conditions precedent to the liability of the insurer.

Conditions may be categorised as either:

1   Conditions precedent to commencement of the policy; or
2   Conditions precedent to the recovery or liability.[90]

8.13 CONDITIONS PRECEDENT TO THE COMMENCEMENT OF THE POLICY

The insurer may insert a condition that acceptance is subject to the payment or receipt of the first premium.[91] In such circumstances, the insurer is not at risk until the condition is satisfied. It operates to extend or suspend the conclusion period, during which time the insured remains under an obligation to disclose.[92] This clause operates as a 'condition precedent to the commencement of the policy and/or the attaching of risk.'[93] In *Administrator General for Jamaica v Life of Jamaica Ltd*,[94] the policy stipulated that it did not commence until the actual payment of the first premium. As the insured died before satisfying the condition, the insurer was held not liable. It is a matter of law for the court to decide whether a policy issued subject to such a condition precedent is a fully concluded contract of insurance, so that the insurer is bound to accept the premium once it is paid, or whether it only constitutes a counter-offer which may

---

85   *Stoneham v Ocean Railway and General Accident Insurance Co.* (1887) 19 QBD 237.
86   Unreported decision, Supreme Court of the Bahamas No. 92 of 1991.
87   *Philips v Baillie* (1784) 3 Doug KB 374, 99 ER 703; *De Hahn v Hartley* (1786) 1 TR 343, 99 ER 1130 (1786).
88   *Conn v Westminster Motor Insurance Association Ltd* [1966] 1 Lloyd's Rep 407.
89   *CTN Cash & Carry Ltd v General Accident Fire & Life Assurance Corp plc* [1989] 1 Lloyd's Rep 299.
90   *Royal Caribbean Hotels v Barbados Fire & Commercial*, Court of Appeal of Barbados No. 1057 of 1988.
91   *Looker v Law Union and Rock Insurance Co. Ltd* [1928] 1 KB 554.
92   See R. Hodgin, *Insurance Law: Text and Materials* (Cavendish Publishing Ltd: 1998), p. 125.
93   *Canning v Farquhar* (1885–1886) LR 16 QBD 727; *Harrington v Pearl Life Assurance Co. Ltd* (1914) 30 TLR 613.
94   Supreme Court of Jamaica No. 40 of 1982.

be accepted by the proposer of insurance by his paying the premium and thereby concluding the contract.[95]

8.14   CONDITIONS PRECEDENT TO LIABILITY OF THE INSURER

Conditions precedent to the liability of the insurer usually relate to ancillary matters such as the claims procedure, the manner in which notice of loss must be given, the particulars and mode of proof of loss required and arbitration clauses. A condition regarding the claims process is not a fundamental to the validity of the contract. Generally the onus of proving breach of a procedural condition is upon the insurer unless a situation shifts the burden and it is clear from the contract of insurance that 'performance is a condition precedent to any claim by the insured.'[96] In *S&T Ltd et al. v West Indies Alliance Insurance Co. Ltd et al.*,[97] the insurer failed to discharge the onus when disputing a claim under a fire insurance policy, alleging, *inter alia*, breach of Condition 11, which required

> on the happening of any loss or damage the insured shall forthwith give notice thereof to the company, and shall within 15 days after loss or damage or such further time as the company may in writing show on that behalf deliver to the company.

In both *Perrier v British Caribbean Insurance Co. Ltd* and *S & T Ltd et al. v West Indies Alliance Insurance Co. Ltd et al.*,[98] the earlier decision of *Welch v Royal Exchange Assurance*[99] was relied upon. In that case, as a result of the insured's breach of a condition precedent to liability, the insured was not entitled to recover. The Barbadian decision of *Royal Caribbean Hotels Ltd v Barbados Fire and General Insurance Co. et al.*[100] surrounded loss and damage to a hotel as a result of Hurricane David. The second defendant, the Bank of Nova Scotia, was the debenture holder and assignee of the policy of insurance. Clause 19 of the policy of insurance provided: 'In no case whatever shall the Company be liable for any loss or damage after the expiration of twelve months from the happenings of the loss or damage unless the claim is the subject of pending action or arbitration.' The insurers successfully refuted liability on breach of the condition, non-compliance with the condition being fatal to the insured's claim. In *Jones v Provincial Insurance Co. Ltd*,[101] a case cited with approval in *M.P.R. Ltd v Bahamas First General Insurance Co. Ltd*,[102] a condition in the policy required the insured to take all reasonable steps to maintain the vehicle in efficient condition. The insurer's argument that this amounted to a condition precedent to the liability of the insurer was accepted by finding that the actions of the insured, by removing the footbrake and driving downhill with passengers, breached the condition. In *M.P.R. Ltd v Bahamas First General Insurance Co. Ltd*,[103] the policy required the insured to use all reasonable diligence and care to keep the house in a 'proper state of repair.' Evidence indicated that the roof was in already in a state of disrepair when trees on an adjoining property fell and further damaged the roof. The Court ruled that the insured was indeed in breach of the condition but that the insurer had waived breach thereof by its offer to repair.

---

95 Supra n. 93.
96 Per Potter LJ in *Virk v Gan Life Holdings plc* [2000] Lloyd's Rep IR 159.
97 Supreme Court of Jamaica Nos S206 and W318 of 1994.
98 Supreme Court of Jamaica No. 3 of 1998.
99 [1939] 1 KB 294.
100 No. 1057 of 1988.
101 [1929] 35 Lloyd's L Rep 135.
102 Supreme Court of the Bahamas No. 92 of 1991.
103 Ibid.

Case law reveals that construction of an insurance policy is not a 'straightforward exercise as judges sitting in the same court may come to different conclusions.'[104] The lack of consistency means that it is difficult to anticipate what consequences will necessarily flow from the insured's breach.[105] Lord Hoffmann, in the House of Lords decision in *Charter Reinsurance Co. Ltd v Fagan*,[106] commented on the inherent difficulties of interpreting language when attempting to determine the contractual intention of the parties. In *Charter*, a case of reinsurance construing the standard clause known as an ultimate net loss (UNL) clause, and in particular the phrase 'actually paid,' the Court noted that the notion of words having a natural meaning is not very helpful since the meaning of a word is sensitive to syntax and context; considering the history, language and commercial background, the word 'actually' was interpreted to emphasise that the loss for which the reinsurer is to be liable is to be met and that the clause did not restrict liability to the amount by which liability of the reinsured for the loss has been discharged. If the insured obtained the information from another source, compliance with the condition may be dispensed with.[107]

8.15 EFFECT OF A BREACH OF A CONDITION

The nature of the condition has an impact on the consequence of breach. The fundamental question is whether the effect of breach of a condition determines the insurer's liability for a particular loss, or whether upon breach the insurer right is restricted to merely claiming damages for such loss. There are three possible constructions: (1) they are conditions precedent to the bringing of the claim, (2) they are suspensive conditions or (3) they are merely procedural conditions giving rise only to a claim for damages. The danger for the insured is that creative drafting may raise the condition from being simply a condition to that of a warranty.[108] In *Cox v Orion Insurance Co. Ltd*, the insurer was entitled to repudiate the entire contract since the term relating to furnishing particulars of loss was stated to be a condition precedent to 'any liability of the company.' If a term is a condition precedent to liability, any breach thereof will necessarily invalidate the policy.[109]

In general, breach of a condition precedent will entitle the insurer to avoid liability for the particular claim, not the contract as a whole, unless of course the policy contains a clause converting all such conditions into conditions precedent to any liability of the company to make any payment.[110] In addition to loss being suffered within the wording of the policy, the insured must satisfy certain contractual requirements in order to present a valid claim. These procedures enable the insurer to investigate the claim and operate as conditions precedent to the liability of the insurer, the breach of which could have dire results for the insured. Close attention must be paid to the manner in which the clause is drafted. In general, a statement that performance is a condition precedent to liability may render that condition a condition precedent to the liability of the insurer. In *London Guarantee Co. v Fearnley*,[111] despite the fact that the obligation was triggered once the insurer had satisfied the claim, the condition in the policy

---

104 J. Lowry and P. Rawlings, *Insurance Law; Cases and Materials* (Hart: 2004), p. 405.
105 See for instance *Conn v Westminster Motor Insurance Association* [1996] 1 Lloyd's Rep 407; *W&J Lane v Spratt* [1970] 2 QB 480.
106 [1997] AC 313.
107 *Luckiss v Milestone Motor Policies at Lloyd's* [1966] 2 All ER 972.
108 *Cox v Orion Insurance Co. Ltd* [1982] RTR 1.
109 *Welch v Royal Exchange Assurance* [1938] 1 KB 757.
110 Supra n. 108.
111 (1880) 5 App Cas 911.

was held nevertheless to be a condition precedent to the liability of the insurer. There was a
fidelity policy enabling the insured to prosecute employees, and when a claim was made he
should give 'all information and assistance to enable the insurer to obtain reimbursement from
the employee of any sums which the insurer was liable to pay.' The majority of the House of
Lords held that the first part of the term was a condition precedent since the policy contained
a general declaration to that effect and the two parts were separate and independent. This
decision can be contrasted with the decision of *Re Bradley and Essex & Suffolk Accident Indemnity
Society*.[112] This concerned a condition in a workman's compensation policy effected by a farmer.
The conditions were stated to be precedent to the liability of the insurer. Condition 5 contained
three sentences. The first provided that the premium was to be regulated by the amount of the
wages and salaries paid by the insured; the second required the keeping of the proper wage
book; and the third required the insured to supply information to the insurers regarding wages
and salaries paid. The insured, who had only one employee, his son, failed to maintain a wages
book, and the insured relied on this to deny liability for a particular claim. By a majority, the
Court of Appeal held that the insured was not guilty of a breach of a condition precedent.
Cozens-Hardy MR held that the first and third parts of condition 5 were incapable of being
condition precedent, while the second part could be. It is difficult to distinguish the case of
Bradley from the earlier decision of *London Guarantee Co. v Fearnley*. Each decision should therefore
be considered in light of the particular wording of the conditions being construed. In *Kazakhstan Wool Processors v Nederlandsche Creditverzekering Maatschappij NV*[113] there was a very wide-ranging
term requiring the insured to fulfil each and every obligation of the claims process, which the
insurer stipulated, before he would pay out upon loss. The Court of Appeal held that such a
term could be a condition precedent to all future liability under the policy. The insured, KWP,
processed wool at a plant in Kazakhstan for export and effected credit insurance with the defendant insurers. Article 13 of the policy provided that:

> Due payment of all premiums (and other charges) specified in Schedule 1, and the due perfor-
> mance and observance of every stipulation in the policy or the proposal, shall be a condition
> precedent to any liability on our part, shall be a condition precedent to any liability on our part.
> In the event of any breach of any condition precedent we also have the right to retain any pre-
> mium paid and give written notice terminating the policy and all liability under it.

Premiums were calculated by reference to monthly premiums submitted by the insured in
respect of the amounts and value of the wool exported. If in any given month no sales were
made, the insured was required to submit a nil return. A claim was met by the insurers, but
soon after KWP filed to submit a return for June 1998. In fact, KWP had ceased trading in May
1998 and failed to make further premium payments. Just before the policy expired in August,
KWP submitted further claims. The insurers gave notice of termination under Article 13 on
the ground of the insured's breaches of conditions precedent. They denied liability relating
to claims relating to the business for which the insured was in compliance with the policy and
requested the return of the earlier payment. KWP argued, *inter alia*, that it was unreasonable
to construe Article 13 permitting the insurers to retrospectively avoid liability in respect of risks
that had attached prior to the breaches of the policy. In some cases, however, the fact that one
clause out of several purports to be a condition precedent may impact on the nature of the
whole conditions, rendering other clauses mere conditions.

A further categorisation can be made. Promises imposed on the insured, first with respect
to the claims procedure which are not fundamental to the validity of the contract, and second,

112 [1912] 1 KB 415.
113 [1999] Lloyd's Rep IR 596.

conditions conferring rights on the insurer, often repeating or enlarging rights bestowed on the insurer by general contract law. Examples include rights of subrogation, the right to control proceedings and conditions relating to double insurance. Such terms, if the wording of the clause so connotes, may amount to a fundamental term. In *Cox v Orion Insurance Co.*,[114] the Court of Appeal held that a breach of a condition relating to the furnishing of particular loss entitled the insurers to treat the whole contract as repudiated because the policy contained a provision making its conditions 'conditions precedent to any liability of the company to make any payment under this policy.' In *Verelest's Administration v Motor Union Insurance Co.*,[115] a motor policy contained a condition precedent that notice should be given as 'soon as possible' following an accident. The insured was killed in India in a motor accident, but it was not until 12 months later that the policy was discovered by her personal representatives. The insurer denied liability for breach of the negotiation requirements.

8.16   INNOMINATE TERMS

The description 'innominate term' has relatively recently crept into the law of insurance as a result of the Court of Appeal decision of *Alfred McAlpine plc v BAI (Run-Off) Ltd.*[116] The phrase is applicable to notice of loss clauses, where the legal consequences depend upon the effects of the breach for the insurers. Repudiation of the claim would be allowed if the breach demonstrated a clear intention by the insured not to continue to make a claim or if it caused the insurer serious consequences. If the effects are not serious, the insurers will have to pay the sum insured and sue the insured for damages for any loss suffered. Where the insurers suffer serious harm, they are entitled to treat the policy as terminated for repudiation or they can repudiate the claim. The condition in the policy required the insured to give notice of any occurrence which may give rise to a claim 'as soon as possible . . . in writing, with full details.' This decision introduces a degree of flexibility to question of remedies.[117] According to Waller LJ, the issue is not simply a matter of black and white – whether it is a condition precedent and a condition simply giving rise to an action for damages. That it is possible for a breach of a condition in some circumstances to be so serious as to give the insurer a right to reject the claim outright,[118] an approach which was later confirmed in *The Mercandian Continent*.[119] In unravelling the law relating to contractual terms, the following principles emerge:

> A promise either contained in the policy or the proposal form and incorporated into the policy may be construed as an affirmative warranty if it relates to past or present facts:
>
> (I)   If the term sufficiently refers to the future then it will be construed as a promissory continuing warranty.
>
> (II) If the language relates to the use of the property insured it is likely to be construed as a clause descriptive of the risk.
>
> (III) A statement in the proposal from can be both a warranty as to past or present facts and a clause descriptive of its use in the future as a clause descriptive of the risk.

---

114 [1982] RTR 1.
115 [1925] 2 KB 137.
116 [2000] Lloyd's Rep IR 352.
117 I. Davies 'Registration Documents and Certification of Title of Motor Vehicles' [2001] *JBL* 489.
118 Waller LJ observed that this remit was not repudiatory in the sense of enabling the insurer to reject the whole claim.
119 *K/S/ Merc-Scandia XXXXII v Certain Lloyd's Underwriters* [2001] EWCA Civ 1275; [2001] Lloyd's Rep IR 563.

(IV) It appears that a statement can be both a continuing warranty and a statement descriptive of the risk.[120]

(V) A distinction exists between conditions precedent to liability and a mere condition which if broken by the insured only gives rise to a claim for damages.[121] It is not always easy to decide whether clauses requiring notice of a claim are conditions precedent to the liability of the insurer under the policy or merely terms of the policy for breach of which the insurer's only remedy is to claim damages for the extra expense flowing from the insured's failure to give notice within a proper time. It is a matter of construing the policy as a whole. It appears that:

   (i)   If the contract states that a condition is a condition precedent or a condition of liability, that is influential but not decisive, especially if the label condition precedent is used indiscriminately;

   (ii)   where individual terms are described as conditions precedent, while others are not, the label will have more weight;

   (iii) Where one clause is labelled a condition precedent and a question arises as to the status of a clause not so labelled, the latter is not, *ipso facto*, precluded from being regarded as such if the wording is apt to make its intention unambiguously clear; the absence of a rubric is not fatal.

8.17   WAIVER OF BREACH

An issue that often arises is whether insurers and/or their agents can waive a breach of a warranty. Section 38(3) of the Barbados Marine Insurance Act expressly stipulates that a breach of a warranty may be waived by the insurer. At first instance in *Royal Caribbean Hotels Ltd v Barbados Fire & General Insurance Co. et al.*, Williams CJ noted that the pleadings did not disclose any facts that could raise the issue of estoppel, but that estoppel could be raised at a later stage with appropriate amendment on the authority of *Parey v Colonial Fire & General Insurance Co. Ltd.*[122] In the Court of Appeal, however, the attempt by the insured to establish waiver and agency on the part of the second defendant failed. The Privy Council decision of *Parey v Colonial Fire and General Insurance Co. Ltd,*[123] on appeal from the jurisdiction of Trinidad and Tobago, surrounded an action for indemnification for a shopkeeper's stock in trade and other items. A fire broke out, destroying a shopkeeper's stock and trade and other items, in which the insured received injuries and later died. The plaintiff, adminstratrix of the insured's estate, served notice of the fire on the insurer within 12 months of the fire. Evidence was submitted that the insurers refrained from admitting the claim before they had received the results of the inquest into the death of the insured, and further, that they had informed the plaintiff of their intentions. As a result the plaintiff, acceding to their wishes, delayed in filing the writ, which was eventually filed more than three years after the fire. The question arose as to whether the waiver of condition 19 was still applicable in view of the delay in filing the writ. The Court found, even though it was not pleaded, that the actions of the insurer amounted to promissory estoppel on which the plaintiff could rely, rather than a waiver of a condition, that quasi or promissory estoppel can be relied on without amendment.

---

120 Supra n. 77. In this case, discussed earlier, if the lorry had been carrying both timber and coal at the time of the accident, applying Lord Buckmaster's reasoning, the insurers would still have been liable because there was no breach of a continuing warranty.
121 *George Hunt Cranes Ltd v Scottish Boiler & General Insurance Co. Ltd* [2002] 1 All ER (Comm) 366.
122 (1972) 22 WIR 480.
123 Ibid.

A request for further information may amount to waiver.[124] This is obviously dependent on the nature of the request. There may be a waiver by conduct if the insurers act in a manner which can only be justified upon the premise that the policy is in force. The insurer in such a case is estopped from contending that the policy is avoided by the breach of condition. The condition precedent may be waived even though the contracting party does not intend his conduct to have that result. In *Toronto Railway Co. v National British & Irish Millers Insurance Co.*,[125] the insurer requested further information and further stated that if the information was insufficient, they would require loss to be ascertained by disinterested appraisers. The correspondence revealed an acceptance of liability. The defendant insurers subsequently refused to pay the claim.

There must be some positive act done which is inconsistent with the avoidance of the policy. In the Jamaican decision of *Perrier v British Caribbean Insurance Co. Ltd*,[126] the defendant insurers insured the plaintiff against loss or damage by fire of several items of goods. Condition 11 of the policy stipulated that

> on the happening of any loss or damage the insured shall forthwith give notice thereof to the company and shall within 15 days after loss or damage or such further time as the company may in writing show on that behalf deliver to the company.

Four generators were destroyed by fire while being stored on the plaintiff's property. The issue was whether there was a breach of a condition precedent to liability by the insured and on the question of damages; whether the value of the generators was to be taken into account. During negotiation the insurer agreed to settle for $300,000, and the issue was whether this amounted to waiver. The replacement cost of the generators was in excess of $3 million. It was argued that since condition 11 related to information in respect to a claim, the claim was for the cost of replacing or reinstating equipment, therefore the price paid by the plaintiff is irrelevant to that determination, and that further, even if there had been breach it had been waived, since the defendants by correspondence proceeded to accept a settlement.[127] It was argued that the question was whether, on an interpretation of the policy contract, the policy was a reinstatement valued policy or an oral policy with an option to reinstate. This, it was contended was material to the information requested in establishing the method valuation applicable. It was held that there was waiver, the defendant was bound by its election – correspondence between the insurer and the insured amounted to waiver.

8.18 CONCLUSION

Discussion reveals that the line between warranties and conditions is imperceptible, and it is often difficult to ascertain the precise nature of a particular term – whether the term is a warranty or a condition – because the language may connote a warranty but when construed in substance it in fact is a condition. Moreover, within warranties the language varies. Authorities which assumed that in non-marine insurance the effect of a breach of a warranty gives the insurer the right to repudiate the policy may now be regarded as wrong.

It is evident that the blurring of the lines between warranties and conditions has complicated the task of ascertaining the true import and nature of warranties and conditions. As

---

124 *Toronto Railway Company & Others v National British & Irish Millers Insurance Co. Ltd* (1914–1915) 3 LTR 555.
125 (1914–1915) 3 LTR 555.
126 No. 1057 of 1985.
127 Supra n. 124.

observed by Lord Goff in the House of Lords decision of *Bank of Nova Scotia v Hellenic Mutual War Risks Association (Bermuda) Ltd, The Good Luck*,[128] there is a marked confusion between conditions as fundamental terms of a contract and conditions precedent. The 'inveterate practice in marine insurance of using the term "warranty" as signifying a condition precedent' is evident in Caribbean jurisprudence. What has been resolved is the effect of a breach of a warranty. In accordance with the leading House of Lords decision of *Bank of Nova Scotia v Hellenic Mutual War Risks Association (Bermuda) Ltd, The Good Luck*,[129] the term 'repudiation' is no longer considered appropriate to insurance contracts upon a literal interpretation of the Marine Insurance Act.[130] The case law indicates that strict compliance with conditions precedent to the liability of the insurer is required.

---

128 Supra n. 2.
129 Ibid.
130 Supra n. 1.

CHAPTER 9

CAUSATION

9.1 INTRODUCTION

The insured must establish that the loss for which a claim is made is proximately caused by an insured peril.[1] Recovery is subject to the parameters of the insurance contract as defined by its contractual terms. The determination of the 'cause' of loss is, however, not always an easy task. A loss may result from a series of events,[2] and as observed by Lord Justice Lindley in *Reischer v Borwick*,[3] it is sometimes difficult to distinguish between causes which cooperate in a given result when they succeed each other at intervals. Further, analysis of what has been called the 'cause-event-result' combination is less than clear. There exists no prevailing agreed and settled criteria for selecting from the existing circumstances, those events genuinely relevant to interpretation and application of the provisions at issue in a given context.[4]

The insured is permitted to be indemnified so long as the loss is caused by an event stipulated by the insurance contract. The event covered – the 'peril' – is known as the proximate cause.[5] Although a 'common sense' approach has distorted analysis described as 'defy[ing] contradiction'[6] – criticised as 'a cloak for intuition when data is lacking,'[7] the rules governing the problem of causation reside within regional marine insurance legislation and the common law, revealing the law occasioning loss relates to personal accident, fire, marine, liability and perils of nature.

9.2 STATUTE

Regional marine insurance legislation simply provides:

> Subject to the provisions of this Act, and unless the policy otherwise provides, the insurer is liable for any loss proximately caused by a peril insured against, but, subject as aforesaid, he is not liable for any loss which is not proximately caused by a peril insured against.

This section represents a codification of the proximate cause rule formulated at common law. Indeed it is the common law which assists in determining what constitutes proximate causation of a loss.[8]

---

1   M. A. Clarke, 'The Proximate Cause in Insurance Law' [1981] *CLJ* 284; J. M. Culp, 'Causation, Economists, and the Dinosaur: A Response to Professor Dray' 49(3) *Law and Contemporary Problems* 23; A. L. Parks, 'Marine Insurance Proximate Cause' (1979) 10 *JMLC* 519.
2   *Dudgeon v Pembroke* (1874) LR 9 QB 581, per Blackburn J, p. 115.
3   [1894] 2 QB 548.
4   J. D. Fraser and D. R. Howarth, 'More Cause for Concern' (1980) 4 *Legal Studies* 131, 138; R. Keeton and A. Widiss, *Insurance Law: A Guide to Fundamental Principles, Legal Doctrines, and Commercial Practices* (West Publishing: 1988), p. 546.
5   Ibid.
6   M. A. Clarke, *The Law of Insurance Contracts* (Lloyds of London Press: 1989), pp. 25–29.
7   Section 59, Barbados Marine Insurance Act, Cap 292.
8   Anguilla Marine Insurance Act RSA 2000 CM 25; Antigua and Barbuda Marine Insurance Act 1959, Cap 711; British Virgin Islands Marine Insurance Ordinance, Cap 257 [1961 Rev.]; Cayman Islands Marine Insurance Act 1959, Cap 711; Dominica Marine Insurance Act 1959, Cap 711 [1961 Rev.]; Grenada Marine Insurance Act No. 5 of 1990, Cap 182; St Kitts and Nevis Marine Insurance Act 1959, Cap 711; St Lucia Marine Insurance Act 1959, Cap 711; St Vincent and the Grenadines Marine Insurance Act,

9.3 COMMON LAW

The proximate cause rule has been called a rule of law.[9] It is a term implied into the contract of insurance as representing the real meaning of the parties. In *Ionides v Universal Marine Insurance Co.*,[10] Willes J declared: 'You are not to trouble yourself with distant causes, or to go into a metaphysical distinction between causes efficient and material and causes final; but you are to look exclusively to the proximate and immediate cause of the loss.'[11] According to *MacGillivray & Parkington*,[12] if the loss or damage is the necessary consequence of the peril insured against under the existing physical conditions, there is *prima facie* damage by that particular peril. Similarly, if the peril is one of the causes in a chain of events following in inevitable sequence, all the causes in the chain are *prima facie* proximate causes of ultimate change. Additionally, in the seminal judgment of Lord Shaw in the House of Lords decision, *Leyland Shipping Co. Ltd v Norwich Union Fire Insurance Society Ltd*,[13] the principle was stated as follows:

> The true and overruling principle is to look at a contract as a whole and to ascertain what the parties to it really meant. What was it which brought about the loss, the event, the calamity, the accident? And this is not an artificial sense, but in that real sense which parties to a contract must have had in their minds when they spoke of cause at all. To treat *proxima causa* as the cause which is nearest in time is out of the question . . . Causation is not a chain, but a net. At each point influences, forces, events, precedent and simultaneous, meet and the radiation from each point extends infinitely.

This formula was applied by the Jamaica Court of Appeal in *Dyoll Insurance Co. Ltd v Cardoza*.[14] In this case, the insured effected a householder's comprehensive policy with the insurers on his premises. Clause 7 of the policy, *inter alia*, contained an exemption for loss or damage caused by subsidence or landslip. In 1998, as a result of unnatural and extreme rainfall, a retaining wall and a swimming pool were damaged. The insured contended that the damage was caused by an insured peril. The insurer, on the other hand, disputed liability contending that the damage was caused by a 'landslip,' which fell within the exclusion clause and thus was not covered by the policy. The Court of Appeal, Justices Downer, Bingham and Panton presiding, reaffirmed the decision of the lower court and found in favour of the insured.[15] In construing the policy the Court of Appeal restated the salient principle that where an exemption clause is clear, the courts will uphold the meaning even if the consequences seem unfair,[16] but that if on the other hand the meaning is ambiguous, the *contra preferentem* rule applies[17] (i.e. the clause is to be liberally interpreted in favour of the insured and the construction more favourable to

---

Cap 105 [1990 Rev.]; Trinidad and Tobago Marine Insurance Act, Cap 45 [1980 Rev.]; Turks and Caicos Marine Insurance Act 1959, Cap 711.

9   *Leyland Shipping Co. Ltd v Norwich Union Fire Insurance Society Ltd* [1917] 1 KB 873.
10   (1863) 14 CB(NS) 259.
11   Ibid., 289.
12   M. Parkington and N. Legh-Jones, *MacGillivray & Parkington on Insurance Law*, 6th edn (Sweet & Maxwell: 1975).
13   [1918] AC 350.
14   No. 137 of 2001.
15   Cooke J:

> I regard slippage as the final step. The prior flooding in my view is the proximate cause. Without the flooding there would have been no slippage without which the damage would not occur. Slippage was the direct result of flooding.

16   *Coxe v Employer's Liability Assurance Corp. Ltd* [1916] 2 KB 629.
17   *Worswick v Canada Fire & Marine Insurance Co.* (1878) 3 OAR 487; *Fitton v Accidental Death Insurance Co.* (1864) 17 CB (NS) 122; 144 ER 50; *Re Etherington & Lancashire & Yorkshire Accident Insurance Company* [1909] 1 KB 591; *Oakleaf v Home Insurance Ltd*, 14 DLR (2d) 535.

the insured must be applied).[18] In finding the word 'landslip' ambiguous in that it 'could mean (i) any landslip whatsoever, (ii) the landslip must be the proximate cause of the damage for it to exclusively effect the flood (iii) a landslip which followed the flood, and was merely incidental to it,' the Court of Appeal ruled that the insurer had failed to discharge the onus to bring itself within the exception,[19] further, that the flood was the proximate cause of the loss and that the landslip or slippage was a mere incidence of the flood – in short, the final link in the chain of circumstances which was brought about, initially, by the flooding.[20] The case law illustrates that the determination of the proximate cause in any situation is a question of fact and it does not signify the last in time but rather the effective, dominant or real cause.[21]

9.4   EXCEPTED PERILS

Where the contract of insurance expressly excludes certain perils, this in effect alters the rules of causation. The insurer's freedom to exclude certain perils is acknowledged in regional marine insurance legislation by the phrase 'unless the policy otherwise provides.'[22] The impact of contractual terms on the question of causation arose for consideration in the decision of *Isitt v Railway Passengers Assurance Co.*[23] Here, the insurers were only liable if the insured 'shall sustain any injury caused by accident . . . and shall die from the effects of such injury.' Isitt fell and dislocated his shoulder. He was put to bed and subsequently died from pneumonia. It was found that he would not have died in the manner in which he did die, if not for the accident, so that the insurers were held liable. Consequently, the 'Issit clause' was developed as insurers, fearful of the *Isitt* decision, started to frame provisions for the very purpose of 'avoiding its effect in the future.'[24] The validity of such a clause was reluctantly upheld by Scrutton LJ in *Coxe v Employers' Liability Assurance Corp. Ltd.*[25] Subsequently, however, in *The Matter of Arbitration Between Etherington & the Lancashire & Yorkshire Accident Insurance Co.,*[26] the clause read:

> this policy only insures against death where accident within the meaning of the policy is the direct or proximate cause thereof, but not where the direct of proximate cause thereof may itself have been disease or other intervening cause, even although the disease or other intervening cause may itself have been aggravated by such accident, or have been due to weakness or exhaustion consequent thereon, or death accelerated thereby.

While out hunting, Etherington fell and the ground being wet, became soaked. As a result of the shock of the fall, the wetting and having to ride home, the insured developed pneumonia and died. Despite the presence of the 'Issit clause,' the insurers were nevertheless held liable. 'Intervening cause' was interpreted restrictively and the 'direct or proximate cause' was construed to cover not only the immediate result of the accident, but all things attendant upon the particular accident.

---

18   Per Bingham J.A, *Dyoll Insurance Co. Ltd v Cardoza*, p. 27.
19   Supra n. 14. E. R. Hardy Ivamy, *General Principles of Insurance Law*, 5th edn (Butterworths: 1986), states that:

> where the insured peril insured against precedes an excepted clause which actually produces the loss, there is a loss within the meaning of the policy if, notwithstanding the operation of the excepted clause, the peril insured against is to be regarded as the proximate cause of loss.

20   4 DLR (2d) 535.
21   *Becker, Gray & Co. London Assurance Corp.* [1918] AC 101.
22   Section 55, Marine Insurance Act (UK).
23   (1889) 22 QBD 504.
24   Per Vaughan Williams LJ, *In the Matter of Arbitration Between Etherington & the Lancashire & Yorkshire Accident Insurance Co.* [1908] 1 KB 591.
25   [1916] 2 KB 629.
26   [1908] 1 KB 591.

Where there are two causes and one of them is expressly covered while the other is expressly exempted, particular attention must be paid to the wording of the policy. The decision of *Dyoll Insurance Co. Ltd v Cardoza*,[27] arising out of the jurisdiction of Jamaica, illustrates that where the loss is as a result of an exempted peril, but the peril was caused by a peril which was covered by the insurance policy, the insurers will be liable. In *Marsden v City & County Insurance Co.*,[28] fire insurers were liable for property damage caused by a mob that had been drawn to the vicinity by a fire in a neighbouring building, the building policy protected a shopkeeper's plate glass against loss or damage arising from any cause with the exception of fire. A fire broke out on a neighbour's property, a mob gathered, rioted and broke the plate glass. The insured was held entitled to recover as the riot, and not the fire, was the cause of loss. The fire merely facilitated the riot. Similarly in *Winicofsky v Army & Navy General Assurance Association Ltd*,[29] a theft policy covered the loss when a shop was burgled during an air raid because, although the loss 'occasioned by the hostilities' was an excepted peril, the cause was theft and the air raid 'merely made the burglar's task easier.'

An illustration of this principle is illustrated in *Dhak v Insurance Co. of North America (UK) Ltd*.[30] Here the assured was covered against a personal accident policy which provided payment in the event of 'Bodily injury resulting in death or personal injury caused directly or indirectly by an accident.' A nurse, who was covered by a personal accident insurance policy, suffered a back injury at work. To ease the pain, she drank a bottle of gin and later died in her sleep from asphyxia. Neil LJ concluded that as a nurse she was aware of the risks associated with heavy drinking and that her deliberate consumption of alcohol was the proximate cause of her death.

9.5   MULTIPLE CAUSES

A difficulty arises when there is more than one proximate cause of the loss and only one of these is an insured peril. Under such circumstances, the recovery of the insured is dependent on whether the other cause is simply not mentioned in the policy or whether it is expressly excluded. Where there are concurrent and effective causes and only one is mentioned in the policy, the insurers must pay.[31] On the other hand, where the other cause is an excepted peril, the insurers will not be liable. The leading authority on point is *Wayne Tank & Pump Co. Ltd v Employers' Liability Association Corp. Ltd*.[32] Here, Wayne Tank was held liable to pay damages to Harbutt's 'Plasticine' Ltd for breach of contract under which they installed new equipment in Harbutt's factory. The equipment was defective and a resultant fire gutted the factory. The fire was attributable to two causes: (1) the defective nature of the equipment used and (2) the fact that one of its employees negligently and without authority turned on the equipment and left it on all night. Wayne Tank were insured by the defendants under a public liability policy 'against all sums which the insured shall become liable to pay as damages as a consequence upon . . . damage to property as a result of accidents.' The policy contained an exemption for indemnity for liability arising from damage caused by the 'nature or condition of any goods' supplied by the insured. Had this not happened, it was likely that the loss would not have occurred, as the equipment would not have been tested under supervision and found to have been defective before any damage occurred.

---

27   Unreported decision, Jamaica Court of Appeal No. 137 of 2001.
28   (1865) LR 1 CP 232.
29   (1919) 88 LJ KB 1111.
30   1996] 2 All ER 609.
31   *J. J. Lloyd Instruments Ltd v Northern Star Insurance Co. Ltd (The 'Miss Jay Jay')* [1987] 1 Lloyd's Rep 32.
32   [1974] QB 57.

The Court of Appeal, applying *Leyland Shipping*, unanimously held that the real cause of loss was the defective nature of the equipment, so that the insurers were not liable. The exclusion clause operated because the dominant and effective cause of the loss was the nature of the goods supplied, the electrical equipment, rather than the negligence of the employee.

9.6   COLLATERAL LOSS

In some instances, loss may be caused not by the insured peril but by efforts to prevent, avert or minimise its effects. Under such circumstances, a distinction must be drawn between an operating peril and the mere apprehension of a peril. According to Scrutton LJ in *Symington & Co. v Union Insurance Society of Canton Ltd*,[33] 'Is it a fear of something that will happen in the future or has the peril already happened and it is so imminent that it is immediately necessary to avert the danger by action?' In *Becker, Gray & Co. v London Assurance Corp.*,[34] the outbreak of war led the master of a ship to put into a neutral harbour to avoid capture and so the voyage was lost. The insurers were not held liable on the policy because the loss was proximately caused by the voluntary actions of the master. This decision can be contrasted with *The Knight of St Michael*,[35] when cargo became overheated and the master unloaded the ship. The insurers were still held liable on the fire policy even though fire had not broken out, because a fire would have started if no action had been taken. It is not certain whether the loss can be construed as falling within the terms of the policy, so that the courts will imply a condition that the insured should take reasonable steps to avert or minimise a loss, since such an obligation could be expressly included in the policy[36] and the broad doctrine of proximate cause can capture such an implied term.[37] But what if the fear is not the subject matter of the insured peril but the fear of danger to others? In the decision of *Khahai v Colonial Life Insurance Co. (Trinidad) Ltd*,[38] employees of an oil refinery in Trinidad and Tobago were commissioned to install a relief valve on a gas line. Hydrogen sulfide gas escaped from a gas line which was supposed to have been completely blocked off. This gas, if inhaled in sufficient quantity, could affect the respiratory system with fatal consequences. In attempting to escape, one of the workers fell and hung unconscious for 15 minutes. The supervisor, who was not wearing a blow mask at the time, went to his rescue along with others. While descending, the supervisor fell to the ground and died on the spot. Prior to his death, the supervisor had effected a life insurance policy with the defendant company. The policy covered accidental death

> as a result, directly and independently of all other causes, of bodily injuries sustained solely through external, violent and accidental means and accidental means provided . . . (6) that death shall not have occurred as a result of . . . inhaling gas whether voluntary or involuntary.

The High Court, finding in favour of the plaintiff, held that the death fell within the ambit of the policy. Justice Ventour, on the issue of foreseeability and dominant cause, stated:

> I do not agree that it was foreseeable that the assured would have slipped and fallen to his death at the time. *Candler v London and Lancashire Guarantee and Accident Co. of Canada* (1963) 404 DLR 408 admirably captures the principle of foreseeability. The facts however are clearly distinguishable

---

33   (1928) 139 LT 386.
34   [1918] AC 101.
35   Ibid.
36   See further H. Bennett, 'Causation in the Law of Marine Insurance: Evolution and Codification of the Proximate Cause Doctrine,' in D. Rhidian Thomas, ed., *The Modern Law of Marine Insurance* (LLP: 1996), p. 173.
37   N. Legh-Jones, J. Birds and D. Owen, *MacGillivray on Insurance Law*, 10th edn (Sweet & Maxwell: 2003), para. 26-18(1).
38   Unreported decision, Trinidad and Tobago Court of Appeal No. 1356 of 1992.

from the instant case. In *Candler* case, the young man deliberately courted the risk of injury when after consuming a quantity of vodka and lime, fell to his death balancing on a 13th storey patio wall. It was held by the Canadian court that his death was not caused solely by accident. I do not think that one could dispute the fact that working in the Petrochemical Industry does carry a degree of risk or what I would prefer to refer to as 'perils of the job' and the maintenance crew . . . did experience the true nature of the peril. . . . On the totality of the evidence I am satisfied on a balance of probability that the assured's death was accidental . . . It was Lord Mac Naughten in the case of *Fenton v Thorley & Co. Ltd* (1903) AC 443 who aptly defined accident as an unlooked – for mishap or untoward event which is not expected or designed.

A fundamental principle in contract law is that all efforts must be taken to mitigate the loss resulting from a breach of contract. It is not clear whether the same principle applies in insurance. Where there is more than one cause and it is impossible to say which is the dominant cause, the original cause dominates unless it merely facilitates the subsequent cause. In practice, this usually arises in relation to a covered loss and an exempted loss, where although the insured has incurred a legal liability, the liability was incurred in a manner excluded from the scope of the policy. In *Leyland Shipping Co. Ltd v Norwich Union Fire Insurance Society Ltd*,[39] their Lordships rejected previous judicial pronouncements which applied the test of last in time and held that the proximate cause is the 'cause which is truly proximate is that which is proximate in efficiency.' However, the so-called accident cases belie this analysis. In *Winspear v Accident Insurance Association*,[40] the policy covered death or injury caused by accidental external and visible means. It excluded any injury caused by or arising from natural disease. The insured, while crossing stream, suffered a fit, fell in and was drowned. The court held that the cause of death was accidental. The drowning, and not the fit, was the proximate cause. In the case of *Lawrence v Accidental Insurance Co.*,[41] the insured suffered a fit while standing on a railway platform, causing him to fall on the track, whereupon he was run over. It was held that being run over was the accident.[42] It appears that the judges in these 'accident' cases were treating proximate as latest cause.

9.7   DETERMINATION OF LOSS

In some cases it may be necessary to determine whether there was an actual loss. In *Moore v Evans*,[43] Banks LJ stated:

> Mere temporary deprivation would not, under ordinary circumstances, constitute a loss. On the other hand complete deprivation amounting to a certainty that the goods could never be recovered is not necessary to constitute loss. It is between these two extremes that difficult cases lie . . . and no assistance can be derived from putting cases which are clearly on the one side or the other of the dividing line between the two.

As to the test for recovery, the decision of *Holmes v Payne*[44] is instructive. In this case, the insured diligently searched for a pearl necklace and could not find it. The necklace was held to have been 'lost' within the terms of the policy.

---

39   Supra n. 13.
40   (1880) 6 QBD 42.
41   (1881) 7 QBD 216.
42   See also on liability insurance the decision of *West Wake Price & Co. v Ching* [1956] 3 All ER 821. Here a liability policy covered negligence of the insured or their employees. There was also evidence that the employee in question was dishonest. The Court held that the policy did not cover combined or mixed causes.
43   [1917] 1 KB 458.
44   Hart and Honeré [1930] 2 KB 301.

9.8 CONCLUSION

It is essential that the loss is shown to have been occasioned by the insured peril. That which is contrary to the proximate cause is excluded via an 'exception clause,'[45] the exception clause operating to impose limits on the cover.[46] The common law illustrates that the solution can be found in the proximate cause rule, although the common sense approach is resorted to, described as a notion necessarily

> a matter of mere impression, or so intuitive that it cannot be further elucidated, at least in its application to standard cases, however, vague a penumbra may surround it. Commonsense is not a matter of inexplicable, or arbitrary assertions, and the causal notions which it employs . . . can be shown to rest, at least in part, on stateable principles.

The guiding common law principle operating in the Commonwealth Caribbean is the proximate cause doctrine. It represents the assumed intentions of the parties as reasonable business people,[47] and as a matter of common sense insurers are only liable for losses which they have agreed to cover. Regional courts apply conventional adherence to established UK decisions.

The House of Lords decision *Leyland Shipping Co. Ltd v Norwich Union Fire Insurance Society Ltd.*[48] is noteworthy, for causation is relative to determining the significance of multiple potential causes.

---

45 B. Coot, *Exemption Clauses* (Sweet & Maxwell: 1964); D. Yates, *Standard Business Contracts* (1968) No. 6 (B) 1.
46 See Chapter 10.
47 Supra n. 36.
48 Supra n. 13.

CHAPTER 10

CONSTRUCTION OF THE
CONTRACT OF INSURANCE

10.1 INTRODUCTION

The construction of the contract of insurance is a question of law. Traditionally, the process simply involved the 'elucidation and application of a number of rules of construction.'[1] However in the United Kingdom there has since been a significant restatement of the approach to the construction of the insurance contract and the principles of construction. The abandonment of the traditional approach has been brought about by a trio of House of Lords cases in the form of *Prenn v Symmonds*,[2] *Reardon Smith Line Ltd v Hansen-Tangen, Hansen-Tangen v Sanko Steamship Co.*[3] and *Investors Compensation Scheme Ltd v West Bromwich Building Society*.[4] The result is that the contract of insurance is now to be construed as a commercial document, free from 'old intellectual baggage of focusing purely on linguistic considerations divorced the contract from its matrix of facts.' Theoretically, this shift in approach is important from the standpoint that historically the court's role was restricted by virtue of the *laissez-faire* philosophy – premised on the viewpoint that parties to the contract of insurance are free to make their own bargain. In this regard, the court's role was viewed as simply to enforce that bargain or, put another way: 'The court cannot either rewrite contracts or impose on parties to them what the court may think would have been a reasonable contract.'[5]

In the Commonwealth Caribbean, there is little to no evidence to affirm the abandonment of statutory aids and traditional canons of interpretation to the question of construction. But Caribbean jurisprudence does indicate that while the accepted canons of interpretation continue to be a useful guide, the question of covered and excepted risks can only be truly understood by paying particular attention to the terms embodied in the contract of insurance. Thus the question becomes what is the scope of that contract as dictated by those terms, that is as an internal exercise rather than a simple external one of applying traditional canons of construction. It is also important to observe the question of construction pervades insurance law and applies to the nature and scope of the insurance as defined by its terms and not purely to the issue of whether recovery is possible.[6]

10.2 STATUTE

Regional insurance legislation provides no guidance on the manner in which insurance contracts are to be construed. This also goes for the Marine Insurance Act requiring the courts to look to the common law for guidance. This having been said, in the Commonwealth Caribbean considerable consumer legislation has recently been enacted modifying contractual terms and the manner in which the contract must set out those terms, in plain and simple language. There is uncertainty whether this legislation applies to insurance contracts. Although insurance falls

---

1 J. Birds, *Modern Insurance Law*, 6th edn (Sweet & Maxwell: 2014), p. 213.
2 [1971] 3 All ER 237.
3 [1976] 3 All ER 570.
4 [1998] 1 All ER 98.
5 Per Mance LJ in *Sinochem International Oil (London) Co. Ltd v Mobil Sales & Supply Corp.* [2000] Lloyd's Rep 339.
6 In *Millers v Sun Alliance (Bahamas) Ltd et al.* (unreported decision, Supreme Court of the Bahamas No. 329 of 1994) the words 'declined or cancelled' applies.

within the definition of a 'service,' in most jurisdictions the legislation does not expressly apply to insurance contracts. By contrast, in the United Kingdom, while Statements of Insurance Practice negated an attempt to bring insurance contracts within the Unfair Contract Terms Act,[7] administrative initiatives reveal a willingness on the part of regulators to bring insurance contracts under the auspices of legislation governing contracts generally[8] and the recently promulgated EC regulations.[9] Apart from the jurisdiction of Guyana, there is no attempt at ensuring that the contract is set out in plain language.[10] There has been considerable consumer legislation enacted in the Commonwealth Caribbean.[11]

Principles of construction: the traditional approach

Generally, the principles of construction applicable to insurance contracts are the same as those applicable to contracts in general. They may be summarised as follows:

1 The intention of the parties must prevail;

2 The whole of the policy must be examined and the policy construed in accordance with the ordinary rules of grammar;

3 The words of the policy must be interpreted in their everyday meaning – a literal approach operates unless the language is unclear, in which case extraneous circumstances may be examined;

4 The ordinary meaning of the words will be adopted wherever possible, but the meaning of a particular word may be limited by its context. In that case, the principle of *generalis specialibus* applies, so that the *ejusdem generis* rule to the effect that where special words are followed by general words, the general words are limited by the preceding specific words;

5 Weight is attached to the fact that the questions are framed by the insurer. In the event of ambiguity therefore the *contra preferentem* rule will be applied so that the clause will be construed contrary to the wishes of the draftsman;

6 Written parts prevail over printed parts as more likely to express the agreement of the parties;

7 The rule against parol evidence applies making oral evidence inadmissible as the basis for varying or contradicting the written word.[12]

Sometimes before the insurance contract can be construed, it is necessary to determine precisely what constitutes the contract of insurance as the terms of the policy and those contained in the proposal form may differ. This necessitates an initial investigation as to priority. Such a

---

7 Unfair Contract Terms Act of 1977, c. 50.
8 The UK Insurance Ombudsman in the Annual Report No. 69 of 1990 stated that the industry agreed to the bound by the spirit of the Unfair Contract Terms Act of 1977.
9 The Unfair Terms Directive 93/13/EC.
10 For a contrary position, see Regulation 6 of the Unfair Contract Terms Directive 93/13/EC. Consider also *Koskas v Standard Marine Insurance Co. Ltd* (1926) 25 LILR 362; (1927) 27 LILR61; where the print was so small that the judge at first instance refused to allow the insurer to rely on a specific condition; *Kausar v Eagle Star Insurance Co. Ltd* [1997] CLC 129.
11 Antigua and Barbuda Consumer Protection and Safety Act, Cap 97; Barbados Fair Competition Act, Cap 326 C No. 19 of 2002; Fair Trading Commission Act, Cap 326 B No. 31 of 2000; Consumer Guarantees Act, Cap 326 D No. 20 of 2002; Consumer Protection Act, Cap 326 No. 20 of 2002; Trinidad and Tobago Consumer Protection and Safety Act No. 28 of 1985; Unfair Contract Terms Act No. 28 of 1985; Misrepresentation Act No. 12 of 1983.
12 E. R. Hardy Ivamy, *General Principles of Insurance Law*, 4th edn (Butterworths: 1979), p. 355.

situation arose in the decision of *Zainool Mohammed v Capital Insurance Co. Ltd & All Trinidad Sugar Estates & Factory Workers' Trade Union*.[13] In *Zainool Mohammed*, arising out of the jurisdiction of Trinidad and Tobago. Here, a conflict existed between the proposal form and the endorsements to and a clause contained in the policy as to who was an 'authorised driver.' The Court ruled, applying the general principles of construction that if there is a final and direct inconsistency between the proposal form and the express condition of the policy, the terms of the policy must prevail. Further, that where clauses of a contract of insurance are in conflict, three rules are applicable to determine which clause shall prevail: (1) the policy shall be construed more strongly against the insurers; (2) where there are printed, written or typewritten words, greater weight is to be given to typewritten words; and (3), where there is more than one document, greater weight should be given to the later in date. It is clear that in *Zainool Mohammed* the Court was striving to determine *consensus ad idem*, so that in cases of conflict written parts will prevail over printed parts as being more likely to express the agreement of the parties.

In *Feanny v Globe Insurance Co. of the West Indies Ltd*,[14] Courtenay J stated on the construction of the proposal form:

> [It] is a basic principle that a fair and reasonable construction must be placed on the questions and answers in the proposal from. In *Condogianis v Guardian Assurance Company* [1921] Vol V.111 LI . L Rep 155 at 156 Lord Shaw said: In a contract of insurance it is a weighty fact that the questions are framed by the insurer, and that if an answer is obtained to such a question which is upon a fair construction a true answer, it is not open to the insuring company to maintain that the question was but in a sense different from or more comprehensive than the proponent's answer covered. Where an ambiguity exists, the contract must stand if an answer has been made to the question on a fair and reasonable construction of that question. Otherwise the ambiguity would be a trap against which the insured would be protected by courts of law.

In situations where there is no conflict, it is necessary to ascertain whether the risk insured against has occurred.[15] There is considerable Caribbean authority illustrating the utility of traditional principles of interpretation in construing the contract of insurance.

10.3   ORDINARY MEANING

The language in a policy of insurance is *prima facie* to be understood in accordance with its ordinary natural meaning. While it is impossible set out an exhaustive guide given the infinite variations in terms or conditions that may arise for consideration, the following terms have been considered in the Caribbean.

10.4   'STORED AND KEPT'

In the Trinidad and Tobago decision of *Solomon Ghany Oil & Engineering Ltd v N.E.M. (West Indies) Insurance Ltd*,[16] the issue arose whether the diesel was 'stored' on the premises in contravention of the terms of the policy. In rejecting the claim for indemnity the insurers argued, *inter alia*, that the plaintiff insured stored on the premises flammable oil in contravention of clause 5(1) of

13   High Court (1990) 1 Trin LR 43.
14   Unreported decision, Supreme Court of Jamaica No. JM 1997 SC 61.
15   P. S-J. H. Langan and P. B. Benson, *Maxwell on Interpretation of Statutes*, 12th edn (Sweet & Maxwell: 1969).
16   Unreported decision, High Court of Trinidad and Tobago No. S3114 of 1986.

the policy. The High Court of Trinidad and Tobago restated established rules of construction, to wit: in a contract of insurance, the first relevant rule of construction is that the apparently literal meaning of the words of warranty must be restricted if they produce a result inconsistent with a reasonable business like interpretation of such a warranty. Applying *Thompson v Equity Fire Insurance Co.*,[17] as to the meaning of the words 'stored or kept,' the High Court held that the phrase connoted a notion of warehousing or depositing for safe custody or keeping for stock in trade so that a small quantity, 'about a gallon or so,' for washing rust off one's hands after handling the oilfield equipment did not amount to the storing of diesel oil,[18] the Court ultimately rejected the insured's claim on other grounds. In *Thompson v Equity Fire Insurance Co.*,[19] a fire policy effected by a shopkeeper exempted the insurers from liability 'while gasoline is stored or kept in the building insured.' The insured had a small quantity of gasoline for cooking purposes. It was held that the insurer was liable for a fire that occurred, as the phrase 'stored or kept' did not apply to trifling amounts.

10.5   'BECOME UNOCCUPIED'

The ordinary natural approach has also been applied to construe the phrase 'become unoccupied.' In the Jamaica Court of Appeal decision of *Swaby v Prudential Assurance Co. Ltd*,[20] a fire policy contained a clause descriptive of the risk, suspending the insurer's liability 'if the building insured . . . become unoccupied and so remain for a period of more than 30 days.' The Court of Appeal, construing the policy, ruled that the phrase 'become unoccupied' implied a change of status, and when applied to a dwelling house connoted that the occupier has ceased to dwell in it. Their view was that such a change does not occur when absence is merely temporary where there is a manifest intention to return and assume control of the building or where adequate provision for its protection was retained,[21] the Court held that the premises were not unoccupied.

Subsequently, in *Dhanpatiya Herman v New India Assurance Co. (Trinidad and Tobago) Ltd*,[22] the insured made a claim for loss under a fire insurance policy for $190,000. The insurers denied liability, claiming that the house had become unoccupied at the time of loss. The evidence revealed that the plaintiff had been living in the United States since 1963 but that she had left her sister and niece in charge of the premises. The issue was whether occupation of premises three nights per week by a caretaker amounted to 'occupation' as required by the policy. It was held that given the circumstances, the building did not become or remain unoccupied for a period of more than 30 days, so the plaintiff was found not to be in breach of the policy. Mr Justice Gregory Smith applied a more open-textured approach and distinguished the earlier decision of *Marzouca*, finding that use of the words 'regular daily presence' in *Marzouca*'s case was not itself definitive of the exact nature of the presence required to fulfil the condition of occupation. In essence, it remained a question of fact, as *Marzouca*'s case did not seek to define occupation but rather it ruled out constructive occupation from the ambit of the clause.

In *Dohlantry v Blue Mounds*,[23] the owners of a farm occupied a house at intervals when they were working on the farm such as during harvesting. They actually resided 1.5 miles from the house in question. It was held that the house was left vacant for 30 days prior to loss. In the

---

17   [1910] AC 592.
18   The plaintiff lost on other grounds.
19   Supra n. 17.
20   (1964) 6 WIR 246.
21   Per Lewis J.A., p. 254.
22   HCA No. 1780 of 1993.
23   (1892) 83 Wis. 181.

Privy Council decision of *Marzouca v Atlantic and British Commercial Insurance Co.*,[24] on appeal from the jurisdiction of Jamaica, the exact clause in a fire insurance policy was considered. Here a hotel was the subject of insurance. It was used as a nurses' home until September 1963 when the nurses moved out. The plaintiff intended to convert the building into residential flats and it was empty until 20 November 1963. A constable was employed as a night watchman but he never entered the building. On 20 November 1963, a contractor began working on the building. Lord Hodson stated that for the occupation to be effectual it must be actual, not constructive. It must involve the regular daily presence of someone in the building. If there is no one present for a continuous period of more than 30 days, there is a breach of condition.[25]

10.6 'THEFT BY FORCIBLE AND VIOLENT MEANS'

The ordinary natural meaning of the expression 'theft by forcible and violent means' was applied in *Dino Services v Prudential Assurance Co. Ltd*[26] so that the term was not satisfied when keys were stolen to gain entry to premises without having to resort to violence. In *British and Foreign Marine Insurance Co. v Gaunt*,[27] an 'all-risks' policy was interpreted as covering all loss to the property insured as is inevitable from ordinary wear and tear and inevitable depreciation or from inherent vice. The insured need only show that the loss was accidental; he need not show the exact nature of the accident or casualty which occasioned the loss.[28]

10.7 'AUTHORISED DRIVER'

In the Barbadian decision of *Weeks v Motor and General Insurance Co. Ltd*,[29] the plaintiff was a passenger in a taxi insured against third party risks with the defendant company. The plaintiff was being given a lift by the driver and had not made any payment for the journey. The taxi collided with a lorry and the plaintiff sustained injuries. She obtained judgment for damages against the driver and then brought an action to recover the sum awarded from the defendant insurance company, relying on Section 9 of the Motor Vehicles Insurance (Third Party Risks) Act of 1952.[30] The policy permitted use for social domestic and pleasure purposes and use for the carriage of passengers or goods in connection with the insured's business. It was held that the effect of Section 9 is to require the owner of the vehicle normally or habitually used for the carriage of passengers for hire or reward, or by reason of or in pursuance of a contract of employment to have a policy in force covering the liabilities specified in the Act. Williams J applied the ordinary natural meaning of the phrase to embrace non-paying passengers: 'If a restrictive application was intended, apt words would have and should have, been chosen.'[31] In *Dillon v Jamaica Co-operative Fire and General Insurance Co. Ltd*,[32] the phrase 'authorised driver' in the contract prohibited unauthorised drivers; the claim was denied.

24 [1971] 1 Lloyd's Rep 449 (PC Jamaica).
25 Ibid., pp. 453–454.
26 [1989] 1 All ER 422.
27 [1921] 2 AC 41.
28 An all-risks policy can be restricted if a limitation is placed on coverage. See *Queensland Government Railways and Electric Power Transmission Pty Ltd v Manufacturers' Mutual Life Insurance Ltd* (1968) 118 CLR 314. An all-risks policy excluded loss or damage arising from faulty design.
29 (1969) 15 WIR 188.
30 No. 22.
31 Ibid., p. 191.
32 (1970) 16 WIR 79.

10.8   TECHNICAL MEANING

The ordinary natural meaning approach will be abandoned where a word to be construed has a technical or legal meaning.[33] This may arise with respect to words outlining cover or exceptions to cover. In this regard, the word 'riot' has repeatedly been the focus of consideration in the Commonwealth Caribbean. Riot legislation exists in many Caribbean territories. In Barbados for instance, the Riots (Prevention Act) of 1967[34] statutorily defines 'riot' as 'where 12 or more being unlawfully, riotously and tumultuously assembled together to the disturbance of the public peace.' The statutory threshold of 12 stands in contrast to the factual circumstances of *London & Lancashire Fire Insurance Co. v Bolands*,[35] where the Court ruled that an exemption clause covering loss caused by or happening as a consequence of a riot applied when four armed, masked men broke a store owner's plate glass. The decision can, however, be understood given the disturbances in Ireland at the time as a result of IRA activity. Although a riot, civil disturbance or commotion is predicated upon the gathering of 12 or more persons in the Commonwealth Caribbean,[36] the statute appears to have been largely ignored. The issue arose for consideration in the Court of Appeal of Trinidad and Tobago of *Grell-Taurel Ltd v Caribbean Home Insurance Co. Ltd & Ors.*[37] Unfortunately, the case turned on whether there was a sufficient causal connection between the question of excepted perils and the loss which occurred, and the reverse burden clause rather than the issue of construction of the policy. In *Grell-Taurel Ltd*, the insured effected a policy of insurance covering the stock and the contents of its premises against loss or damage. Condition 6 of the policy excluded cover for any 'loss or damage occasioned by or through or in consequence, directly or indirectly . . . of insurrection.' As a result of the Muslimeen uprising of 1990 in Trinidad and Tobago, the insured's premises were looted by persons not involved in the insurrection. The insurer was held entitled to reject liability, not on the construction of the term 'riot' but on of whether there was a sufficient causal connection between the question of excepted perils and the loss which occurred and the reverse burden clause. In *Brodie & Rainer Ltd v British Guiana & Trinidad Mutual Fire Insurance Co. Ltd*,[38] disturbances broke out in the city of Georgetown, Guyana, during the course of which the plaintiffs' premises, fittings and stock were almost completely destroyed by fire. In construing the policy, the court had regard to the judicial definition of 'riot' as laid out in the earlier decision of *Field v Metropolitan Police District Receiver*.[39] Adopting in substance Hawkins's definition, the court concluded that in order to constitute a riot, 'five elements were necessary: (a) three persons at least must take part; (b) there must be a common purpose; (c) there must be execution or inception of the common purpose; (d) there must be an intent to help one another by force if necessary against any person who may oppose them in the execution of their common purpose; (e) there must be force or violence used in the execution of the common purpose not merely used in demolishing but displayed in such a manner as to alarm at least one person of reasonable firmness and courage.[40]

The Court held that, on the facts, a riot had occurred. On the issue of whether the damage was as a result of an excepted peril the Court ruled that the fire originated and was in blaze

33   *Deutsche Genossenschaftsbank v Burnhope* [1995] 4. All ER 717; *Pan Am v Aetna Casualty* [1974] 1 Lloyd's Rep 232; *Hayward v Norwich Union Insurance Ltd* [2001] Lloyd's Rep IR 410; See also Wasik [1986] *JBL* 45.
34   Cap 171.
35   [1924] AC 836.
36   Antigua and Barbuda Riot Act, Cap 383; Barbados Riots (Prevention Act) of 1967, Cap 171; Belize Riots Compensation Act, Cap 338 [2000 Rev.]; British Virgin Islands Riot Act, Cap 69 [1991 Rev.]; Dominica Riot Act Chapter 10:02 [1990 Rev.]; Jamaica Riot Act [1973 Rev.]; St Kitts and Nevis Riot Act, Cap 72 No. 6/643.
37   (2001) 62 WIR 384.
38   Unreported decision, British Guiana LRBG 72 of 1966.
39   [1907] 2 KB 853.
40
       A number of questions in the cross-examination of witnesses for the defendants was directed to show that passersby who were not engaged in the breaking into of premises joined in the looting.

during the riot. That fire spread to the plaintiffs' premises by the operation of natural forces only, without the intervention of anything to change its character or identity.

Hence, despite the statutory assistance provided by riot prevention legislation, there is little indication of its relevance to the interpretation of the term 'riot' in the Caribbean.

10.9   CONTEXT

The ordinary meaning of a word may not be adopted where the context requires otherwise. This approach was applied in the Jamaican decision of *Dyoll Insurance Co. Ltd v Cardoza.*[41] In *Dyoll*, a decision which is also instructive on the principles of causation, the insured effected a householder's comprehensive policy which contained an exemption clause for loss or damage caused by subsidence or landslip. As a result of unnatural and extreme rainfall, damage was caused to a retaining wall on the insured premises. The insured contended that the damage was caused by an insured peril. The insurer on the other hand, disputed liability contending that the damage was caused by a 'landslip,' which fell within the exclusion clause and thus was not covered by the policy. In construing the policy, the Court of Appeal restated the salient principle that where an exemption clause is clear, the courts will uphold the meaning even if the consequences seem unfair,[42] but that if on the other hand the meaning is ambiguous, the *contra preferentem* rule applies.[43] The Court of Appeal found that the insurer had failed to discharge the onus to bring itself within the exception.[44] 'Landslip' construed as a term which should be approached with common sense, as a small land-slide, a rapid downward movement under the influence of gravity of a mass of earth on a slope.[45] The dictionary was resorted to for the meaning of 'flood' and the English decision of *Young v Royal Sun Alliance*,[46] as something which is a natural phenomenon which has some element of violence suddenness or largeness about it.

In *Young v Sun Alliance & London Insurance*,[47] the insured's household policy insured him against loss arising from, *inter alia*, 'storm, tempest, or flood.' The insured returned home to discover his house was flooded. The house was built on a meadow and water had seeped into the premises and caused damage to the ground floor bathroom, three inches deep. The Court of Appeal rejected the insured's claim for indemnity. Applying a contextual approach, the term 'flood' was held to take the character of 'storm' and 'tempest,' importing a notion of violence and abnormality.

In this regard I would adopt the following passage appearing at p. 248 in Vol I of Russell On Crime (12th edn) adopting 1 Hawkins c 65, s 3– If any person seeing others actually engaged in a riot, joins them and assists them therein, he is as much a rioter as if he had first assembled with them for the same purpose, inasmuch as he had no pretence that he came innocently into the company, but joined himself to them with an intention of seconding them in the execution of their unlawful enterprise. And it would be endless, as well as superfluous, to examine whether every particular person engaged in a riot were in truth one of the first assembly, or actually had a previous knowledge of the design.

41   Jamaica Court of Appeal No. 137 of 2001.
42   *Coxe v Employer's Liability Assurance Corp. Ltd* [1916] 2 KB 629.
43   *Worswick v Canada Fire & Marine Insurance Co.* (1878) 3 OAR 487; *Fitton v Accidental Death Insurance Co.* (1864) 17 CB (NS) 122; 144 ER 50; *Re Etherington & Lancashire & Yorkshire Accident Insurance Company* [1909] 1 KB 591; *Oakleaf v Home Insurance Ltd*, 14 DLR (2d) 535.
44   E. R. Hardy Ivamy, *General Principles of Insurance Law*, 6th edn (Butterworths: 1986) states that where the insured peril insured against, precedes an excepted clause which actually produces the loss, there is a loss within the meaning of the policy if, not withstanding the operation of the excepted clause, the peril insured against is to be regarded as the proximate cause of loss.
45   *Oddy v Phoenix Assurance Co. Ltd* [1966] 1 Lloyd's Rep 134.
46   [1976] 3 All ER 561.
47   [1977] 1 WLR 104.

10.10 *CONTRA PROFERENTEM*

Construction of the *contra proferentem* rule requires words to be construed against the person drafting them, where they are ambiguous and capable of more than one meaning. Although in most cases this means against the insurer, in principle the rule may operate against the insured regarding any words of contract for which he is primarily responsible, including statements defining the scope of the risk. In *English v Western*,[48] a motor policy effected by a 17-year-old youth covered his liability for injury to all persons except, *inter alia*, in respect of 'death or injury to any member of the assured's household' traveling in the car with the insured. He negligently injured his sister when she was his passenger. The insurers argued that they were not liable to indemnify the insured against his liability to her by virtue of the above exception. It was held that the expression 'any member of the assured's household of which the assured was the head' was equally capable of meaning 'any member of household of which the assured was a member.' It was therefore ambiguous and the meaning more favourable to the insured, the former meaning, was adopted, so that the insurers were liable. In *Houghton v Trafalgar Insurance Co. Ltd*,[49] an exception in a motor policy provided 'Any load in excess for which it was constructed.' The insurers argued that the carriage of six persons instead of five was within the exception. The Court found that this was not a 'load.'

The ambiguity should be apparent on the face of the document. In accordance with the Judicial Committee of the Privy Council decision of *Melanesian Mission Trust Board v Australian Mutual Provident Society*,[50] it is not the function of the court, when construing a document, to search for an ambiguity. Nor should the rules which exist to resolve ambiguities be invoked in order to create an ambiguity which, according to the ordinary meaning of the words, is not there. So the starting point is to examine the words used in order to see whether they are clear and unambiguous. The question of construction is a question of law and once a word has been judicially considered, in accordance with the doctrine of precedent, the rule should be followed.[51]

10.11 ACCIDENT

The term 'accident' covers unintentional acts which may arise from various scenarios. The diverse nature of injuries either partial or severe, culminating in bodily harm, death associated with intractable psychiatric post-traumatic stress disorder (PTSD) all have to be dealt with. So accident may be thought of as the inevitable consequence of a deliberate foreseeable act for example, in *Dhak v Insurance Co. of North America (UK) Ltd*,[52] a nurse experiencing severe back pain drank a bottle of gin to ease the pain and died from asphyxiation. The death was foreseeably the inevitable consequence of a foreseeable event. In *Page v Smith* [1995] 2 All ER 736, the House of Lords was concerned there with damages for personal injury, not merely bodily injury. Nevertheless, Lord Lloyd, giving the majority judgment, said: 'In an age when medical knowledge is expanding fast, and psychiatric knowledge with it, it would not be sensible to commit the law to a distinction between physical and psychiatric injury.'

48 [1940] 2 KB 156.
49 [1954] 1 QB 247.
50 [1997] 2 EGLR 128.
51 Birds, supra n. 1, p. 212.
52 [1996] 1 Lloyd's Rep 632.

Problems arise as the policy may limit the operation of the term 'accident' by specific language. We may think of meaning with respect to 'accident' as any loss resulting from, or caused by accidental means, an event occurring without specific intent, accidental happenchance – all these are phrases, some occurring fairly commonly in insurance policies. It is the problem of defining 'accident' which causes the courts difficulties. The need for definition occurs most frequently in policies of personal accident insurance, motor vehicle policy coverage and in situations which embody a personal accident component as well as policies of liability insurance. These situations prove to be quite common hence our need to be aware of the difficulties presented.

The core issue is succinctly well described by Birds[53] in this quote:

> insurance *prima facie* covers only unintentional acts . . . so one problem is how the presence of the word 'accident' qualifies this. Another is that even a deliberate act by someone may well be accidental from the point of view of the victim. Similarly, an insured may be engaged in a deliberate course of conduct when something happens which he did not intend. Is this an accident? It is suggested that the answers to these and other problems are best considered by a separate examination of first, those first party insurances where the description 'accident' is to be found, and second, cases of third party or liability insurance where the liability of the insurer to indemnify exists only if the insured acted accidently.

Clear-cut as this may seem, the apparent definition or distinction here described has not been uniformly adopted.

10.12 PRINCIPLES OF CONSTRUCTION: THE MODERN APPROACH

A trio of House of Lords cases – *Prenn v Symmonds*,[54] *Reardon Smith Line Ltd v Hansen-Tangen, Hansen-Tangen v Sanko Steamship Co.*[55] and *Investors Compensation Scheme Ltd v West Bromwich Building Society*[56] – has brought about a change in the traditional approach. Although the modern approach still has as its objective ascertainment of the intention of the parties as reflected in the insurance contract, the practice of focusing purely on linguistic considerations and divorcing the contract from its matrix of facts has 'long since passed.'[57] As a result, the old intellectual baggage has given way to a common sense approach, examining the circumstances of the particular contract. Lord Hoffmann in *Investors Compensation Scheme Ltd v West Bromwich Building Society*[58] summarised the law as follows:

> The result has been, subject to one important exception, to assimilate the way in which any serious utterance would be interpreted in real life . . . The principles may be summarised as follows:
>
> (1)   Interpretation is the ascertainment of the meaning which the document would convey to a reasonable person having all the background knowledge which would reasonably have been available to the parties in the situation in which they were at the time of the contract.
>
> (2)   The background was famously referred to by Lord Wilberforce as the 'matrix of fact' but this phrase is, if anything, an understated description of what the fact background may

---

53   Birds, supra n. 1, p. 218.
54   Supra n. 2.
55   Supra n. 3.
56   Supra n. 4.
57   *Prenn v Simmonds* [1976] 1 WLR 1381.
58   Supra n. 4.

include. Subject to the requirement that it should have been reasonably available to the parties and to the exception to be mentioned next, includes absolutely anything which would have affected the way in which the language of the document would have been understood.

(3) The law excludes from the admissible background the previous negotiations of the parties and their declaration of subjective intent. They are admissible only in an action for rectification. The law makes this distinction for reasons of practical policy and, in this respect only legal interpretation differs from the way we would interpret utterances in ordinary life. The boundaries of this exception are in some respects unclear.

(4) The meaning which a document (or any other utterance) would convey to a reasonable man is not the same thing as the meaning of the words. The meaning of words is a matter of dictionaries and grammars; the meaning of the document is what the parties using those words against the relevant background would reasonably have been understood to mean. The background may not merely enable the reasonable man to choose between the possible meaning of words which are ambiguous but even (as occasionally happens in ordinary life) to conclude that the parties must, for whatever reason, have used the wrong words or syntax (see *Mannai Investment Co. Ltd v Eagle Star Life Assurance Co. Ltd* [1976] 3 All ER 352.

(5) The 'rule' that words should be given their 'natural and ordinary meaning' reflects the commonsense proposition that we do not easily accept that people have made linguistic mistakes, particularly in formal documents. On the other hand, if one would nevertheless conclude from the background that something must have gone wrong with the language, the law does not require judges to attribute to the parties an intention which they plainly could have had. Lord Diplock made this point more vigorously when he said in *Antaios Cia Naviera SA v Salen Rederierna AB, The Antaios* [1984] 3 All ER 229 at 233 [1985] AC 191 at 201.

... if detailed semantic and syntactical analysis of words in commercial contract is going to lead to a conclusion that flouts business common sense, it must be made to yield to business common sense.

Lord Hoffmann applies a purposive approach, to the contract of insurance as a commercial contract. In *Jumbo King Ltd v Faithful Properties Ltd*,[59] Lord Hoffmann opined that the overriding objective in construction is to give effect to what a reasonable person rather than a pedantic lawyer would have understood the parties to mean. Therefore, if in spite of linguistic problems the meaning is clear, it is that meaning which must prevail. Lord Hoffmann later qualified his earlier position in his dissenting judgment in *Bank of Credit and Commerce International SA (In Liquidation) v Ali*[60] by stating that the factual background to which reference could be made was only such as the reasonable person would regard as being relevant. Lord Hoffmann's judgment provides a road map for the interpretation of insurance contracts – advising that they should be construed to make good commercial sense.

10.13 CONCLUSION

The new – or if you prefer, current – approach to construction of the contract of insurance recognises implicitly the imbalance that exists between the insured and the insurer, an imbalance entrenched by the proliferation of standard form contracts, drafting techniques like declaration clauses and basis of contract clauses and the operation of the doctrine of *uberrimae fidei*.[61] In

---

59 FACV 000007/1999.
60 [2001] 2 WLR 535.
61 See further, *Solomon Ghany Oil Engineering Ltd v N.E.M. (West Indies) Insurance Ltd* (unreported decision, Trinidad and Tobago High Court No. S3114 of 1996); *Bowe v British Fidelity Assurance Ltd* (unreported decision, Supreme Court of the Bahamas No. 372 of 1999).

the Caribbean, there is no comprehensive control of policy terms and conditions.[62] Insurance contracts are regulated primarily by insurance statute. To determine whether a specific loss falls within the ambit of a particular policy, one must apply the general principles of contract construction.

The absence of self-regulatory mechanisms like 'Statements of Insurance practice' or Codes combine with the fact that the insured consumer cannot tangibly take advantage of the rise in consumerism evident in the plethora of consumer legislation enacted.[63] Among these are the establishment of consumer tribunals and anti-trust or fair trade legislation[64] underscores this point. Actually, in some cases, regional consumer legislation expressly excludes an application to contracts of insurance.[65] It is this difficulty in ascertaining a *consensus ad idem* ideology within insurance law that demands a departure from traditional rules of construction.

---

62 Consider Section 155 of the St Lucia Insurance Act No. 6 of 1995, which simply provides that all policies must be in clearly legible letters.
63 Barbados Consumer Guarantee Act No. 21 of 2002; Consumer Guarantees Act, Cap 326 D No. 20 of 2002; Consumer Protection Act, Cap 326 No. 20 of 2002; Electronic Transactions Act, Cap 308 B No. 2 of 2006.
64 Barbados Fair Competition Act No. 19 of 2002; Jamaica Fair Competition Act of 1993.
65 Consider the Antigua and Barbuda Unfair Contract Terms Act, Cap 450; Consumer Protection and Safety Act, Cap 97; Misrepresentation Act No. 7 of 1992; see also Trinidad and Tobago Misrepresentation Act No. 12 of 1983; Consumer Protection and Safety Act No. 30 of 1985.

CHAPTER 11

THE CLAIMS PROCEDURE

11.1   INTRODUCTION

The procedure for claiming under a contract of insurance is dependent on the nature of the policy, the nature of the risk insured against and any conditions within the policy imposed on the insured by the insurer. The fundamental distinction in insurance law is that between life insurance and indemnity insurance. There are several types of life insurance, ranging from pure whole life, where there is an undertaking to pay a certain sum on the death of the life insured so that the claims process would require, *inter alia*, proof of death; to endowment insurance where proof of the attainment of a certain age is required. In indemnity insurance, proof of the peril insured against is required. It is important therefore to consider the nature of the policy and the nature of entitlement to the policy monies in addition to any condition outlining the procedure to be followed in the case of loss.[1] Conditions outlining the claims process, as we saw in Chapter 10, enable the insurer to investigate the claim and often operate as conditions precedent to the liability of the insurer.

Regional Insurance Acts provide little assistance on the procedure to be followed at the claims stage. Statutory intervention is restricted to permitting payment of policy monies without evidence of probate or letters of administration up to a given threshold,[2] enabling the insurer to retain the policy monies or to use policy proceeds to offset a debt owing to the insurer and provisions requiring the insurer to give notice where proof of age of the life insured is a condition precedent to the insurer's liability.[3] Additionally, regional statutes expressly overrule the doctrine of privity by bestowing a right on a workman who has been injured on insured premises to pursue a claim directly against the insurer.[4] Consequently, the procedure to be followed by the insured when submitting a claim is a matter of common sense and the construction of the insurance contract in accordance with existing common law.

11.2   COMMON LAW

Notice clause

Insurance contracts often contain a notice clause requiring notification to the insurer that a loss has occurred. Oral notice of loss will suffice unless written notice is expressly stipulated. 'A provision requiring notification of loss within a specific time period will be interpreted as a condition precedent to the liability of the insurer.'[5] Such a condition must be strictly complied

---

1   See Chapter 10.
2   Section 101, Barbados Insurance Act No. 32 of 1996, Cap 310; Section 132, Jamaica Insurance Act No. 26 of 2001.
3   Section 130, Guyana Insurance Act No. 20 of 1998.
4   Section 100, Barbados Insurance Act No. 32 of 1996, Cap 310; Section 154, Guyana Insurance Act No. 20 of 1998.
5   J. Birds, *Modern Insurance Law*, 7th edn (Sweet & Maxwell: 2007), p. 241 notes that

> In the absence of any specific term in an insurance policy, it is undecided whether, upon suffering a loss, an insured is bound to claim for the loss within a reasonable time on pain of the claim being denied, or whether it is sufficient merely to claim before the statutory limitation period expires.

with and the insurer is entitled to avoid liability for the loss if the insured fails to fulfil this condition. It may however also be regarded as an innominate term, and if the consequences of breach so merit, the insurer will be entitled to repudiate liability.[6] Where there is no stipulated time period and the policy contains a condition precedent that notice should be given as 'soon as possible following an accident,' the court will assess the factual circumstances to determine what is reasonable.

Once a notice clause is clear and unambiguous, it must be strictly complied with. In *Verelest's Administration v Motor Union Insurance Company*,[7] the policy placed an obligation on the insured to give notice in writing 'as soon as possible.' The insured was killed in India as a result of a motor accident. It was not until some 12 months later that the policy was actually discovered by the insured's personal representatives. The insurer denied liability on the basis of breach of the negotiation requirements, arguing that knowledge of the accident, not knowledge of the existence of the policy, should be the triggering event for the negotiation period. The Court rejected this argument, finding for the personal representatives. Applying a subjective construction to the term 'as soon as possible,' the Court strictly construed the clause against the insurer.

In the absence of statutory restrictions, the insurer has significant freedom when drafting the terms and conditions of insurance policies. Notice requirements may range from specifying a place of notice, for example the company's head office,[8] to a specific time period within which a claim must be lodged, normally within 14 days. With respect to time limits, there is considerable English and Commonwealth Caribbean case law on point. One such English decision is that of *Adamson v Liverpool London & Globe Insurance Co.*,[9] which has implications for progressive or staggered perils. In *Adamson*,[10] a cash in transit policy contained a condition to the effect that

> The insured shall immediately upon the discovery of any loss, give notice thereof to the company . . . The company shall be under no liability hereunder in respect of loss which has not been notified to the company within 15 days of its occurrence.

Over a period of two years, an employee of the insured embezzled money entrusted to him for the purchase of National Insurance stamps. When the theft was eventually discovered, at a point obviously outside the 15-day period, the insurer was immediately notified.

The Court of Appeal of Barbados was presented with an opportunity to construe the implications of a notice of loss clause in *Royal Caribbean Hotels v Barbados Fire & Commercial et al.*[11] In *Royal Caribbean Hotels*, loss and damage occurred to a hotel on the south coast of Barbados as a result of Hurricane Allen. The second defendant, the Bank of Nova Scotia, was the debenture holder and assignee of the policy of insurance. Clause 11 of the policy required written notification of loss within 15 days. Clause 19 of the policy of insurance provided: 'In no case whatever shall the Company be liable for any loss or damage after the expiration of twelve months from the happenings of the loss or damage unless the claim is the subject of pending

---

6   Birds, ibid., p. 212 notes that

> In the absence of any specific term in an insurance policy, it is undecided whether, upon suffering a loss, an insured is bound to claim for the loss within a reasonable time on pain of the claim being denied, or whether it is sufficient merely to claim before the statutory limitation period expires.

   Cassel v Lancashire & Yorkshire Accident Insurance Co. (1885) 1 TLR 495.
7   [1925] 2 KB 137.
8   *Brook v Trafalgar Insurance Co* (1946) 79 Ll. L.R. 365.
9   [1953] 2 Lloyd's Rep 355.
10 Ibid.
11 Ibid.

action or arbitration.' The insurers refuted liability for breach of a condition. The Court of Appeal of Barbados observed that the utility of the notice is to give the company an opportunity to investigate and adjust the damages at an early date. Thus the insured's non-compliance therewith was fatal to his claim for indemnification. Whereas in *Ennia General Insurance Co. v Astaphan & Co.* (1970),[12] the Court of Appeal of Dominica took into account the sheer chaos in the aftermath of the destruction of Hurricane David in Dominica, which had caused untold devastation over the island with several people killed or injured. In *Barbados Fire & General*, no such consideration was invoked. Admittedly the devastation Hurricane David caused in Dominica dwarfs the minor damage Barbados suffered as a result of Hurricane Allen. But more importantly, the decision can be understood as illustrating the strictness with which Courts will interpret such a condition, only in very narrow circumstances will this approach be disturbed, so that a failure to comply, however 'inadvertent or excusable,'[13] will entitle the insurer to avoid liability.'

In the Caribbean, unlike in the United Kingdom, there are no Statements of General Insurance Practice operating alleviating the burden placed on the insured by interpreting 'as soon as' to mean as soon as 'reasonably possible.' Although the insurer must not impose unreasonable requirements,[14] he has a large degree of freedom in this respect.

11.3   PARTICULARS OF LOSS

Apart from notifying the insurer upon occurrence of loss, the insured must also provide particulars of the loss. Normally this requires the insured's completion of a claim form and submission of documentary evidence detailing the loss.[15] The burden of proof that loss has occurred falls squarely on the insured. The guiding principle: the insured must provide 'sufficient detail to enable the insurers to form a judgment as whether or not a loss has been sustained.'[16] The condition 'full particulars,' when present in the insurance contract, has been interpreted as meaning the 'best particulars which the assured can reasonably give.'[17] A condition that the insured give such proof and information as may reasonably be required is more expansive. It is a question of fact to be gathered from the circumstances of the case, so for instance particulars of the insured's bank account may be required where the insurance contract renders such an inquiry necessary.[18] Despite strict rules regarding compliance, the insured's duty to notify may be discharged by a third party, as for instance a taxi man or policeman in the case of a motor vehicular accident, once the insurer receives all necessary information within the stipulated time.[19]

Where the policy contains a co-operation clause, this is also subject to strict compliance.[20] Co-operation clauses are frequently found in liability policies, whereby the insured is required to co-operate by, *inter alia*, refraining from reaching a settlement with a third party or by agreeing not to take steps which may jeopardise the interests of the insurer.

---

12   Court of Appeal of Dominica Civil Appeal Nos 8 and 16 of 1984, DM 1988 CA 1.
13   Birds, supra n. 5, p. 254; *Cassel v Lancashire & Yorkshire Accident Insurance Company* (1885) 1 T.L.R. 495.
14   *Braunstein v Accidental Death Insurance Co.* (1861) 1 B & S 782.
15   *Watts v Simmons* (1924) 18 Ll L Rep 87.
16   *Mason v Harvey* (1853) 8 Exch 819 at 820, per Pollock C.B.
17   Ibid.
18   *Welch v Royal Exchange Assurance* [1939] 1 KB 294.
19   *Lickiss v Milestone Motor Policies* [1966] 2 All ER 972.
20   *London Guarantee Co. v Fearnley* (1880) 5 App Cas 911.

11.4   ARBITRATION

Arbitration clauses embodied in the contract are usually construed as conditions precedent to recovery of the insured's loss. Failure to submit to arbitration in accordance with an express term bars the insured from recovery.[21] In the decision *Motor Union Insurance Co. v Linzey*,[22] on appeal from the jurisdiction of the Windward Islands and Leeward Islands, the insured's motor car was insured for an additional premium covering risk of injury to passengers. The insured claimed for the unpaid balance on the amount of a judgment which a passenger in his motor car obtained against him. The passenger had recovered £1,054 6s 4d. The agent had failed to inform the insured that the risk was limited to £500 per passenger in respect of any one accident. The policy contained a clause which provided that all differences arising out of the policy should be referred to arbitration. The insured did not refer the matter to arbitration and brought an action for unpaid balance on the amount of a judgment which a passenger had obtained against him. The Federal Supreme Court upheld the arbitration clause allowing the appeal by the insurance company and held that the matter should have been referred to arbitration.

An arbitration clause restricts the ability of the insured to sue under the policy. An action to enforce an arbitration award in the insured's favour, is however, allowed.[23] As arbitration takes place outside a court of law, it avoids both the expense and delay of litigation. The court, however, has limited jurisdiction to interfere with arbitration awards. There is no inflexible rule of construction.[24] Thus an arbitrator's award can only be set aside in well-defined circumstances.[25] This is aptly illustrated in the case of *National Sugar Co. v American International Underwriters (Jamaica)*.[26] Here arbitration proceedings were brought by the appellants to determine whether a bridge came within the definition of buildings. The arbitrator had found that the bridge was not part of the property insured by the policy and that the insurers were not liable to the insured in respect of damage caused to the bridge. The Court of Appeal, in the judgment delivered by Justice Carey, restated the established principle that unless it appears on the face of the award that the arbitrator has proceeded on principles which were wrong in law, conclusions as to the construction of the deed must be accepted. Following established guidelines, the Court noted that it was settled law – the court cannot interfere with an arbitrator's award merely on the ground that it would have come to a different conclusion. Where a specific question of law has been referred to the arbitrator, the court will not interfere unless the arbitrator acted illegally.

11.5   PROOF OF DEATH

In life insurance, the terms of the policy dictate the procedure to be followed on death of the insured. Generally, where a claim by death arises under a life policy, an official certificate of death should be furnished to the insurance company within a specified time period.[27] Some

21   See the Guyanese decision of *Elphage v Federal Life and General Insurance Co. v* [1964] LRBG 76.
22   Supra n. 21; WIR 34; MS 1959 FSC 1.
23   *Scott v Avery* (1856) 5 HLC 811.
24   *Kelantan Government v Duff Development Co.* [1923] All ER 349.
25   *British Westinghouse Electric and Manufacturing Co. v Underground Electric Railways Co. of London* [1912] AC 673; *Re King and Duveen & Ors* [1913] 2 KB 32; *Champsey Bhara & Co. v Jivraj Balloo Spinning and Weaving Co. Ltd* [1923] AC 480; *F. R. Absalom Ltd v Great Western (London) Garden Village Society Ltd* [1933] AC 592.
26   JM 1990 CA No. 78.
27   *Hadenfayre Ltd v British National Insurance Society Ltd* [1984] 2 Lloyd's Rep 393.

insurance companies also require a declaration by a disinterested party. Where the insured has disappeared for an extended period, an application to the court can be made for a declaration of presumption of the death of the insured.[28] In *Chard v Chard*,[29] cited and applied in the Guyanese decision of *Demerara Bauxite Co. v Henry and Allicock*:[30]

> the issue whether a person is, or is not, to be presumed dead is generally speaking, one of fact, and not subject to a presumption of law. To that there is an exception which can be assumed without affecting the present case. By virtue of a long sequence of judicial statements, which either assert or assume such a rule, it appears accepted that there is a convenient presumption of law applicable to certain cases of seven years' absence where no statute applies. The presumption in its modern shape takes effect without examining its terms too exactly substantially as follows: where as regards 'AB' there is no acceptable affirmative evidence that he was alive at some time during a continuous period of seven years or more than if it can be proved first, that there are persons who would . . . [have likely] . . . heard of him over that period, secondly, that those persons have not heard of him, and thirdly, that all due inquiries have been made appropriate to the circumstance, 'AB' will be presumed to have died at sometime within that period.

Demerara involved an action for trespass to lands. The defendant sought to justify the trespass by, *inter alia*, laying claim by the right of intestate succession to a portion of the estate and prescriptive title. Applying the decision of *Chard v Chard*, it ruled that while conditions (1) and (2) were established, the court was unable to confidently assert that condition (3) had been established. Consequently the court found that there was insufficient evidence for the claimants to claim on intestacy.

Leave to swear death is possible after the expiration of seven years where the best possible enquires and searches have been made.[31] The claimant may not have to wait for seven years to elapse before applying to the court for leave to swear death, if there is strong circumstantial evidence that the insured is dead.[32] An application for the presumption of death must be made to the court, accompanied by an affidavit. After establishing proof of death, the insurer may pay the policy monies to the insured, despite not having received a grant of probate or letters of administration.[33]

11.6 PROOF OF SURVIVAL AND ENTITLEMENT

In the case of a life annuity policy, payment by an insurance company is dependent on survival. A Life Certificate is required, sworn by an independent person, usually an attorney and/or doctor. In order to discharge its obligations under a policy, the insurer must be satisfied the person claiming entitlement is indeed so entitled. This requires identification of the relevant claimant, the beneficiary or personal representative of the deceased trustees or executors under

---

28 *Demerara Bauxite Co. v Henry & Allicock* (1965) 23 WIR 1. Where a will, validly executed, is not forthcoming on the testator's death, it is presumed to have been destroyed by the testator unless there is sufficient evidence to repel such a conclusion. *Re Sargeant* (1975) 27 WIR 40. The onus of proof of circumstances sufficient to rebut the presumption is on the person propounding the will; *Allan v Morrison* [1900] AC 604. For authority on where a duplicate will had been submitted in probate, *Hapijan Sattar v Sarojni Dass* (1991) 44 WIR 257, the presumption of the destruction of the will *animo revocandi* may be rebutted by the fact that the beneficiary under the will had lived with the testatrix for most of her life.
29 [1955] 3 All ER 721.
30 (1965) 23 WIR 1.
31 *Re Phene's Trust* [1870] LR 5 Ch App 139; *Prudential Assurance Co. v Edmonds* (1877) 2 AC 487; *Lal Chand Marwari v Mahant Ramrup Gir* (1925) 42 TLR 159; *Chard v Chard* [1956] P 259.
32 C. H. Denbow, *Life Insurance Law in the Commonwealth Caribbean* (Butterworths: 1984), p. 138.
33 Section 132, Jamaica Insurance Act No. 26 of 2001.

the will who have obtained probate, where it is not dispensed with by statute. According to *Braunstein v Accidental Death Insurance Company*,[34] the standard of proof is of such a nature as a reasonable man will consider satisfactory.

11.7 FRAUDULENT CLAIMS

Apart from the formal requirements dictated by the insurance contract, public policy and its abhorrence of fraudulent claims also applies during the claims process. Whether a claim is fraudulent or not is a question for the jury. There is an abundance of West Indian authority on the requirements necessary for pleading fraud.[35] Justice Langrin, in *S & T Ltd et al. v West Indies Alliance Insurance Co. Ltd et al.*,[36] commenting on the varieties of fraud, noted that the claim may be fraudulent in that the assured has suffered no loss within the meaning of the policy, or that although he has suffered a loss, it was not caused by the peril insured against. It may contain false statement of fact or it may be supported by fraudulent evidence. Fraudulent claims may be brought about in a variety of ways, ranging from the deliberate intentional act which brings about the peril insured against, to the situation where the insured succumbs to the temptation to exaggerate the claim. In *S & T Ltd et al. v West Indies Alliance Insurance Co. Ltd et al.*,[37] fraud was established enabling the insurer to reject the plaintiff's claim of indemnity.

At this juncture, the focus is on exaggerated or inflated claims. The fundamental principle of insurance law is that the insured should be indemnified against his actual loss and no more.[38] The insured therefore is not to make a profit or gain out of insurance; such loss or damage to be calculated at the time of loss or damage and not when the policy was effected.[39] Insurance policies often contain terms that specifically address the consequences of making a fraudulent claim.[40] As stated by Mr Justice Willes in *Britton v Royal Insurance Co.*:[41]

> The law is, that a person who has made a fraudulent claim should not be permitted to recover at all. The contract of insurance is one of perfect good faith on both sides, and it is most important that such good faith be maintained.

11.8 UTMOST GOOD FAITH

The duty of utmost good faith survives after the making of the contract. However, there is considerable uncertainty as to the content of the duty or as to the remedy for breach of the duty at the post-contractual claims stage. Hence, it is not clear whether there is a duty to disclose co-extensive with that which exists before the contract of insurance is entered into, as opposed to a rather different obligation to make full disclosure at the claims stage.[42] Early West Indian authorities suggest that fraudulent claims entitle the insurer to avoid the contract *ab initio*, even

---

34 (1891) 1 B & S 782.
35 See for instance *Alleyne v Clico International General Insurance Ltd*, BB 2004 CA 23; *Solomon Ghany Oil & Engineering Ltd v N.E.M. (West Indies) Insurance Ltd*, TT 2000 HC 93; *Hosein & Co. v Goodwill Life*, TT 1990 HC 165; *Thomas v Stoutt* (1997) 55 WIR 112; *Gleaner Co. v Abrahams* (2003) 63 WIR 197.
36 JM 1998 SC 3.
37 Ibid.
38 *Castellain v Preston* (1883) 11 QBD 380.
39 *Leppard v Excess Insurance Co.* [1979] 2 All ER 668.
40 *Britton v Royal Insurance Co.* (1866) 4 F & F 905.
41 (1866) 4 F & F 905.
42 See also early UK common law, *Levy v Baille* (1831) 7 Bing 349; *Goulstone v Royal Insurance Co.* (1858) 1 F & F 276; *Britton v Royal Insurance Co.* (1886) 4 F & F 905.

where there is no express clause in the policy. In the Guyanese decision of *Pereira v Hand-In-Hand Mutual Guarantee Fire Insurance Co*,[43] Justice Sheriff states:

> Bearing in mind that the obligation assumed by an insurance company is to make good the losses actually and *bona fide* incurred, it is essential for a plaintiff to observe good faith in rendering his claim and to be accurate as the circumstances of the case permit.

In *Mustapha Ally v Hand-In-Hand Insurance Co*,[44] also arising out of the jurisdiction of Guyana, the appellant effected a policy of insurance with the respondent company to cover stocks of paddy and empty bags stored in his rice mill. A fire occurred destroying some paddy and a number of empty bags. In making his claim under the policy, the appellant so exaggerated his claim that the trial judge disallowed recovery even of the actual loss. The Court of Appeal, reaffirming the decision of the High Court, ruled that once a fraudulent claim is made, the contract of insurance becomes absolutely void, not voidable.

> The submission that the respondents (the insurance company) had not exercised their option to avoid the contract within a reasonable time and had therefore waived their right to do so cannot be considered sound as the evidence indicates that the company was pursuing a course of enquiries right up to December 18, 1963, when their solicitors, in a letter addressed to the appellant's solicitor, made it clear that after consideration of all the evidence the company had arrived at the conclusion that the claim was excessive and fraudulent.

The simplicity of the judgments in these early Caribbean decisions belie the complexity of the scope and application of a post-contractual duty of good faith. As summed up by Lord Justice Mance in *Agapitos v Agnew (The Aegeon)*:[45]

> The opacity of the relevant principles – whether originating in venerable but cryptically reasoned common law cases or enshrined, apparently immutable, in section 17 of the Marine Insurance Act, 1906 – is matched only by the stringency of the sanctions assigned.

11.9 APPLICATION OF THE MARINE INSURANCE ACT TO FRAUDULENT CLAIMS

A question generally arises whether a breach of the duty of utmost good faith at the claims stage entitles the insurer to (1) avoid the entire contract *ab initio*; (2) only repudiation from the date of the breach of the duty; or (3) whether the insurer is restricted to merely repudiating the claim. The answer resides in part, in determination of the auxiliary, narrow, but fundamental question whether the Marine Insurance Act applies at the post-contract stage to the effect that a breach of the duty of utmost good faith at the claims stage entitles the insurer to avoid the entire contract. The Marine Insurance Act is a codification of the law of marine insurance. The law is, in general, no different from that of other forms of insurance in so far as the duties in relation to 'good faith, disclosure and representation are concerned.'[46] Section 20 of the Barbados Marine Insurance Act[47] provides: 'A contract of marine insurance is a contract

---

43 Ibid.
44 Guyana (1968) WIR.
45 Per Mance LJ, *Agapitos v Agnew* [2003] QB 556.
46 Per Longmore LJ in *K/S Merc-Scandia XXXXII v Certain Lloyd's Underwriters and Others* [2000] 2 All ER (Comm) 731.
47 Cap 292.

based upon the utmost good faith; and if the utmost good faith is not observed by the other party, the contract may be avoided.'

The question whether avoidance operates only from the date of the fraud or whether in addition, the insurer may avoid the whole contract retrospectively entitling the insurer to avoid the contract *ab initio* arose in *Black King Shipping Corp v Massie (The Litsion Pride)*.[48] In this case, Mr Justice Hirst adopted the notion of culpability to the effect that a fraudulent claim could amount to a breach of duty under the Marine Insurance Act of 1906, entitling the insurer to avoid the contract *ab initio*.[49] The position adopted in *The Litsion Pride* was subsequently disapproved by the House of Lords in *Manifest Shipping Co. v Uni-Polaris Shipping Co. (The Star Sea)*.[50] In *The Star Sea*, the insured's ship was destroyed by fire. The insurers refuted the claim on the ground that during negotiations after the loss, the insured failed to disclose facts relating to similar fires that had damaged other ships also owned by him. The defendants contended that there was a positive duty of fair dealing and disclosure, any breach of which would amount to constructive fraud giving rise to a Section 17 remedy of an entitlement to avoid the contract. The House of Lords ruled that culpable non-disclosure was insufficient to attract the drastic consequence of avoidance contemplated in Section 17 of the 1906 Marine Insurance Act. The House of Lords, however, did not resolve the debate on the ambit and nature of the post-contract duty of good faith, so the issue continues to be litigated.

In *Agapitos v Agnew (The Aegeon)*, the Court of Appeal, *inter alia*, considered whether and in what circumstances the common law rule and/or Section 17 can apply in the event of the use of fraudulent means or devices to promote a claim, which claim may prove at trial to be in all respects valid and, if so, whether the application of the rule and the Marine Insurance Act ceases with the commencement of litigation. Mance LJ reinforced the stance adopted in *The Star Sea* and tentatively found that the Section 17 duty has no application to fraudulent claims, rather that the common law fraudulent claim rule, that of forfeiture of the claim, should be applied in a case where fraudulent devices are used.

It is clear that Section 17 of the 1906 Marine Insurance Act (Section 20 of the Barbados Marine Insurance Act) does not apply to a breach of utmost good faith at the claims stage and no question of avoidance of the whole contract arises. In the Commonwealth Caribbean the position is that in the case of fraudulent claims, the Marine Insurance Act has no application at the post-contractual stage. The appropriate avenue for the insurer is to seek protection under the common law instead.

11.10   COMMON LAW

At common law, a distinction is drawn between fraudulent claims and 'culpable or negligently' submitted claims within which there exist various degrees of fraud, and as recent litigation suggests, the categories are constantly expanding.[51] Exaggerated claims can arise where the assured clearly intended to defraud the insurers;[52] where the overestimate of the loss is so excessive as to lead to the inevitable inference that the claim was fraudulent; where the insured cannot have made the claim honestly but must have intended to defraud the insurers; where the overestimate, though not deliberately put forward with manifest fraudulent intent of inducing the

---

48   [1985] 2 Lloyd's Rep 437.
49   Ibid.
50   Supra n. 48.
51   *Manifest Shipping Co. v Uni-Polaris Shipping Co. (The Star Sea)* [1997] 1 Lloyd's Rep 360.
52   Supra n. 40.

insurers to pay the full amount claimed, is designedly made for the purpose of fixing a basis upon which to negotiate with the insurers the claim is rendered void. Where it results from an honest over-estimate of the loss due to a mistake, recovery may be available.

Fraud is clearly established where the insured intends to defraud the insurer or puts forward false evidence. With respect to culpable or negligent claims, in *Sofi v Prudential Assurance Co.*,[53] the Court of Appeal found that the insured had exaggerated the contents of his suit cases but did not equate the overstated loss with fraud. Thus, despite the overstatement, the insured was able to recover. This decision can be contrasted with that of *Galloway v Royal Guardian Royal Exchange (UK)*, where the whole claim was forfeited.[54] In *Galloway*, the insured claimed for losses following a burglary under a householder's insurance. There was a genuine loss of £18,143, but £2,000 related to a computer that had not been lost and the receipt of its purchase had been forged. The forgery therefore amounted to a material misrepresentation. The insured claimed under the policy, although the deception was eventually discovered and the claimant convicted of fraud. The Court of Appeal held that the fraud tainted the whole contract. Lord Woolf MR opined that the purpose of the law was to discourage fraudulent claims and crafted a formula: that a fraudulent claim representing 10 per cent of the whole was regarded as substantial. Millett LJ's approach was that 'substantial' ought not to be tested by reference to the proportion of the entire claim represented by the amount of the fraudulent claim, on the ground that this could lead to the absurd result that the greater the genuine loss, the more fraudulent the claim could be without penalty. The correct approach was to consider whether the making of the claim was sufficiently serious to justify stigmatising it as a breach of the insured's duty of good faith so as to avoid the policy. Despite the differences in approach, both judges found that the whole claim was avoided because of the breach of duty of utmost good faith.

Taking the principle in *Galloway* to its logical conclusion, in the case of co-insurance where a fraudulent claim is made by one insured but not the other, the rule of law discouraging a fraudulent claim applies. This rule directed at the deterrence of false claims means an innocent co-insured will be deprived of recovery. This is illustrated in *Direct Line Insurance plc v Khan*,[55] where a fire occurred at the property owned by a husband and wife which was covered by an insurance policy on the house and contents. The husband made a claim under the policy for rent alleged to be payable for alternative accommodation. He pretended that the property belonged to a friend and forged a receipt for rent and deposit. In fact, the husband owned the property. The insurer disputed the claim and sought summary judgment for the amounts paid on the reinstatement of the property, replacement of contents and the rent payable under the false rental agreement. Insurers successfully argued that the insured lost all right to recover under the policy if a material part of the claim, that is *non de minimis* part of the claim which he makes, is fraudulent. This argument was based on *Galloway v Guardian Royal Exchange (UK)*,[56] the court ruled that there was nothing in the *Manifest Case* which detracts from the authority of *Galloway v Royal Guardian Royal Exchange (UK)*,[57] the public policy rule operated to prevent the wife from recovering under the policy.

The ambit and nature of the post contractual duty arose again for consideration in *Agapitos v Agnew (The Aegeon)*. Here Mance LJ complicated matters by drawing a further distinction between fraudulent claims in the narrow sense of no or exaggerated loss and the use of fraudulent devices, regarded as a 'sub-species' of making a fraudulent claim where the insured

53 [1993] 2 Lloyd's Rep 559.
54 [1999] Lloyd's Rep IR 209.
55 *Direct Line Insurance plc v Khan* [2002] Lloyd's Rep 364.
56 Supra n. 54.
57 Ibid.

embellishes the facts surrounding the claim, by some lie. In *Agapitos v Agnew (The Aegeon)*,[58] the distinction was made between material fraud and fraudulent devices. 'Material fraud' was described as any fraud during the life of the contract, the consequences of which are so serious that the insurer would be entitled to terminate the contract for breach.[59] The term 'fraudulent devices' on the other hand applies to any device which is used to promote what is in essence a dishonest claim. In this case, the insured's claim was genuine but was made through the use of fraudulent devices and means. Describing fraudulent devices as when the insured believes that he has suffered the loss claimed but seeks to improve or embellish the facts surrounding the claim by some lie,[60] Mance LJ importantly reasoned on the scope and application of the Marine Insurance Act and the inter-relationship with the common law. Concluding that the Marine Insurance Act did not apply, he stated:

> In the *Star Sea* . . . Lord Clyde said that to confine section 17 to the pre-contract stage now appears to be past praying for. Lord Scott accepted the section's post-contractual application . . . Lord Hobhouse, as I see it, proceeded on the same basis . . . Lord Justice Longmore commented in the *Mercandian Continent* that this Court should now proceed on that basis, and I for my part, while expressing the hope that the House of Lords judicially or Parliament legislatively might one day look at the point again, agree we should do so . . . It is convenient at the outset to consider two points on which the scope of the common law rule is not clear. The first is whether a claim, which dishonestly believed in when initially presented, may become fraudulent for the purposes of the rule, if the insured subsequently realizes that it is exaggerated, but continues to maintain it. The second is whether the fraud must relate, in some narrow sense, to the subject matter of the claim, or may go to any aspect of its validity, including therefore a defence. The first point was left open by Lord Scott in *The Star Sea* . . . But I believe that the correct answer must be in the affirmative. As a matter of principle, it would be strange if an insured who thought at the time of his initial claim that he had lost property in a theft, but then discovered it in a drawer, could happily maintain both the genuine and the now knowingly false part of his claim without risk of the application of the rule. Further, if and in so far as the use of fraudulent devices may invoke the fraudulent claim rule – an issue to which I come at greater length below – it would again be artificial to distinguish between the use of such devices before and after the initial making of any claim. Such devices are a not unfamiliar response to insurers' probing the merits of a claim . . . As to the second point, a claim cannot be regarded as valid, if there is a known defence to it which the insured deliberately suppresses.

Lord Justice Mance goes on to suggest a solution blurring the line between fraudulent claims and fraudulent devices:

> a) To recognise that the fraudulent claim rule applies as much to the fraudulent maintenance of an initially honest clam as to a claim which the insured knows from the outset to be exaggerated; b) to treat the use of fraudulent devices as a sub-species of making a fraudulent claim – at least as regards forfeiture of the claim itself in relation to which the fraudulent device or means is used. (The fraudulent claim rule may have prospective aspect in respect of future, and perhaps current claims, but it is unnecessary to consider that aspect or its application to case of use of fraudulent devices). c) to treat as relevant for this purpose any lie, directly related to the claim to which the fraudulent device relates, which is intended to improve the insured's prospects of obtaining a settlement or winning the case, and which would, if believed, tend, objectively, prior to any

---

58 [2002] EWCA Civ 247; [2002] Lloyd's Rep IR 573.
59 See for instance *K/S Merc-Scandia v Certain Lloyd's Underwriters* [2001] 2 Lloyd's Rep IR 563.
60 Mance LJ considered that *K/S Merc-Scandia v Certain Lloyd's Underwriters* [2001] 2 Lloyd's Rep IR 563, was an unusual case where the insured's deceit was aimed at a third party claimant. Noting that the decision offered no guidance to the appropriate approach on the use of fraudulent devices, he concluded that Section 17 duty has no application to fraudulent claims.

final determination at trial of the parties' rights, to yield a not insignificant improvement in the insured's prospects – whether they be prospects of obtaining a settlement, or a better settlement, or of winning at trial. d) To treat the common law rules governing the making of a fraudulent claim (including the use of fraudulent device) as falling outside the scope of section 17 . . . on this basis no question of avoidance *ab initio* would arise.

11.11 SUMMARY

The duty of utmost good faith has a different application and content depending on the stage of the contract. The judicial consensus appears to be that the duty of disclosure as contemplated by the Marine Insurance Act, expires when the contract of insurance is concluded, except in the case of renewal of the policy. Where the duty as contemplated by Section 20 applies, it has retrospective effect enabling the aggrieved party to rescind *ab initio*. This consequence is appropriate where the want of good faith has preceded the conclusion of the contract and has been material to the making of that contract. Where good faith occurs later at the claims stage fettered by Section 23 of the Barbados Marine Insurance Act, it becomes anomalous and disproportionate.

With respect to the common law, the situation is unclear. A claim which is knowingly exaggerated does not necessarily disqualify the insured from any recovery.[61] At common law there must be a connection between the fraud and the claim for the fraudulent claim rule to apply. Under this rule, no distinction is made between the use of 'fraudulent device' before and after the initial making of the contract. The law forfeits not only that which is known to be untrue, but also any genuine part of the claim. A claim for loss, known to be non-existent or exaggerated, will amount to a fraudulent claim where it is substantial, not immaterial and if it had an effect on the insurer's conduct. A fraudulent claim exists where the insured claims, knowing that he has suffered no loss, or only a lesser loss than that which he claims or is reckless as to whether this is the case. The 'bite' of the fraudulent claim rule is to forfeit even the genuine part. It must occur in relation to the making of the claim and relates to a part of the claim which when viewed discreetly, is not itself immaterial or unsubstantial. Since the decision of *Agapitos v Agnew (The Aegeon)*,[62] a distinction must be made between fraudulent claims and fraudulent devices. It appears that the use of a fraudulent device does not attract treatment parallel to fraudulent claims. A Distinction exists between fraudulent claims, in the narrow sense of where there are no or exaggerated losses and the use of fraudulent devices. 'A fraudulent device is used if the insured believes that he has suffered the loss claimed, but seeks to improve or embellish the facts surrounding the claim, by some lie.'

An underling recurrent theme in the common law is the overall policy consideration – to discourage the making of fraudulent claims. The insured should not be allowed to think that if the fraud is successful, he will gain and if it is unsuccessful, he will lose nothing.

11.12 AFFIRMATION OF THE CONTRACT

An important consideration at the claims stage is the judicial recognition of rights at variance with policy provisions. Rather than treat the contract of insurance as being avoided by a

---

61 B. Soyer, 'The Star Sea – A Lone Star?' [2001] *LMCLQ* 428.
62 Supra n. 58.

breach of warranty or on the basis of breach of condition, insurers are entitled to treat the contract as subsisting. Judicial recognition of rights at variance with policy provisions include waiver, estoppel and rights based on unreasonable delay in processing an application for insurance. Where the insurer has a right to avoid the contract, but nevertheless elects to honour the contract this is known as waiver. It is dependent on knowledge of the breach and either express election or such act as would convince a reasonable man that election had taken place. Waiver is the abandonment of a right in such a way that the other party is entitled to plead the abandonment by way of confession and avoidance if the right is thereafter asserted and is either expressed or implied from conduct. Waiver must always be an intentional act with knowledge, where the conduct of the defendant leads the other party to believe that the strict legal rights under the contract will not be insisted upon.'[63] In *Lickiss v Milestone Motor Policies*,[64] the insured failed to comply with a clause relating to notification of loss. However, the insurers were subsequently informed by the police. The insured in turn wrote to the insured requesting a meeting in order to arrange the defence. It was held that this amounted to a waiver. In the Bermudan decision of *Whittington v Hartford Fire Insurance Company*,[65] a fire occurred on the plaintiff's premises while a policy of insurance was still in force. Letters were exchanged between the lawyer for the insured and counsel for the insurer regarding the claim for damage. A clause of the policy provided that notification was to take place within 12 months. The issue was whether the telephone conversations amounted to waiver. The Supreme Court applied the reasonable man test, stating that the plaintiff failed to take the steps that a reasonably prudent man would have taken to protect his rights. Mere delay, however, on the part of the insurer will not amount to a waiver. In *Allen v Robles*,[66] a delay of some four months was held by the Court of Appeal as not to amount to affirmation. In order to constitute affirmation of the policy there must be knowledge on the part of the insurer combined with some express or implied conduct leading a reasonable insured to conclude that the policy subsists in full. *Bawden v London Edinburgh and Glasgow Assurance Co.*[67] is instructive on the role an intermediary can play in imputing knowledge to the principal insurer. Where the insurer fails to repudiate the whole policy upon learning of the breach, then such conduct may be regarded by the courts as an election to affirm the contract.[68]

Estoppel on the other hand is wider in ambit than waiver and does not depend on the knowledge of the person estopped. Estoppel occurs where either by words or the conduct of the insurer, the insured has been induced to believe that the insurer will not rely on his strict legal right. In *Lakhan v United Security Life Insurance Co.*,[69] where the issue was whether the policies were still in force on the death of the life insured, Warner J opined that 'the plaintiff here cannot recover unless he is able to make out estoppel precluding the claimant from asserting that the policies had ceased to be in force before the death of the assured.'[70] The High Court of Trinidad and Tobago held that as estoppel had not been specifically pleaded and the policies had ceased to be in force several months before the death of the assured.

63 *Edgar v Demerara Mutual Life Assurance Society*, St Lucia High Court Suit No. 160 of 1989; see also *Tuky Air Transport Inc. v The Liquidator of Edinburgh Insurance Co. Ltd (In Liquidation)* (unreported decision British Virgin Islands High Court No. 3 of 1984).
64 [1966] 2 All ER 972.
65 *Gray v Barr* [1971] 2 QB 554.
66 [1969] 1 WLR 1193.
67 Ibid.
68 *West v National Motor and Accident Insurance Union* [1955] 1 WLR 343.
69 TT 1989 HC 8.
70 Section 125, Jamaica Insurance Act No. 26 of 2001.

11.13   LOST POLICIES

Where a policy has been lost, stolen or destroyed, in the case of a life insurance policy, a policyholder or a person claiming the benefit of policy monies, may apply in writing for a replacement policy.[71] The insurance company also has the option of paying the monies into the court.[72] The insurer is under an obligation, not to issue a replacement policy unless and until it has received sufficient proof of the validity of the person's claim in respect of the policy.[73] A court, in awarding judgment to a plaintiff, may, with the consent of the insurer and the insured, order specified payments with interest over a stipulated period, instead of a lump sum.[74]

11.14   CONCLUSION

The question of the principles governing procedure to be followed when claiming under a policy of insurance is answered by an application of the common law. The policy will invariably contain a condition outlining the degree and nature of notice. It is clear that the courts construe such clauses as a condition precedent to the insurer's liability, and they must be strictly complied with. Whether or not there has been a breach of the condition is a question of construction and in so doing, the courts will generally have regard to the purpose of the particular provision. These conditions ordinarily outline the notice to be given to the insurers in the event of loss, particulars of loss and the procedure to be adopted to resolve disputes by way of settlement or arbitration. There is no assistance from regional consumer legislation or from statements of insurance practice so that the terms of the contract must be construed solely from the Insurance Act.

---

71   Section 125, Jamaica Insurance Act No. 26 of 2001.
72   Section 131, Jamaica Insurance Act No. 26 of 2001.
73   Section 131(2), Jamaica Insurance Act No. 26 of 2001.
74   Section 133, Jamaica Insurance Act No. 26 of 2001.

CHAPTER 12

PUBLIC POLICY

12.1 INTRODUCTION

Public policy is an amorphous concept which has been described as an 'unruly horse.'[1] It can arise at any juncture in the insured/insurer relationship from inception to the claims stage. In this chapter the focus is on the fundamental principle of insurance law, that the insured must not voluntarily bring about the insured event. This principle is acknowledged in regional marine legislation. For instance, Section 59(2)(a) of the Barbados Marine Insurance Act[2] provides:

> the insurer is not liable for any loss attributable to the wilful misconduct of the assured . . . but, unless the policy otherwise provides, he is liable for any loss proximately caused by a peril insured against, even though the loss would not have happened but, for the misconduct or negligence of the master or crew.

Assisting principles as to the scope and application of public policy emerge from the common law. The orthodox position at common law is the 'public conscience test' as postulated by Lord Mansfield CJ in *Holman v Johnson*,[3] to the effect that 'no court will lend its aid to a man who founds his cause of action upon an immoral or illegal act.'[4] Accordingly, where the loss is as a result of the insured's criminal conduct, the courts will not allow the legal process to be abused by allowing the insured to enforce a claim: 'the human mind revolts at the very idea that any other doctrine could be possible in our system of jurisprudence.'[5] The equitable maxims *ex turpi causes non oritur action* ('no action can arise from a wrongful cause') and 'a man may not profit from his own crime or wrong' pervade the common law.[6] The anomaly exists, however, that wilful and deliberate acts of a third party are normally expressly covered by liability insurance. This is suggested by the language of the Marine Insurance Act. Further, where loss is occasioned by the insured's negligence,[7] or if the insured adopts steps to reduce the loss but ends up increasing the degree of loss,[8] once these acts do not break the chain of causation the insurer will not necessarily be exempted from liability. The point here is that there is a fine line between acceptable and unacceptable conduct and according to the rule in *Garner v Moore*,[9] the court will consider the gravity of the illegal conduct; intentional illegality is considered worse than negligent illegality.

The discussion on public policy is also relevant to fraudulent claims as the insured's duty of utmost good faith continues beyond the point when the contract of insurance is concluded and renewed and operates when an insured seeks to claim against the insurer for loss. The

---

1   Per Burrough J in *Richardson v Mellish* (1824) 2 Bing 229, p. 252.
2   Ibid.
3   (1775) 1 Cowp. 341.
4   The relevance of the public conscience test may have to be re-evaluated in light of the House of Lords decision of *Tinsley v Milligan* [1994] 1 AC 340.
5   *In the Estate of Cunigunda (Otherwise Cora) Crippen, Deceased* [1911] 108, per Evans LJ, p. 112.
6   M. Clarke, 'Illegal Insurance' [1987] *LMCLQ* 210; M. A. Clarke, 'Insurance of Wilful Misconduct; the Court as Keeper of the Public Conscience' [1996] 7 *Insurance L.J.* 173.
7   *Harris v Poland* [1941] 1 KB 462; *Amey Properties Ltd v Cornhill Insurance plc* [1996] LRLR 259; *Gunns v Par Insurance Brokers* [1997] 1 Lloyd's Rep 173; see also Adams, 'Reasonable Care Provisions, the Courts and the Ombudsman' [1998] *JBL* 85.
8   *Canada Rice Mills Ltd v Union Marine and General Insurance Co.* [1941] AC 55.
9   [1984] 1 All ER 1100.

precise nature of the application of the equitable maxims remains unclear; as the common law demonstrates, there are differences in the court's interpretation and application.[10] Debate revolves around the question whether public policy is simply the correct construction of the contract[11] or, alternatively, whether public policy arises as a requirement external to the contract of insurance.

Notwithstanding ambiguities surrounding interpretation and effect of public policy, it is clear the nature of its application depends on the underlying contract. It is readily discernable that a distinction exists between first party and third party insurance. The approach that leads to the distinction is not without its critics. In *Gardner v Moore*,[12] Lord Denning reasoned:

> I can see no reason in public policy for drawing a distinction between one kind of wrongful act, of which a third party is an innocent victim, and another kind of wrongful act; between wrongful acts which are criminal on the part of the perpetrator and wrongful acts which are not crimes, or between wrongful acts which are crimes of carelessness and wrongful acts which are intentional crimes. It seems to me to be slightly unrealistic to suggest that a person who is not deterred by the risk commits grievous bodily harm would be deterred by the possible risk of life imprisonment.[13]

12.2   FIRST PARTY INSURANCE

As a general rule, it is irrelevant if the loss is as a result of the insured's negligence,[14] but insurance does not cover losses deliberately caused by the insured.[15] It is also important to consider precisely who the 'beneficiary' is. If an insured is claiming in respect of a loss suffered solely by him, then it appears that the insured will be barred from recovery if the loss is a result of his deliberate act.[16] In the case of first party insurance, the equitable maxim will operate to preclude recovery by the insured,[17] and it appears that conduct evincing a significant degree of moral turpitude, such as 'murder reduced to manslaughter by provocation, would be sufficient to bar recovery.'[18]

12.3   DELIBERATE ACTIONS BY THE INSURED

As observed by the High Court in the Trinidad and Tobago decision of *Solomon Ghany Oil & Engineering Ltd v N.E.M. (West Indies) Insurance Ltd*,[19] there is a presumption in every insurance contract that the assured cannot by 'his own intentional act bring about the event upon which the insurance money is payable and then recover under the policy.'[20] Policies of insurance

---

10 *Richardson v Mellish* (1824) 2 Bing 229 at 252; see further W. Gellhorn, 'Contracts and Public Policy' (1935) 35 *Colum. L. Rev.* 679; J. Shand, 'Unblinkering the Unruly Horse: Public Policy in the Law of Contract' (1972) 30 *CLJ* 144.
11 *Beresford v Royal Insurance Co. Ltd* [1938] AC 586, per Lord Atkin, p. 595.
12 Supra n. 9.
13 Ibid.
14 *Tinline v White Cross Insurance Association* [1921] 3 KB 327; *James v British General Insurance Co. Ltd* [1927] 2 KB 311.
15 *Geismar v Sun Alliance and London Insurance* [1977] 2 Lloyd's Rep. 62; *Euro-Diam Ltd v Bathurst* [1987] 2 All ER 113.
16 Supra n. 11.
17 *W. H. Smith v Clinton* (1908) 99 LT 840; *Geismar v Sun Alliance and London Insurance* [1977] 2 Lloyd's Rep 62.
18 C. H. Denbow, *Life Insurance Law in the Commonwealth Caribbean* (Butterworths: 1984), p. 144.
19 TT 2000 HC 93 HCA No. S3114 of 1996.
20 *Bell v Carstairs* (1811) 14 East 374; 104 ER 646; *Beresford v The Royal Insurance Co.* [1938] AC 586.

usually contain an express clause forfeiting recovery 'where the loss or damage was occasioned by the wilful act, or connivance of the insured,' mirroring the fundamental principle contained in regional marine insurance legislation. If the insured's actions were meant to reduce loss and ended up playing a role in the creation of loss, the act may not necessarily preclude the insurers' liability, if that act was reasonable in the circumstances and the insured peril was operating; as when the ventilators in a cargo hold were closed to prevent the entry of seawater during a heavy storm and this caused the cargo to overheat.[21] Thus, it has been held that indemnity insurance covering libel is unenforceable where the libel was intentional,[22] and a beneficiary under an insurance policy who murdered the life insured will be precluded from recovering under an insurance policy.

As reflected in Section 59(2) of the Barbados Marine Insurance Act, insurance is often designed to cover losses caused by a third party's wilful or negligent actions.[23] Because of the nature of insurance, it is necessary to pay particular attention to the nature of the offence.

12.4   CRIMINAL ACTS

If the deliberate act of the insured is criminal in nature, then even where the insured's act did not proximately cause the loss, a claim may be denied on the basis of public policy. It is important that the act be deliberate, as if the act is deliberate but not criminal, the insurer remains liable. Conversely, if the act is criminal but not deliberate, then the insurer is not liable.[24] The line between unenforceable and enforceable claims is imperceptible to say the least. In *Geismar v Sun Alliance & London Insurance Ltd*,[25] the insured smuggled several items of jewellery into the United Kingdom without declaring them and paying the requisite excise duty. As a result, the jewellery was liable to forfeiture. The jewellery was among items subsequently stolen and the insured made a claim under a theft policy. It was held that the insured could not recover, as to allow such recovery would enable the insured to benefit from his own deliberate criminal act. This decision can be contrasted with the Court of Appeal decision of *Euro-Diam Ltd v Bathurst*.[26] Here a wholesaler of diamonds insured a shipment of diamonds to West Germany. The wholesaler had misrepresented the value of the diamonds to German customs, although there had been no misrepresentation to the insurer. The diamonds were subsequently stolen from the customer's warehouse. Despite the fact that the insured had understated the value of the diamonds and that the transaction was illegal under West German law, the Court held that the insured was entitled to recover under the insurance policy,[27] since the customer and not the insured benefitted from the illegality. The Court ruled that the right to possess goods will be enforced even if the customer came into possession of those goods by way of an illegal contract, so long as it is not necessary to use the illegal contract to enforce the claim. The *ex turpi causa* rule did not prevent the insured in *Euro-Diam* from recovering.

There is authority to the effect that merely because goods are bought with proceeds obtained through the sale of an illegal cargo, this will not prevent a claim on the theft of those goods. The rationale for this principle is that to hold otherwise would necessitate an in-depth

---

21   Supra n. 8.
22   *W. H. Smith v Clinton* (1908) 99 LT 840.
23   *Schiffshypothekenbank Zu Luebeck AG v Compton (The 'Alexion Hope')* [1988] 1 Lloyd's Rep 311.
24   *Turner v Estate of Turner*, 454 N.E.2d 1247 (1983).
25   [1977] 3 All ER 570.
26   [1987] 2 All ER 113; [1987] 2 WLR 517.
27   For a criticism of this ruling, see the House of Lords decision of *Tinsley v Milligan* [1994] 1 AC 340.

examination of 'the past conduct of the assured in order to see whether or not, by their former transactions in life, they had illegally acquired the funds with which the goods insured were purchased.' In order for a right to money or property to be unenforceable, in accordance with *St John Shipping Corp. v Joseph Rank Ltd*,[28] the money or property must be 'identifiable as something to which but for the crime, the plaintiff would have had no right or title.'[29]

The problem remains one of identifying the precise degree of connection needed between the crime and the loss, in order for the claim to be defeated. Earlier in *Thackwell v Barclays Bank plc*,[30] it was stated that the court would not simply deny a remedy to the plaintiff whose claim was based on an illegal act but would look at the quality of that act and would consider whether in all the circumstances it would be an affront to the public conscience, in the sense of indirectly assisting or encouraging the plaintiff in his criminal act. This principle was subsequently applied and expanded upon by Kerr LJ in *Euro-Diam*, concluding that while deceiving German customs was reprehensible, it did not benefit the insured and had no bearing on the loss.

12.5 NEGLIGENT ACTS

The insurer will be liable for loss caused by the insured's negligence unless expressly exempted by the insurance policy,[31] so that an insurer has been held liable where the insured negligently lit a fireplace, forgetting that she had previously hidden her jewels there.[32]

An insurance policy may contain a clause to the effect that the insured must take 'reasonable care to avoid loss.' It appears that despite the presence of such a clause, the insurer will still be liable in employers' liability and property insurance unless the conduct is reckless. 'Reckless' has been interpreted as 'acting with actual recognition that a danger exists, not caring whether or not harm is averted.'[33] In motor insurance, on the other hand, the insurers will not be liable if the loss was caused by the negligent maintenance of the vehicle but will be liable if it is caused by insured's negligent driving.[34] The courts have adopted different approaches to the construction of such clauses. It depends upon the nature of the policy and whether a broad construction of the phrase 'to reasonably avoid loss' would be repugnant to the whole purpose of the policy. In *Sofi v Prudential Assurance Co. Ltd*,[35] a theft policy required the insured to take 'all reasonable steps to safeguard any property insured.' The insured parked his car in a car park, locked £42,035 worth of jewellery in the glove compartment of the car and then left the car for 15 minutes, during which time the jewels were stolen. Nevertheless, the insurers were held liable as it could not be established that the insured acted recklessly in assuming that the jewellery was safer in the car. However, in *Gunns v Par Insurance Brokers*,[36] the insured, who was a jeweller, locked his jewels in a safe which the insurer considered inadequate and failed to set the alarm system, the insured's conduct was held to be reckless and the insurers were found not liable on the policy.

28 [1957] 1 QB 267. For a criticism of this ruling, see the House of Lords decision of *Tinsley v Milligan* [1994] 1 AC 340.
29 Ibid. per Devlin J, p. 292.
30 [1986] 1 All ER 676.
31 *Attorney-General v Adelaide Steamship Co. Ltd* [1923] AC 292.
32 *Harris v Poland* [1941] 1 KB 462.
33 Per Diplock LJ in *Fraser v B.N Furman (Productions) Ltd, Miller Smith & Partners (A Firm) Third Party* [1967] 1 WLR 898 at 906.
34 *Amey Properties Ltd v Cornhill Insurance plc* [1996] LRLR 259.
35 [1993] 2 Lloyd's Rep 559.
36 [1997] 1 Lloyd's Rep 173.

12.6 SUICIDE

The historical position is reflected in the House of Lords decision of *Beresford v Royal Insurance Co.*[37] Here the insured effected a number of insurances on his own life. The insured committed suicide and the personal representatives sought to recover. The policies contained a clause which provided:

> If the life or lives of any one of the lives insured shall die by his own hand, whether sane or insane within one year from the commencement of the assurance, the policy shall be void as against any person claiming the amount hereby insured.

The House of Lords, despite the express provision, refused to uphold the contract which was considered to be contrary to public policy. In so doing, the House of Lords relied on the age-old principle that even if there was no express reference to suicide, intentional suicide by a man of sound mind would preclude the representatives from claiming. This presumption rests on the ordinary principles of insurance law that an assured cannot profit by his own deliberate act.

> On ordinary principles of insurance law, if an assured by his own deliberate act, cause the event upon which the insurance is payable. It is assumed that the insurers have not agreed to pay on that happening. Public policy applies *ex post facto*.

Society's perception of suicide has since changed so that unless the policy expressly precludes recovery for suicide, suicide no longer enables the insurer to avoid the contract of insurance.[38] In 1961, the United Kingdom passed the Suicide Act, which abolished suicide as a crime.[39] In the Commonwealth Caribbean, most Insurance Acts contain a provision similar in nature to Section 162 of the Barbados Insurance Act, which states:

> A policy shall not be avoided merely on the ground that the person whose life is insured died by his own hand or act, sane or insane, or suffered capital punishment if upon the true construction of the policy, the company thereby agreed to pay the sum insured in the events that have happened.[40]

This section can be regarded as expressed acceptance of the *lassiez-faire* freedom of contract principle by sanctioning a contract that provides for payment in the event of suicide.

12.7 MURDER, MANSLAUGHTER AND OTHER CRIMES

Aiding and abetting suicide, however, remains a crime. In *Dunbar (Administrator of Dunbar) v Plant*,[41] a man and a woman agreed on a suicide pact, tied rocks to their feet and plunged into the river Thames. As a result, the man died but the woman survived. The man's estate disputed the woman's entitlement as beneficiary under a life insurance policy. Despite the fact that the woman was guilty of the crime of aiding and abetting, the Court of Appeal, by a majority of 2:1, upheld her claim to the insurance monies. It is important to note that the Court arrived at

---

37 [1938] AC 586.
38 Belize Insurance Act, Cap 127.
39 9 & 10 Eliz. 2 c. 60 (1961).
40 Section 164, Trinidad and Tobago Insurance Act of 1980 Chapter 84:01; Section 126, Jamaica Insurance Act No. 26 of 2001.
41 Supra n. 36.

its decision after exercising its discretion and modifying the forfeiture rule under Section 1(1) of the Forfeiture Act of 1982.[42] Mummery LJ stated:[43]

> It is sufficient that a serious crime has been committed deliberately and intentionally. The references to acts or threats of violence in the cases are explicable by the facts of those cases. But in none of those cases were the courts legislating a principle couched in specific statutory language. The essence of the principle of public policy is that (a) no person shall take a benefit resulting from a crime committed by him or her resulting in the death of the victim and (b) the nature of the crime determines the application of the principle. On that view the important point is that the crime that had fatal consequences was committed with a guilty mind (deliberately and intentionally). The particular means used to commit the crime (whether violent or non-violent) are not a necessary ingredient of the rule. There may be cases in which violence has been used deliberately without an intention to bring about the unlawful fatal consequences. Those cases will attract the application of the forfeiture rule. It does not follow, however, that when death has been brought about by a deliberate and intentional, but non-violent, act (e.g. poison or gas) the rule is inapplicable.

The result is that in the case of assisted suicide the person who is complicit in the suicide will not recover. In *Dunbar (Administration) v Plant*,[44] the forfeiture rule was modified. This rule precludes those who have unlawfully killed from acquiring a benefit as a result of their own act. It was held that the rule applied to the survivor of a suicide pact as well as to someone convicted of murder or manslaughter. In the United Kingdom, the Forfeiture Act 1982 allows a court, in cases other than murder, to modify the forfeiture rule. In determining whether to apply its discretion under the Act, the Court will first determine whether the rule applies and then consider matters such as the offender's moral culpability, the financial position of the offender, and particularly in spousal manslaughter, the treatment of the offender by the deceased. There is no comparable statute operating in the Caribbean. In *Davitt v Titcumb*,[45] two parties purchased a house which was partly financed and supported by an endowment policy. One party murdered the other and, once the mortgage lender had been repaid, a surplus sum remained. The personal representatives of the deceased successfully argued that the murderer should not be entitled to take his share, 'for to do otherwise would run counter to the reasoning that underlies the rule of public policy.'

In *Cleaver et al. v Mutual Reserve Fund Life Association*,[46] the executors of James Maybrick sued on a life policy which he had effected in favour of his wife who had been convicted of his murder. The objection that the executors were suing to enforce a trust in favour of the wife was overcome by holding that the wife could get no benefit from her crime, but that, her interest failing, the executor could recover for the benefit of the testator's estate. It should be noted that on the principle stated, it is not a question of refusing to enforce a contract made by the criminal. The doctrine avoids a testamentary gift, and it would appear to be immaterial whether or not the criminal is aware of the intended gift. If there is no knowledge, then arguably the supporting inducement to commit the crime does not exist.

12.8   INVOKING PUBLIC POLICY AS A DEFENCE

There is a danger for the insurer to invoke its own non-compliance with the statute as a defence in order to avoid its obligations under the insurance contract. An insurer is precluded from

---

42   1982 S1(1)–(2).
43   [1998] Ch 412.
44   [1997] 4 All ER 289.
45   Supra n. 26.
46   [1892] 1 QB 147.

relying on its non-compliance with the statute in order to avoid its obligations to the insured,[47] and the equitable maxim 'he who comes to equity must come with clean hands' or the common law maxim, *nullus commodum capere potest de injuria sua propria* ('no one can gain an advantage by his own wrong'). This can be seen in the Guyanese decision of *Guyana National General Insurance Co. Ltd v Moore et al.*,[48] where the plaintiff company sought a declaration that it was not an authorised insurer under the Insurance Act and consequently its operations were illegal, void and *ultra vires* its powers. Vieira J refused to 'countenance such disgraceful conduct.'

Lord Esher MR in *Cleaver v Mutual Reserve Fund Life Association*[49] opined;

> No doubt there is a rule that, if a contract be made contrary to public policy, or if the performance of a contract would be contrary to public policy, performance cannot be enforced either at law or equity: but when people vouch that rule to excuse themselves from the performance of a contract, in respect of which they have received the full consideration, and when all that remains to be done under the contract is for them to pay money, the application of the rule ought to be narrowly watched, and ought not to be carried a step further than the protection of the public requires.

Thus an attempt by either the insured or the insurer to utilise public policy so as to avoid compliance with a ruling will be defeated by an overriding public policy consideration against such action.

12.9   COMMON LAW: THE PUBLIC CONSCIENCE TEST

At common law, there is considerable doubt whether public policy operates as an external principle, to restrain against the furtherance of a crime, or whether it is simply an application of the rule that the courts will endeavour to adopt as an interpretation against the enforcement of claims based on the criminal act of the insured.[50] The orthodox position was laid down by Lord Mansfield CJ in *Holman v Johnson*[51] to the effect that 'no court will lend its aid to a man who founds his cause of action upon an immoral or illegal act.' The public conscience test was been disapproved by the House of Lords in *Tinsley v Milligan*,[52] which has forced reconsideration of the nature of public interest. In *Tinsley*, a house was acquired by two people but placed in the name of only one person so as to facilitate a fraudulent claim for a social security benefit. The House of Lords held that when the house was acquired a resulting trust was created, so that the owner of the legal title became a trustee for the other, who could claim under the trust without having to rely on the original illegal contract. Further, that the only defence to the plaintiff's claim that the other party could raise would be based on an illegal agreement and therefore, would not be countenanced by the court.

Thus the courts will not enforce an illegal contract provided the claim can be made without relying on that contract. The majority of the House of Lords took the view that if an illegal contact was executed and property rights created, the plaintiff could recover the property,

---

47   See *R v Wilson Scher* and *Ackman v Policyholders Protection Board* [1993] 4 All ER 840.
48   [1969] Guy LR 91.
49   Supra n. 46.
50   R. A. Buckley, 'Social Security Fraud as Illegality' (1994) 110 *LQR* 3; N. Cohen, 'The Quiet Revolutuion in the Enforcement of Illegal Contracts' [1994] *LMCLQ* 163; M. Halliwell, 'Equitable Proprietary Claims and Dishonest Claimants: A Resolution?' (1994) 58 *The Conveyancer* 62; H. Stowe, 'The "Unruly Horse" Has Bolted: *Tinsley v Milligan*' (1994) 57 *MLR* 441.
51   Supra n. 3.
52   [1994] 1 AC 340.

unless in order to prove the right the plaintiff had to rely on evidence of the illegality.[53] This approach introduces a degree of flexibility. A strict application of the public conscience rule would have rendered the whole contract unenforceable, whereas instead an investigation is conducted as to determine whether the enforcement of property rights was tainted by the illegal act. Birds contends that *Tinsley v Milligan* should affect only cases where a contract is unlawful from its inception. Since the House of Lords did not expressly overrule the decision of *Thackwell v Barclays Bank plc*,[54] it may be that the public conscience test will still apply in cases of tort actions for negligence and conversion.

While *Tinsley* has placed a gloss on the application of the public conscience test, prior to the House of Lords decision, there was difficulty in distinguishing between enforceable and unenforceable due to claims as a result of the fine distinction between two seemingly indistinguishable decisions of *Geismar v Sun Alliance & London Insurance Ltd*[55] and *Euro-Diam Ltd v Bathurst*.[56] These cases made it necessary for a determination to be made whether there is a direct relationship between the illegal act and the insurance contract. In *Euro-Diam* there was no connection, so that the insurers remained liable on the contract. In *Geismar*, however, the insurance contract was directly related to the illegal act. Public policy cannot be used as a defence, to excuse the performance of a contract,[57]

> but when people vouch that rule to excuse themselves from the performance of a contract, in respect of which they have received the full consideration, and when all that remains to be done under the contract is for them to pay money, the application of the rule ought to be narrowly watched, and ought not to be carried a step further than he protection of the public requires.[58]

Where issues of illegality are raised, the courts have steered a middle course between two unacceptable positions. On the one hand it is unacceptable for a court of law to assist in the enforcement of an obligation which the law forbids, while on the other hand, in the words of Bingham LJ, 'it is unacceptable that the court on the first indication of unlawfulness affecting any aspect of a transaction, draw up its skirts and refuse all assistance to the plaintiff.'

12.10   THIRD PARTY INSURANCE

With respect to third party insurance, the general principles applicable to first party insurance apply. In the case of murder, a person who is lawfully entitled to the policy proceeds under a life policy will have that right forfeited on the grounds of public policy if he is criminally responsible for the death of the life insured.[59] As Lord Fry stated, no system of jurisprudence can, with reason, include amongst the rights which it enforces, directly resulting to the person asserting them from the crime of that person.[60] This principle logically applies to joint policies where one person murders the other.[61] In the case of criminal conduct falling short of murder,

53   The minority view, as expressed by Lord Goff, narrowly applied the public conscience rule, so that since the property rights were created by an illegal contract, they should be left as they were.
54   Supra n. 30.
55   [1977] 2 Lloyd's Rep 62.
56   [1987] 2 All ER 113.
57   Ibid.
58   *Cleaver v Mutual Reserve Fund* [1892] 1 QB 147, per Lord Esher MR at 151.
59   Supra n. 18.
60   Supra n. 58; *Re Barrowcliff* (1927) SASR 147; *Schobelt v Barber* (1967) 60 DLR (2d) 519.
61   *Re Barrowcliff* (1927) SASR 147; see also *Minasian v Aetna Life Insurance Co*. 3 N.E.2d 17.

the authorities are not as clear. In *Gray v Barr Prudential Assurance Co. Ltd,*[62] the appellant was covered by an accident indemnity insurance policy, indemnifying him for all sums which he shall become legally liable to pay as damages in respect of bodily injuries to any person caused by accident. The insured's wife was allegedly having an affair with Gray. Barr, believing his wife was there, entered into a farm house with a loaded gun and fired a shot into the ceiling with the intention of frightening the occupant. The occupant grappled the gun and during the ensuing scuffle, the insured fell, the gun went off and the occupant was killed. Barr was acquitted of murder and manslaughter but was successfully sued under the Fatal Accident Act,[63] and the dependents were awarded £6,000. Barr sought indemnification under the insurance policy. The Court of Appeal was confronted with two issues. First, was the death as a result of an accident? Second, could public policy be invoked to prevent such indemnification? The Court held that the occupant's death had not occurred as a result of an accident because Barr had entered the house with a loaded shotgun with the intention of frightening Gray and had fired shots into the ceiling. More importantly, the court went further and declared that it would have been against public policy to require the insurer to indemnify Barr against Gray's dependents.

It is difficult to understand this decision in light of the finding that the death resulted from an accident. The insurer's refusal of indemnity, especially in light of the fact that the insurer had for several years been in receipt of Barr's premiums, ultimately results in the frustration of innocent dependents of the deceased and the potential to undermine the business efficacy of indemnity insurance.[64] But the word 'accidents' does not include injury which is caused deliberately or intentionally. If a man shoots another in self-defence or under gross provocation, the death is not caused by accident. It is caused by a deliberate act, no matter how justifiable or excusable it may be. But, if a man shoots another whilst out shooting pigeons without intention, being grossly negligent, the death is caused by accident, even though it be manslaughter. 'Crimes of violence particularly when committed with loaded guns, are of amongst the worst curses of that age.' While it may well be very much in the public interest that such actions be deterred,[65] the question must be raised whether a husband spouse is likely to be deterred by the possibility of being denied indemnity? Unlikely perhaps, since surely, not even life imprisonment appears to operate as a deterrent in such circumstances.

12.11   MOTOR MANSLAUGHTER

Rather than applying the sliding scale of seriousness beyond which point the insured is not entitled to be indemnified, as suggested by *Gray*, jurisprudence on motor manslaughter indicates that the public policy prohibition against a man profiting from his own crime is overshadowed by the competing, overarching consideration (i.e. the plight of the innocent victim). The courts therefore will consider the effect of non-enforcement on third parties not only on the victims but on the society as a whole. In a case of motor insurance, the primary purpose of compulsory motor vehicle liability insurance is to compensate innocent victims who have been injured. In that regard, it is distinguishable from ordinary insurance and there is no reason why the victim's right to recover from the insurer should be dependent on whether the insured's conduct was intentional or negligent.

---

62   [1971] 2 All ER 949.
63   1969 and 1976.
64   Shand, supra n. 10.
65   Ibid.

The operation of this principle can be seen in *Tinline v White Cross Insurance Association Ltd*,[66] where the insured, a speeding motorist who killed one pedestrian and injured two others and who was convicted of manslaughter involving gross or reckless negligence, was held nevertheless to be entitled to be indemnified. In determining whether the insurers were liable on a personal accident policy, a distinction was made between an intentional and an accidental act. In the case of the former, the policy would not protect him as a man driving a motorcar at an excessive speed intentionally runs into and kills a man, the result is not manslaughter but murder. Manslaughter is the result of an accident and murder is not, and it is against accident and accident only that an indemnity policy insures. Similarly, in *James v British General Insurance*,[67] the insured was able to recover against sums which he should become liable to pay to third parties as compensation for accidental personal injury. In both of these cases, the insured drove recklessly and killed innocent accident victims and, in both cases, the insured was convicted of manslaughter. It is difficult to reconcile these cases with the case of *Gray v Barr*. In *Hardy v Motor Insurance*,[68] the driver was convicted of wounding with intent to commit grievous bodily harm. The Court of Appeal held that although the driver's deliberate and criminal act precluded indemnity from the insurers for any damage already paid to the victim, if the victim was unable to recover compensation from the driver, then the victim could proceed against the Motor Insurer's Bureau. It is important to note that in the Commonwealth Caribbean there is no Motor Insurer's Bureau or similar body providing compensation for accident victims. In *Gardner v Moore*,[69] the driver of the vehicle was convicted of inflicting grievous bodily harm. The driver was convicted of maliciously inflicting grievous bodily harm. On the issue of public policy, Lord Denning stated:

> I can see no reason in public policy for drawing a distinction between one kind of wrongful act, of which a third party is an innocent victim, and another kind of wrongful act; between wrongful acts which are crimp on the part of the perpetrator and wrongful acts which are not crimes, or between wrongful acts which are crimes of carelessness and wrongful acts which are intentional crimes. It seems to me to be slightly unrealistic to suggest that a person who is not deterred by the risk commit grievous bodily harm would be deterred by the possible risk of life imprisonment.

12.12   FRAUDULENT CLAIMS

The principle of public policy logically extends to the question of fraudulent claims. Fraudulent claims may be brought about in a variety of ways; ranging from the deliberate, intentional act which brings about the peril insured to the situation where the insured succumbs to the temptation to exaggerate the claim. As a result of the decision of *Castellain v Preston*,[70] the guiding principle of insurance law is that the insured should be indemnified against his actual loss and no more. The insured is not entitled to recover where, in the case of property covered by a fire policy, the loss has been occasioned by deliberate arson.[71]

The Bahamian decision of *Bethel v Gresham Fire & Accident Insurance Society*[72] is instructive on the standard of proof in alleging criminal conduct. In this case, the plaintiff was a shopkeeper

---

66   [1921] 3 KB 327.
67   [1927] 2 KB 311.
68   Supra n. 62.
69   [1984] AC 549.
70   (1883) 11 QBD 380.
71   *Britton v Royal Insurance Co.* (1866) 4 F & F 905.
72   [1979–1980] 1 LRB 280.

who carried on a business in Nassau selling souvenirs and clothing. In June 1978, while the plaintiff was not in the Bahamas, a fire occurred at the plaintiff's shop in which a substantial portion of her stock was destroyed. An investigation showed that the fire was deliberately started and that there were no signs of forcible entry to the shop. The plaintiff held a policy of insurance with respect to the business which made provision for the period within which the claims must be lodged, and the plaintiff was required to substantiate her claims as a condition precedent. The plaintiff commenced proceedings, claiming $50,000. The defendant insurer denied liability, claiming that it was fraudulent in that the insured conspired with persons unknown to cause the fire and that she failed to comply with conditions precedent in the policy of insurance. The court held in favour of the plaintiff, that the defendant on the facts had failed to discharge the burden of proof necessary to establish so grave a charge as conspiracy to commit an offence of arson.[73] Although there was a breach of the conditions precedent contained in the policy of insurance, the defendant had by its conduct waived its position in that regard. Since the plaintiff did not give a clear presentation of damage sustained, the duty of the court in assessing the amount due to the plaintiff would be restricted to the material placed before it together with such evidence which was produced. In *Solomon Ghany*, Justice Moosai outlines the degree of the burden of proof placed the insurer to establish fraud. Typical examples of fraud include allegations of arson as in the cases of *Solomon Ghany*[74] and *Hossein v Goodwill Life Insurance*,[75] or where the value of items was over-estimated or claims for items that were never owned.

12.13 CONCLUSIONS

At common law, there is considerable doubt as to whether public policy operates as an external principle, to restrain against the furtherance of a crime, or whether it is simply an application of the rule that the courts will endeavour to adopt an interpretation against the enforcement of claims based on the criminal act of the insured.[76] The orthodox position, as laid down by Lord Mansfield CJ in *Holman v Johnson*,[77] to the effect that 'no court will lend its aid to a man who founds his cause of action upon an immoral or illegal act,' has been disapproved by the House of Lords in *Tinsley v Milligan*. While introducing a degree of flexibility, if the entire contract is tainted by the illegal act, the contract cannot be supported. The conclusion seems to be that:

1   At common law, it is important to ascertain the relationship between the crime and the loss. In *Euro-Diam* there was no such connection, so that the insurers remained liable on the contract. In *Geismar*, however, the court ruled that the insurance contract was directly related to the illegal act so that the insurer was entitled to deny recovery.

2   The court will examine the quality of the act and consider whether in all the circumstances it would be an affront to the public conscience to allow relief.[78] A conviction for manslaughter will not automatically signify that the insurer is not liable; the nature of the crime itself will dictate whether public policy considerations will operate.

---

73   *Slattery v Mance* [1962] 1 All ER 525.
74   TT 2000 HC 93.
75   [1990] 3 Carib. Comm Law Rep 163; TT 1990 HC 165.
76   Supra n. 50.
77   (1775) 1 Cowp. 341.
78   *Thackwell v Barclays Bank plc* [1986] 1 All ER 676.

3   Is the person seeking indemnity guilty of deliberate, intentional and unlawful violence, or threats of violence? If he was, and death resulted, then however unintended the result was, the courts will not entertain a claim for indemnity.

4   With respect to first party insurance, the question is whether the insured is claiming in respect of a loss suffered solely by him, and if so, was it the result of his deliberate act? Deliberate acts are not covered by the insurance contract.

5   The nature of the deliberate act is important. Is the offence criminal, and if so, is it serious enough to merit the claim being defeated? There is a distinction between murder and manslaughter.[79] The court will look to the nature of the insured's act and, having decided that a crime has been committed, even if there is no criminal conviction, the court will then determine whether the insured should be denied a claim under the insurance policy.

6   In the case of suicide, operation of Section 162 of the Barbados Insurance Act, which permits recovery regardless of whether the suicide was 'sane or insane,' once the terms of the contract so permit. Thus the deliberate suicide is not debarred. In other words, was the insured's commission of a crime or tort deliberate?

7   Is there an overarching need to compensate the victim? In motor insurance cases, the courts have focused on the need to compensate the victim.[80]

8   Public policy cannot be used as a defence to excuse the performance of a contract,[81] but when people vouch that rule to excuse themselves from the performance of a contract, in respect of which they have received the full consideration, and when all that remains to be done under the contract is for them to pay money, the application of the rule ought to be narrowly watched, and ought not to be carried a step further than the protection of the public requires.[82]

9   Where issues of illegality are raised, the courts have steered a middle course between two unacceptable positions. On the one hand, it is unacceptable for a court of law to assist in the enforcement of an obligation which the law forbids, while on the other, in the words of Bingham LJ, 'it is unacceptable that the court on the first indication of unlawfulness affecting any aspect of a transaction, draw up its skirts and refuse all assistance to the plaintiff.'

---

79   *Gray v Barr* [1971] 2 QB 554; see J. A. Jolowicz, 'Liability Insurance – Manslaughter – Public Policy' [1970] *CLJ* 194; Fleming, 'Insurance for the Criminal' (1971) 34 *MLR* 176; Shand, 'Unblinkering the Unruly Horse: Public Policy in the Law of Contract'; R. A. Hasson, 'The Supreme Court of Canada and the Law of Insurance 1975' (1976) 14 *Osgoode Hall L.J.* 769.
80   *Tinline v White Cross Insurance Association Ltd* [1921] 3 KB 327; *Hardy v Motor Insurer's Bureau* [1964] 2 QB 745; *Gardner v Moore & Another* [1984] All ER 1100.
81   *Cleaver v Mutual Reserve Fund Life Association* [1892] 1 QB 147.
82   Supra n. 58, per Lord Esher MR at 151.

CHAPTER 13

INTERMEDIARIES

INTRODUCTION

The composite term 'intermediary' embraces the functionaries agent, broker, sales representative, adjuster, insurance consultant or any such other person carrying on business connected with insurance as may be prescribed.[1] So important is the role that intermediaries play that it is difficult to envisage a circumstance in insurance without the involvement of some sort of intermediary at some stage of the insurer/insured relationship. Indeed, *Ward v New India Assurance Co. (Trinidad and Tobago) Ltd*[2] reveals (1) the importance of the intermediary's role in the conclusion of insurance contracts, (2) imputation of knowledge to his principal and (3) the potential for actions to give rise to estoppel and/or waiver, thereby precluding the insurer from rejecting a claim, Unfortunately, despite the intermediary's importance in the Caribbean, unlike the position elsewhere there is no comprehensive statutory regulation of intermediaries, so that a great deal of reliance must instead be placed on the common law and the general rules of agency.

13.1   STATUTE

The regulation of intermediaries in the Commonwealth Caribbean is via statute and the common law. Regional Insurance Acts play a marginal role in this regard, their application being largely restricted to the formalities of registration and the qualification of insurance personnel. It is important for regulatory purposes to first ascertain exactly who is an intermediary. A logical and convenient starting point is the definition section contained in the Insurance Act.[3] Minor differences in regulatory approach exist. This necessitates, in the context of the regional operation of insurance business, regard to the specific Act in each territory in which the insurance company operates. Accordingly, with respect to the definition of a broker, under the Guyana Insurance Act,[4] a broker is defined as a person who as an individual contractor brings together, with a view to the insurance of risks, persons seeking insurance and insurance undertakings and carries out work preparing contracts of insurance, but does not include an insurance agent. In Barbados and Jamaica, a broker is defined as '[any person] who in any manner solicits, negotiates or procures insurance or the renewal or continuance thereof on behalf of insurers or on behalf of agents or who arranges insurance business on behalf of prospective policyholders.'[5] Differences in approach are also discernible with respect to the definition of agents. In Barbados and Jamaica, an 'agent' is defined as an individual, form or body corporate appointed by an insurer and not being an employee of the insurer, to solicit applications for insurance or negotiate insurance on behalf of the insurer and, or authorised to do so by the insurer, to effectuate and countersign insurance contracts.[6] In Guyana, an 'agent'

---

1   Section 2, Jamaica Insurance Act No. 26 of 2001.
2   (2005) 70 WIR 48.
3   Section 2, Barbados Insurance Act No. 32 of 1996; Section 2, Guyana Insurance Act No. 20 of 1998; Section 2, Jamaica Insurance Act No. 26 of 2001.
4   Insurance Act No. 20 of 1998.
5   Supra n. 2.
6   Section 2, Barbados Insurance Act No. 32 of 1996; Section 2, Jamaica Insurance Act No. 26 of 2001.

means any person who holds an appointment in writing from an insurer enabling him to place insurance business with that insurer, but does not include an insurance broker. In some jurisdictions, the legislation also defines a 'sub-agent.' A sub-agent is defined in Barbados, for instance, 'as any person appointed by an insurer, an agent or broker to solicit applications for insurance or to negotiate insurance on behalf of the insurer, the agent or the broker as the case may be.' There is no statutory definition of a salesman in Guyana, but in Barbados and Jamaica, a 'salesman' means an individual employed by an insurer, an agent or broker to solicit applications for insurance or to negotiate insurance on behalf of the insurer, the agent or broker as the case may be.[7] Essentially, differences in statutory language notwithstanding, an insurance broker is an independent contractor who procures insurance contracts on his own behalf. As the definition suggests, the factual circumstances may render the broker the agent of either the insured or the insurer.

It is clear that there is a divergence between the layman's perception of an agent and how the agent is actually treated in law. The man on the street invariably views the agent as an 'insurance agent,' ergo under the insurer's employ. But as the statute indicates, the agent is treated as the agent of the insured. Further, the statutory definition while useful is not conclusive so that the factual circumstances must be examined in light of the relevant common law in order to resolve questions of the scope and ambit of the intermediary's authority.

As stated earlier, there is no comprehensive structure governing insurance intermediaries in the Caribbean.[8] Against the background of a weak regime, the Insurance Act of Guyana stands out. In Guyana, the schedule to the Insurance Act outlines a code of conduct for brokers.[9] In addition to Part XIV of the Act,[10] Schedule 4 provides, *inter alia*, that brokers shall at all times conduct their business with utmost good faith; do everything possible to satisfy the insurance requirements of their clients; and shall place the interest of those clients before all other considerations and refrain from making any misleading representations in their advertising.[11] It further requires brokers to provide advice objectively and independently with due care and diligence and to explain, on request, the differences in the type of insurance.[12] Brokers shall ensure that all work carried out in connection with their business shall be properly supervised and shall ensure that their employees are made aware of these regulations.[13] It is important to observe that the code of conduct is expressly stated to be 'illustrative only of the conduct which is considered to be in the best interest of the public and the insurance brokers and other persons concerned with their conduct,'[14] and further that it applies to brokers, not agents or salesmen.

Statutory regulation is predicated the registration, registration operating as a filter, weeding out undesirable applicants and serving as an initial regulatory device. An application for

---

7   Supra n. 2.
8   In St Lucia Insurance Act No. 26 of 2001 [Rev.], Chapter 12:08 2014, Part V.
9   Section 88, Guyana Insurance Act No. 20 of 1998, Schedule 4.
10 Part XIV of the Insurance Act contains the provision regulating brokers in Guyana. Section 88 of the Act authorises the Commissioner to issue a code of conduct of brokers registered under this Part which is substantially similar to the content as set out in Schedule 4. Section 81 of the Act stipulates that only corporations or partnerships registered with and authorised by the Commissioner may carry on insurance business as a broker in Guyana. Section 82 provides for the registration of existing brokers within three months of the commencement of the Act. An application must be made in the prescribed manner accompanied with a fee of $50,000 payable to the Commission. By virtue of Section 83, brokers must have indemnity insurance at a minimum of $10 million but not more than $250 million. A broker shall for the purposes of receiving a premium be deemed to be the broker of the insurer notwithstanding a condition or stipulation to the contract in accordance with Section 90.
11 Rule 2.
12 Rule 3(b).
13 Rule 3(c).
14 Rule 1.

registration must be made to the relevant regulatory authority in the prescribed manner, accompanied by the requisite fee.[15] Section 70 of the Jamaica Insurance Act provides:

> No person shall, in relation to insurance business of any class specified in section 3(1) carry on or purport to carry on business as, or act in the capacity of, an insurance intermediary, unless he is registered under this Part to do so.[16]

The bifurcated approach adopted by the Guyana Insurance Act demands that insurance agents registering must pay a filing fee of $2,000, while the filing fee for a broker is $50,000.[17] All regional Insurance Acts attempt to ensure the quality of actors involved in the industry. The registrant must possess the minimum statutory qualifications and satisfy the 'fit and proper' test in order to perform his functions under the Act. Registration is a prerequisite, the statutory requirements are mandatory and a failure by the intermediary to register under the Insurance Act will render the intermediary personally liable. In some jurisdictions the consequences are severe. In Jamaica, on summary conviction, the intermediary will be personally liable to a fine not exceeding $3 million or to imprisonment for a term not exceeding three years or to both such fines and imprisonment.[18]

The regulator's role in registering brokers came under review in the Bahamian decision of *Johnson v The Registrar of Insurance and the Attorney General*.[19] In this case, the plaintiff applied to the Registrar of Insurance for registration under Section 29(2) of the Bahamas Insurance Act.[20] The registrar rejected the applicant's application as although it was found that the applicant satisfied Section 29(2)(a) in that he had adequate knowledge of the insurance business having previously worked in the business, he was unable to satisfy the registrar as to his compliance with Section 29(b) '[that] he [was] of good character.' Consequently, the registrar rejected the applicant's application. The plaintiff, on an application for judicial review, sought to compel the Registrar to reconsider his application. The High Court of the Bahamas ruled against the applicant, finding there had been no breach of the rules of natural justice so that the registrar's refusal to register an agent was upheld. As we saw in Chapter 1 with respect to the registration of insurers, the rules of natural justice under administrative law operate to measure the actions of the supervisor.

One area where Insurance Acts in the Commonwealth Caribbean notably intervene is in insurance premium payment by the insured to the agent.[21] In this regard, statute expressly abrogates the common law principle that an agent is assumed to be the agent of the insured and renders the agent as the agent of the insurer for the purposes of the receipt of premium. Thus, Section 79 of the St Lucia Insurance Act provides:[22]

> an insurance agent, an insurance broker or an insurance salesman is guilty of an offence where he received money from a client for an account of an insurer and fails to pay over the same less any commission and other deduction within 30 days after demand for payment is made in writing.[23]

---

15 Section 71, Jamaica Insurance Act No. 26 of 2001.
16 Act No. 26 of 2001; Sections 81 and 92, Guyana Insurance Act No. 20 of 1998.
17 Section 82.
18 Section 70(2), Jamaica Insurance Act No. 26 of 2001; Section 76 of the St Vincent and the Grenadines Insurance Act No. 45 of 2003, imposes a penalty of $10,000 and/or imprisonment for 12 months or both.
19 No. 640 of 2002.
20 Ch 317.
21 Section 90, Barbados Insurance Act No. 32 of 1996; Section 39, Dominica Insurance Act No. 17 of 1974 Chapter 78:49.
22 St Lucia Insurance Act, Cap 12:08 [2001 Rev.].
23 Section 90, Barbados Insurance Act, Cap 310; Section 82(1), Jamaica Insurance Act No. 26 of 2001.

A failure by the agent to pay the said premium to the insured within the stipulated time period will render the agent personally liable. The utility of these provisions is obvious. The insurer is not free to assert the non-receipt of the premium in order to avoid its obligations under the contract of insurance where the premium has been already been paid by the insured, to the agent. Instead, the statutory solution is to impose personal liability on the agent, where he fails to pay over premium within a stipulated time period: 15 days in Barbados and 30 days in St Lucia.[24] Apart from the agent being subject to personal liability for failure to turn over premiums paid in respect of an insurance policy, in some jurisdictions an agent will be rendered personally liable to the insured for unauthorised contracts in the same manner as if he were the insurer. The basis of the liability is knowingly procuring by fraudulent representation, the contract of insurance.[25]

13.2   PRE-REFORM

The Marine Insurance Act

> an agent to insure is presumed to know every circumstance that in the ordinary course of business ought to be known by or to have been communicate to, him; and (b) every material circumstance that the assured is bound to disclose, unless it comes to his knowledge too late to communicate it to the agent. Further, section 23 (1) provides: – 'Every material representation made by the assured or agent to the insurer during the negotiations for the contract, and before the contract is concluded, must be true; and if a representation is untrue the insurer may avoid the contract.'

The Marine Insurance Act emphasises the importance of the role of the agent.

13.3   COMMON LAW

The common law illustrates that the role of intermediary has an impact on (1) the conclusion of the insurance contract, (2) imposition of knowledge and (3) the creation of waiver and estoppel.

Conclusion of the contract of insurance

As discussed in Chapter 3, there is *dicta* to the effect that an informal agreement by word of mouth can support a contract of insurance for a line of insurance to protect the risk in the meantime, if made by an authorised agent of the insurer. In such circumstances, the insurer will be liable in the event of loss.[26] Although in St Lucia's decision of *Edgar v Demerara Mutual Life Assurance Society*,[27] Matthew J found that the insurer's agent had no authority to enter into an oral agreement as the particulars of the contract, the amount of premium and the nature of

---

24   Section 94, Barbados Insurance Act, Cap 310; Section 83, Jamaica Insurance Act No. 26 of 2001; Section 73, St Lucia Insurance Act No. 6 of 1995.
25   Section 84, Jamaica Insurance Act No. 26 of 2001.
26   *Mayne Nickless Ltd v Pegler* (1974) 1 NSWLR 228. Here, the insured purchased a car and the vendor immediately arranged for insurance over the telephone. A binding contract of insurance seems to have been accepted before the issue of the cover note and before the policy was issued.
27   High Court of St Lucia 1991.

the risk had not been established, in *Murfitt v Royal Insurance Co.*,[28] however, the agent was held to have implied actual authority to enter into temporary oral contracts of fire insurance. The importance of establishing agency is also brought to light by *Tuky Air Transport Inc. v The Liqui-dators of Edinburgh Insurance Co. Ltd*,[29] a case from the British Virgin Islands. In *Tuky*, the plaintiff had filled out a blank proposal form for the issuance of the policy in the presence of a broker/agent. At the time of the trial, although the form had been completed in blue ink, red and black ink were discovered in addition to the blue ink on the proposal form. Bertrand J ruled, on the filling out of the proposal form, that the agent was not a dual agent but was the agent of the insurance company. Further, the High Court reiterated the fundamental principle that there can be no agency or relationship of principal and agent in regard to an act unless the alleged principal actually or ostensibly authorised or appointed the alleged agent to perform the act for or on behalf of the alleged principal or unless the alleged principal subsequently ratified the act purported to have been performed on his behalf. The fact that an agent is entrusted with blank cover notes will be sufficient to confer upon the agent, implied actual or apparent authority. In *Mackie v European Assurance Society*,[30] the actions of the principal in supplying the agent with cover notes conferred authority on him to bind the principal.[31]

Imposition of knowledge

From the insured's perspective, his success in alleging that the insurer is bound because of the actions of the intermediary with respect to any of the circumstances outlined is dependent on the existence of an agency relationship between the agent and the insurer as principal. It can be maintained that the insurer was seized with knowledge of information disclosed to the agent. As contained in the Marine Insurance Act, where an insurance is effected for the assured by an agent, the agent must disclose to the insurer, and every material circumstance that is known to himself and an agent to insure is presumed to know every circumstance that in the ordinary course of business ought to be known by or to have been communicate to him. In accordance with Section 23(1) of the Barbados Marine Insurance Act, 'every material representation made by the assured or agent to the insurer during the negotiations for the contract, and before the contract is concluded, must be true; and if a representation is untrue the insurer may avoid the contract.'

While regional marine insurance legislation makes reference to the agent, the essence of the principal/agent relationship must be gathered by applying the common law. In order for the insured to successfully establish that a disclosure to the agent is tantamount to a disclosure to the insurer, an agency relationship must be in existence. Agency is a question of fact to deter-mined on a consideration of the factual circumstances of the case. The fundamental question is, whose agent is the agent? As a general rule, only the agent under the direct employment or control of the insurer is the agent of the insurer, and even he may not at all times when dealing with an insured, be regarded as the insurer's agent. While regional insurance legislation sheds

---

28 (1922) 38 TLR 334.
29 [1988–1989] 1 *Carib. Comm. L. Rev.* 263.
30 *Mackie v European Assurance Society* (1869) 21 LT 102.
31 *Adams-Eden Furniture Ltd v Kansa General Insurance Co.* [1977] 2 WWR 65, Manitoba CA; *Anglo-African Merchants Ltd v Bayley* [1970] 1 QB 311 [1969] 2 All ER 421 [1969] 2 WLR 686, Megaw J; *Con-Stan Industries of Aus-tralia Pty Ltd v Norwich Winterthur Insurance (Australia) Ltd*, 64 ALR 481, Australia High Court; *Inniss v Belgrave* (2002) (unreported decision, Court of Appeal of Barbados magisterial appeal 9 of 1999); *Pelter v University of the West Indies* (1994) Barbados LR 175, Barbados CA; *Ramsey v St James Beach Hotels Services Ltd* (2002) (unreported decision, Court of Appeal of Barbados magisterial appeal 4 of 1999); *Stockton v Mason* [1978] 2 Lloyd's Rep 430 [1979] RTR 130, England CA.

light, *prima facie*, on the existence or non-existence of a master/servant relationship for certain categories of intermediaries, it is towards the common law that the answer to the question 'whose agent is the agent?' lies. In the oft-cited decision of *Bawden v London, Edinburgh & Glasgow Assurance Co.*,[32] a proposal for accident insurance was effected by a proposer who was illiterate and had only one eye. This fact was known to the agent of the insurers who completed the proposal form for him. The form, however, warranted that the proposer had no physical deformity, which was obviously incorrect. Subsequently the insured suffered an accident in which he lost sight in the other eye. It was held that the insured could recover under the policy for total loss of sight. The agent's knowledge of the truth at the time of the proposal was imputed to the insurer. *Bawden* has, however, been distinguished in subsequent decisions. In *Newsholme Bros v Road Transport & General Insurance Co.*,[33] in a proposal for motor insurance, incorrect answers relating to previous losses were warranted to be true. The agent who filled in the proposal form knew the truth. Although he was not authorised to effect either temporary or permanent insurance, he was employed by the insurers to canvass for proposals. Scrutton LJ in the Court of Appeal delivered the leading judgment, finding in favour of the insurer on the basis that since the agent filled in the form at the request of the proposer, for that purpose he must have been acting as the agent of the proposer and not of the insurers. Further, that on the contract principle established in *L'estrange v Graucomb*,[34] a man who has signed a document without reading it could not escape the consequences of his negligence. Greer LJ also relied upon the agency point, but he laid greater emphasis upon another reason, namely, that to allow evidence of what the agent actually knew to be introduced would be a violation of the parol evidence rule, whereby oral evidence is generally inadmissible to vary the terms of a written contract. Here the proposal form was part of the contract because, as usual, it contained a basis of contract clause so that its terms constituted warranties. Greer LJ was thus able to distinguish the *Bawden* case on the grounds that in the latter case, because of the special circumstances of the proposer's illiteracy, the court could rightly ignore the parol evidence rule or put a special meaning on the words used in the contract. In contrast, Scrutton LJ came very close to saying that the earlier *Bawden* decision was incorrect.[35] It appears that in Canada the decision in *Newsholme Bros* has been effectively overruled by the Court of Appeal decision of *Stone v Reliance Mutual Insurance Society*.[36] Here the claimant's fire policy with the defendants lapsed. An inspector employed by the defendants called on the claimant's wife and persuaded her to effect a new policy. On the proposal form the answer 'none' was put to a question asking for details of lapsed policies and previous claims. This was incorrect, as the claimant had previously made a claim on the defendants and thus obviously had insured with them. The inspector had filled in the proposal form as he was instructed to do by the insurers. It was held that the insurers could not avoid liability for loss. Megaw and Stamp LJJ regarded the case as turning on its special facts, namely, that the inspector was actually authorised to fill in proposal forms. Lord Denning's judgment turned on the authority of the agent, not simply as regards the imputation of knowledge of the agent, but also because the agent had the requisite authority to represent that the form had been correctly filled in. The decision of *Stone* can be regarded as merely an exception to the general rule. The decision must be understood on the basis of the special facts and there is no mandate for

---

32   [1892] 2 QB 534.
33   [1929] 2 KB 356.
34   [1934] 2 KB 394.
35   Arguably in the United Kingdom, the transferred agency aspect of the rule in *Newsholme Bros* has been effectively overruled in respect of life insurances that fall within the definition of investments under the Financial Services Act 1986. Section 44 of this Act seemingly provides for a wide statutory authority for an 'appointed representative' under the Financial Services and Markers Act 2000.
36   [1972] 1 Lloyd's Rep 469.

regarding the decision in *Stone* as overruling that in the earlier decision of *Newholme Bros*. The latter remains authoritative, but there are exceptions in the case of illiterate and possibly poorly educated proposers and, possibly, where the agent in question is more than a mere canvassing agent but can be regarded as having some authority to vary the terms of the contract.

These cases indicate that the question of whether disclosure to an agent amounts to a disclosure to the insurer rests on the authority of the agent. Further support for this rule can be seen from the Dominican decision of *Baptiste v British American Insurance Co. & White*.[37] The judgment makes no reference to the earlier decisions of *Bawden* or *Newsholme*. Instead, Justice Berridge simply states:

> I consider that it is highly improbable that any salesman, notwithstanding the fact that it was suggested that he was at the time somewhat junior, would resort to the somewhat unorthodox procedure of talking insurance to a prospective purchase by way of reference to an existing policy: Indeed it may be said that the more junior the salesman the more likely he is to have consulted his sales presentation which the plaintiff had with him rather than a policy issued to another.

Thus despite the obvious illiteracy of the proposer in *Baptiste*, the agent was held to be the agent of the insurer. In the Court of Appeal decision of *Caribbean Atlantic Life Assurance Co. v Nasseif*,[38] also arising out of the jurisdiction of Dominica, an agent innocently misrepresented that if the insured purchased a policy of insurance, the premiums were tax deductible. The agent was held to be skilled in insurance matters while the insured was a person ignorant of the law, so that the insurance company was held liable and the premiums were recoverable. Seemingly the status of the insured in this case was taken into account.

A useful decision, although arguably the unusual facts of the case limit its utility, is the unreported decision of *Hypolite v Demerara Mutual Life Assurance Society Ltd*[39] arising out of St Vincent and the Grenadines, where the Supreme Court availed itself of opportunity to elucidate on the question of agency. In *Hypolite*, the appellant engaged the respondent as an insurance consultant agent and/or broker to secure insurance coverage for certain contract work. The respondent issued to the appellant a cover slip which contained the following statement: 'Principal: To be advised as required by contract.' In fact, there was no principal in existence for whom the defendant acted. During the currency of the cover slip, the appellant's property was damaged by flood causing special damages of over $700,000. In disputing liability, the defendant insurers contended, *inter alia*, that the premium had not been paid and disputed the degree of damage alleged to have been suffered. On the issue of whether the defendant, as a mere broker, could be sued successfully for losses as if he were a principal insurer, the court held that the respondent can be sued for breach of warranty that he had authority to make the contract. The Court held that the defendant, as a broker, could be sued as an agent for an undisclosed or non-existent principal for the breach of warranty that there was a principal, and is equally liable where an undisclosed principal has not consented or authorised the contract to be made on his behalf. Further, *dicta* in *Hypolite* supports the proposition that on the issue of whether in the absence of a claim in negligence or fraudulent or negligent misrepresentation or breach of warranty of authority, the plaintiff has any cause of action against the defendant, the Court found that the agent's liability is strict and does not depend on negligence or fraud.

The case law is replete with attempts by the insured to claim that the agent's knowledge of a particular fact amounted to the insurer's knowledge or that the actions of an agent amounted

---

37   Unreported decision, High Court of Dominica Suit No. 120 of 1966.
38   DM 1970 CA 6.
39   Unreported decision, St Vincent and the Grenadines High Court Civil Appeal No. 25 of 1993 [95-03-20].

to a waiver by the insurer. Determination of an agent's usual authority is a question of fact and will obviously vary with the nature of the office held by him and established usage in the commercial community.

Creation of waiver and estoppel

More often than not, when waiver or estoppel is pleaded it is based on the actions of the agent. As seen from Chapter 7, rather than treat the contract of insurance as being avoided by a breach of warranty or on the basis of breach of condition, insurers are entitled to treat the contract as subsisting, notwithstanding the breach by the insured. Waiver is defined as where the insurer has a right to avoid the contract, but nevertheless the actions of the intermediary amount to an election on the part of the insurer to honour the contract.[40] In order to constitute affirmation of the policy, there must be knowledge on the part of the insurer combined with some express or implied conduct leading a reasonable insured to conclude that the policy subsists in full. Estoppel, on the other hand, is wider in ambit than waiver and does not depend on the knowledge of the person estopped. Estoppel occurs where either by words or the conduct of the insurer, the insured has been induced to believe that the insurer will not rely on his strict legal right.

At the core of the discussion of whether the intermediary's knowledge will be imputed to the principal or whether his action will amount to waiver or estoppel is the question of agency.

13.4   AUTHORITY OF THE AGENT

As Justice Hanschell succinctly states in the Barbadian decision of *Forde v The British Guiana and Trinidad Mutual Fire Insurance Co. Ltd*:[41]

> Every agent who is authorised to conduct a particular trade or business, or generally to act for his principal in matters of a particular nature, or to do a particular class of acts, has implied authority to do whatever is incidental to the ordinary conduct of such a trade or business, or of matters of that nature, or is within the scope of that class of acts, and whatever is necessary for the proper and effective performance of his duties; but not to do anything that is outside the ordinary scope of his employment and duties.

An agent does not have authority to do anything that is outside the ordinary scope of his authority.[42]

Actual authority

Actual authority may be express or implied. Express actual authority may be conferred on the agent, orally or in writing. Implied authority, on the other hand, arises by virtue of the position

---

40   *American Life Insurance v Sumintra* (1983) 37 WIR 242; *Edgar v Demerara Mutual Life Assurance Society*, St Lucia High Court Suit No. 160 of 1989; see also *Tuky Air Transport Inc. The Liquidator of Edinburgh Insurance Co. Ltd (In Liquidation)* (unreported decision of the British Virgin Islands High Court No. 3 of 1984).
41   Ibid.
42   *Linford v Provincial Horse & Cattle Insurance Co.* (1864), 34 Beav 291, 5 New Rep 29, 11 LT 330, 28 JP 803, 10 Jur NS 1066, 55 ER 647.

held by the agent. The common law doctrine of implied actual authority or usual authority arises where an agent is given actual authority, but the precise scope of that authority is not defined and therefore needs to be implied or inferred from the surrounding circumstances of the position. It is binding between the company and the agent and between the company and others.[43]

Apparent or ostensible authority

Apparent or ostensible authority is often wider than actual authority. It is the legal relationship between the principal (the insurer) and the policyholder (the third party) created by a representation made by the principal to a given fact, and in fact acted upon by the policyholder that the agent had the authority to enter into a contract of the kind entered into. In *Freeman & Lockyer (A Firm) v Buckhurst Park Properties (Mangal)*,[44] Lord Justice Diplock laid down four criteria which assist in the determination of apparent or ostensible authority.

(1)   A representation was made to the outsider that the 'agent' had authority to enter into a contract of the kind in dispute on behalf of the company;

(2)   This representation was made by a person who had actual authority to manage the business of the company either generally, or in respect of the matters to which the contract relates;

(3)   The outsider was induced by such representation to enter into the contract;

(4)   The company had the capacity either to enter into a contract of the kind sought to be enforced or to delegate authority to an agent, to enter into a contract of that kind.

Generally apparent or ostensible authority concerns the exercise of a power that an agent of that class would not normally be expected to have, but which the principal has held out the particular agent as having. This is also known as agency by estoppel, and rests on the statements or conduct by the principal. The basis of the rule is that where a third party deals in good faith with an agent, in reliance on the credentials with which he has been entrusted by his principal, his principal is estopped from his agent's authority. Accordingly, an insurance company may be estopped by reason of ostensible authority from denying that an agent has passed on information to them. Thus in *Wing v Harvey*,[45] the agent had authority to accept premiums on his company's behalf and paid them to his directors, aware at the time that the insured had broken a condition of the policy, so that the assured was entitled to rely on the agent passing on his knowledge to the directors. By accepting the premium through their authorised agent, the insurer was therefore taken to have affirmed the policy. In *Evans v Employer's Mutual*[46] it was held that where it must have been clear to a clerk of the insurer from perusing a claim, that an answer in the proposal form was untrue, the agent's knowledge amounted to knowledge by the company and that they had then to elect whether to continue with the contract.[47] The result is that the insurer, as principal, will be bound by an agent's acts carried out within the scope of his actual or apparent authority. However, knowledge of the agent is never imputed when the agent is acting in fraud of his principal. In *Wing v Harvey*,[48] a life policy provided that it would become void if the assured traveled beyond the limits of Europe without the insurer's

---

43   *Hely & Hutchinson v Brayhead Ltd* [1967] 1 QB 549.
44   (1964) 2 QB 480 [1964] 1 A.
45   [1936] 1 KB 505.
46   Ibid.
47   *Avery v British Legal Assurance* [1918] 1 KB 136; *Holdsworth v Lands and Yorks Insurance* [1907] 23 TLR 521; *Blackley v National Mutual Life Association of Australia* [1972] NZLR 1038.
48   (1854) 5 De GM & G 265.

consent. An assignee of the policy subsequently informed an agent of the insurer that the life assured had taken up residence in Canada. For some time after this, before the life assured died, premiums were received by the insurer. It was held that the insurer had waived the breach of warranty; they were deemed to know what their agent knew and having accepting premiums subsequently, could not rely upon the breach. The degree of knowledge that will be imputed to the insurer depends upon the status of the agent receiving it. In other words, upon his actual or apparent authority. In *Wing v Harvey*,[49] the agent was the local representative of the insurer at a branch office. A mere canvassing or soliciting agent ordinarily not be regarded as having such broad authority, since it would be tantamount to variation of the terms of the policy. But such an agent probably has authority to receive disclosures of material facts.

The Barbadian decision of *Forde v The British Guiana and Trinidad Mutual Fire Insurance Co. Ltd*[50] applied the leading authorities of *Newsholme Bros v Road Transport & General Insurance Co. Ltd*[51] and *Wing v Harvey*.[52] In *Forde v The British Guiana and Trinidad Mutual Fire Insurance Co. Ltd*,[53] which stands as authority for the rule that an agent for an insurance company has no implied authority to waive a forfeiture of a policy,[54] the plaintiff insured her dwelling-house with the defendant insurance company against damage by fire. The policy of insurance was subject to the condition that the policy was of no effect if the building became unoccupied and remained so for a period of more than 30 days. The plaintiff's building was damaged by fire after remaining unoccupied for 30 days. The defendant insurer contended that the policy of insurance had ceased to attach to the said dwelling-house at the time when it was burnt. The plaintiff, on the other hand, argued that the actions of the insurer's agent, by visiting the dwelling-house and assessing the damage, when a second fire occurred on 8 November 1960, that the defendant by its agent had waived the forfeiture. The Supreme Court of Barbados held that the policy of insurance had ceased to attach to the dwelling-house as the agent had no authority, express or implied, to waive the forfeiture.[55] The Court paid special regard to the fact that the agent under consideration was an ordinary local agent of an insurance company is not, without special authority, authorised to bind the company by a contract to grant a policy. Local agents are employed to obtain proposals and forward them to their principals and to accept premiums on policies which have been issued by their principals. *Wing v Harvey*[56] was explained and distinguished, citing *dicta* in *Newsholme Bros v Road Transport & General Insurance Co. Ltd*:[57]

> The case is only an authority for the proposition that if an event has happened after the issue of the policy which would make the policy void, and the company with notice of the event which avoids the policy renews the contract by receiving the premium to cover a further period of insurance, it will be deemed to have effected the insurance on the term that the conditions will not be insisted on.

---

49 Ibid.
50 Unreported decision, Supreme Court of Barbados 1964.
51 Supra n. 33.
52 Supra n. 48.
53 Supra n. 50.
54 *British Industry Life Assurance Co. v Ward* (1856), 17 CB 644, 27 LTOS 81, 20 JP 391, 139 ER 1229, 29 Digest (Repl) 72, 241; *Wing v Harvey* (1854), 5 De GM & G 265, 2 Eq Rep 533, 23 LJ Ch 511, 23 LTOS 120, 18 Jur 394, 2 WR 570, 43 ER 872, LJJ, 29 Digest (Repl) 72, 242.
55 *Ashworth v Builders Mutual* (1873), 17 American Reports; *Simmonds v Cockell* [1920] 1 KB 843; *Linford v Provincial Horse and Cattle Insurance Co.* (1864), 34 Beav 291; *British Industry Life Assurance Co. v Ward*, 139 ER 1229; *Wing v Harvey* (1854), 5 De GM & G 265; *Newsholme Bros v Road Transport & General Insurance Co. Ltd* [1929] All ER 442.
56 Supra n. 48.
57 Supra n. 33.

Another instructive decision emanating from the Caribbean is the case of *Rambally v Barbados Fire and General Insurance Co. Ltd et al.*[58] This case on indemnity insurance on a building, housing a bakery and restaurant in Castries, St Lucia, which was destroyed by fire. There was an insurance policy in existence that covered loss or damage by fire, flood and other perils. The issues that arose for consideration were, *inter alia*, whether the insurance brokers were agents of the insurers or the insured, and thus whether the insurers were bound by the promises and representations, acts or conduct of the agent. On the question of agency, the plaintiffs attempted to establish that the agent was the agent of the insurers on the ground that the insurers had provided the agent with application forms and had the authority to collect premiums for the insurers in addition to a 10 percent commission for business placed with the company. The Court, reaffirming that the burden of proof was upon the claimants to establish on the balance of probabilities that the brokers were serving two masters, commented that a broker may not act for both parties to a transaction unless he fully discloses all material facts to both parties and obtains their informed consent to his so acting, any custom to the contrary will not be upheld. The Court ruled that the broker remained the agent of the insured, a fact not disturbed by the collection of premiums by the agent and the payment of commissions.[59]

It is settled law, as authoritatively laid down in *Anglo-African Merchants v Bayley*,[60] that a failure by the agent to secure express and full informed consent amounts to a breach of duty.[61] The principle that there can be no agency without consent of the principal was succinctly expressed by Lord Person in the House of Lords decision of *Garnac Grain Co. Inc. v H.M.F. Faure & Fairclough Ltd*,[62] to wit:

> The relationship of principal and agent can only be established by the consent of the principal and agent. They will be held to have consented if they have agreed to what amounts in law to such a relationship, even if they do not recognise it themselves and even if they have professed to disclaim it.

In a situation where there is no agency relationship, any person acting without authority of an alleged disclosed or undisclosed principal who performs or purports to perform an act for or on behalf of an alleged principal, represents and warrants that he has the alleged principal's authority to do so.[63] The House of Lords held that a broker who applied to the Bank of England for a power of attorney for the sale of Consols, wrongly believing himself to have been instructed by the stockholder, was liable to indemnify the bank against the claim of the stockholder on the ground that he must have been taken to have given an implied warranty that he had authority. The agent's liability is strict, is not fault based and is not dependent on negligence.

---

58 Unreported decision, High Court of St Lucia No. 1179 of 2000.
59 It is a long-standing rule of English law that the broker is remunerated not by the assured but by the insurer, by means of deduction of commission from the premium, and that commission is earned where the broker is responsible for arranging insurance. The rule is anomalous in that it contravenes the general equitable principle that the agent must not receive payment from the third party, but it is well established despite occasional *dicta* to the contrary. The level of commission is agreed between the insurer and the broker, although the assured can apparently demand to be informed of what has been agreed and can object to excessive remuneration, and where the Financial Services Act 1986 (UK) applies he has a statutory right to know. As the rule is derived either from custom or implied term, it can accordingly be ousted by an express arrangement to the contrary. R. Merkin, *Colinvaux's Law of Insurance*, 7th edn (Sweet & Maxwell: 1997), p. 330, paras 15–37.
60 Per Megaw J [1969] 2 All ER 421 at 429.
61 *Halsbury's Laws of England*, 4th edn (Butterworths: 1989), Vol. 25, para. 397:

> If a person wishing to obtain insurance of a non-marine character employs an insurance broker as distinct from going direct to the insurers of their agents, the broker is his agent and the ordinary law of agency governs the responsibility of the proposer for the acts and omissions of the broker.

62 [1968] AC 1130.
63 *Starkey v Bank of England* [1903] AC 114.

Apart from the obvious situation where agency is pleaded, attempts are often made to assert agency outside the stated category of intermediaries as defined in the Insurance Act. Such an attempt was made in *Royal Caribbean Hotels Ltd v Barbados Fire & General Co. et al.; Bank of Nova Scotia*.[64] In this case, the insured hotel which was subject to a mortgage was damaged by Hurricane Allen. As the insurance premiums were paid by the mortgagee bank, an attempt was made to hold the mortgagee responsible for fulfilling the conditions under the policy. At trial, the judge found the bank negligent. On appeal, the judgment was overturned, finding that the mortgage clause did not make the mortgagee the insured. Rather, as a mere assignee, his claim is subject to be defeated by any act of the mortgagor which would entitle the insurer to reject liability. Addressing the issue of whether the banks owed a duty of care to notify the insurer within the prescribed manner and within the prescribed time, applying the Privy Council decision in *Tai Hing Cotton Mill Ltd v Lui Chong Hing Bank Ltd & Ors*,[65] the Court of Appeal refrained from embarking on an investigation for liability in tort where parties are in a contractual relationship. Echoing the words of Lord Scarman, the plaintiff cannot rely on the law of tort for which was expressly or impliedly it has contracted with the bank. As to whether alternatively such a duty could be implied in the contract, the court noted that the effect of the term sought to be implied must be one without which the whole transaction would become 'inefficacious, futile and absurd.' Thus, the Court of Appeal ruled that there was no need to imply those terms to give it business efficacy as it could be read quite reasonably and sensibly on the premise that the plaintiff itself would look after such matters. The duty remained on the plaintiff to notify the insurer forthwith and to make the claim within the prescribed period.

13.5   CONCLUSION

The discussion reveals that intermediaries are regulated for the most part by common law, specifically the rules of agency at common law and the Insurance Act. As far as regional Insurance Acts are concerned, they govern the formalities of registration and the qualification of insurance personnel. As noted earlier, in the jurisdiction of Guyana the schedule to the Insurance Act, albeit not binding and being illustrative only,[66] provides a code of conduct for brokers and requires them to conduct their business with utmost good faith, to do everything possible to satisfy the insurance requirements of their clients, to place the interest of those clients before all other considerations and to refrain from making any misleading representations in their advertising.[67] Apart from Guyana, regional insurance law's role is limited to registration and the initial qualifications of insurance personnel. It is logical, therefore, for there to be considerable reliance on the common law. The common law and the traditional rules of agency assist in ascertaining whose agent is the agent for the purposes of receipt of premiums, disclosure and the question of waiver.

---

64   Court of Appeal No. 31 of 1992.
65   [1986] 1 AC 80.
66   Rule 1.
67   Rule 2.

CHAPTER 14

SUBROGATION, MEASURE OF
LOSS AND REINSTATEMENT

14.1 INTRODUCTION

Subrogation is an equitable doctrine adopted solely for the purpose of preventing the insured from recovering more than full indemnity. It does so by placing the insurers in the position of the insured.[1] While the elements of an insurer's cause of action are based upon equity, satisfaction is achieved through law.[2] The doctrine of subrogation is applicable in a variety of situations, but it is not available to life insurance[3] or personal accident insurance.[4] A plethora of regional case law, such as *Musson (Jamaica) Ltd v Clarke*,[5] *Royal Caribbean Insurance Ltd v Marcial*[6] and *Walwy. v Archibald and RBTT Bank (SKN) Ltd*,[7] suggest not only an adherence to British jurisprudence but also the existence of various circumstances which can give rise to subrogation.

Regarding the measure of loss, not only must one consider the value of the subject matter lost or damaged, but the provisions of the insurance policy which may contain average clauses, excess and franchise clauses, salvage and reinstatement. This is complicated when payments are made by third parties.[8] Early on, in the Barbadian decision of *Oliver v New India Assurance Co. Ltd*,[9] Hallinan CJ asserted:

> (i) the burden of proving the value of the vehicle at the time of its loss was on the appellant; (ii) the admitted total loss not only established the event in which an indemnity was payable under the contract of insurance, but the character of the article lost was *prima facie* evidence that it was of same value.

In the recent Bermudian case of *Argus Insurance Co. Ltd v Somers Isles Insurance Co. Ltd et al.*[10] resting on priorities, Kawaley CJ stated: 'The general rule as regards priorities when an insured makes a recovery from a third party and his own insurer has a subrogation claim that if the insured makes a recovery from a third party, after the insurer has made a payment under the policy, the assured can retain what he has recovered until he is fully indemnified.' He holds the rest subject to any equitable lien in favour of the insurer up to the value of the insurer's payment. The assured is however, entitled to deduct the costs of recovery from the third party before he is obliged to account to the insurer.[11]

---

1 R. Hasson, 'Subrogation in Insurance Law – The Critical Evaluation' (1985) 5 *OJLS* 416.
2 R. Hodgin, *Insurance Law: Text and Materials* (Cavendish Publishing Ltd: 1998), p. 563.
3 *Solicitors & Central v Lamb* (1864) 1 De GJ & Sm 251; *John Edwards & Co. v Motor Union Insurance Co. Ltd.* [1922] 2 KB 249.
4 *Morris v Ford Motor Co.* [1973] 2 All ER 1084, CA.
5 JM 2016 CA 85.
6 TT 1991 HC 63.
7 KN 2014 CA 2.
8 *See Argus Insurance Co. Ltd v Somers Isles Insurance Co. Ltd et al.* (Supreme Court of Bermuda No. 6 of 2012). The general rule as regards priorities:

> If the insured makes a recovery from a third party, after the insurer has been compensated the assured is, however, entitled to deduct the costs of recovery from the third party before he is obliged to account to the insurer made a payment under the policy, the assured can retain what he has recovered until he is fully indemnified, but he holds the rest subject to any equitable lien in favour of the insurer up to the value of the insurer's payment.

9 BB 1961 HC 23.
10 BM 2014 SC 91.
11 J. Birds, B. Lynch and S. Milnes, *MacGillivray on Insurance Law: Centenary Edition*, 12th edn (Sweet & Maxwell: 2012), para. 23-068.

As previously stated, since regional common law from Montserrat, Jamaica, Trinidad and Tobago and the Organisation of Eastern Caribbean States (OECS) portray respect for British jurisprudence in shaping and explaining its operation, it is useful to outline the foundation.

14.2   NATURE AND ORIGIN

The insurer's right of subrogation is considered as the 'fundamental correlative of the principle of indemnity.'[12] Although often referred to as a right, it is actually more in the 'nature of a restitutionary remedy.'[13] Some decisions refer to this as a common law doctrine arising as an implied term in every contract of indemnity insurance.[14] In *Napier v Hunter*,[15] however, the House of Lords unanimously held that the right of the insurers was an equitable proprietary claim. According to Lord Justice Templeman:

> The principles which dictated the decisions of our ancestors and inspired their references to the equitable obligations of an insured person towards an insurer entitled to subrogation are discernible and immutable. They establish that such an insurer has an enforceable equitable interest in the damages payable by the wrongdoer.

The implications of the right of subrogation being regarded as an equitable proprietary claim are that the insurers' right cannot be defeated if the insured, who is in receipt of the monies, goes bankrupt or becomes insolvent.[16] Further, any unconscionable conduct on the part of the insurer will not defeat the insurer's right of subrogation, but an ancillary claim for breach of implied term will be available to the insured.[17]

The other view is to consider the right of subrogation as a legal right supported by equity. It is a right that can be modified, excluded or extended by the contract of insurance.

Considering the approach adopted by Caribbean jurists to the question of subrogation, it is useful perhaps to outline the history of the doctrine. The principle of subrogation was applied as far back as the eighteenth century in *Randal v Cockran*[18] in the United States concerning perils associated with the Civil War. Lord Hardwicke L.C. referred to the insurers as having the 'plainest equity' to enforce subrogation rights. In *Mason v Sainsbury*[19] and *Clark v Inhabitants of Blything*[20] protests mushroomed into riots, occasioning looting and loss. The insureds submitted a claim which was satisfied by the insurers. Subsequently, an attempt was made to sue the local authorities as they were seen as being statutorily liable for the damage under the Riot Act 1714. The authorities denied the action since the claimants had been indemnified by the insurers, but in both cases it was held that this was no defence. The insurers, 'standing in the insured shoes,' are entitled to recover and pursue civil litigation.

In the seminal nineteenth-century decision of *Castellain v Preston*,[21] a vendor of a house in the midst of a contract for sale was insured against fire. Brett LJ clarified the principle, stating:

---

12   J. Birds, *Modern Insurance Law*, 6th edn (Sweet & Maxwell: 2014), p. 295.
13   J. Lowry and P. Rawlings, *Insurance Law Cases and Materials* (Hart: 2004), Chapter 12.
14   See the judgment of Lord Justice Diplock in *Yorkshire Insurance Co. v Nisbet Shipping Co.* [1962] 2 QB 330 at 339.
15   [1993] 2 WLR 42.
16   *Re Miller, Gibb & Co.* [1957] 1 WLR 703; *England v Guardian Insurance Ltd* [2000] Lloyd's Rep IR 404; see further Mitchell [1993] *LMCLQ* 192.
17   *Banque Financière de la Cité v Parc (Battersea) Ltd* [1998] 1 All ER 737.
18   (1724) 27 ER 916.
19   (1782) 99 ER 358.
20   (1823) 2 B & C 254.
21   (1883) 11 QBD 380.

as between the underwriter and the assured, the underwriter is entitled to the advantage of every right of the assured, whether such right consists in contract, fulfilled or unfulfilled, or in remedy for tort capable of being insisted on or already insisted on, or in any other right, whether by way of condition or otherwise, legal or equitable, which can be, or has been exercised or has accrued, and whether such right could or could not be enforced by the insurer in the name of the assured by the exercise or acquiring of which right or condition the loss against which the assured is insured, can be, or has been diminished.

Earlier in the nineteenth century, the House of Lords affirmed in *Burnand v Rodocanachie & Sons & Co.*[22] that the insured is required to account to the insurer for sums received in diminution of his loss, but not for sums which are properly regarded as gifts. In this case, underwriters valued policies of insurance (including war risks) on cargo, which was subsequently destroyed by a Confederate vessel. The underwriters compensated the insured on the actual total loss according to the valued amounts, which were less than the real value. After the conclusion of the Civil War, the United States established a compensation fund under an Act of Congress. Under this Act, the insured was paid the difference between their real total loss and the sum received from the underwriters. Regarding whether the underwriters were entitled to recover the compensation from the insured, the House of Lords held they were not so entitled. Lord Blackburne avowed: 'We do not pay the money for the purpose of repaying or reducing the loss against which the insurance company have indemnified, but for another and a different purpose, it effectually prevents the right arising.'[23] In *Burnand*, payment was held to be an *ex gratia* payment.

In the Caribbean, an acute reliance on British and Commonwealth decisions is exhibited,[24] as confirmed in *Musson (Jamaica) Ltd v Clarke*:[25]

a close study of the English decisions, and those of other common law jurisdictions, reveals a reasonably developed and systematic complex of rules. It shows that the principle of unjust enrichment is capable of elaboration and refinement. It presupposes three things. First, the defendant must have been enriched by the receipt of a benefit. secondly, that benefit must have been gained at the plaintiff's expense. Thirdly, it would be unjust to allow the defendant to retain that benefit. These three subordinate principles are closely interrelated and cannot be analysed in complete isolation from each other. Examination of each of them throws much light on the nature of restitutionary claims and the principle of unjust enrichment.[26]

Elsewhere, *Patent Scaffolding Co. v William Simpson Construction Co.*,[27] *AFG Insurance Ltd v City of Brighton*[28] and *Welch Foods, Inc. v Chicago Title Insurance Co.*[29] indicate the presence of the doctrine in the United States, Canada and Australia which provide assistance. In *Patent Scaffolding Co. v William Simpson Construction Co.*,[30] Justice Lavenski R. Smith maintains

the elements of an insurer's cause of action based upon equitable subrogation are these: the insured has suffered a loss for which the party to be charged is liable, either because he is a wrongdoer whose act or omission caused the loss or because he is legally responsible to the insured for the loss caused by the wrongdoer; (2) the insurer, in whole or in part, has compensated the insured for the same for which the party to be charged, is liable; (3) the insured has an

---

22 (1882) 7 App Cas 333.
23 Ibid., 341.
24 *Colonia Versicherung AG and Others v Amoco Oil Co.* [1996] EWCA Civ 1002.
25 Supra n. 5.
26 Per Brooks J.A.
27 64 Cal Rptr 187 (California Court of Appeal, 1967).
28 (1972) 126 CLR 655 (High Court).
29 17 SW3d 467 (Supreme Court of Arkansas, 2000).
30 Supra n. 27.

existing, assignable cause of action against the party to be charged, which action, the insured could have asserted for his own benefit had he not been compensated for his loss by the insurer; (4) the insurer has suffered damages caused by the act or omission upon which the liability of the party to be charged depends; (5) justice requires that loss should be entirely shifted from the insurer to the party to be charged, equitable petition is inferior to that of the insurer; (6) the insurer's damages are in a stated sum, usually the balance it has paid to its insured, the payment was not voluntary and was reasonable.

With respect to (6) above, *Burnand v Rodocanachie & Sons & Co.* is clearly a case that reflects a payment that was *voluntary and was reasonable*. The US government was under no liability to pay the money, which could only really be described as amounting to an *ex gratia* payment.

14.3   STATUTE

Section 83 of the Barbados Marine Insurance Act[31] outlines the process of subrogation. It provides:

(1)   Where the insurer pays for a total loss, either of the whole, or, in the case of goods, of any apportionable part of the subject-matter insured, he thereupon becomes entitled to take over the interest of the assured in whatever may remain of the subject-matter so paid for; and he is thereby subrogated to all the rights and remedies of the assured in and in respect of that subject-matter as from the time of the casualty causing the loss.

(2)   Subject to the foregoing provisions, where the insurer pays for a partial loss, he acquires no title to the subject-matter insured, or such part of it as may remain, but he is thereupon subrogated to all rights and remedies of the assured in and in respect of the subject – matter insured as far as the assured has been indemnified, according to this Act, by such payment for the loss.

14.4   PRINCIPLES

There are essentially two limbs to the doctrine of subrogation: (1) the insurer may recover from the insured any sum which the insured recovers from a third party in diminution of his insured loss; and (2) the insurer may require the insured to join in an action against a third party from whom he has the opportunity to recover such sums. *Royal Caribbean Insurance Ltd v Marcial*[32] illustrates that the insurer is entitled to recover from the insured any payment which the insured has received which goes towards the diminution of loss. In *Yorkshire Insurance Co. Ltd v Nisbet*,[33] a ship insured for £72,000 was damaged after a collision with a Canadian Navy ship. The insurers paid for total loss. The cause was negligence and the Canadian government subsequently paid compensation in Canadian dollars. Due to changes in the exchange rate by the time of payment, the payment was worth £127,000. The insured was prepared to hand over £72,000, but the insurers sought to claim the whole amount. Diplock J rejected the insurers' claim, stating the purpose of the doctrine is to ensure that insurers receive up to the amount which they have paid out, but no more; this demonstrates the extent of the doctrine.

Several Caribbean decisions on subrogation are attributable to property loss and motor vehicular claims. Relating to the former, as stated in the recent Court of Appeal decision in

---

31   Cap 249.
32   Supra n. 6.
33   [1961] 1 Lloyd's Rep. 479.

Walwyn v Archibald & RBTT Bank (SKN) Ltd[34] arising from the jurisdiction of St Kitts and Nevis, subrogation by itself does not require an agreement or a contract. The facts surrounded Mr. Archibald, who agreed to purchase a large amount of land on Nevis ('the Property') from a realtor. It was secured by a loan for five years. The issue was whether the claimant was in breach of her fiduciary duty by placing a major part of proceeds of sale towards the payment of her loan. The claimant was found in breach of her fiduciary duty as solicitor to give full disclosure from the conflict of interest that arose; subsequently the claim was dismissed. In dismissing the claim, Chief Justice Pereira stated subrogation by itself does not require an agreement or a contract. It arises by operation of law. As Lord Diplock put it in the House of Lords decision in *Orakpo v Manson Investments Ltd & Ors*:[35]

> There is no general doctrine of unjust enrichment recognised in English law. What it does is to provide specific remedies in particular cases of what might be classified as unjust enrichment in a legal system that is based on the civil law. There are some circumstances in which the remedy takes the form of 'subrogation,' but this expression embraces more than a single concept in English law. It is a convenient way of describing a transfer of rights from one person to another, without assignment or assent of the person from whom the rights are transferred and which takes place by operation of law in a whole variety of widely different circumstances.

In *Royal Caribbean Insurance Ltd v Marcial*,[36] subrogation was denied as the transaction with the third party was in breach of the terms of policy. Permanand J in *Royal Caribbean Insurance Ltd v Marcial*[37] notes:

> The only question is what was the state of the insurers' mind at the time of making the payment. If at that time they believed on the facts as present to their minds, that they were liable to pay, it is immaterial whether they did not know and could not have known the true facts till after the payment, or whether they had known them previously and, but for their carelessness, would have know them at the time, or whether they could, if they had made enquiries, have discovered them before payment.[38]

Hence, according to Ivamy, the right to recover money paid by mistake

> arises only where the mistake is one of fact. It is immaterial how the mistake came to be made. It may be due to fraud on the part of the assured, or merely to ignorance, inadvertence, or for-getfulness on the part of the insurers.[39]

Payment by third parties is problematic. There is no doubt that if a stranger pays off a bank loan, the bank's remedies are subrogated in favour of the stranger whether or not there is notice to the borrower or any agreement on the part of the borrower. In *England v Guardian Insurance Ltd*,[40] the relationship between subrogation claims and the rights of ancillary assistance were considered.[41]

---

34 Supra n. 7.
35 [1977] 3 All ER 1 at 7.3.
36 Supra n. 6.
37 Ibid.
38 See *Murfitt v Royal Insurance Co. Ltd* (1922) 38 *The Times Law Reports* 334, where the plaintiff had insure his orchard which abutted on a railway station and was informed by the defendants' agent that he was covered by insurance but before the policy was issued fire destroyed the orchard and the defendants refused to pay as it stated that its agent could not have so contracted. The court held that the defendants' agent had implied authority to make the contract and the plaintiff was entitled to recover.
39 E. R. Hardy Ivamy, *General Principles of Insurance Law*, 4th edn (Butterworths: 1979).
40 [2000] Lloyd's Rep IR 404.
41 The claimants brought an action against the insurers and those allegedly responsible for the damage. It involved a complex scenario of contributory negligence between two parties' payments into court. The

In *Morris v Ford Motor*,[42] an issue emerged which involved employer-employee relationships. Here the defendants engaged the third party, a firm of cleaners to clean their factory. The third party agreed to indemnify the defendants against all losses arising from the cleaning, even if caused by the defendant's negligence. The claimant was an employee of the third party and was injured by the negligence of a fourth party who was also an employee of the defendant. The claimant succeeded against the defendant on the ground of vicarious liability. The defendant, relying on the indemnity clause, succeeded after joining the third party., the defendant would perhaps have had a *Lister v Romford Ice and Cold Storage Co. Ltd*[43] action against the fourth party.[44] Hollings J held in favour of the third party, acting through the defendant as nominal client. The fourth party appealed, but the majority of the Court of Appeal rejected the argument and subrogation was denied. Importantly, several questions on the origin and basis of the doctrine of subrogation were then addressed. Lord Denning MR's statement provides insight into the equitable nature and origin, stating the exercise of subrogation rights resides within the discretion of the court rather than being a matter of right. On the rather special facts of the case, Lord Denning held that it would not be equitable to allow the exercise of subrogation rights. Whilst the conclusion that was reached is likely to strike lawyers as a desirable one, it is submitted that the reasoning employed is not fully developed as it might appear to be. Lord Denning does not distinguish in his judgment between the two limbs of subrogation, which is unfortunate because an examination of the history of subrogation appears to support the conclusion that the two limbs have different origins. The first limb has its origin in the two decisions of the Court of Kings Bench mentioned above, and it is disputable that the Court of Kings Bench was a common law court. It is scarcely surprising that a remedy which operated against the defendant's property rather than his person should have been available in the common law courts.

The origin of the second limb emanated in *Randal v Cockran*;[45] some assistance towards the correct classification of this limb may perhaps be obtained by considering the nature of the remedy involved. It is a remedy which operates upon the person of the defendant rather than upon his property, since it requires him to do something. Thus it is by its nature likely to have been a remedy granted by the courts of equity rather than by the courts of common law. It is of course this limb which Lord Denning was considering in *Morris*, and it therefore seems likely that he was right to assume that the case before him was governed by equitable considerations. However, it should be assumed that the same is true of the first limb of the doctrine.

---

insurers' lien took priority over the Legal Aid Board's statutory charge because the money could not be said to have been 'recovered' by the insured until that lien had been discharged. At the same time the lien was a matter of equity, and it was open to the court to decide how much of the money should be subject to the lien. In making this decision, the court should allow the deduction by the insured of legal costs reasonably incurred in attempts to recoup the loss from elsewhere, even if those attempts had been unsuccessful, provided that the court was satisfied that in the circumstances it would be inequitable to allow the insurer to benefit from the sums received without giving credit for the expenses incurred in securing those sums.

42 [1973] 2 All ER 1084.

43 [1956] UKHL 6. Martin Lister and his father Martin Lister, working for the Cold Storage company, were driving a waste disposal lorry. They went to a slaughterhouse on Old Church Road, Romford. When they were entering through the gates to the yard, the father got out ahead and the son, driving, backed over him. McNair J awarded the father two thirds of the compensation to reflect the father's contributory negligence. The insurers, who paid £1,600 and costs, sued the son in the name of the company (which was not consulted) by right of subrogation.

44 The House of Lords held that contracts of employment contain an implied term that an employee owes a duty to take reasonable care of the employer's property and in the performance of his tasks. So the lorry, which was entrusted to him, was used carelessly when Martin ran over his father. This meant the son was responsible, and because no term could be implied that an employee may be indemnified by the employer or his insurance, the son would have to pay the insurance company back.

45 Supra n. 22.

Having paid under a policy of insurance, the insurer acquires the right to stand in the insured's shoes and institute proceedings against the third party. Subrogation applies to all types of insurance that are contracts of indemnity. It does not apply to life insurance or *primae facie* accident insurance.[46] However, the concept is not exclusive to insurance.[47] In the *locus classicus* House of Lords decision of *Burnand v Rodocanachie & Sons & Co.*,[48] Lord Blackburn explained the application of subrogation in the following way:

> The general rule of law and its obvious justice is that where there is a contract of indemnity (it matters not whether it is a marine policy, or a policy against fire on land, or any other contract of indemnity) and a loss happens, anything which reduces or diminishes that loss reduces or diminishes the amount which the indemnifier is bound to pay; and if the indemnifier has already paid it, then, if anything which diminishes the loss comes into the hands of the person to whom he has paid it, it becomes an equity that the person who has already paid the full indemnity is entitled to be recouped by having that amount back.

14.5 THE INSURED CANNOT MAKE A PROFIT

If the insured would have been double indemnified if he had kept the insurance monies, this rule is subject to a qualification as the insured is accountable only when he has been fully indemnified. If he received an *ex gratia* payment, this may not necessarily be taken into account, and if there is a surplus the insured is entitled to retain any surplus after the insurer has received its money.

14.6 CONDITIONS FOR SUBROGATION

The insurer's rights can be no greater than the insured's rights. If the insurer has extinguished all rights against a third party, the insurer has no right of subrogation but has a right of action against the insured.[49] Where the insured was compensated from the third party and relinquished right of action against the third party, the insured is liable to repay the insurer. If the insured agreed to accept a lesser amount than that to which he was entitled, the insurer is entitled to recoup the difference from the insured. In the case of deductibles, where the insured by virtue of the terms in the motor insurance policy, for instance, accepts a certain threshold of the damage, he may commence an action against the other party for the amount, but by doing so he relinquishes any subrogated rights for a greater amount.[50] If the subrogated amount exceeds the indemnity paid, the question as to who is entitled to the surplus is generally dependent on the terms of the policy. In *Yorkshire Insurance Co. v Nisbett Shipping Co. Ltd,*[51] because of currency fluctuations in the damage award, the insured was held to be entitled to the excess, as according to Lord Justice Diplock, 'subrogation cannot produce for the insurer more than the sum he paid out.'

---

46 *Theobald v Railway Passengers Assurance Co.* (1854) 10 Exch 45. But consider *Glyn v Scottish Union & National Insurance Co.* (1963) 40 DLR (2d) 929, where the right of subrogation applied to medical payments under a motor insurance policy.
47 See Lord Diplock in *Orapko v Manson Investment* [1977] 3 WLR 229 at 234.
48 (1882) 7 App Cas 333.
49 *West of England Fire Insurance Co. v Issacs* [1897] 1 QB 226.
50 *Hayler v Chapman* [1989] 1 Lloyd's Rep 490.
51 [1962] 2 QB 330.

Subrogation applies to all contracts of insurance. Ever since the decision of *Castellain v Preston*,[52] the guiding principle of insurance law is that the insured should be indemnified against his actual loss, and no more. The insured is not to make a profit/gain out of insurance. The loss or damage is calculated at the time of loss/damage and not when the policy was effected. Insurance companies support the doctrine of subrogation as it enables them to recoup their losses, reduces the costs of insurance and prevents premiums from increasing. On the other hand, there is the argument that subrogated claims are only worth pursuing if the defendant is also insured and that subrogated claims add to the costs of the loser's bill.[53]

14.7   THE PRINCIPLE OF INDEMNITY

The constant thread throughout insurance law is that insurance is a contract of indemnity, so that the insured shall recover no more than his loss and is prohibited from making a profit out of insurance. Brett LJ in *Castellain v Preston* stated:[54]

> In order to give my opinion upon this case, I feel obliged to revert to the very foundation of every rule which has been promulgated and acted on by the courts with regard to insurance law. The very foundation, in my opinion, of every rule which has been applied to insurance law is this, namely, that the contract of insurance contained in a marine or fire policy is a contract of indemnity, and of indemnity only, and that this contract means that the assured, in case of loss against which the policy has been made, shall be fully indemnified, and shall never be more than fully indemnified. That is the fundamental principle of insurance, and if ever a proposition is brought forward which is at variance with it, that is to say, which either will prevent the assured from obtaining a full indemnity, that proposition must be certainly wrong.

This having been said, it is difficult for the profit motive to be totally eradicated from the contract of insurance. Apart from the fact that with regard to life insurance, the contract is not a contract of indemnity as there is no value on life; where goods are replaced, the replacement of an old item with a new one necessarily involves some degree of profit element.

14.8   CO-INSUREDS

Co-insurance must not be confused with double insurance or contribution. It describes a situation where the interests of two parties are covered by a single policy. The issue that arises with respect to subrogation is whether, if only one of the parties is responsible for the loss, can the insurer subrogate against the other party? In *Petrofina (UK) Ltd v Magnaload*,[55] the main contractor effected 'all-risks' insurance against loss or damage caused to property. The insured under the policy were stated to include the main contractor and sub-contractors. The sub-contractors were employed to carry out certain aspects of the work. Due to their negligence, damage was caused to the property and the insurers paid. The insurers then sought to subrogate against the defendant's sub-contractors. The defendant argued that they were insured under the same policy. The Court denied the insurer the right of subrogation because, on the wording of

---

52 Supra n. 21.
53 S. R. Derham, *Subrogation in Insurance Law* (Law Book Co: 1985); C. Mitchell, *Law of Subrogation* (Clarendon: 1994). For a criticism of the doctrine see Hasson, supra n. 1.
54 Supra n. 21 at 386.
55 [1983] 2 Lloyd's Rep 91.

the policy, the defendants were covered by the policy. Mr Justice Lloyd based his decision on 'commercial convenience' (i.e. the simplicity in the head contractor securing a single policy as opposed to each individual contractor effecting separate insurance, resulting in extra paper work, an overlapping of claims and cross claims in the result of an accident). This principle is dependent on the wording of the policy. In *National Oilwell (UK) Ltd v Davey Offshore Ltd*,[56] the scope of the insurance did not cover the specific loss attributable to the defendant's negligence, so that the insurer was entitled to subrogation.[57]

14.9   LANDLORD AND TENANT SITUATIONS

It is necessary to construe both the insurance policy and the lease/agreement in order to determine whether the landlord's insurer is entitled to subrogate against the tenant.[58]

In the leading decision of *Lord Napier and Ettrick v Kershaw*,[59] the House of Lords construed the idea of indemnity in light of the contract, so that rights of subrogation arose once the insurers had satisfied their obligations under the contract, even though the insured's loss might not have been fully covered.[60] This case concerned the difficulties experienced in the Lloyd's market in the 1980s. The insureds were members of a Lloyd's syndicate (the 'names'). A managing agent negligently wrote policies without adequate reinsurance coverage. The names were covered under the agent's insurance. Further, they shared with the agent the premiums and where liable to pay claims issued under the policies of the agent. The names suffered a net underwriting loss of £160,000. Under the stop loss insurance the name agreed to bear the first £25,000. The stop loss insurers and the appellants paid to the name £100,000, being the fixed amount of the limit which exceeded the excess of £25,000. The agent paid £116 million to the solicitors of the plaintiffs. The issues that arose for consideration were (1) how much was payable to the stop loss insurers by way of subrogation and (2) were the stop loss insurers entitled to be paid the amounts found due to them by way of subrogation out of the damage award now held by the solicitor of the plaintiffs. Lord Justice Templeman found the names acted as their own insurers for the first £25,000 and as their own insurers for loss in excess of £125,000. Thus, they were not entitled to a better position than they would have been in. Hence 'The insured is not entitled to be indemnified against a loss which he has agreed to bear'[61] On the question of whether the insurers had an interest in the monies held by the solicitor, Lord Justice Templeman held that the stop loss insurers had an interest in the right of action possessed by the name against the agent.

> It may be that the common law invented and implied in contracts of insurance a promise by the insured person to take proceedings to reduce his loss, a promise by the insured person to account to the insurer for moneys recovered from a third party in respect of the insured loss and a promise by the insured person to allow the insurer to exercise in the name of the insured person rights of action vested in the insured person against third parties for recovery of the insured loss if the insured person refuses or neglects to enforce those rights of actions. There must also

56   [1993] 2 Lloyd's Rep 582.
57   See also *Stone Vickers Ltd v Appledore Ferguson Ship Builders Ltd* [1992] 2 Lloyd's Rep 578.
58   In *Mark Rowlands v Berni Inns* [1985] 3 All ER 473, the lease provided that the tenant was to contribute to the insurance and was to be relieved from repairing obligations should there be damage by fire and that the landlord would expend any insurance monies to repair the building; subrogation rights were denied. See also *Barras v Hamilton* [1994] SLT 949.
59   [1993] AC 713.
60   C. Mitchell, 'Defences to an Insurer's Subrogated Action' [1996] *LMCLQ* 343.
61   Supra n. 59 at 731.

be an implied a promise by the insured person that in exercising his rights of action against third parties he will act in good faith for the benefit of the insurer so far as he has is indemnified the insured person against the insured loss.[62]

Where the insured person has been paid policy monies by the insurer for loss, in respect of which the insured person recovers damages from a wrongdoer, the insured person is guilty of unconscionable conduct, if he does not procure and direct that the sum due to the insurer shall by way of subrogation be paid out of damages.

> damages payable by the wrongdoer to the insured person are subject to an equitable lien of charge in favour of the insurer. The charge is imposed by equity because the insurer, once he has paid under the policy, has an interest in the right of action against the wrongdoer and an interest in the establishment, quantification, recovery and distribution of the damages awarded the wrongdoer.[63]

14.10   CONTRIBUTION

Ancillary to the right of subrogation is the concept of contribution. This is a term used in marine and non-marine insurance to describe the right of an insurer, when he has discharged their liability to the assured, to call on another insurer to bear his portion of the loss.

Where the policy is a valued policy, there is a stipulated ceiling; the stipulated sum is paid in the event of total loss. Such policies are common in indemnity insurance. The replacement principle invariably operates in relation to goods, where for example if a TV is damaged, it will be replaced by one of new or equivalent value. In a sense, the insured will benefit, having received more than true indemnity. In *Leppard v Excess Insurance Co. Ltd*,[64] the insured bought a remote country cottage for £1,500 in 1972. In 1994 he insured it for its replacement value totaling £10,000. The policy contained a provision reserving for the insurer the option of payment, reinstatement or repair. In 1975 the plaintiff increased the value to £14,000. Later that year the cottage was destroyed. The agreed cost of reinstatement was £8,694 taking into account betterment (improvement). However, the insurers discovered that the cottage was for sale at the time of the fire and due to difficulties he was experiencing with the neighbour he would have accepted £4,500. In this case, the issue was whether on the true construction of the insurance policy the plaintiff was entitled to require the defendants to pay him the cost of reinstatement of the cottage. If the answer was no, then the second question was whether the amount of loss actually suffered by the plaintiff was £8,694 or the figure of £3,000. The insurer offered the site value (i.e. £3,000, not £4,500). The Court of Appeal held that the amount of loss was £3,000, taking into account that the plaintiff himself was ready and willing to sell the property for £4,500 or less.

In *Orakpo v Barclays Insurance Services & Another*,[65] the plaintiff insured a grossly exaggerated amount of his claim, alleging dry rot and damage to furniture. Lord Staughton stated:

> I am not convinced that a claim which knowingly exaggerated in some degree should, as a matter of law, disqualify the insured from any recovery. If the contract says so well and good – subject

62   Ibid., 736.
63   Ibid., 738.
64   [1979] 2 All ER 668.
65   [1995] LRLR 443 CA.

always to the unfair contract terms Act. But I would not lend the authorities of this court to the doctrine that such a term is imposed by law.

There is a tendency for some people to put forward inflated claims. These cases illustrate that the courts, rather than treating the principle of utmost good faith as expiring upon the conclusion of the contract, regard the duty as continuing up until the circumstances of casualty. Hoffmann LJ in the aforementioned case noted that

> the insurance company should be able to trust the assured to put forward a claim in good faith. Any fraud in making the claim goes to the root of the contract and entitles the insurer to be discharged. One should naturally not readily infer fraud from the fact that the insured has made a doubtful or even exaggerated claim.[66]

In the case of total loss, the market value of the destroyed property generally provides adequate compensation. The sum insured represents the maximum amount recoverable. In the case of partial loss, the cost of repairing is the general principle subject to the principle of betterment. The equitable doctrine of subrogation prevents the insured from recovering more than full indemnity. In the House of Lords decision of *Burnand v Rodocanachie & Sons & Co.*,[67] Lord Blackburn stated:

> The general rule of law (and its obvious justice) is that where there is a contract of indemnity (it matter not whether it is a marine policy, or a policy against fire on land or any other contact of indemnity) and loss happens, anything which reduces, or diminishes that loss reduces or diminishes the amount which the indemnifier is bound to pay; and if the indemnifier has already paid it, then, if anything which diminishes the loss comes into the hands of the person to whom he has paid it, it becomes an equity that the person who has already paid the full indemnity is entitled to be recouped by having that amount back.

14.11 MEASURE OF LOSS

Valued policies

The valued policy does not consider the actual value of the insured property at the time of the loss; instead the total loss mandates the total payment. Valued policies are commonly found in indemnity insurance where a valuation of the subject matter is undertaken, constituting conclusive evidence as to the measure of the indemnity under that insurance policy,[68] in the absence of mistake or fraud, where that subject matter is totally destroyed by an insured peril. Where the subject matter insured is partially destroyed, any agreed value attaching to the property will be apportioned. The calculation of the indemnity payable for partial loss of property where there is a stipulated value under a policy of insurance is the true value less the true value damage divided by the true value preceding damage multiplied by the agreed value.

(True value less true value damage)
True value preceding damage   ×   agreed value

---

66   Ibid.; J. Birds, *Modern Insurance Law*, 7th edn (Sweet & Maxwell: 2007), pp. 292–293.
67   Per Lord Blackburne (1882) 7 App Cas 333 at 339.
68   Birds, supra n. 66.

In *Elcock v Thomson*[69] Morris J considered the agreed value of property which was partially destroyed by fire, stating:

> the assured are entitled to be indemnified in respect of the depreciation which was caused by fire, and, in quantifying such depreciation, the insurable value of the mansion as agreed by the parties cannot be set aside and disregarded. I observe that, at the end of the schedule to the policy, in the words by which such agreement as to value is expressed, it is stipulated that in the event of loss, the property would be assumed to be of the value recorded and would be assessed accordingly.

Unvalued policies

Where the policy contains no stipulated value, the amount recoverable by the insured is dependent on whether there has been total or partial loss. In the event of total loss, the amount payable is the value of the property at the time[70] and place[71] it was destroyed. In the event of partial loss the amount payable to the insured is the difference in value of the property before and after it was destroyed.[72] In *Leppard v Excess Insurance Co. Ltd*, the policy contained a standard clause that provided that the insurers 'at their option by payment, reinstatement or repair indemnify the insured in respect of a loss or damage caused by the . . . [perils].' The defendant insurers contended that the plaintiff insured was entitled to recover only his actual loss, which was the market value of the cottage at the time of the fire, agreed at £4,500, less the agreed site value of £1,500. The Court of Appeal upheld this principle, reaffirming that the insured can only recover his actual loss, even where the policy expressly stated that the full value of the property is to be deemed to be the reinstatement cost.

Salvage

Where property insured is damaged or destroyed by an insured peril for which the insurer either pays the insured or reinstates or repairs that property, the debris vests in the insurer to obtain what he can for its salvage. Similarly, where goods are damaged to such an extent that the insurer replaces them, the damaged goods vest in the insurer upon replacement or monetary payment under the policy. It would be an infringement of the principle of indemnity to do otherwise. Transference of the right of salvage from the insured upon loss to the insurer upon payment[73] is optional. The insurer may prefer not to assume responsibility over the salvage.[74] Additionally, the insurer may allow the insured to retain salvage, adjusting his claim by allowing a reasonable sum for salvage value.

---

69   [1949] 2 KB 755.
70   *Chapman v Pole* (1870) 22 LT 306.
71   *Rice v Baxendale* (1817) 7 H & N 96.
72   *Leppard v Excess Insurance Co. Ltd* [1979] 2 All ER 668.
73   *Randal v Potter* (1873) LR 6 HL 83.
74   *Allgemeine Versicherungs Gesellschaft Helvetia v Administrator of German Property* [1931] 1 KB 672. Goods were insured with neutral underwriters against war risks. – Abandonment of goods to underwriters on payment for total loss. The right of underwriters to recover proceeds from Administrator of Enemy Property-Trading with the Enemy (Amendment) Act, 1914, Sect. 6:

> No person shall by virtue of any assignment of any debt or chose in action . . . made or to be made in his favour by or on behalf of an enemy . . . have any rights or remedies against the person liable to pay, discharge or satisfy the debt, chose in action . . . unless he proves that the assignment . . . was made by leave of the Board of Trade.

Average clauses

Where the insured property is under insured and the policy is subject to average, the insured is entitled to recover the proportion that his loss bears to the risk known to the insurer, and upon which the insurer assessed the premium. The insured is deemed to be his insurer with respect to the balance. Additionally, fire insurance policies invariably contain average clauses where two or more policies are held covering the same risk. In the absence of an average clause, the insured may recover the full sum insured once the under insurance does not amount to a non-disclosure of a material fact. The average clauses may be a *pro rata* average clause or first condition of average clause which is generally inserted in non-floating policies. Upon a loss the clause reduces the indemnity payable under the policy in direct proportion to the amount that the insured is under insured. A second condition of average clause, which is not truly an average clause but rather a clause excluding property already covered by another policy of lesser scope,[75] regulates payment to be made by several insurers of the lost or damaged property.

14.12   EXCESS AND FRANCHISE CLAUSES

Excess and franchise clauses define the scope of the indemnity granted under the policy and operate to limit the amount an insured is entitled to recover. The courts regard such clauses as representing a bargain struck between the parties to the insurance contract.[76] Excess clauses or 'deductibles,' common in motor, household and third party insurance, generally provide that the insured will bear the first X amount of dollars of each and every claim under the policy. The issue of construction of such clauses arose in the decision of *Australian & New Zealand Bank Ltd v Colonial & Eagle Wharves Ltd*.[77]

14.13   REINSTATEMENT OR REPLACEMENT

Insurance policies may contain a clause indicating that the insurers may, at their option, reinstate or replace the property damaged or destroyed instead of paying the amount of the loss or damage. Such a clause may be accompanied by special provision indicating the reinstatement or replacement value. In the Jamaican decision of *Perrier v British Caribbean Insurance Co. Ltd*,[78] four generators were destroyed by fire while being stored on the plaintiff's property. On the question of whether the insurers were liable to indemnify the insured at the 'book value' of an estimated $300,000 or whether the insurers were liable for the replacement costs of the generators, which was considerably higher, in excess of $3 million. The Court applied the formula prescribed in *Leppard v Excess Insurance Co. Ltd*:[79]

> The undamaged value before the loss to be taken at the market value immediately before the loss occurred. The assured is not entitled to take the cost price or the cost of construction or manufacture as conclusive evidence of the value of the property at the time of the fire. It may be prima facie evidence but it must be remembered that (1) the assured may have paid more

---

75   D. C. Jess, *The Insurance of Commercial Risks Law and Practice* (Butterworth: 1993), p. 128.
76   *Bartlett & Partners Ltd v Meller* [1961] 1 Lloyd's Rep 487.
77   [1960] 2 Lloyd's Rep 241.
78   JM 1994 SC 79.
79   Supra n. 64.

than its value (2) the market value may since have fallen since the time of purchase (3) wear and tear or damage different from that insured against may have depreciated the value of the particular property. Conversely, the property may have risen in value but the condition that the property is insured only for the value declared by the assured either in the proposal or elsewhere.[80]

The Supreme Court of Jamaica thus took into account the market value of the damaged goods immediately before the loss was sustained, adjusted for the depreciated value for storage and lack of use and held that the price paid for the generators was not determinative of the issue, and that the replacement value should be used.[81] If the property is wholly destroyed, the company may, if they think fit, replace it by other things which are equivalent to the property destroyed, instead of paying the amount of the loss, or of the goods insured and damaged and not destroyed by fire. The company may exercise their option and reinstate them, or in other words may repair them and put them in the state in which they were before the fire.[82] In *Brown v The Royal Insurance Co.*, it was stated that the defendant was bound by its election if the insured elects to reinstate.[83] In *Perrier*[84] it was stated that a breach by the insured of a condition precedent can invalidate the insurance contract, however the insurer can waive the breach and therefore affirm the policy. Waiver cannot take place unless the insurer is aware of the facts which constituted the breach.[85]

14.14   CONCLUSION

The principle of subrogation is a latent, inherent ingredient of the contract of indemnity.[86] It arises where there is an obligation on the insurer to indemnify the insured. It does not become operative or enforceable until actual payment has been made, at which time equity previously held in suspense, 'grasps and operates the assureds' choses in action.'[87] It derives from the original contract and gain for payment. A wealth of regional authority speaks to the operation of subrogation: *Musson (Jamaica) Ltd v Clarke*,[88] *Royal Caribbean Insurance Ltd v Marcial*[89] and *Walwyn v Archibald & RBTT Bank (SKN) Ltd*[90] reveal the significance of British jurisprudence. Regional common law from the jurisdictions of Montserrat, Jamaica, Trinidad and Tobago and the OECS depict reverence to the Commonwealth jurisprudence in shaping the doctrine of subrogation. While helpful on the definition of subrogation, they fail to definitively illuminate on the operation, ambit, effect of the assignment, under insurance and availability of defences for wrongdoers. It is therefore imperative that recourse continue to be had to the extra territorial jurisprudence.

---

80   M. Parkington and A. O'Dowd, *MacGillivray & Parkington on Insurance Law*, 7th edn (Sweet & Maxwell: 1981), p. 643, para. 1564.
81   Law Reform Miscellaneous Provision Act and the Bank of Jamaica Act, where discussed in relation to the award of interest.
82   Per Lord Esher, *Anderson v The Commercial Union Assurance Co.* (1886) 55 QBD 1216, p. 1248.
83   *Anderson v The Commercial Union Assurance Co.* (1886) 55 QBD 146; *Brown v The Royal Insurance Co.*, 120 ER 1131.
84   Per Langrin J, *Perrier v British Caribbean Insurance Co.*, JM 1994 SC 79.
85   *Locker & Woolf v Western Australia Insurance Co. Ltd* (1936) 1 KB 408.
86   Per Justice McCardie, *John & Co. v Motor Union Insurance Co. Ltd* [1922] 2 KB 249.
87   Ibid.
88   Supra n. 5.
89   Supra n. 6.
90   Supra n. 7.

In sum, as stated by Bishop J in *Lascelles De Mercado & Co. Ltd v King Et.*[91]

The right of subrogation is in my view not available as a defence by a third party. The effect of payment by the insurers is to subrogate them to the rights of the assured in respect of the subject matter and the insurers become entitled to stand in the shoes of the assured. An action may be brought on behalf of the insurers to enforce the rights to which they are subrogated. The third party who remains responsible to the assured has for the resulting loss, cannot avoid or defend his liability on the ground that the assured had already been fully indemnified by the insurer. If this could be a good defence then the third party would be reaping the benefit of a policy without having paid any premium whatsoever.

---

91   LC 1968 HC 35.

INDEX